ELLERY QUEEN

The Art of Detection

MYSTERY FICTION

Publish and Perish (1975)
Corrupt and Ensnare (1978)
The 120 Hour Clock (1986)
The Ninety Million Dollar Mouse (1987)
Into the Same River Twice (1997)
Beneficiaries' Requiem (2000)
Night of Silken Snow and Other Stories (2001)
Leap Day and Other Stories (2003)
Night Forms (2010)

NONFICTION ON THE MYSTERY GENRE

Royal Bloodline: Ellery Queen, Author and Detective (1974)
The Sound of Detection: Ellery Queen=s Adventures in Radio (1983)
Cornell Woolrich: First You Dream, Then You Die (1988)
The Sound of Detection (revised and expanded edition) (2002)
Cornucopia of Crime (2010)

ON MOVIES

The Films of Hopalong Cassidy (1988)
Bar-20: The Life of Clarence E. Mulford, Creator of Hopalong Cassidy (1993)
The Films of the Cisco Kid (1998)
Joseph H. Lewis: Overview, Interview and Filmography (1998)
Paul Landres: A Director' Stories (2000)
Hopalong Cassidy: On the Page, On the Screen (2008)
The Cisco Kid: American Hero, Hispanic Roots (2008)

ANTHOLOGIES & COLLECTIONS (EDITED OR CO-EDITED)

The Mystery Writer's Art (1970)
Nightwebs by Cornell Woolrich (1971)
The Good Old Stuff by John D. MacDonald (1982)
Exeunt Murderers by Anthony Boucher (1983)
Buffet for Unwelcome Guests by Christianna Brand (1983)
More Good Old Stuff by John D. MacDonald (1984)
Carnival of Crime by Fredric Brown (1985)
Hitchcock in Prime Time (1985)
The Best of Ellery Queen (1985)
Leopold's Way by Edward D. Hoch (1985)
Darkness at Dawn by Cornell Woolrich (1985)
The Adventures of Henry Turnbuckle by Jack Ritchie (1987)
Better Mousetraps by John Lutz (1988)
Mr. President—Private Eye (1988)
Death on Television by Henry Slesar (1989)
Little Boxes of Bewilderment by Jack Ritchie (1989)
The Night My Friend by Edward D. Hoch (1991)
The Anthony Boucher Chronicles 2001-02
Night & Fear by Cornell Woolrich (2004)
Tonight, Somewhere in New York by Cornell Woolrich (2005)
The Keeler Keyhole Collection by Harry Stephen Keeler (2006)
Love and Night by Cornell Woolrich (2007)

ELLERY QUEEN

The Art of Detection

Francis M. Nevins

PERFECT CRIME BOOKS

Crime@PerfectCrimeBooks.com

Cover Photo courtesy of The Frederic Dannay Literary Property Trust.

Perfect Crime Books™ is a registered Trademark.

Printed in the United States of America.

Library of Congress Cataloging-in-Publication Data
Nevins, Francis M.
Ellery Queen: The Art of Detection / Francis M. Nevins
ISBN: 978-1-935797-47-0

First Edition: January 2013

In memory of Patty

ELLERY QUEEN

The Art of Detection

INTRODUCTION

ONCE UPON A TIME, back in the Reagan era, I wrote a book called *Cornell Woolrich: First You Dream, Then You Die* (1988). Are you familiar with everything bagels? I wanted that literary doorstop to be the Woolrich everything book, with answers to almost any imaginable question about the haunted recluse I've called the Hitchcock of the written word. This present tome I want to be the Ellery Queen everything book, an equally comprehensive account of Frederic Dannay and Manfred B. Lee, the two first cousins from Brooklyn who, using the name Ellery Queen for both their protagonist and their joint byline, wrote some of the most complex and involuted detective novels of the genre's golden age.

I think I just heard a question. "Hey, didn't you do that book already, back in the Watergate era?" Well, sort of. But as I got older I became convinced that I hadn't done all that good a job. Fred Dannay was the public face of Ellery Queen, and in the years after we met he became the closest to a grandfather I've ever known, but I never really got to know the much more private Manny Lee. He and I had exchanged a few letters, and we met briefly at the Edgars dinner in 1970, but he died before we could meet again. Because of his untimely death *Royal Bloodline* (1974) inadvertently gave the impression that "Ellery Queen" meant 90% Fred Dannay. One of the most important items on my personal bucket list was to do justice to Manny. Thanks largely to the memoirs published by his son Rand Lee, along with the Dannay-Lee correspondence in *Blood Relations*, edited by Joseph Goodrich (2012), and the correspondence between Manny and Anthony Boucher, which is archived at Indiana University's Lilly Library, I've come to a much clearer understanding of Manny, of who he was and how he lived and worked and thought. *The Art of Detection* improves on *Royal Bloodline* in all sorts of ways but for me this one is the most important. In addition it provides much more detail on subjects like the EQ radio series (1939-48) and the decades-long interaction between the cousins and Boucher. And of course it covers all sorts of subjects that postdate the early 1970s, like the EQ TV series with Jim Hutton, and Fred's third marriage and last years and death.

When I first discovered the Ellery Queen novels, that byline was a household name. It still was when I first met Fred Dannay. I can't believe that in my lifetime the Queen name has (except in Japan) been so completely forgotten. Maybe, just maybe, with the publication of *Blood Relations* last year, and of my book now, and of Jeffrey Marks' biography-in-progress two or three years from now, I'll live to see the return of Ellery Queen to the public eye where the name belongs.

***

The cousins who wrote as and about Ellery Queen were often involved in so many activities at the same time that it proved impossible to keep strictly to chronological order throughout this book. It would have been intolerably confusing, for example, to break up my account of Columbia's EQ movie series of 1940-42 with a discussion of the landmark Queen anthology *101 Years' Entertainment* (1941), or to put the material on Queen's novel *The Murderer Is A Fox* (1945) in the middle of the section on the Queen radio show during that season. Two particular subjects—the story of *Ellery Queen's Mystery Magazine* during Fred Dannay's forty years as editor and the story of my own relationship with Fred—I've relegated to Appendixes. My decision to do so raises no problems with the material on Fred and me, but I found that I had to repeat a few paragraphs in the *EQMM* appendix that also appear in the main body of the book. This overlap is deliberate, not an oversight, and intended to keep readers from having to flip back and forth between one part of the book and another.

A book of this sort can't be written without a great deal of help. A small army of men and women assisted in one form or another, from the late 1960s when I began work on *Royal Bloodline* to the summer of 2012 when I put the final touches on *The Art of Detection*. I have marked with asterisks the names of those no longer with us. My deepest thanks to Robert C.S. Adey; Dale Andrews; Jon L. Breen; *Robert E. Briney; *Ray B. Browne; J.R. Christopher; William Contento; J. Randolph Cox; Rose Dannay; David L. Godwin; Joseph Goodrich; Martin Grams, Jr.; Douglas G. Greene; Michael Grost; *Edward D. Hoch; Allen J. Hubin; Janet Hutchings; Marvin Lachman; William Nadel; Otto Penzler; Kurt Sercu; Charles Shibuk; Steven Slutsky; *Sydney Smith; *Ray Stanich; Steven Steinbock; *Eleanor Sullivan; *Julian Symons; Saundra Taylor; Arthur Vidro; Rev. Robert E. Washer; *Phyllis White; and Donald A. Yates. I owe a special debt of gratitude to Douglas and Richard Dannay and Rand B. Lee, without whose co-operation I could not have quoted at such length from the correspondence of and between their fathers, and who generously provided some of the rarest photographs reproduced in this book. Most of all I am debt to Frederic Dannay (1905-1982) and Manfred B. Lee (1905-1971), without whom there would have been nothing to write this book about.

FRANCIS M. NEVINS
St. Louis, Missouri
July 24, 2012

CHAPTER ONE

The Brooklyn Cousins Mystery

ONE NOON DURING the late spring or early summer of 1928, two cousins in their early twenties met for lunch at an Italian restaurant in midtown Manhattan. Over a spicy antipasto one of them—later neither could remember which—mentioned that he'd seen an announcement in the morning *Times* about a $7,500 mystery novel writing contest sponsored jointly by *McClure's Magazine* and the publishing firm of Frederick A. Stokes. By the time they'd set down their last cups of coffee, the cousins had not only decided to enter the competition but had devised the nucleus of a plot. "It was a lark," Frederic Dannay recalled 51 years later. "We had no intention in the world of doing more than one book." Lark it may have been but they took it dead seriously, working frantically on evenings and weekends and holidays over the next several months, writing in the one cousin's office or the other's or wherever they could get together for a few hours, pushing themselves to complete the manuscript before the contest deadline of December 31, 1928. "I remember Manny Lee had to go to a wedding in Philadelphia during the time we were writing it," Fred Dannay told a *Playboy* interviewer in 1979. "And I had to go with him, to the wedding of a complete stranger, just so we wouldn't lose the time it took to get there and back on the train." At times they were tempted to scrap the project but by then, as

Dannay put it during a visit to the San Diego campus of the University of California in 1977, they had "reached a point of no return where if we stopped all the work would be wasted, and it seemed that it would be reasonable to go on and finish it." They completed the manuscript on December 30, 1928, turned it in on the following day—the last day entries could be submitted—and, as Fred said at the University of California, "sat back with a sigh of relief to await the outcome." That was how Ellery Queen was born, as the detective (and detective novelist) within the novel and as the joint pseudonym of the authors.

***

The young men who called themselves Frederic Dannay and Manfred B. Lee were born nine months and five blocks apart, in Brooklyn's teeming Brownsville district. Lee, the older cousin, was born Manford Lepofsky on January 11, 1905. His parents, Benjamin and Rebecca (Wallerstein) Lepofsky, were Russian Jewish immigrants with Socialist interests and a family tradition of disdain for organized religion. It was said that each year on Yom Kippur one of Benjamin's brothers would stand on the steps of the local synagogue and eat a ham sandwich. Small wonder that they didn't give their newborn son a traditional Jewish name! As an adult Manford came to detest his birth name, telling one of his sons that Rebecca "must have gotten it from some damn romance novel." But her doctor didn't think the name appropriate for a Jewish child and took it upon himself to register the boy's birth certificate under the name Emanuel Lepofsky.

Rebecca and her sister Dora were the daughters of Russian Jewish immigrants named Leopold and Rachel Wallerstein, and Dora had married Meyer H. Nathan, a liquor salesman. On October 20, 1905, a little more than nine months after the birth of the Lepofsky child, the Nathans had a son whom they named Daniel. However, Mrs. Nathan was using the same doctor who had attended her sister, and this Ben Casey of the Brownsville tenements also frowned on Daniel as a name for a Jewish child (perhaps because the book of Daniel isn't part of the Tanakh, the Hebrew bible proper, but only of the Apocrypha) and changed it on the birth certificate to David Nathan. Eventually both cousins opted for names of their own choosing.

***

"My family moved to the small upstate town of Elmira, New York, when I was a baby," Dannay recalled in his seventies, "and the twelve years I spent there were a great gift. Elmira was bisected by the Chemung River, and I lived a Tom Sawyer boyhood in one of Mark Twain's hometowns. My cousin stayed in Brooklyn and became streetwise, while I was sort of a country bumpkin." In a 1944 reminiscence he described vividly what that boyhood was like.

> When I was a child my family lived in a small town in western New York. I didn't realize it then, but I was given a colossal gift early in life—a Huckleberry Finn-Tom Sawyer boyhood spent, by a strange coincidence, in the very town in which Mark Twain lived shortly before I was born.
>
> Does any man with a spark of boyhood still in his heart ever forget his home town? No—it's an unconquerable memory. Most of us never return, but none of us forgets.
>
> I remember we had a river at our back door—the gentle Chemung. I remember how, in the cycle of years, the spring torrents came down from the hills; how they overflowed our peaceful valley—yes, over the massive concrete dikes that towered with grim Egyptian austerity above the shallow bed of the Chemung. I remember how old man river burst through our back door, flooding our kitchen and parlor, driving us—temporary refugees—to our top floor. Happy days for a wide-eyed boy, proud in his hip boots and man's southwester, with the prospect of daily trips by rowboat—voyages of high adventure—to the nearest grocer!
>
> I remember the unpaved streets—the heavily rutted road that slept in the sun before our house. I have a queer memory about those ruts. Every 4th of July we boys would plant our firecrackers deep in the soft earth of those ruts. Then we'd touch our smoking punks to the row of seedling fuses, run for cover, and watch the "thunderbolts" (that's what they were called in those days) explode with a muffled roar and send heavenward—at least three feet!—a shower of dirt and stones. It wasn't so long after the

Spanish-American War that we couldn't pretend we were blowing up the *Maine*—in some strangely perverted terrestrial fashion only small boys can invent.

I remember the long walks to and from public school—three miles each way, in summer mud and winter drifts; the cherry trees and apple trees and chicken coops and dogs—the long succession of dogs ending with that fine hunter that was killed by a queer-looking machine called an "automobile." I remember the all-day trips to the brown October hills, gathering nuts; the wood fires and the popping corn; the swimming hole that no one knew about but ourselves; the boyhood secret society and its meeting place in the shed behind my best friend's house.

His best friend in Elmira was named Ellery.

Such was the childhood of Daniel Nathan, who roamed the woods and fields, took part in elaborate business adventures with his playmates (like exhibiting the ghost of Long John Silver for a two-cent admission fee), and, as the son of the town liquor dealer, enjoyed the prestige of being the only boy in the community who was allowed into saloons.

Meanwhile the Lepofskys remained in Brooklyn, raising their son in what he later called "a typical *Sidewalks of New York* atmosphere." But the allusion to the old ballad is misleading. The Brownsville section of Brooklyn was a rough environment, and early in life the boy performed an inner emigration. "I knew I was going to be a writer from the time I was eight years old," he said in 1969. "I think boys of American Jewish background can't take the brutality of the streets and turn for refuge to books." In summertime he went upstate to Elmira to visit his cousin— usually for a week, but in 1914 for the entire vacation—and the boys would spend their leisure competing against each other in games of oneupmanship which they would continue playing, in altered forms, during their more than forty years of collaboration as writers.

In 1917 the Nathan family moved back to Brooklyn and into the house of Danny's maternal grandparents, the Wallersteins, which was in a neighborhood several steps up from Brownsville. That winter, while 12-year-old Danny was in bed suffering from an abscess of the left ear that periodically afflicted him, one of his aunts walked into his cubbyhole sickroom and handed him a book which she'd borrowed from the neighborhood public library. It was Conan Doyle's *Adventures of Sherlock Holmes*, and it changed his life. Young Danny had been a voracious reader—of Dumas' *The Three Musketeers* and the books of Horatio Alger, Jules Verne, and James Fenimore Cooper, of Viking legends and the adventures of Tom Swift and the Rover Boys, Frank Merriwell and Baseball Joe, Tarzan and Peck's Bad Boy, of the multi-colored Andrew Lang fairy tale collections and the Oz stories of L. Frank Baum—but until that winter day his only exposure to crime fiction had been in the form of silent cliffhanger serials like *The Exploits of Elaine* (1915). Reading those fabulous adventures of Sherlock Holmes, which he devoured in one gulp, so fired the boy's imagination that the next morning he slipped out of the house and down to the library, where he wangled a card and stripped the shelves of all the Holmes books he could lay his hands on. A year or so later, while exploring the bookcases in the house of one of his uncles, he stumbled upon *Master Tales of Mystery* (ed. Francis J. Reynolds, 1915), a three-volume anthology of short stories bound in rich blue cloth which introduced him to Anna Katharine Green and Baroness Orczy's tales of the Old Man in the Corner and Arthur B. Reeve's scientific detective Craig Kennedy and Jacques Futrelle's Thinking Machine. The Elmira bumpkin quickly became an unquenchable fan of the genre that was to shape his life.

With the return of the Nathans to Brooklyn there developed a powerful friendship between the boys. "We were cousins," Fred Dannay said more than sixty years later, "but we were closer than brothers." Besides having mutual interests in typical teen-age concerns like baseball, they also shared a passion for detective fiction. Both of them attended Boys' High, and as early as 1920, Dannay remembered, while "walking together to and from high school, and while sitting together on streetcars in bad weather," he and his cousin began "to experiment with ideas, to play with the strings of plot." They planned to write a tale of murder in the public library but changed their minds. "A public library was dear to our hearts, it was our treasure-house, our fountain of life. It was too sacred a place to be defiled by crime, and murder in a public library was unthinkable." They changed the crime scene to a museum and imagined a locked-room situation, "a room in the museum, with all doors and windows locked on the inside, and a body found dead behind a desk." The solution? The murderer had hidden inside a suit of armor all day, stepped out of the armor that night, killed the victim, stepped back into the armor, slipped through a convenient hole in the floor to the room below, and somehow or other escaped from the museum. "I can recall, almost as if it were last week," Dannay wrote in 1979, "the two of us strolling home, discussing heatedly, sparking ideas, laughing at the patently ridiculous suggestions, and finally coming up with" their masterstrokes.

Manford Lepofsky graduated from Boys' High and went on to New York University's Washington Square College, working as a Western Union messenger for pocket money, eventually leading a five-piece jazz band. His major was English and he was in his final semester and about to graduate *summa cum laude* when he confided in Professor James Buell Munn (1890-1967), his faculty adviser and mentor and later the chair of Harvard University's English department, that someday he hoped to become a professor of literature at his alma mater. "Manny," the older man told him gently, "no Jew is ever going to get tenure in the New York University system." Soon afterward an embittered Lepofsky legally adopted the most un-Jewish name he could think of that would allow him to keep his nickname: Manfred Bennington Lee. Manfred means man of peace and may also have been intended as homage to the hero of Lord Byron's romantic poem. His new dream was to become "the Shakespeare of the 20th century."

Daniel or David Nathan had written verse since his early teens and, during his years at Boys' High, aspired to become a poet. He brought in some money for the family working after school as a soda fountain clerk, but the coming of Prohibition put his father out of the liquor business and forced Danny to quit Boys' High before graduation. "At the end of my third year in high school my family was in financial straits so desperate that I had to help out. In 1921 jobs were easy [to find], even if you were sixteen years old." Dannay's first full-time position was as a bookkeeper, and over the next seven years he hopped from job to job. In time family finances improved to the point where he received his high school diploma and then enrolled in a few courses at the Art Students' League. That experience, he said in 1979, convinced him that "I could not be happy if I wasn't a first class painter, but I could be a second class writer and be happy."

Around the middle of the decade Daniel Nathan followed in his cousin's footsteps and took the name of Frederic Dannay, the first name in honor of the composer Chopin and the second a combination of the first syllables of his birth name. In 1926 he married Mary Beck, the first of his three wives, and by 1928 he was working as a copywriter and art director for a New York advertising agency. Lee had graduated from NYU in 1926 and then entered the business world, although his mother had wanted him to go on to law school. Sometime that year, Lee traveled to Philadelphia with his friend and fellow band member Hyman Miller and met Hy's youngest sister. Betty Miller (1909-1974) and Manny Lee were married in 1927 and moved into an apartment on Ocean Avenue in Brooklyn. Manny supported the family writing publicity releases for the Manhattan-based Pathé movie studio. His office and Fred Dannay's were only a few blocks apart, and the cousins met for lunch almost every day. They called each other Man and Dan or Manny and Danny.

In the late 1920s the foremost detective novels in the United States were the best-selling Philo Vance books, written by art critic Willard Huntington Wright (1888-1939) under the pseudonym of S.S. Van Dine, and among the subjects Dannay and Lee discussed over their meals was the possibility of collaborating on a detective novel of their own, this time not a teen-age fantasy but a serious book in the Van Dine manner, complete with super-intellectual sleuth and reams of erudite deduction. But it was the announcement of the $7,500 prize contest that catalyzed them into serious action and gave birth to Ellery Queen, author and detective.

With their backgrounds in advertising and publicity, the cousins decided to take great pains over the name of their protagonist. "What we wanted," Dannay said on TV's *Dick Cavett Show* in 1978, "was a name which, once heard, read, or seen in print, would have a mnemonic value and remain in the person's memory." It had to be slightly unusual, easy to remember and rhythmic in sound, and after a few false starts like James Griffen and Wilbur See, they had it. Ellery had been the name of Dannay's best friend in Elmira, and he admired both the magazine editor Ellery Sedgwick and the poet William Ellery Leonard. How they chose the character's last name was explained by Manny's daughter Patricia Lee Caldwell (1935-   ).

> My mother told me that the families used to get together a lot over the weekends. . . . One weekend cousin Fred and Manny were playing cards. . . . I think she said it was bridge. . . . [T]hey suddenly looked at the picture cards and they said: "Yeah, wait, the picture cards. Maybe this will give us something." And they suddenly decided it

would be Ellery King . . . but it didn't seem quite right, and so they diddled around with it a little and they said: "No, Queen. Queen!"

It was indeed a name whose sound meshed perfectly with the sound of Ellery. As the cousins reiterated in later interviews, they had no idea at the time that the word was a derogatory synonym for homosexual.

The $7,500 prize consisted of $5,000 which *McClure's Magazine* was offering for serial rights to the winning manuscript plus $2,500 which Stokes was putting up for hardcover rights. The contest was open to all comers, established professionals as well as beginners, but in order to make sure that all entries would receive equal consideration, the sponsors had adopted a rule that each entry had to be submitted under a pseudonym. "We both had our personal ambitions," Dannay said in 1979, referring to his own desire to be recognized as a poet and Lee's to be the Shakespeare of his time, "so we were perfectly content not to make known who we were." But instead of picking a pseudonym out of a hat, the cousins hit upon the brilliant idea of using Ellery Queen as their own joint byline as well as the name of their detective. As fans of the genre they knew that readers of detective fiction tended to remember Sherlock Holmes and Philo Vance, not Sir Arthur Conan Doyle and S.S. Van Dine. But, they reasoned, people couldn't forget their pseudonym if they used the same name for themselves and their character. The only precedent for this device was the ever-popular Nick Carter pulp stories which had been turned out by a variety of hands for Street & Smith Publications under the Nicholas Carter house name since the 1880s. No individual mystery writer had done it before, and it must have contributed hugely to the cousins' success.

After submitting *The Roman Hat Mystery* they continued with their jobs in advertising and publicity and waited for word of the contest results—and heard nothing. In his 1977 University of California interview, Dannay described what happened next.

> We sat back and waited and actually forgot about the contest. And about three months later—this would be somewhere around March 1929—we had our usual lunch, and one of us—I don't remember again which one—said:

"Say, what ever happened to that contest that we went into and submitted a manuscript to?" And whoever asked that, I said: "You know, I think I'll go out and call the agent who was in charge."

All the manuscripts had been given to the Curtis Brown literary agency, which represented both the publisher Stokes and *McClure's*. So I went out to the lobby of the restaurant, to a public phone, and called up the agent, a man named Mr. Rich whom I had never seen. And I said to him: "We submitted a manuscript to the contest and we haven't heard a word in three months." He said: "Under what name did you submit it?" I said: "Ellery Queen." And there was a pause, an ominous pause on the phone. And he said: "Can you come over right away?" I said: "We sure can." So I went back and told Manny that we were supposed to see Mr. Rich.

We finally got there. Mr. Rich's office was Old Curiosity Shop on a small scale, absolutely cluttered, mostly with manuscripts stacked more than waist-high everywhere on the floor. We met Mr. Rich, who had a long full Dickensian beard, and he said to us: "Now this is not for public report, but confidentially, you have won the contest, and it will be publicly reported in a few days, and I congratulate you."

So Manny and I walked out on Cloud Nine. And we said to ourselves: "We have to commemorate this event." So we went into Dunhill's [the New York tobacconist shop] and bought each other a pipe and had the initials EQ put on the stem of each pipe. Manny had his till the day he died. I either lost mine or had it stolen from me. . . .

In any event, we waited a couple of days for the public announcement, and it never came. So we called up Mr. Rich again, and he said: "Can you come over right away?" And we said: "We sure can." We went over to see Mr. Rich, and he said: "Since I last talked to you something terrible has happened. *McClure's* has gone bankrupt."

The magazine's assets had been taken over by another magazine,

The Smart Set, whose editors had decided to award the prize to another manuscript more suited to that periodical's female readership. That was the bad news. The good news was that the Stokes editors liked the Queen novel enough to publish it anyway, provided the cousins would accept a picayune advance of $200 apiece. "We with great dignity said that if they wanted to publish the manuscript the least they could do for us was to publish it ahead of the prize winner, which they agreed to do."

Dannay in his seventies was philosophical about having won the contest only to lose it. As he said on *The Dick Cavett Show*:

> We thought at the time that it was a terrible blow from fate. . . . Seventy-five hundred dollars, to us at least, was a considerable amount of money. What we had planned to do was to pack up our families, give up our jobs, go to the south of France, where at that time there were many American expatriate writers, and write in the south of France. And of course when we lost the contest and lost the first prize we had to stay with our jobs. And that actually was the best thing that ever happened to us. Because I think if we had gone to the south of France we'd have frittered the money away, produced no work, whereas the way it happened, we buckled down and started a career.

True to its word, Stokes published *The Roman Hat Mystery* on August 15, 1929, a few months before it issued *Murder Yet to Come* by Isabel Briggs Myers (1897-1980), the winner of the $7,500 price. I happen to own a copy of Myers' book. It's a creaky old-dark-house melodrama featuring a ruby stolen from a Hindu temple, an enigmatic turbaned butler, a lot of hypnotized characters making idiots of themselves, and an excruciatingly obvious Least Likely Suspect whose guilt is exposed by Peter Jerningham, witty playwright and amateur sleuth. Myers favored an overwrought silent-movie kind of prose, redeemed only by one unforgettable sentence: "For a moment he gave all his attention to passing a milk truck that was bottling up traffic on our side of the pike." After a second Jerningham exploit, *Give Me Death* (Stokes, 1934), Myers vanished from the genre, although years later she became famous in her own right as the originator (with her mother Katharine Cook Briggs) of the widely used Myers-Briggs Type Indicator personality inventory.

Myers' contributions to the literature of crime can be summed up in one paragraph of moderate length. Giving an account of Ellery Queen's contributions will take a book. This book.

CHAPTER TWO

Enter Ellery I

BUT FIRST, A DETOUR.

The life and work of the author who overwhelmingly influenced the early Ellery Queen novels are most fully explored in John Loughery's Edgar-winning biography *Alias S.S. Van Dine: The Man Who Created Philo Vance* (Knopf, 1992), but a much briefer account will do us here. Willard Huntington Wright (1888-1939) was an erudite art critic whose faith in the values of Western civilization was destroyed by the carnage of World War I. He withdrew into a shell of detachment, but in 1923 the combination of overwork, despair and cocaine drove him into a nervous breakdown. Forbidden to read "serious" literature during his two-year convalescence, he amassed and devoured a huge library of mystery fiction, studied the aesthetics of the genre, and amused himself by creating his own fictional detective, who would carry erudition and cerebration—and detachment from the obscene mess of humankind's struggles—to undreamt-of heights. Finally Wright arranged a lunch date with Maxwell Perkins of Charles Scribner's Sons and gave the legendary editor his lengthy outlines for three novels about the projected sleuth. Perkins agreed to publish the novels when completed. Those books made history, propelling Wright's pseudonym S.S. Van Dine onto the best-seller lists and turning his hypercerebral hawkshaw Philo Vance into a household name.

Van Dine's early novels—*The Benson Murder Case* (1926), *The "Canary" Murder Case* (1927), *The Greene Murder Case* (1928), *The Bishop Murder Case* (1929)—were consumed by readers of the late Twenties with incredible gusto but are not highly regarded today. Plot flubs, wooden characterizations, leaden prose, Vance's infuriating mannerisms and encyclopedic footnoted disquisitions on intellectual trivia which interrupt the already snail-paced story at regular intervals—these flaws make it almost an act of penance to read Van Dine today. They also make it too easy for us to forget that almost singlehandedly he created the skeletal structure of that noble subspecies of mystery fiction, the formal deductive puzzle, which during the Thirties would be fleshed out and perfected by Golden Age giants like John Dickson Carr, Agatha Christie and, of course, Ellery Queen.

Today that form is all but extinct and few remember what a crackle of intellectual excitement filled the best detective fiction of those years. Delectable frustration consumed reader and sleuth as both discovered an entanglement wrapped inside every complication and a conundrum within every enigma. With unshakable determination the protagonist would sift through masses of bizarre circumstances and conflicting testimony, much of it flat lies and the rest even at best (to quote the novelist and whodunit fan Vladimir Nabokov) "shaped by the teller, reshaped by the listener, concealed from both by the dead man of the tale." Then at the most perplexing point in the investigation, the detective would announce: Now I see. And readers would experience a sense of awe as he (in those days it was almost always a man) unfolded his solution, setting each fact and clue in its logical niche and giving a name to the murderer. That, friends, was the formal deductive puzzle. That's the kind of book Van Dine wrote, and influenced Fred Dannay and Manny Lee to write better. In Fred's words: "He influenced us because he made so much money; and then, the kind of thing he did appealed to us in those days. It was complex, logical, deductive, almost entirely intellectual."

Although superior to the Philo Vance best-sellers in plotting, characterization and style, the early Queen novels were influenced by Van Dine in all sorts of ways. The strict Queen title-pattern, *The Adjective-of-Nationality Noun Mystery*, is clearly derived from Van

Dine's *The* Six-Letter-Word *Murder Case* pattern. Each of the principal characters surrounding Vance has a close analogue in the Queen novels: District Attorney Markham and Inspector Queen; blockheaded Sergeant Heath and concrete-brained Sergeant Velie; Dr. Doremus and Doc Prouty for the examination of corpses at the most awkward times; Currie the Vance butler and Djuna (named, Dannay told me, for the avant-garde novelist Djuna Barnes) the Queen houseboy.

Philo Vance's exploits were narrated by his ever-present but never noticed attorney S.S. Van Dine, who served as both Watson and the supposed author. Dannay and Lee had the exploits of Ellery Queen put before the public by a characterless acquaintance signing himself J.J. McC but, in a stroke of genius, improved on Van Dine by using the same byline, Ellery Queen, for both supposed author and supersleuth. Both Van Dine and McC informed their readers in Prefaces that the names Philo Vance and Ellery Queen were pseudonyms adopted to protect the identities of the respective sleuths, both of whom were alleged to be living in retirement in Italy (Ellery with a bride and an infant son!).

The most important element the young cousins borrowed from Van Dine was his concept of the detective as a towering intellectual, full of scholarly quotations, interested not in people but only in abstract problems. Observe Ellery walking on stage in *Roman Hat*:

> There was a square cut to his shoulders and an agreeable swing to his body as he walked. He was dressed in oxford grey and carried a light stick. On his nose perched what seemed an incongruous note in so athletic a man—a pince-nez. But the brow above, the long delicate lines of the face, the bright eyes were those of a man of thought rather than action.

His father, Inspector Richard Queen of the NYPD, is described in the same scene as "a small, withered, rather mild-appearing old gentleman" who walks "with a little stoop and an air of deliberation that somehow accorded perfectly with his thick grey hair and mustaches, veiled grey eyes and slender hands. . . ." Ellery usually calls him "pater" or "Inspector darling."

In their last active years as mystery writers the cousins came to despise the Harvard-educated dilettante bibliophile who is here called

Ellery I. Dannay described him to an interviewer from *MD*, the medical magazine, as "really a most unpleasant character," and Lee ridiculed him as "the biggest prig that ever came down the pike." But those novels of Queen's first period are among the most richly plotted specimens of the Golden Age deductive puzzle at its zenith, bursting with bizarre circumstances, conflicting testimony, enigmatic clues, alternative solutions, fireworks displays of virtuoso reasoning, and a constant crackle of intellectual excitement. Most of the distinctive Queen story motifs—the negative clue, the dying message, the murderer as Iago-like manipulator, the patterned series of clues deliberately left at crime scenes, the false answer followed by the true and devastating solution—originated and were given classic treatment in these books of the first period.

If one element more than any other made the Ellery Queen novels stand out from the rest of the detective fiction of the Golden Age between world wars, it was the cousins' insistence on playing fair with the reader. "We stressed fairness to the reader," Dannay said in 1979, "in the sense that in the Golden Age type of detective story, the reader had to know everything that the detective knew, and therefore had an even chance of beating the detective before the solution was given at the end of the book." And they did play the game with scrupulous fairness, not only presenting all the facts honestly (albeit with a great deal of trickiness on occasion) but stopping most of the novels at a certain point to issue a formal "Challenge to the Reader" to solve the puzzle ahead of Ellery. The odds of course were stacked in favor of the house, and when Fred Dannay once boasted to a *Look Magazine* interviewer that Queen was always "completely fair to the reader," Manny Lee rightly interjected: "We are fair to the reader only if he is a genius."

Shall we enter Queenland?

***

The first Ellery Queen "problem in deduction" was *The Roman Hat Mystery* (1929), set in the late Twenties when romantic gangster melodramas were popular on the silent screen (as witness Josef von Sternberg's visually dazzling *The Docks of New York* and *The Drag Net*) and on the live stage. *Gunplay*, a show of this sort, is being performed before a well-filled house at the Roman Theater, on 47th Street west of Broadway, on the evening of Monday, September 24. (During the 1920s that date fell on a Monday only in 1928, the year *Roman Hat* was written, and 1923.) Near the end of Act Two a scream tears through the audience and the lights snap on. The occupant of LL32, the leftmost seat in the rear aisle, is found poisoned in his seat. Inspector Queen and his team are summoned and Ellery comes to the theater with them. The body belongs to Monte Field, a shady criminal lawyer. The seven seats nearest the corpse are vacant although box-office records show all seven had been paid for. Field is in evening clothes but his top hat is missing. There's a woman's evening bag in his pocket and a half-empty ginger ale bottle under his seat. An usher has been standing at each exit since the play began and the ticket seller swears no one left by the front door, ergo the murderer must still be in the theater. Among the playgoers that evening are several with reason to want Field dead, including a former underworld client, a former law partner, and a society girl engaged to one of the actors in the play. When the investigators visit Field's apartment and office, they encounter an angry mistress, a suspicious valet, a set of books on handwriting analysis, and several more missing toppers. Various suspects are caught in lies while being questioned or later.

The solution, which consumes roughly 9% of the book's wordage, is surprising, fair to the reader, and much more controversial today than it was 80-odd years ago. Why? Because it involves race.

> Inspector Queen: ". . .[T]o make it short and ugly, [one suspect] has a strain of negroid blood in his veins. . . . [T]here was definite documentary evidence . . . to prove that his blood had the black taint. I needn't explain what it would have meant . . . to have the story of his mixed blood become known. . . ."
>
> Assistant District Attorney Cronin: "Black blood, eh? . . . Poor devil."
>
> District Attorney Sampson: "You would scarcely guess it from his appearance. . . . He looks as white as you or I."
>
> Inspector Queen: "[He] isn't anywhere near full-blooded Negro. . . . He has just a drop in his veins—just a drop, but it would have been more than enough [to ruin him]."

This is precisely the detached, intellectualized take on race one would expect in a formal deductive puzzle of the time: not racist but not outraged or even upset by the racism of the society, stoically accepting as unalterable that (in Richard's words to Ellery) "there's little justice and certainly no mercy in this world." A more palatable outlook will be found in the mature Queen novels of Period Three.

The plot of *Roman Hat* required a poison that would kill with split-second accuracy under precisely specified circumstances. Having no medical expertise themselves, Dannay and Lee consulted Professor Alexander Goettler, the chief toxicologist for the City of New York, who advised them to use tetra ethyl lead, a component of gasoline whose exact chemical workings were still something of a mystery to scientists. Fred and Manny followed Goettler's suggestion and gratefully dedicated their book to him. Their debut novel was a relatively minor title on Stokes' 1929 list and received little promotion or advertising from the publisher. But the publicity-intoxicated cousins hyped the book on their own by writing pseudonymous letters to newspapers, accusing "Queen" of disclosing dangerous information about tetra ethyl lead to potential murderers in real life. Years later they learned that the controversy had prompted secret conferences among oil company executives on how to deal with this problem. The book wound up selling about 8,000 copies in its original edition. "In a word," Dannay said in 1943, "that was sensational." "It was a minor miracle," Lee chimed in modestly.

***

Fred and Manny weren't so imprudent as to abandon their secure jobs and become full-time writers on the strength of one fairly successful novel. "We buckled down and did more work," Fred said, "producing a second and third book by working nights and weekends." *The French Powder Mystery* (1930) was inspired when one of the cousins passed a department store display window and stopped to look at an exhibit of contemporary apartment furnishings which included a Murphy bed. We open on the morning of Tuesday, May 24. (During the 1920s that date fell on a Tuesday only in 1927 and 1921, but *French Powder* clearly postdates *Roman Hat*. Go figure.) A high-level police conference is being held at the Queens' apartment on the top floor of a three-family brownstone on West 87th Street, "a man's domicile from the piperack over the hearth to the shining sabers on the wall." On the agenda is the question of what strategy to adopt against a certain large drug ring. But the Queens are diverted from narcotics to murder (or are they?) when the body of Winifred Marchbanks French tumbles out of a concealed wall bed in the display window of French's Department Store, terrifying the model demonstrating furniture inside the window and the crowd watching from outside. Ellery and Richard Queen are quickly propelled into the intrigues within tycoon Cyrus French's family—his wife, his daughter, his mysteriously absent stepdaughter, the wife's first husband and her brother—and into the equally complex intrigues among the board of directors, security staff and other members of French's business family. The huge store all but becomes a character in its own right as Ellery and his father uncover one tiny clue after another. A lipstick in the dead woman's purse doesn't match the color of her lips. A piece of green felt protecting the underside of an onyx bookend is not the same shade as that on the matching bookend. A hat and a pair of shoes are not quite where they should be, while a few grains of powder are where they should not be. Out of such minutiae Ellery forges a chain of iron logic in a climax which Anthony Boucher, in his lifetime and now the foremost commentator on the genre, praised as "probably the most admirably constructed denouement in the history of the detective story." The name of the murderer is kept concealed throughout 35 closely printed pages of explanation until the novel's last two words.

***

The Dutch Shoe Mystery (1931) opens on a raw Monday morning in January—whose date the cousins wisely decline to provide—as Ellery drops into the Dutch Memorial Hospital in the east Sixties to pick the brains of a medical friend. Dr. Minchen mentions that emergency surgery is about to be performed on Abigail Doorn, the hospital's founder and principal support, and invites Ellery to watch the operation from the upstairs gallery. As Doorn relatives and retainers converge on the hospital to await the outcome, a mysterious visitor insists on seeing Dr. Janney, the operating surgeon, even though surgery is about to begin. When Janney returns to the operating theater and Mrs. Doorn's stretcher is wheeled in from the anteroom, she is dead, but not from organic causes. Someone strangled her with picture wire while she was in the anteroom lying on her stretcher. Inspector Queen and his team arrive. The testimony of several witnesses seems to establish that only

Janney, who was well remembered in Mrs. Doorn's will, could have committed the murder. Janney swears he was with his mysterious visitor at the time of the crime, claims that someone disguised as him entered the anteroom and strangled the old lady, but refuses to say who his visitor was. Meanwhile the police learn that a loanshark with strong reason to want Mrs. Doorn dead was having his appendix removed at the Dutch Memorial Hospital at the time of the murder; that several doctors and several Doorn family members have motives of hatred or gain and no alibis; that there's a strange connection between the hospital diagnostician and Mrs. Doorn's companion, a religious fanatic; and that the family lawyer destroyed certain papers shortly after the murder. As the complexity of the puzzle grows, we find a 14-page "Interlude" chapter, printed on pages with extra-wide margins "for the use of the reader in jotting down his personal notes about the solution." (Within a few years, Fred Dannay was to become such a reverent bibliophile that he would have eaten the pages rather than have them published that way.) After a second strangulation in the hospital, Ellery offers his solution, based on a pair of starched white trousers and a pair of white canvas shoes and accounting brilliantly for everything. Well, *almost* everything.

Take a close look at the diagram of the hospital, printed at the front of *Dutch Shoe*, and you'll notice an oversight which no one seems to have spotted for decades after the book's publication. The diagram does not show a door connecting the main operating room and the west corridor, but there simply has to be one. It's referred to twice (on pages 27 and 49 of the first edition) and it's the only way Inspector Queen could have entered the anteroom from the amphitheater, as he does on page 50, unless he walked through the wall like Superman. Catching occasional tiny flaws like this one is among the many joys of reading early Ellery Queen novels.

Are there also flaws in the medical background? *Dutch Shoe* was dedicated to a physician who apparently gave the cousins technical advice, but after its publication they received a ten-page letter from a Chicago doctor, Maurice B. Wolff, disputing their notions of what was possible in a hospital setting. Fred and Manny didn't agree with all of Dr. Wolff's points but answered his letter courteously, and from that time until Wolff's death years later he was their expert on all medical aspects of the Ellery Queen series.

***

In the early 1960s, 10- or 11-year-old Rand Lee discovered that his father was a famous author and Manny explained to him a little about Ellery Queen. Rand asked if he could read a Queen novel. Manny: "Well, which one would you like to start with?" Rand: "With the first one." Manny: "Oh, son, that awful thing!" Rand insisted and Manny gave him a copy of *Roman Hat*. "It was indeed a dreadful book," Rand wrote in 1999, "and the next one, *The French Powder Mystery*, wasn't much better. . . . I found the vast casts of characters impossible to keep track of, the convoluted plots impossible to follow, the mannered writing peculiar, and smart-alecky Ellery with his Twenties pince-nez peculiarly unattractive." As we've seen, both Manny and Fred in middle age came to agree with that estimate of their youthful novels. Many of us who discovered first-period Queen at a more auspicious time in their lives would beg to differ. Still and all, the first three Ellery Queen novels were not in the same league with the eight that were to come out in 1932 and 1933.

CHAPTER THREE

The Year of Abundance

I<small>T WAS IN</small> 1931, some time after the publication of *Dutch Shoe*, that, as Fred Dannay told a *Playboy* interviewer, "our agent said to us, in more earthy language than I will give to you now, fish or cut bait." The agent's words as Fred gave them to me were: "Shit or get off the pot." He and Manny decided—a bold decision indeed in the pit of the Great Depression—to make it as professionals or go broke. Once the cousins discovered that without day jobs to slow them down they could turn out a 90,000-word detective novel every three months, they agreed that four new Ellery Queen books a year would glut the market. Therefore they adopted a second pseudonym and launched a new detective character, who lasted for four novels (three of them sharing a common title pattern) and then was terminated irrevocably. Or was it irrevocable?

To publish the new series they chose Viking and for their new joint byline Barnaby Ross. Perhaps this was an echo of the building in Elmira known as Barnaby's barn, which Fred often played in as a child. The Foreword to *Roman Hat* had contained an oblique reference to the first puzzle Ellery had solved, "the now-ancient Barnaby-Ross murder-case." The cousins resurrected the name "deliberately," Fred wrote many years later, "so that eagle-eyed, elephant-memoried students of the genre could some day establish a remote connection between Ellery Queen and Ellery Queen's other pen name."

For their new series character they devised Mr. Drury Lane, an ambivalent gentleman they later described as "half ham and half ruffed grouse . . . mountebank and genius, and quite the most extraordinary detective who ever lived (except, perhaps, one who shall be nameless)." Renowned as a Shakespearean actor but forced into retirement by total deafness, Lane has recreated an Elizabethan village community on his acreage above the Hudson. The village is dominated by Lane's private castle, The Hamlet, and populated by down-and-out theatrical folk who earn their keep by sporting period costumes and Shakespearean names. But this power-driven tyrant wants more: "From obeying the jerk of the master's strings, I now have the impulse to pull the strings myself, in a greater authorship than created drama." The leitmotif of his existence is power—to stir audiences with his performances, to control his villagers' lives totally, and, in a mad oedipal rivalry with Shakespeare's shade, to intervene in real-world dramas and in a sense rewrite them. And you thought Ellery I was difficult to like? Decades later, movies like Hitchcock's *Rear Window* and stage plays like Shaffer's *Sleuth* made it more commonplace to identify the detective's impulse to rummage through others' lives with the dark side of human nature, but during the Golden Age of the formal deductive puzzle it was the height of radicalism. And yet despite their implicit criticism of the genre's authoritarian tendency, at least the first two Drury Lane novels are richly plotted masterworks, with all the facts presented trickily but fairly so that the reader might play the game along with the detective and perhaps (if the reader was a genius) beat him to the solution.

The Tragedy of X (1932) opens with a biographical sketch of Lane and his letter to the NYPD offering the solution to an unsolved murder case. When his deductions prove right, Inspector Thumm and District Attorney Bruno visit The Hamlet to meet the old mastermind, thank him, and ask his help on a problem even more bewildering. We flash back to four days earlier and eavesdrop on a cocktail party thrown by sadistic and lecherous stockbroker Harley Longstreet to celebrate his engagement to a much younger woman and make his guests squirm. Among those invited are Longstreet's browbeaten partner, his former mistress, a man who's in love with the woman he wants as his next mistress, a former lover of his present fiancée, and a corrupt politician who blames the brokers for ruinous losses in the market. After cocktails Longstreet insists that everyone go along with him to a dinner party in New Jersey. When a sudden thunderstorm makes it impossible to get a taxi for the trip to the ferry, they all board a crosstown trolley. The packed streetcar is lurching west towards the ferry slip when Longstreet reaches into his pocket and suddenly falls into the aisle, his hand pricked and bleeding in a dozen places. Once on the scene, Inspector Thumm searches the dead man's pockets and finds a cork ball riddled with needles, each one coated at both ends with pure nicotine poison. But there are too many suspects with motive and opportunity and his investigation founders. When Thumm and Bruno have recounted these facts, Drury Lane announces that he believes he knows the murderer but, due in roughly equal parts to his analysis of the situation and his lust to exercise power, refuses to say more. The next evening there's a second murder, the victim thrown from the upper deck of a ferry and crushed to pulp as the boat pulls into the Weehawken slip. Later come a spectacular murder trial, a disturbing conversation aboard a New Jersey commuter train, a third murder committed within a few feet of Lane himself, and finally, during another train ride, the unmasking.

The Tragedy of X introduced into the cousins' repertoire two motifs that were to become hallmarks. One, which they borrowed from Conan Doyle's *The Valley of Fear* (1915) and recycled throughout the novels of their first period, can't be discussed without ruining several of those books for those not yet familiar with them. The other, on which Dannay and Lee played variations for the rest of their careers, is the dying message clue. During a night journey on the Weehawken local which one commuter will not live to complete, Drury Lane and others involved in the case have a conversation about the last moments before death which is as central to Queen as is the locked room lecture in *The Three Coffins* (1935) to the works of John Dickson Carr. "There are no limits to which the human mind cannot soar," Lane declares, "in this unique, godlike instant before the end of life." *The Tragedy of X* offers a superb plot-puzzle, the rationale for dozens of future dying message stories and a disturbing study of power. It also recreates vividly a vanished time when the Depression racked the economy and ruthless businessmen lived by the tooth-and-claw rules of brute unregulated capitalism, and when American cities and suburbs were linked by streetcars, ferries, electric interurban lines, commuter trains — by a mass transit system that worked, and in this novel lives again.

***

This first Barnaby Ross novel was followed up by perhaps the finest Ellery Queen novel of Period One. *The Greek Coffin Mystery* (1932) begins with blind art dealer Georg Khalkis dying of heart failure in the library of his West 54th Street brownstone. Three days later the coffin is taken to the church graveyard next door and lowered into the family crypt. When the burial party returns to the house, the attorney for the estate discovers that the steel box containing Khalkis' will is missing from the wall safe. The police are summoned but after two days the box is still missing. At a conference called to discuss the case are Inspector Queen and his young and cocksure son, who has just begun to apply his talents to crime problems. Ellery deduces that the box must be inside Khalkis' coffin. An exhumation order is obtained, the coffin is opened, and inside the investigators find not the will but the decaying corpse of a second man, strangled to death and lying on top of Khalkis' body. Inspector Queen and his men soon unearth a cornucopia of counterplots inside the Khalkis household and an assortment of intrigues outside, many rooted in the theft of a Leonardo from a British museum. After about 130 pages Ellery proposes a devilishly ingenious solution based on the amount of tea water in a percolator and the color of a dead man's tie, but he soon learns that this version of events was prepared for him to find by "the player on the other side." This is the first of four solutions to the Khalkis case, each one radiating outward from those that went before and accounting for more of the total picture. The fourth explanation alone embraces the entire brain-boggling web of plot and counterplot, described by Ellery as "a complex plan which requires assiduous concentration for complete comprehension," and reveals, with total fairness to the superhumanly alert reader, a stunning surprise murderer.

Greek Coffin may well be the most involuted, meticulously constructed detective novel published during the genre's Golden Age. But it's not quite flawless. Anyone who studied Latin in high school — as Fred and Manny apparently didn't — is likely to raise an eyebrow or two at the moment in Chapter 31 when Ellery tries to quote the ancient proverb *Ne quid nimis* (nothing too much, moderation in all things) but renders it as *Ne quis nimis* (which is gibberish) and then translates it as a completely different ancient proverb, "Know thyself" (in Latin, *Nosce teipsum*). Other gaps in Ellery's supposedly all-encompassing fund of knowledge will be found in later Queen novels.

***

The Barnaby Ross byline returned a few months later on the spine of one of the most darkly brilliant detective novels ever written. Most of *The Tragedy of Y* (1932) unfolds in a mansion on Washington Square and among the members of a doom-haunted family worthy of Eugene O'Neill. Head of the clan is the wealthy and ruthless Emily Hatter, whose first husband died mysteriously long ago and whose daughter by that marriage, Louisa Campion, was born blind and mute and went deaf the day she turned eighteen, "as a sort of birthday gift from the dark gods who seemed to rule her destiny." For the 37 years of Emily's marriage to the unworldly chemist York Hatter she made her second husband's life one long hell. One child of that second marriage is a hopeless alcoholic whose sons, aged 13 and 4, are willful sadists. Another child of the marriage is a vicious and frigid tramp. "Mad as a Hatter" is not a humorous expression here.

A fishing trawler off the Atlantic coast discovers a shapeless body identified as York Hatter, who had vanished several weeks before. A suicide note is found but an autopsy proves that the cause of death was poison. Emily identifies her husband's body without hesitation and without a tear. Two months later, on a Sunday afternoon, someone adds strychnine to Louisa Campion's egg nog, which Emily's teen-age grandson snatches and gobbles up before falling to the floor, screaming. Inspector Thumm seeks advice from Drury Lane, who warns that the poisoner will probably try to kill Louisa again. After two more months, Lane is summoned to Washington Square. Someone has bludgeoned old Emily to death in her bed with a strange weapon indeed: York Hatter's mandolin. Louisa slept in the same room with her mother and even touched the murderer's face but the investigators get nowhere, although a box of spilled talcum powder and some tiptoeing footprints give Lane ideas which he refuses to share with Thumm. Slowly we experience a sense of the imbecility of these crimes which matches our growing understanding of the filth and perversion eating away at the Hatter family, which for Dannay and Lee seems to be a paradigm of American society, its members rotting with greed, sadism and inertia, consenting for the sake of expected inheritances to endure love-hate relationships with each other and with the bitch goddess of wealth and property who rules the roost. The Hatters' sickness isn't some naturalistic venereal disease but a disease of human nature and the human condition. "Good God," District Attorney Bruno gasps on learning the murderer's identity, which was peculiarly horrible in 1932 although the shock was later blunted by other authors' use of the same device. "Not a very good God," Lane replies. "Not to that poor . . . creature." *The Tragedy of Y*'s distrust and despair of human nature will surface again and again in later Ellery Queen novels, as will the theme of Iagoesque manipulation, although here the Iago figure is dead before the story begins.

***

The cousins closed out this most abundant year with perhaps the bloodiest of all pure detective novels, *The Egyptian Cross Mystery* (1932). On a chill Tuesday morning between Christmas and New Year's, Ellery and his father arrive at a muddy West Virginia crossroads where a branch road leading to the village of Arroyo forms a T with the main highway. At the junction stands another T, a signpost with a crossbar. A few hundred feet away is a third T, smeared in blood on the front door of Andrew Van, the hermit-like atheist who served as Arroyo's schoolteacher. On Christmas morning a fourth T had been found, a T that had once been a man, a beheaded and crucified body nailed to the doorpost and identified as Van. It's this crime that has brought the Queens to Arroyo.

At the inquest they hear evidence that a limping foreigner was searching Van's house late on December 24, and that a local medicine man calling himself Ra-Harakht the Sun God had employed one Velja Krosac, a limping foreigner who had vanished on Christmas Eve. The case dies and six months pass before Ellery reads that the maker of T's has returned. The body of Thomas Brad, wealthy rug merchant and checkers enthusiast, has been found beheaded and lashed to a totem post on his own Nassau County estate, only a few miles from an island nudist colony run by a certain Harakht. There are also a slew of suspects in Brad's house and neighborhood: his wayward wife, his lovelorn daughter, his ex-convict chauffeur, his ambitious business manager, his often absent partner. Among the clues are a red checker, a pipe filled with the wrong tobacco, a misplaced rug, the remnants of a checker game and the remnants of a Montenegro blood feud. More beheadings follow before Ellery's deductions unmask the serial crucifixionist.

Certainly there's more carnage here than in any other Queen novel, but the physical horror of these crimes is necessary to the ingenious variations of the Conan Doyle *Valley of Fear* gambit on which the solution rests. There are also more plot problems here than one expects in early Queen. The middle chapters are only distantly related to the novel as a whole, and there's a character who should have starved to death while he was a prisoner alone in a cave but on whose body there were no signs of captivity. But with its exceptionally large and well-handled cast, labyrinthine plot and vivid evocation of several socially, economically and geographically disparate milieus, *Egyptian Cross* remains one of the finest Queen novels of Period One.

***

By 1932 "Ellery Queen" had attained such eminence in the genre that Columbia University School of Journalism invited "him" to deliver a lecture on mystery writing. Neither Dannay nor Lee particularly wanted to go that day, so they flipped a coin to see who would do the honors. Manny lost the toss and went up to Morningside Heights to lecture as Queen, wearing a black mask for the occasion since the author's identity was still being kept under wraps. Not to be outdone, Fred bought his own mask and started to make public appearances as the hot new detective novelist Barnaby Ross.

Manny's Columbia gig came to the attention of W. Colston Leigh, the proprietor of a well-known lecture bureau, who put the cousins under contract and, over the next two years, sent them out together on several cross-country speaking tours, with Fred posing as Ross and Manny still playing Queen, both men sporting what Fred described as "domino masks with little ruffles at the bottom so that no part of our faces, except the glasses over the masks, could be seen." They would appear on the lecture platform as rival mystery writers and challenge each other's skill as detectives, with Ross tossing off clues in a complex murder case and defying Queen to solve it on the spot. "It was really a vaudeville act," Fred remarked in 1970, and the whole performance was intensively rehearsed before the cousins hit the road. Soon they had developed a knack for reacting spontaneously to each other's verbal cues during interviews, so that one reporter in the late 1930's wrote:

[They share an] intellectual Siamese twinship that binds them together. . . . Their minds blend so easily and naturally that a third person, talking to them, gets the slightly uneasy impression that he is conversing with one man. Never prompting each other by as much as a glance (in one hour-long interview neither one ever addressed the other), one would begin a sentence, in the middle of which the other would hook on a subjunctive clause, with the first reappearing in the caboose of the train of their thought.

Their lecture tours as Queen and Ross were so convincing to audiences that they often posed a credibility problem which the cousins once described for the press in a series of those alternating segments.

Dannay: "Almost everywhere we went as Ellery Queen and Barnaby Ross we were asked to work on some local mystery."

Lee: "But we remembered [S.S.] Van Dine's experience when he undertook to solve a murder mystery out in Jersey."

Dannay: "He worked long and hard at it and was getting nowhere . . ."

Lee: ". . . when along came a flatfoot who didn't know the difference between analytical deduction and pustular acne . . ."

Dannay: ". . . and solved it in two hours."

Whenever they were asked to play real-life detectives, their invariable response was to extemporize some fast double talk and then politely inquire the way to the nearest exit.

In time these little games focused a good deal of attention on the masked authors. As veterans of the advertising business, Fred said in 1979, he and Manny "were advertising-minded, and while we didn't intend our hiding behind a mask or hiding behind a pseudonym to create publicity, whether we intended it or not it did create publicity, and the more publicity it created the more successful we were." Soon rumors began to appear in print that Ellery Queen was none other than

S.S. Van Dine and that lurking behind the mask of Barnaby Ross was the celebrated raconteur Alexander Woollcott.

The cousins' lives would follow the same pattern in 1933—a great deal of time on tour plus four detective novels—but in that year they would also launch two new ventures. One was to continue throughout their careers; the other, brief as it was, shaped the career of one cousin for much of the rest of his life.

CHAPTER FOUR

Novels, Stories and a Magazine

L ATE IN 1932, at the instigation of their agent, Dannay and Lee had begun to think about writing Ellery Queen short stories, with the hope of earning astronomical amounts from slick-paper magazines like the *Saturday Evening Post*. But Ellery's first short adventure wound up in an ephemeral pulp (alongside stories by Dorothy L. Sayers, Earl Derr Biggers and Sax Rohmer) whose check for $35 had to be shared by Fred, Manny and the agent, and another early tale seems never to have appeared in a magazine at all. The first eleven Queen short stories were collected in book form in 1934 and will be covered in the chapter devoted to that year. But three and perhaps four of them were written in 1933, along with two more Ellery Queen novels for Stokes, two more Barnaby Ross books for Viking, and four issues of a magazine that will be taken up later in this chapter. Plus all those tours!

***

In the third Drury Lane novel, *The Tragedy of Z* (1933), the cousins dropped the somber impersonal narrative of the first two tragedies, which are now said to have taken place ten years earlier, and substituted the more sprightly first-person narration of Inspector Thumm's daughter. Lovely Patience Thumm has returned to New York after several years in Europe and rejoined her father, now retired from the NYPD and running his own detective agency. Taken to meet Drury Lane and former District Attorney Bruno, now governor of New York, she quickly proves herself a first-rate sleuth. From The Hamlet the Thumms proceed to upstate New York's Tilden County, the Inspector having been retained by the part owner of a local marble quarry to find out why the firm has been awarded so many state contracts. Then a state senator is stabbed to death in his study amid clues such as a piece of a carved toy chest, a footprint trodden in ashes, and a jagged scratch on a forearm. The police seize on ex-convict Aaron Dow as the obvious murderer, and the local prosecutor, who stands to gain politically by the senator's death, puts the one-eyed one-armed derelict on trial. Patience insists that the evidence if properly interpreted proves Dow innocent and asks Drury Lane's help, but the race against time is complicated by a prison break, a second murder, and a chain of events originating at the turn of the 20th century in, of all places, Viet Nam. In one of the genre's most chilling denouements, Lane reconstructs the case and unmasks the killer in the execution chamber of the prison moments before Dow is to be fried.

Frankly, *The Tragedy of Z* is something of a comedown from its predecessors. Except for one brief scene, Drury Lane is kept offstage until almost halfway through the book, and Patience Thumm is hardly a substitute, especially since she shares the tendency of Ellery I to talk in book-length sentences. One of the major flaws in the novel's construction is that a dedicated and incorruptible warden discovers a message smuggling system within his prison and does nothing about it, for no better reason than that the plot requires the system to be still operational later on. But the two death-house sequences are as bone-chilling as anything in the literature of suspense, and the clues Lane collates at the climax are planted with unobtrusive brilliance.

***

The American Gun Mystery (1933) is set at a huge rodeo, "ripped up from its alkaline soil and transplanted bodily—horses, lariats, steers, cowboys and all—to the stony soil of the East" or, more precisely, to the Colosseum, New York's newest and largest sports arena. The premier attraction of Wild Bill Grant's rodeo during its New York engagement is Buck Horne, the legendary star of countless silent cowboy films until age and the talkies laid him low. (Anyone remember William S. Hart?) His old amigo Grant is staking Horne to a comeback, not only out of friendship and hope of profit but because a marriage is expected between young Curly Grant and Horne's adopted daughter Kit, an actress in Western films. Among the 20,000 spectators at the rodeo's opening night are Ellery and Richard Queen. In the first event Horne is supposed to lead forty riders in a hell-for-leather chase around the arena. But when the riders draw their pistols and shoot as one man into the air, the aged horseman thirty feet ahead of them suddenly falls to the tanbark and is crushed under the hooves of 41 horses. Ellery and his father leap into the arena, start investigating at once, and quickly establish that the victim was shot with a .25 automatic. But after a bone-numbing search of the Colosseum and every person in it the weapon remains invisible. Frustrations and false leads breed like rabbits as Ellery and Richard pursue separate lines of inquiry. Only after a second rodeo murder, under almost identical circumstances including the vanished .25, does the truth come out.

The solution of *American Gun* is certainly fair to the reader but again depends on Conan Doyle's *The Valley of Fear*. The murder motive is woefully weak and Ellery never explains how the culprit managed to get the victim into the position required for the plan. The boxing counterplot that fills out the middle chapters isn't related to the basic storyline. And Ellery shows himself to be as ignorant of film technique as he was of Latin in *Greek Coffin*. In Chapter 6 he describes a shoot-em-up in which Kit Horne, galloping down a hillside, drew her pistol and shot through the strands of rope with which the villain was hanging the hero. Since Kit and her revolver and the rope were all distinctly visible throughout the scene, he deduces that she must have fired a real bullet in the film. As if any director could have captured all those elements in one take! "Nevertheless," Ellery then concedes, "I grant the possibility of a trick. . . ." To which his father rightly retorts: "Darned decent of you."

***

By far the weakest of the Barnaby Ross novels is *Drury Lane's Last Case* (1933), which is set in the near future. Ex-Inspector Thumm and his daughter are still running their detective agency. Patience no longer functions as first-person narrator but continues to sound as pretentious as Ellery I, even when presenting a fine feminist manifesto to her adoring boyfriend. "But the only thing that differentiates us from the lower primates is the power of reasoning, and I don't see why the mere fact that a woman is biologically different from a man should prevent her from cultivating her mind." The puzzlement begins when a strange man sporting a blue and green beard pays Thumm $1,000 to hold a manila envelope containing, so the client claims, a clue to a secret worth millions. Three weeks later Thumm gets tangled in the case of a guard who vanished from the Britannic Museum while the curator was giving a guided tour to a sightseeing-busload of Indiana schoolteachers. It soon turns out that the sightseeing group included two extra men, one of whom did not return from the museum. Either he or the other unknown apparently broke into one of the museum's glass cases, removed a valuable Shakespeare folio, replaced it with another of much greater value, and next day returned the stolen folio to the museum. Drury Lane, a financial patron of the Britannic, joins the investigation along with Thumm and Patience and a young Shakespeare scholar smitten with the Inspector's daughter. Two bibliomaniac brothers on the trail of some new information about Shakespeare himself further thicken the plot. Eventually the man with the dappled beard and his envelope are found to be connected with the Britannic mystery.

There are plenty of bizarre events in the first three-quarters of *Drury Lane's Last Case* but many of them remain either inadequately explained at the denouement or dependent on absurd motives. No one is murdered until late in the game, but the killer's identity is a stunt rather than a logical outgrowth of the plot, and the climax depends on Shakespearean "facts" that Fred and Manny made up out of whole cloth. There are two fine sequences (the deductions from the Saxon Library notepaper and the matter of the ax-man and the alarm clock) which would have made excellent Ellery Queen short stories, but this is the single novel from Period One that might better have remained unwritten.

***

The death of Drury Lane at the end of the book would seem to establish unequivocally that Dannay and Lee intended to end the series at that point. In fact they had planned to resurrect him for more novels, but a dispute with Viking, which was publishing the series, caused them to change their minds.

In the second half of 1933 Fred and Manny set out to launch an ambitious new periodical. In Manny's words: "*Mystery League* magazine was the child of the Queen imagination and early ambition. It was published on the proverbial shoelace . . . and [Fred and I] were its entire staff . . . ; we did not even have a secretary. We selected the stories, prepared copy, read proofs, dummied, sweated, . . . and almost literally swept out the office as well." The debut issue (October 1933) contained the complete text of their own latest novel, making *Drury Lane's Last Case* available to any reader with a quarter to plunk down at his or her favorite newsstand. The people at Viking grew understandably angry at this unintended but unauthorized competition with the $2.00 hardcover edition the firm was about to publish. Fred and Manny were forced to accept some unfavorable revisions in the royalty clauses of their contract with Viking, and the dispute convinced them that as long as Drury Lane was already dead he might just as well be kept in his grave.

***

In *The Siamese Twin Mystery* (1933) Ellery and his father are returning from a Canadian vacation when they're trapped by a forest fire on the side of Arrow Mountain. Their only hope of survival is to drive up to the mountain top. Long after dark they discover a house on the peak of the mountain, whose entire base is now ablaze. Ellery and Richard are grateful for the hospitality of retired surgeon Dr. John Xavier and his strange family, but soon find several reasons to feel uneasy. Who is the vicious fat man wandering around the mountain? Why were several rings stolen from the household in the past week? Who is the extra woman hiding in an upstairs bedroom? And who or what is the crablike creature that scuttles through the corridors at night? The next morning Dr. Xavier is found shot to death in his study, a game of solitaire laid out in front of him, a torn half of the six of spades clenched between his fingers. By now the fire has sealed off the mountaintop so it's up the Queens to solve the crime alone, without help from the police. Despite the steadily nearing flames a second murder soon follows, this time with half a jack of diamonds in the victim's hand.

The fire reaches the house and everyone still alive flees to the cellar and waits to be eaten by the flames. Previously Ellery had determined to preserve some remnants of civilized tradition at the edge of chaos. "Get as much of your clothing off *as you decently can*," he had told the male and female firefighters. To the abject Smith he had said: "You're the type, old friend, who loses his head at the last moment and goes about bashing his brains out against the nearest wall. I'll thank you to remember that you've a certain amount of sheer pride to live up to." Now, in the basement, Ellery undertakes to keep his companions' minds from the terrible death that is minutes away by deducing the identity of the double murderer among them—a pointless exercise intended only to "lighten the last hour with a game of wits." He knows that what he's doing is absurd and wishes "with fierce yearning that at this moment, when their attention was wholly caught, when for the fluttering instant they turned their faces away from death, that death would come crashing and smoking upon them through a collapsed ceiling, so that their lives might be snuffed out with no warning and no pain." Yet, like a proud French aristo facing Mme. Guillotine, he will not betray his ideal of human excellence as long as a thread of life is in him. In what can legitimately be called an existential detective novel, Dannay and Lee balance perfectly the nobility and the lunacy in this confrontation of Enlightened Man and death.

Siamese Twin is not as richly plotted as earlier Queen books and would be no longer than a novelette were it not for the fire sequences, but the detection and the fiery background are necessary to each other and to the theme of the power and emptiness of reason in the face of death. On the puzzle level, this novel offers some dazzling variants on the false confession gambit and, for the first time in a novel about Ellery and his father, a series of wonderfully involuted Dying Message clues. It's by far the finest of the four novels of 1933 and among the finest of Period One.

***

The four issues of *Mystery League* were dated consecutively from October 1933 to January 1934, the first three running 160 pages apiece, the last 128 pages. In addition to *Drury Lane's Last Case* as by Barnaby Ross, the October issue included three excellent short stories—Dashiell Hammett's "Nightshade," Dorothy L. Sayers' "Suspicion," and Queen's own "The Glass-Domed Clock"—plus a column of criminous criticism and gossip and a potpourri of brain-teasers. The issue closed with an editorial, "Through the Looking Glass," which seems to be the first Queenian use of a motif from one of Fred Dannay's favorite authors, Lewis Carroll.

The following issues featured much less well-known contributors, no doubt because the top names like Agatha Christie were beyond reach of the magazine's modest budget. The full-length novel in the November 1933 issue was Phoebe Atwood Taylor's *The Riddle of Volume Four,* which was published in book form under her pseudonym Alice Tilton as *Beginning With a Bash.* Also included were short stories by English authors G.D.H. & M.I. Cole and Henry Wade, plus Part I of *Drums Beat at Night,* a serial by Gavin Holt (Charles Rodda), plus more brain-teasers and another column of gossip and critique, this one titled "To the Queen's Taste." The complete novel for December 1933 was Brian Flynn's *The Spiked Lion,* and the three new short stories included one by a young man named Thomas Walsh who was soon to become a top name in the field. Part II of Gavin Holt's serial was supplemented by another helping of "To the Queen's Taste" shoptalk, another assortment of puzzles, and, for the first and only time in *Mystery League,* a "Reader's Corner" letter column. In the somewhat smaller farewell issue of January 1934 there was still room for a complete novel (B.G. Quin's *The Mystery of the Black Gate*), two short stories, and the final installment of *Drums Beat at Night,* not to mention a final potpourri of brain-teasers and a final "To the Queen's Taste" column. A fifth number of the magazine was assembled, Fred Dannay told me, but never printed. Commercial flop though it was, *Mystery League* offered Fred a crash course in editorial arts that would serve him well about eight years later.

CHAPTER FIVE

Exit Ellery I

ONLY ONE ELLERY QUEEN NOVEL appeared the following year but it must have made more money for Fred and Manny than any that came before it since a condensed version in the high-paying *Redbook* (June 1934) preceded hardcover publication. Most of *The Chinese Orange Mystery* (1934) takes place on the 22ⁿᵈ floor of Manhattan's Hotel Chancellor, which houses both the office of Donald Kirk—wealthy young publisher, socialite, jewel and stamp collector—and the huge apartment Kirk shares with his sister, his wheelchair-bound father, and the fiery old philologist's private nurse. At 5:44 p.m. on a brisk fall day, a stout middle-aged man of excruciatingly ordinary appearance steps out of the elevator and asks Mrs. Shane, the floor clerk, to direct him to Kirk's office. Osborne, Kirk's secretary, informs the stranger that Mr. Kirk is out and ushers him into a luxurious waiting room where the newcomer sits down, alone. During the next hour several of Kirk's acquaintances—including his fiancée's brother, a woman novelist and an international adventuress—drop into the office looking for him, but he remains out. He arrives at 6:45, accompanied by his friend Ellery Queen, to find the waiting room transformed into something out of Lewis Carroll: the rug turned upside down, pictures and clock facing the walls, floor lamps standing on their shades, every movable object in the room either inside out or backside front. Lying on the overturned rug, his brains splattered with a blow from the fireplace poker, is Mr. Nobody from Nowhere, the nameless visitor on nameless business. Every article of clothing—collar, shirt, coat, trousers, shoes—is on him backwards. There's no necktie on the body or in the room but the peelings of a tangerine are found in a fruit bowl. Two ornamental African spears have been thrust up the dead man's trouser legs, out at the waist and under his reversed suit jacket, with the blades sticking out of his lapels like horns growing on the back of his neck.

If the entire story of the man who was backwards even approached the craftsmanship and bizarrerie of the early chapters, *Chinese Orange* would rank as one of the all-time great detective novels. What we get after the superb opening, however, is a series of excursions into philately, sex, Chinese culture, blackmail and missing Hebrew biblical commentaries, none relevant to the murder except that by amazing coincidence each involves some element that is, in one sense of the word or another, backward. Despite the usual Challenge to the Reader, not even the genius reader Manny Lee postulated could have imagined the outlandish physical manipulations on which the solution hinges. A simple police laboratory examination of the two spears under magnification would have disclosed physical traces of the truth, but for obvious reasons no such examination is made. And why did the murder victim tell his associates so much about his plans when nobody in his circumstances would have confided in anyone? *Chinese Orange* may well have been the most financially successful Queen novel of Period One but it's also one of the weakest.

***

In 1933 Dannay and Lee had written the first three short stories about their character and seen two of them published in magazines. Early the following year they decided to write more: enough to fill a book. That book was *The Adventures of Ellery Queen* (1934). The title of the collection was meant to evoke Conan Doyle's *Adventures of Sherlock Holmes*, and the title of each story was ritually preceded by "The Adventure of . . ." which we shall omit here. The tales range from superb to substandard but every one of them has plenty of meat on its bones. Seven were first published in *Mystery*, a pulp widely distributed in America's drugstores; one in *Great Detective,* one in the debut issue of the cousins' own *Mystery League*, and the most recent of the group in *Redbook*, the only one of the four periodicals that paid top dollar. One seems never to have appeared in a magazine at all. If printed in *Adventures* in the order of their first publication, which presumably mirrors the order in which they were written, the sequence would have been as follows:

???	The African Traveler
Apr 1933	The One-Penny Black
May 1933	The Teakwood Case
Oct 1933	The Glass-Domed Clock
Apr 1934	The Three Lame Men
May 1934	The Hanging Acrobat
Jun 1934	The Two-Headed Dog
Aug 1934	The Bearded Lady
Sep 1934	The Invisible Lover
Oct 1934	The Seven Black Cats
Oct 1934	The Mad Tea-Party

Why they were printed in haphazard order remains a puzzlement.

"The African Traveler" (no prior magazine publication) finds Ellery as Professor of Applied Criminology, taking his students to the scene of a murder his father is investigating and later arguing alternative solutions with his class. The hotel-room bludgeoning of a lecherous salesman turns up a neat variant on the old cliché of the watch that stopped when the victim died, but there are just too many coincidences and implausible events in this one.

In "The Hanging Acrobat" (*Mystery*, May 1934, as "The Girl on the Trapeze"), a far superior story, Ellery and the Inspector probe the backstage murder of a promiscuous trapeze star and learn much about the sociology of vaudevillians and the art of knot-making before Ellery deduces which of the victim's amorous co-workers put the rope around her neck. "I'm not really concerned with the moral aspects of crime," he announces at the end. But he soon would be.

The earliest published Queen short story, "The One-Penny Black" (*Great Detective*, April 1933), offers a neat blend of the classic Six Napoleons and Purloined Letter situations. A stamp initialed by Queen Victoria and worth $30,000 is stolen from a dealer, the thief is chased into a bookstore but escapes, and during the next few days everyone who purchases from the store a copy of a certain best-seller is visited by a thief who steals nothing but that book. Ellery employs a battery of psychological deductions to wrap up the case.

"The Bearded Lady" (*Mystery*, August 1934, as "The Sinister Beard") is Queen's earliest Dying Message short story, and one of the finest. The murderee is a doctor and amateur painter, embroiled in an intra-family war over legacies, whose last act before being stabbed to death in his studio was to paint a beard on a portrait of Rembrandt's wife. The gruesome family of suspects echoes the mad Hatters in *The Tragedy of Y* but the solution and Ellery's reasoning are brilliantly original.

In "The Three Lame Men" (*Mystery*, April 1934) Ellery and his father are confronted with bizarre evidence indicating that a trio of cripples kidnapped a prosperous banker from his love nest and left his paramour to suffocate to death on her gag. Ellery's more rational reading of the evidence vindicates the prime suspect and deftly exposes a surprising murderer. "I feel sorry for [the killer's wife]," Richard says at the end. To which Ellery replies: "You always were a sentimentalist."

"The Invisible Lover" (*Mystery*, September 1934, as "Four Men Loved a Woman") brings Ellery to Corsica, New York, a somnolent hamlet of 745 souls, to tackle the murder of an artist who was staying in the local boardinghouse and romancing his landlord's lovely daughter. An attorney who was engaged to the young woman had made threats and owned the murder gun, which he admits no one could have taken from him during the crucial period. Ellery rearranges the boardinghouse furniture and unearths a meticulously wrought frame-up whose frustration somehow convinces him that there is a God.

In "The Teakwood Case" (*Mystery*, May 1933, as "The Affair of the Gallant Bachelor") Ellery is asked to look into a series of jewel thefts in an exclusive apartment house and finds his father trying to solve a strangulation in the same building, the only clue being a missing teakwood cigarette case. After a second murder committed almost under the Queens' noses, Ellery clears up all the crimes, but his reasoning and the whole story seem to presuppose a clairvoyant criminal.

"The Two-Headed Dog" (*Mystery*, June 1934) opens with Ellery stopping over at a remote New England inn whose proprietor tells him of some weird events that took place there several months before, involving a vanishing red-bearded stranger and a murdered dog. The host insists that unearthly noises have come ever since from the cabin where Redbeard had stayed. A few hours later another guest at the inn is found in his cabin with his throat slashed. A worn spot on a rug leads Ellery to a peculiarly inhuman murderer in this most atmospherically chilling of the eleven stories.

"The Glass-Domed Clock" (*Mystery League*, October 1933) is the most elaborate of all the Queen Dying Message stories and probably the finest. A curio dealer is found bashed to death in his shop. Evidence indicates that with his last ounce of strength he had smashed a glass jewel-case, clutched at a large amethyst with his left hand, crawled over to a pedestal, knocked the titular clock to the floor and died with his right hand resting on it. The case is further complicated by a silver loving-cup, an exiled Russian nobleman, a poker game and five birthday messages. Ellery's magnificent solution shows the cousins' genius for using mesmeric but fair indirection to conceal the obvious answer in plain sight.

"The Seven Black Cats" (*Mystery*, October 1934, as "The Black Cats Vanished") opens with Ellery visiting a pet shop on a routine errand and hearing about a miserly old invalid who is known to be a cat-hater but phones in an order once a week for a black green-eyed tomcat. Going to the apartment shared by the invalid and her sister, Ellery finds both women vanished and the black cat beaten to death in the bathtub. Before the end of the day he's also found a vicious murderer of people, although he never does find an acceptable motivation for the murder of the cat or the second human.

In "The Mad Tea-Party" (*Redbook*, October 1934), which was Fred Dannay's favorite short tale from this period and another proof of his fondness for Lewis Carroll, Ellery is invited to a Long Island house party that is to feature a private performance of *Alice in Wonderland*, but festive spirits are dampened when the host vanishes the morning after Ellery arrives. Then comes the delivery of a series of packages containing pairs of shoes, cabbages, chessmen and other bizarre objects. Ellery's solution of the mad events is astoundingly simple, although it presupposes a secret closet without a *raison d'être*. The tale indeed owes much to Carroll but Ellery's psychological war against his adversary is inspired by Poe's "Thou Art the Man."

***

The requirements of the slick magazines, in one of which "The Mad Tea-Party" had first appeared, drove a radical change in the direction of Queen's work that began to emerge around this time. His next novel, which like *Chinese Orange* first appeared in condensed form in *Redbook*

(April 1935), expresses the cousins' growing dissatisfaction with the strict chess problem in the Van Dine mold, and we can infer that the end of Period One is in sight. *The Spanish Cape Mystery* (1935) is set on a private peninsula thrusting out into the Atlantic. At the far end of the cape sits the sprawling hacienda of Walter Godfrey, a hermit-like Wall Street pirate who putters around his beloved rock gardens in filthy overalls, with lordly indifference to the guests his young wife has invited to the Cape: an obese and overwrought matron, a savage cowboy millionaire, a former musical comedy star, a young man in love with Godfrey's daughter, and a ruthless professional lover calling himself John Marco. It's Marco who is found one morning on the private beach terrace, strangled by a coil of wire. His hat is on his head, his ebony stick in his right hand, a black opera cloak is draped about him, but beneath the cloak he's stark naked. Ellery is visiting in the area and is enlisted by the local police but is faced with other questions besides who done it. Why did a one-eyed giant kidnap Walter Godfrey's brother-in-law shortly before the murder? Why did Mrs. Godfrey invite complete strangers as house guests? Why did they accept the invitations? Why is every woman in the house terrified by Marco's death? And why did the murderer strip Marco of every stitch of clothing except hat, stick and cloak? Ellery's solution is relentlessly logical and scrupulously fair, but one can sense the cousins' realization that they are fast exhausting the possibilities of the formal deductive puzzle. This is the fourth of their novels since 1932 that rests on the gambit whose *locus classicus* is Conan Doyle's *The Valley of Fear*, and the wary reader of other Period One books can figure out the truth before finishing fifty pages.

In Chapter 15 Ellery states his Period One credo: "My work is done with symbols . . . not with human beings. . . . I choose to close my mind to the human elements and treat it as a problem in mathematics. The fate of the murderer I leave to those who decide such things." But at the end of the book, realizing that he's exposed a murderer whose act was justified if any crime ever was, he renounces his old self. "I've often boasted that the human equation means nothing to me. But it does, damn it all, it does!" In *Spanish Cape* there is no price to pay since we are assured that on the known facts no local jury will convict the murderer. We haven't yet reached novels like *Ten Days' Wonder* where the misuse of Ellery's mind kills people, but we are clearly very close to the end of one of the great sustained endeavors in the history of crime fiction.

CHAPTER SIX

The New EQ

THE QUEEN OUTPUT from 1936 to the end of the decade is so different in content, style, form and motifs from what went before as to constitute a second period. S.S. Van Dine, the major influence on the "complex, logical, deductive, almost completely intellectual" Queen novels of Period One, had lost much of his appeal by the time this period began, for whodunit readers in general and for Dannay and Lee as well. During the years that are bracketed together as Queen's second period, what radically reshaped the cousins' fiction was not the example of any other writer but the requirements of two extremely well-paying media to which they'd begun to sell very late in Period One: the slick-paper magazines like *Redbook* and *Cosmopolitan*, and the movies.

In 1979 Dannay described his and Lee's second-period strategy as follows: "We loosened the construction . . . ; we put more emphasis on character development and background; we put more emphasis on human-interest situations. And what we were doing, frankly, was to aim at getting magazine serialization, which paid very good money in those days, and to sell to the movies, which was the only other means of getting extra money. . . . We turned to commercialism because we frankly wanted to make more money." Compared with the great detective novels of Period One, most of what the cousins wrote in the later 1930s suffers from intellectual thinness, an overabundance of so-called love interest (meaning a tedious boy-meets-girl counterplot), and characters all too obviously tailored to please story editors in the slick magazine suites and the studios. But in the longer view they succeeded at least partially in opening up the formal deductive puzzle and making room within its cerebral rigor for more of the virtues of mainstream storytelling. Ellery II was no longer a priggish Philo Vance derivative like Ellery I but had taken several steps along the road to recognizable humanity.

Those whose horizons are limited to prose fiction may have the impression that Dannay and Lee were loafing during Period Two since during those years they produced just five novels, plus a handful of short stories which were collected in 1940 (along with the last short exploits of Period One) as *The New Adventures of Ellery Queen*. In fact Fred and Manny were not slacking off but investing much of their time in media that were new to them.

One of these was the Broadway stage. At the request of producer Jed Harris, Dannay and Lee collaborated with professional playwright Lowell Brentano on *Danger, Men Working*, a stand-alone effort about three would-be dramatists who encounter murder while trying to come up with a mystery plot. The play opened in Baltimore on February 6, 1936 but closed after a few nights there and in Philadelphia. A movie sale later in the year generated a small amount of money for the cousins. Their unhappy experience with the live stage was more than matched by their misadventures in movieland.

***

"[A] benediction upon the head of whoever invented the cinema. May he be thrice blessed!" Ellery I had exclaimed in Chapter 21 of *The American Gun Mystery* (1934), the year before the movie industry began trying to convert EQ to celluloid. The cousins had nothing to do with these attempts, and Fred once told me that if he was watching TV in bed at night and a Queen-based movie came on, he'd duck under the covers.

In 1935 a new studio called Republic Pictures was created by former tobacco mogul Herbert A. Yates out of the remains of several low-budget outfits like Liberty, Monogram and Mascot. Among devotees of the so-called B Western, Republic is a legend, the home to shoot-em-up stars like John Wayne, Gene Autry and Roy Rogers and cliffhanger serial heroes like Zorro and The Lone Ranger. Very few of the studio's non-Westerns are highly regarded today; certainly not the two that we briefly consider here.

The Spanish Cape Mystery (1935), nominally based on the then most recent Queen novel, came to Republic from its Liberty component. Lewis D. Collins directed from a screenplay by Albert DeMond which was somewhat faithful to the book, although censorship required that the body of John Marco be found not naked but wearing bathing trunks under the opera cloak. Helen Twelvetrees was given top billing as Stella Godfrey (Rosa Godfrey in the novel), with Donald Cook coming in second as Ellery, who passionately romances Ms. Godfrey as he never did in the novel. Guy Usher was shoehorned into the continuity as Inspector Queen, who hadn't appeared at all in the book. Featured in the cast were Berton Churchill (Judge Macklin), Betty Blythe (Mrs. Godfrey) and Huntley Gordon (David Kummer). Loudmouthed Sheriff Moley, whom Ellery allows to take credit for solving the mystery, was played by Harry Stubbs. Outdoor sequences were shot in the seaside community of Laguna. As usual in Hollywood versions of detective novels, large chunks of the reasoning were axed.

The following year Republic came out with a sequel. *The Mandarin Mystery* (1936) was ineptly adapted by four screenwriters (John Francis Larkin, Rex Taylor, Gertrude Orr and Cortland Fitzsimmons) who took the impossible crime element out of the plot of *The Chinese Orange Mystery* and thereby scuttled its *raison d'être*. Ellery was played by Eddie Quillan, a vaudeville hoofer type whose oafish smirks and incessant wisecracking suggest that he landed the part on the basis of his initials. In the role of Inspector Queen was the marginally more adequate Wade Boteler. Charlotte Henry (Josephine Temple), Franklin Pangborn (Mellish), Rita LeRoy (Martha Kirk) and George Irving (Dr. Alexander Kirk) rounded out the cast. The whole mess was directed by Ralph Staub.

If nothing else, these films brought Queen's work to the attention of other and bigger studios. Over the next few years Fred and Manny were invited to Hollywood for three stints as screenwriters, a term apiece at Columbia, Paramount and MGM. We'll soon take a closer look at how the cousins collaborated; suffice it for now to say that their work methods tended towards the argumentative, often disturbing people in neighboring offices. At one point the Paramount mimeograph department, which gave forth a constant clatter from dozens of machines, complained about the noise Fred and Manny were making.

In an interview with the press after returning from one of these excursions they described their impressions in their own brand of crosstalk.

> Dannay: "There's enough material in Hollywood for a thousand books."
>
> Lee: "Don't let anyone tell you that fantastic stories of Hollywood are exaggerated."
>
> Dannay: "They don't tell the half of it. Our first assignment was to do a racing story."
>
> Lee: "Neither of us had ever seen a horse race and we haven't yet."
>
> Dannay: "But we found a man who knew racing from the ground up, lived with him for three days and nights, and wrote the picture."
>
> Lee: "Which delighted the producer."

Actually the racing screenplay was shelved, and the cousins received not a single screen credit for their work on movies of the late Thirties. "The place was filled with crazy people," Dannay said in 1979. "I told Manny even if I had to dig ditches for the rest of my life, I wasn't coming back." But while at MGM they met two young contract actors who, at least in Fred's mind, would have been perfect for the part of Ellery: Franchot Tone and Walter Pidgeon. And the cousins' Hollywood experiences would contribute heavily to some of their novels and stories of Period Two.

***

It's convenient, and conventional, to treat that period as beginning with *Halfway House* (1936), the first Queen novel to break the chain of nationality titles and the first to appear in condensed form before book publication in that top-of-the-line slick magazine *Cosmopolitan* (June 1936). But the "Problem in Deduction" subtitle from all the Period One novels, and the Challenge to the Reader from most of them, remain intact. And, as Ellery in the Foreword points out to that Period One mainstay J.J. McC, there's no reason why the book couldn't have been titled *The Swedish Match Mystery*. The movement to Period Two is a gradual evolution, not a sudden change of course.

On his way back to New York, Ellery stops off for dinner at a restaurant in Trenton, New Jersey and happens to encounter Bill Angell, a long-unseen college friend who is now practicing law and social activism in Philadelphia. Bill's sister Lucy is married to often absent traveling salesman Joe Wilson, who for undisclosed reasons has asked to meet privately with his brother-in-law that evening at a remote house on the shore of the Delaware River. As Bill drives up to the meeting place, he hears a scream and sees a female figure rush out the front door into a huge cream Cadillac and race away. As Bill discovers when he enters, the house is a shabbily furnished hovel except for a rich fawn wall-to-wall carpet. On the center table is a chipped plate containing twenty burnt paper-match stubs. Near it lies a bloody paperknife, a tiny cone of cork impaled on its point. Behind the table lies Joe Wilson, who tells Bill with his last breath that he was stabbed by a veiled woman. Bill phones Ellery as well as the police. At the crime scene Ellery makes some crucial observations. The dead man's suit is of very poor quality but several other suits in the house bear the label of the most exclusive private tailor in New York. There is no food or bed in the shack but a sailboat with an outboard motor is in the boathouse at the river's edge. A rusty nude figurine, part of an auto radiator cap, is discovered in the muddy driveway. What most astonishes Ellery is that he knows the dead man: not as Joe Wilson the impecunious peddler but as Joseph Kent Gimball of Park Avenue, husband of socialite Jessica Borden Gimball and stepfather of lovely Andrea Gimball.

The murder of the man with two wives and two lives, in the halfway house between New York and Philadelphia where he was both of his identities and neither, seems on all the evidence to be the work of Lucy Wilson, who has ample motive and no alibi and whose car is proven by muddy tire-tracks and the rusty figurine to have been on the scene although she denies knowing anything of Joe's double life. The middle chapters are taken up with her trial and Bill Angell's defense of his sister in court, while Ellery is off on his own, trying to pry Andrea Gimball's hidden knowledge out of her. After several weeks he returns to Halfway House to set an elaborate psychological trap for the real killer.

Even without the brain-bruising webwork of *The Greek Coffin*

Mystery and *The Tragedy of X*, there are a few cracks in the foundation of *Halfway House*. How did the murderer know that Wilson/Gimball would be at the house that night? Why did he plan the crime so that the dead man's double life was bound to be exposed even though the killer had every reason in the world *not* to want Jessica's bigamous marriage revealed? Still and all, the plot is intriguing (though unworkable except at a time when women's skirts were ankle length), the solution is closely reasoned and the clues subtly planted, especially the incident of Pierre the obliging tobacconist. All things considered, this novel marks a smooth transition to Period Two.

***

Between *Halfway House* and the next Queen novel a brief paragraph appeared in *Publishers Weekly* (October 10, 1936), revealing the long-concealed identities behind both the Queen and the Barnaby Ross bylines. Clearly the cousins felt they no longer needed such publicity stunts. And that next novel *The Door Between* (1937), which first appeared in condensed form in *Cosmopolitan* (December 1936), is unequivocally a work of Period Two, with the Challenge to the Reader omitted, deduction taking a back seat to intuition, plot subordinated to characterization and relationships, and "love interest" on every page.

Karen Leith had come to the U.S. from Japan in 1927, after her expatriate father's death, and sequestered herself in a house in Greenwich Village from which then came forth a series of incredibly beautiful novels. To celebrate her winning the major American prize in literature, her publisher arranges a party in the Japanese garden behind her prim house in Washington Square. Among the lesser guests is Ellery, who gets to meet both Miss Leith and her fiancé, Dr. John MacClure, a man worn out by years of search for a cancer cure, who treats money and fame and life with detached scientific aloofness. (A sort of medical Philo Vance?) Ellery doesn't get to meet MacClure's young niece Eva but she meets young society doctor Richard Scott and is soon engaged to him.

Some time later, while MacClure is off on an ocean voyage, Eva and Dick decide to get married right after he returns and she dashes downtown to share the news with Karen Leith. The maid tells her that Karen is busy writing and Eva waits in the sitting room next to Karen's bedroom-study. After a long silence from within, she steps into the inner room and finds Karen lying on the dais behind her desk, stabbed in the throat with a half-scissors. Being as brainless as most heroines of the female-oriented mystery novels of the time, Eva fingers the weapon, gets blood all over her hand and presents a perfect picture of a murderess caught in the act to the strange young man she suddenly sees watching her from the doorway. Being as brainless as most male leads in that subgenre of crime fiction, private detective Terry Ring instantly concludes that the young woman is innocent and sets out to rearrange the evidence so as to suggest an outside assailant.

Terry's and Eva's efforts to deceive Inspector Queen and Ellery consume as much of this novel as the gradual revelation of skeletons in the Leith and MacClure family closets. Among the puzzlements are the rock that broke Karen's window while she lay dying, the pet jay that vanished from the death room and reappeared downstairs, the woman with the short right leg who'd been living in Leith's attic, and a 20-year-old "accident" in Japan. At the climax we are introduced to the Two Solutions device that will recur in countless later Queen novels: Ellery explains the crime to the satisfaction of everyone but himself, then later reveals to the murderer alone a second and more stunning solution.

The cousins were quite right to drop the Challenge to the Reader this time, for Ellery's solution is so intuitive as to suggest Maigret rather than the logical successor to Sherlock Holmes. There's also a troublesome flaw in the murderer's plan, which would have gone up in smoke if Karen Leith had acted naturally and written the kind of note that Ellery produces at the denouement. And the triangle Eva/Terry Ring/Richard Scott is almost identical to the triangle Andrea Gimball/Bill Angell/Burke Jones in *Halfway House*. *The Door Between* is not major Queen but it's a major step forward in the evolution of the new EQ.

***

March 1937 saw the release of the movie based on the failed stage play *Danger, Men Working* which the cousins had written in collaboration with Lowell Brentano. *The Crime Nobody Saw* (Paramount, 1937) was directed by Charles Barton from a screenplay by Bertram Millhauser. *The Film Nobody Saw* might have been a better title. Aspiring dramatists Nick Milburn (Lew Ayres), Babe Lawton (Eugene Pallette) and Horace Dryden (Benny Baker) have received a $500 advance to write a mystery play, but so far they haven't written a word and their wealthy backer

(Ferdinand Gottschalk) is demanding his money back. In desperation they rent an apartment and try to come up with a plot. A drunken neighbor wanders into their room and passes out on the floor. When they find $15,000 in his pockets, inspiration strikes and they decide to build their play around the premise that he's a blackmailer who's been murdered. The soup hits the fan when they discover that their visitor really has been murdered. The movie aimed at laughs but failed to get any.

**

Later that year Fred and Manny decided to use their Hollywood experiences in an Ellery Queen novel. Their decision paid off in the sense that once again a condensed version appeared in *Cosmopolitan* (December 1937) before the book was published in hardcover. But the characters in *The Devil To Pay* (1937) are little more than molds waiting to be filled by movie actors and its plot is nowhere near complex enough for a full-length novel. The scene is Sans Souci, a Hollywood hilltop development consisting of four faux-Spanish mansions and a central swimming pool. Middle-aged millionaire sportsman Rhys Jardin occupies one house, along with his daughter Valerie and his confidant/athletic trainer Pink and a platoon of servants. Across the pool is the abode of Solomon Spaeth, an obese and ruthless tycoon who lives with his "protégée" Winni Moon and—when he hasn't stormed out of the house after a political argument—his son Walter, a left-wing cartoonist. Proletarian principles have not kept Walter from falling in love with that daughter of privilege Val Jardin. Solly Spaeth had persuaded Rhys Jardin to invest in the gigantic Ohippi hydro-electric development project but had sold out his own interest at a huge profit just before the Ohippi machinery and plants were ruined by floods. While mobs of ruined investors converge on Sans Souci, the now bankrupt Rhys Jardin has two violent arguments with Solly Spaeth and Walter threatens his father over the debacle. Meanwhile an acquaintance of Walter's has arrived in town to write screenplays for the Magna studio, a luxuriantly bearded fellow who eschews polysyllables. His name? Ellery Queen.

Solomon Spaeth is found in his study, dead of a stab wound with a molasses stain at its edge. A 17th-century Italian rapier is missing from the collection on the study wall. The gatekeeper tells Inspector Glücke that he saw Rhys Jardin enter the grounds just before the murder but Val knows the visitor was Walter Spaeth, wearing her father's torn camel's-hair coat. Walter doesn't admit the truth and refuses to explain why but asks Val to trust him and keep silent. The young couple discover Rhys' bloodstained coat and the missing rapier, both planted in Jardin's closet, but the police find the same objects a few minutes later. Ellery enters the case to help Val clear her arrested father but has to break down the interconnected lies of Val, Rhys and Walter before tying together the two-fingered handprint, the Indian club dropped down a sewer, the tear in a terrace awning and the pair of cracked binoculars as he identifies the murderer.

The main problem with *The Devil To Pay* is that Ellery just isn't Ellery any more. Change his name to Charlie Brown and, except for the denouement scene, you'd never identify him with the protagonist of the earlier Queen novels. And the clichés breed like rabbits, with Hollywooden misunderstandings between the cute young couple, an unmasked killer who aims a weapon at the sleuths and snarls "Don't move," and True Love triumphant at the fadeout. The agony of the Depression is supposed to be central but we see no more real pain or despair than the most reactionary front office would allow. Instead the tears are reserved for the tragic plight of the Jardins, reduced to the penury of a five-room apartment, one car and one measly quasi-servant. "It's like a movie, thought Walter gloomily." And that's precisely the problem: Fred and Manny shrank their world to Hollywood's dimensions in hopes of a movie sale. Result: dreadful book, no movie. At least not officially.

***

In the years since he and Manny Lee had quit their day jobs, Fred Dannay had become a fervent bibliophile, with the goal of owning a copy of every collection of detective-crime short stories ever published. This ambition in turn led him to think of himself not just as an author but as an anthologist of detective fiction, and over the next several decades he was to edit dozens of such volumes. In the introduction to the first of these he set forth his credo that an anthology should not be a miscellaneous grab-bag of stories, as so many in fact were, but should "possess a unique central idea to hold it together, to differentiate it from any other anthology ever published." The structural principle of

Challenge to the Reader (1938) involved changing the names of each of the 25 detectives who appeared in the book, leaving it to the reader to identify both the sleuth and the author of each tale. The unforeseen result was that the book was cut off from any conceivable audience. Those who hadn't before read detective stories couldn't play the game, and for those who had read even a few the game was too simple to play, especially since the names of supporting characters like Lestrade, Flambeau and Sergeant Velie remained unaltered. It took the Stokes company several years to sell out the original edition of this anthological misfire.

***

If we can make one novel out of our misadventures in movieland, Fred and Manny must have asked each other sometime in the middle months of 1938, why not two? They lucked out in the sense that *Cosmopolitan* once again paid them handsomely to publish a condensation (October 1938) before their next book's hardcover appearance. *The Four of Hearts* (1938) finds Ellery still sitting around the Magna studio after several well-paid weeks of doing nothing. Finally Jacques Butcher, the studio's vice-president and reigning boy wonder—modeled, Fred told me, on Irving Thalberg, whom he and Manny had met during their stint at MGM—finds work for his new screenwriter. Ellery is assigned to collaborate on the script of a blockbuster biopic dealing with Magna's own leading star families, the Royles and the Stuarts, whose highly publicized feud has cheered the hearts of Hollywood gossip columnists for two decades. While researching the subject, Ellery does something that would have been inconceivable in Period One. He falls in love with one such columnist, lovely and reclusive Paula Paris, who offers him inside information on debonair Jack Royle and his son Ty and on gorgeous Blythe Stuart and her daughter Bonnie. Suddenly Jack and Blythe discover and admit to each other that despite twenty years of feuding they are and always have been in love. The Magna publicity office goes ecstatic and plans a mammoth public wedding for the stars at an airfield, to be followed by a flight in Ty Royle's plane to a no less public island honeymoon. The only cloud on the horizon is the strange series of playing cards that Blythe Stuart has been receiving in the mail, one card even delivered to her at the airfield just before the wedding. After the ceremony everyone toasts the happy couple and the red-and-gold monoplane takes off. Then Ty Royle, who's supposed to be piloting the plane, is found bound and gagged in the hangar. The plane never reaches Honeymoon Island but is located that night on a plateau not far from the remote mountain estate of Blythe Stuart's hypochondriac father. Whoever flew the craft is gone and Jack and Blythe are found in the plane's cabin, dead of morphine poisoning. Ellery's informal investigation of the murders ticks off the harried Inspector Glücke but unearths some offtrail clues: a set of filed-down typewriter keys, a threatening letter to a dead woman, a frightened old man running around in a thunderstorm wearing a flying helmet, a glass of iced tea. While sifting the evidence and bewailing the snail's progress of his own romance with Paula Paris, Ellery also hunts for a way to sabotage the budding love affair between Ty Royle and Bonnie Stuart, which he believes is a source of extreme danger to them both. Finally, knowing who the murderer is but lacking evidence, Ellery arranges an elaborate charade to make him attempt another double murder.

The Four of Hearts boasts a number of skillfully planted clues, an exceptionally well-concealed murderer, and a complex plot bristling with legal subtleties, but much of the book is only vaguely relevant to the plot. Dannay and Lee threw every imaginable ingredient into their mixture: a wacky-humor opening, three separate love stories, a barrage of movieland patter, and a deadly serious multiple murder scheme. In the first chapter Hollywood is made to seem absurd, in the funeral sequence it's presented as sick, when Paula Paris is involved it's warm and wonderful. The abrupt changes of tone from farce to grief to light romance to rigorous reasoning are grating, and the meant-to-be-made-into-a-movie aura prevents one from taking the book with full seriousness. On the other hand, the disunity of tone enables the cousins to plant clues unobtrusively in the chapters we're tempted to read with relaxed minds. On re-reading those chapters we can learn a great deal about the murderer's reactions to unforeseen developments by taking a closer look at dialogue which, the first time around, we dismissed as Hollywood banter. If nothing else, *The Four of Hearts* offers a fine cockeyed view of the big studios and a wild roller-coaster ride through the celluloid Wonderland.

***

By 1938 detective fiction was in its golden age, and followers of the genre could count on between one and four books a year from John

Dickson Carr, Agatha Christie, Erle Stanley Gardner, Rex Stout, and of course Dannay and Lee. Meanwhile a young executive in the Columbia Broadcasting System's programming department was toying with the concept of a new kind of radio drama. George Zachary (1911-1964) had been associated until then with CBS musical variety series like *99 Men and a Girl*, which featured the Raymond Paige orchestra and "the incomparable Hildegarde." What he really wanted was to produce and direct an hour-long detective series that would invite listeners to match wits with the protagonist and, if they were very smart and very lucky, beat him to the solution of the week's mystery. What he required to realize this dream was a writer who knew the genre well and could turn out a 60-minute script each week. No one of that description was working in dramatic radio, a medium still in its adolescence at the time, with mystery series few and far between. The spooky anthology *Lights Out!* was doing well, as were the cop show *Gang Busters* and the newshawk series *Big Town* and of course the weird weekly exploits of *The Shadow*, portrayed in 1937-38 by a young genius named Orson Welles. But except for an occasional cycle of adventures of Sherlock Holmes, who debuted over the airwaves in 1930, radio had no genuine detective programs at all.

If we are to believe the unsigned article in *Radio Varieties* for March 1940, Zachary spent night after night sitting up

> until the early hours of the morning, reading mystery author after mystery author, looking for the one perfect writer who could turn out a complete detective story every week, make it puzzling enough to intrigue the radio audience, and yet fair enough so that they could solve it if they marshaled all the facts correctly.

The clear implication of this article is that Zachary knew next to nothing about the detective fiction of his time and didn't have sense enough to seek advice from fans of the genre, for according to *Radio Varieties* it was only "after reading some 200 odd stories" that he "stumbled upon the first of the mysteries connected with Ellery Queen." This tidbit smacks of publicity hype, but in any event once Zachary had read a few Queen novels and realized that their "Challenge to the Reader" device was the precise literary equivalent of his own plan to enlist the radio audience as detectives, he got in touch with Dannay and Lee and proposed to make their character the star of his own weekly series on CBS.

At first the cousins were reluctant. They knew nothing about radio writing and were being offered a starting salary of just $25 a week to learn the ropes. Then—and most of this reconstruction is informed guesswork—they must have thought long and hard about their economic situation and their professional goals. Between them they had a wife, an ex-wife and four children to support. Twenty-five dollars was only ten less than they'd received for the first Ellery Queen short story six years before, and currently the short adventures of their character were appearing in slicks that paid top prices. But the audience for a successful radio program could be counted in the millions, astronomically larger than the readership of the most profitable Queen novels. And the cousins had already proved their own and Ellery's ability to change with the times and the needs of different media when they'd converted him from the Philo Vance clone of the early books to the slick magazine and Hollywood sleuth of Period Two. So why not invest some time and energy and give this new form of storytelling a try?

First of course they had to learn the fundamentals of writing for radio. This they did by turning out a number of scripts, without credit and at minimal pay, for two existing crime series. One of these was *Alias Jimmy Valentine* (1937-1939), a program produced by soap-opera specialists Frank and Anne Hummert and very remotely based on the O. Henry short story "A Retrieved Reformation" which had earlier spawned a popular song, a stage play and three silent movies. Bert Lytell starred as a reformed safecracker who helped the police by not quite legal means. In his introduction to *Cops and Robbers* (1948), a paperback collection of O. Henry's crime stories that he had edited, Dannay claimed that he and Lee wrote "weekly scripts" for this series. The only episode known to be theirs is the one broadcast November 21, 1938.

Alias Jimmy Valentine has long been forgotten but the other series on which the cousins honed their radio-writing skills was that audio immortal *The Shadow*. How much they enhanced the saga of that mysterious character with the power to cloud men's minds will probably never be known for sure. When I asked Fred he couldn't remember any episode titles he and Manny had written, nor even whether The Shadow was being played by Orson Welles or his successor Bill Johnstone when the cousins' scripts were aired. It now seems clear that they made their contributions to *The Shadow* during the 1938-39 season, the first of five in which Johnstone played the character. Radio scholar William Nadel has pinpointed between eight and eleven episodes, broadcast between November 1938 and March 1939, that were probably the cousins' work, but no business papers have yet come to light that would let us know for sure.

***

A little more than two months before the Ellery Queen series debuted, Dannay and Lee became involved in another radio venture which to the end of his life Fred believed to be one of the most fascinating experiments in the medium's history. *Author! Author!* was an impromptu mélange of game and panel show which the cousins created and sold to the Mutual network. It debuted on April 7, 1939 under the sponsorship of the B.F. Goodrich Rubber Company and with Robert Lewis Shayon as director. The moderator for the series was humorist S.J. Perelman, although light-verse wizard Ogden Nash took Perelman's place one week. Dannay and Lee, billed respectively as "Mr. Ellery" and "Mr Queen," served as permanent panelists, and the guests each week were media figures like Dorothy Parker, Heywood Broun, Moss Hart and George S. Kaufman, Mark and Carl Van Doren, Fannie Hurst, Erskine Caldwell and Quentin Reynolds. The format of the program was described by the announcer as "a fiction funfest." Each week's show would begin with a dramatized version of some inexplicable event. Here's an example, employed on the first program (which has survived on audio) and summarized by Dannay exactly forty years later for David Behrens of *Newsday*:

> A young man arrives for the reading of his uncle's will. The only heir, he is desperately in need of money to cover gambling debts. The will gives him a choice: Accept $10,000 in cash or the contents of an envelope. He opens the envelope, which is empty, with no stamps or writing on it. "I will take the envelope," he says.

At this curtain line the sketch would end and the moderator would challenge each of the week's four panelists—Fred, Manny, and two guests who varied from program to program—to devise on the spot a set of circumstances that would make sense of the scene. Fred's explanation for his own example was as follows:

> The young man could not wait for his uncle to die. He killed him instead. The murder was committed with a slow-working poison placed on an envelope in his uncle's study. But the uncle realizes his nephew's evil deed and scrawls a revision in his will, to create a malicious dilemma. His nephew has to choose between $10,000 in cash or the chance to recover the only evidence of the murder—the uncle's final revenge.

After each panelist had offered an ad lib rationale for the situation, everyone would proceed to attack the others' constructions and defend his or her own. At the end of the first broadcast the announcer invited listeners to send in their own impossible story situations, with B.F. Goodrich promising $25 for each one used on the air. The panel members seemed to have a marvelous time heckling each other, but the whole concept presupposed an absurdly mechanical approach to storytelling and offered little to the millions of listeners who had no desire to hear writers match wits. Surprisingly, *Author! Author!* survived for almost a year before vanishing into the ether.

***

The next Queen novel returned Ellery from the movie capital to New York, but the tone of *The Dragon's Teeth* (1939) comes straight out of Hollywood's screwball comedy films of the late Thirties. The chapter titles are atrocious puns as in "The Devil To Pay," and Ellery is still little more than a receptacle for the personality of a movie star. The Queens are hardly present in the book's first half, in which we meet a new protagonist. Beau Rummell, who is both a lawyer and a ditchdigger and also a detective wannabee, meets Ellery and they decide to form their own agency. A few months later Cadmus Cole, an eccentric retired millionaire, retains the firm of Ellery Queen, Inc. to perform a task after his death whose nature he refuses to disclose now. Six weeks pass and Cole is reportedly buried at sea after suffering a heart attack on his yacht. His will reveals that the Queen firm's mission is to locate his two long-lost nieces, who will inherit his fortune if (a) they are and forever remain unmarried, and (b) they agree to live together for a year on his Tarrytown estate. Beau, for his own good reasons calling himself Ellery Queen, locates Kerrie Shawn, the younger cousin, and they promptly fall in love. Margo Cole, the other cousin, is located in Paris, comes to New York and also starts making eyes at "Ellery." The women's stay at the Tarrytown estate is punctuated by some near-fatal "accidents" aimed at Kerrie, and since the survivor cousin takes all under the Cole will, Margo is the prime suspect. When she is herself shot to death in front of Kerrie, the false Ellery frantically contracts the true EQ to bail out his beloved. Making all sorts of deductions from toothmarks on a pen-and-pencil set, Ellery unmasks the villain and brings the lovers and the Cole millions together.

With its farcical love and money problems and its neat variants on Conan Doyle's *Valley of Fear* gambit before the brilliant final resolution, *The Dragon's Teeth* is okay as light entertainment, but plotwise it's—dare I say it?—full of cavities. The obvious explanation of the evidence is wrong, but only a dentist could possibly figure out why. Queen doesn't seem to realize that the entire Cole will, to which the only available witness was also a main legatee, would almost certainly have been denied probate at the time (although the rule today is different in many jurisdictions), or that even if the will as such were valid, the courts would have thrown out its anti-marriage clause as a violation of public policy. An even bigger legal blunder is found in Chapter II, which presupposes that without a dead body the prosecution can't establish *corpus delicti* in a murder trial. Both the attempted asphyxiation of Kerrie Shawn and the murder of Margo Cole are possible only because the killer, in Raymond Chandler's phrase, had God sitting in his lap. It may not be coincidence that, among the five Queen novels of Period Two, this one alone was not published in condensed form by *Cosmopolitan* (or any other magazine) before it came out as a book.

***

Dannay and Lee were well along on their next novel when one or both of them picked up the latest *Saturday Evening Post* and noted with dismay that Agatha Christie in *And Then There Were None*, which the *Post* was running in five installments (between May 27 and June 24), had come up with the exact same plotline. This explains why there was no new Queen novel for 1940. In fact, except for four new short sports mysteries about Ellery which appeared in *Blue Book* during the second part of 1939, not a word of new prose fiction by the cousins appeared until well into 1942.

The only new Queen title published in 1940 was the cousins' second story collection, which reached book length after the four sports tales of 1939. *The New Adventures of Ellery Queen* (1940) lacks the unified style and content of the first *Adventures* or of later Queen collections but contains some top-notch stories.

The volume leads off with a short novel, perhaps the finest mystery ever written at that length. In "The Lamp of God" (*Street & Smith's Detective Story Magazine*, November 1935, as "House of Haunts") a desperate phone call from an attorney friend takes Ellery out to the raw January snowscape of Long Island. The patriarch of the maniacal Mayhew family is believed to have hidden a fortune in gold somewhere in the Poesque old mansion where he had lived and recently died, and attorney Thorne suspects that certain of the old tyrant's relatives are bent on finding and taking the treasure before it can be turned over to the old man's long-lost daughter. After a raw-nerved evening with an obese doctor, a demented old lady and an enigmatic young hired man, Ellery and the others go to bed but awaken to an event that convinces them the world has gone mad. The entire huge black house of old Sylvester Mayhew, next door to where they've been sleeping, has vanished in the night.

Unlike the vast majority of earlier Queen tales, "The Lamp of God" has a strong religious dimension. Ellery is described as "that lean and indefatigable agnostic" and says of himself: "If I were religiously inclined . . . if I, poor sinner that I am, possessed religious susceptibilities, I should have become permanently devout in the last three days." Elsewhere he remarks: "No riddle is esoteric . . . unless it's the riddle of God; and that's no riddle—it's a vast blackness." This is one of the finest pieces of atmospheric writing in the genre, evoking chills that rise off the page into our bones. With imagery of light against darkness, sun against cold, reason against the absurd, Queen summons up the terror of a universe abandoned to the demonic, then exorcises it through the rigorous use of the instrument given us by "chance, cosmos, God, whatever you may choose to call it": the enlightening human mind.

The titles of the next four stories in *New Adventures* are prefaced with the Holmesian "The Adventure of . . . ," which shall be omitted here, and unaccountably presented in haphazard rather than chronological order. "The Treasure Hunt" (*Street & Smith's Detective Story Magazine*, December 1935) presents Ellery with twin missions: to find the rope of pearls that one of retired General Barrett's house guests filched from his daughter's bedroom, and to identify the thief. He devises a treasure hunting game as a psychological trap and solves the case neatly and quickly. In "The Hollow Dragon" (*Redbook*, December 1936) the theft of a soapstone doorstop brings Ellery to the home of a wealthy Japanese importer in financial straits. Some deductions from an almanac (which the reader doesn't get to see) lead him to the thief and the motive and also to an unsuspected murder. Ellery is again described as a "notorious heretic" but stands up against the vilifications of Eastern religion indulged in by Miss Letitia Gallant, one of Queenland's most obnoxious Christians.

In "The House of Darkness" (*American Magazine*, February 1935) Ellery takes his houseboy Djuna for a day's outing at a surrealistic amusement park where a murder is committed, requiring our detective to deduce who did it and how the killer was able to put four lethal bullets into his victim's back in total darkness. The motif of red-green color-blindness from *The Greek Coffin Mystery* pops up again here in a different but equally ingenious way. That tale is a tightly plotted gem, but "The Bleeding Portrait" (*American Cavalcade*, September 1937, as "The Gramatan Mystery") is a dull disaster. Vacationing in the artists' summer colony of Natchitauk, Ellery becomes entangled in the amorous problems of a lovely woman, the jealous rages of her husband, and the legend of a portrait that is said to bleed whenever a female member of the family has been unfaithful. A slick-magazine aura hangs over this nothing tale like thin smog.

New Adventures concludes with Ellery's four most recent cases, appearing here in their proper order, each one involving a crime connected with a major sporting event. Try to imagine Philo Vance, the original model for Ellery, enjoying a baseball game or, God save us, a boxing match, and you'll appreciate how far the character has evolved in ten years. "Man Bites Dog" (*Blue Book*, June 1939) is set in the Polo Grounds during a World Series game between the Yankees and the Giants. The actual Series of that year was between the Yanks and the Cincinnati Reds and consisted of four games, all of which the New York team won—two on their own turf on October 4 and 5, two in Cincinnati on the 7th and 8th—but the story of course was written far in advance of the event. In a box near that of Ellery and his father, a baseball great of yesteryear drops dead after mistakenly picking up and eating his estranged wife's frankfurter. Ellery's frantic desire to get back to his seat for the final innings doesn't keep him from brilliantly analyzing a tight-packed and devious plot. No one would use that phrase to describe "Long Shot" (*Blue Book*, September 1939, as "The Long Shot"). Ellery is back in Hollywood, visiting craggy old John Scott's horse-breeding ranch to research a racing screenplay to which (like his creators before him) he's been assigned. There he gets ensnared in the love problems of the old man's daughter, who wants to marry a stablehand, and in a plot to kill or maim Danger, Scott's prime thoroughbred. With silly characters, a less than fair plot (why weren't we told that there were powder burns around that wound?), and a solution very similar to that of "The Hollow Dragon," this horse tale is—if I may be permitted—a dog.

In "Mind Over Matter" (*Blue Book*, October 1939) Ellery attends the world heavyweight championship boxing match and later discovers the stabbed body of the vicious dethroned champ in a parking lot but seems much more concerned to locate his missing camel's hair coat than to find the killer, because he knows that when he has the one he'll have the other. This one boasts a superb tight-knit plot with not a word wasted and is a pure joy to read even if you've never seen a boxing match in your life. *New Adventures* closes with "Trojan Horse" (*Blue Book*, December 1939, as "The Trojan Horse"), in which the theft of eleven matched sapphires from a wealthy old grad and football buff mars the traditional Rose Bowl game on New Year's Day. Ellery deduces the thief and the gems' hiding place without leaving his box seat. The story makes an unspectacular but not unpleasant coda to Period Two in the Queen career.

CHAPTER SEVEN

How Did They Do It?

IN 1939 FRED and Mary Dannay and their children, six-year-old Douglas and newborn Richard, were living the suburban life in Great Neck, Long Island. Fred continued to collect stamps and write poetry in odd moments and was progressing toward his ultimate goal as a bibliophile, owing a copy of every book of detective-crime short stories ever published. By that time Manny Lee was divorced from his first wife and living in an apartment at 1050 Park Avenue. Between visits from his daughters Jacquelin and Patricia he played the violin and added to his already sizable collection of classical record albums. But there was little leisure for either cousin. They were putting in average twelve-hour workdays at home and meeting weekly to consolidate their material at one or another nondescript office—first at 545 Fifth Avenue, later in the Fisk Building near Columbus Circle—which was rented under the name of Ellery Queen. The atmosphere of the office tended to be thick with tobacco smoke (both men alternated between Pall Malls and pipes, with cigars thrown in for good measure), and its floor was home for a tattered brown envelope labeled IDEAS.

How did they collaborate? Or, more precisely, what was each cousin's function in the Ellery Queen partnership? Literature abounds with authors who insisted that such questions shouldn't be asked. "If you collaborate," said Jorge Luis Borges, "you have to forget you have an identity. If you are to work successfully in collaboration, you shouldn't think whether you said that or whether I said it." "If you collaborate with someone at all," added W.H. Auden, "you form a third person who is entirely different. Critics like to play the game of what is by me and what is by him with a collaboration and they're wrong 75 per cent of the time." These strictures did not stop reporters throughout the cousins' decades as co-authors from repeatedly asking them how they worked together. Their replies varied. Sometimes they'd toss back questions of their own.

> Dannay to a *New Yorker* interviewer in 1940: "Did you ever ask Hecht and MacArthur how they collaborated?"
> Lee: "Or Nordhoff and Hall?"

In 1978 Dannay told Dick Cavett:

> Our own method was to write a complete outline before the finished work was started, and the complete outline could easily have been 20,000 words, the outline covering not only the details and the sequence of events but broken down into scenes, with character sketches and dialogue and so on. That's the only way I know how to work.

Sometimes they'd drop a tantalizing clue and then throw dust in the interlocutor's eyes with one of their crosstalk acts. They told John Bainbridge, who was profiling then in 1943 for *Life*, that they'd begin with "a 25,000 word outline, complete to a full description of the last false suspect," and then proceed to the full-length version of the novel, which usually ran about 100,000 words. But exactly who does what? Bainbridge asked.

> Lee: "In its simple form our collaboration is like this: one of us does a plot and shoots it off to the other for writing."
> Dannay: "Or one of us writes a plot and the two of us start writing."

Lee: "Sometimes one of us writes a plot and the two of us tear it to pieces."

Dannay: "Other times the two of us write a plot and one of us tears it to pieces."

The only conclusion a bewildered Bainbridge could reach was that "apparently one partner is strong on plots, the other on writing."

On some occasions they'd reply in terms of their divergent personalities.

Lee to Israel Shenker of *The New York Times* in 1969: "[Fred's] a very clever, driving kind of individual and a perfectionist. I'm a perfectionist too, but I tend to be more of an extrovert. I've always thought I have a sense of humor. Whether he does he'll have to tell you."

Dannay to Graham Lord of the London *Sunday Express* in 1970: "We're two entirely different people, with different philosophies and make-ups. I'm quieter and more introverted while Manny is more impulsive and tends to speak a very earthy language. He's louder, more aggressive."

Dannay to Paul Bargren of the Waukesha (Wisconsin) *Freeman* in 1979, after Lee's death: "I am more of an indoors, introspective country person, and Mr. Lee was streetwise, citified, an outdoor person."

On other occasions their response would be framed purely in terms of logistics.

Dannay to Lord of the London *Sunday Express* in 1970: "We've used every collaboratory system invented by the mind of man. We've worked in the same room, at the same typewriter, and separately. We've worked in the same city and three thousand miles apart. The only difference then was that the telephone bills were bigger."

And once in a while their answer would evoke memories of the oneupmanship games they'd played as children during Manny's summer visits to Fred in Elmira. Witness this bit of crosstalk from an interview with the medical magazine *MD* in 1965.

> Dannay: "The truth is, we are competitors and always have been. We are always trying to out-top each other."
>
> Lee: "We fight each other. We've been fighting each other for thirty-nine years. We have basically different attitudes toward the detective story."
>
> Dannay: "We have basically different attitudes toward everything."

And:

> Dannay to Robert W. Wells of the Milwaukee *Journal* in 1979: "We collaborated for forty-three years, but we were as much competitors as collaborators. He brought a certain sharpness to our writing that otherwise wouldn't have been there. Each of us was always trying to top the other, and I think it showed. We were always battling each other to do the best we could, and competition brings out more creative energy."

But the bottom line tended to be the same in every interview. "We will never reveal how we work," Fred exulted to Israel Shenker of the New York *Times* in 1969, "at least [not] until we hang up our gloves." And he gave the British journalist Graham Lord a dose of the same medicine the following year: "I don't know why we don't answer it and I don't mean to be mysterious but we just don't. Perhaps it's psychological." More likely it stemmed from their backgrounds in advertising and publicity and their calculation that keeping a veil of secrecy drawn over their division of labor would keep readers interested in their output. In any event Fred carried on the policy after Manny's death, claiming it was what his cousin had wanted.

But the truth was deducible, at least in skeletal form, to anyone who read the cousins' remarks with the infinite care of a mystery fan determined to beat Ellery to the murderer's identity. Here are two clues from the last years of Manny Lee's life.

Lee to Shenker of the *Times*, 1969: "In the beginning we'd plot together and write together. But Fred and I never agreed on anything."

Dannay to Lord of the *Sunday Express*, 1970: "In time we've mellowed and our quarrels have got less frequent. But once we were almost as bad as Gilbert and Sullivan, who wouldn't even talk to each other and had to pass each other handwritten notes."

It was to Shenker that Manny revealed that when he and Fred were working at Paramount as screenwriters, in an office directly underneath the studio's mimeograph department which generated a permanent clatter from the scores of duplicating machines, *"they* complained about the noise *we* were making."

The conclusion is inescapable (as Ellery I might have put it) that in their salad days Fred and Manny fought like a pair of wildcats. So why did they continue to collaborate at all? That's an easy one: they literally couldn't afford to stop.

Dannay to Wells of the Milwaukee *Journal*, 1979: "We had manufactured a benevolent Frankenstein's monster. If we ever considered a divorce—well, it would have been easier for a husband and wife to part than for us. We had a valuable property in Ellery Queen and we couldn't let go of it."

But why couldn't they let go of it? Why couldn't they have agreed that one of them would do this Ellery Queen novel from start to finish and the other the next? Since these were supremely rational men we must adopt the working hypothesis—again as Ellery I might have put it—that they had considered the possibility and rejected it. The question that logically follows this conclusion all but asks itself: on what grounds could they conceivably have rejected such an eminently sensible solution to their problem? And the answer virtually shouts back at us that they must have rejected it because it wouldn't have worked; in other words, because for reasons of talent, temperament, whim or whatever, *each of them believed that he couldn't complete a piece of fiction without the other.*

John Bainbridge of *Life* inadvertently hit the nail on the head in

1943: plotting was the strong suit of one cousin, prose the forte of the other. Which cousin performed which function? A year or two after Manny Lee's death Fred Dannay told me, and he approved of the way I explained it in *Royal Bloodline* (1974):

> As a general principle the conceptual work on a Queen novel—themes, plotting, basic characters, deductions, clues, etc.—is by and large the creation of Dannay, while the detailed execution, the fleshing out of character and incident and the precise choice of words, was by and large the creation of Lee.

It was Fred who wrote the 25,000-word skeletons that John Bainbridge mentioned, and Manny who put the meat on the bones. In an article about Ellery Queen in *TV Guide* for October 11, 1975, Manny's son Rand Lee confirmed this account: "Cousin Fred plotted all the novels and short stories, creating the characters and providing Dad with detailed skeletons that Dad fleshed out. Their talents determined this arrangement. I'm sure Dad could never have come up with the sort of plots Fred did."

What inspired Fred to devise those plots? At least when he was young, it was often other detective novels. We've noted the recurring gimmick in several early Queens that clearly came from Conan Doyle's *The Valley of Fear*. Almost as influential on Fred was the long forgotten but once popular F. Van Wyck Mason (1897-1978), whose series sleuth was military intelligence officer Hugh North. *The Vesper Service Murders* (1931), second in the long series of North novels, contains the germs of several early Queen plots. Its clue of the train conductor's ticket punch became central to *The Tragedy of X* (1932); its rural climax with North and everyone else in the cast menaced by a forest fire was echoed in *The Siamese Twin Mystery* (1933); and its color-blindness gimmick was the grandfather of all the variations Fred played on that theme over four decades. No doubt other plots were inspired in other ways, but books like these were crucial.

Exactly when the cousins hit upon their method of collaboration remains unclear, but it apparently evolved during Period Two and was firmly in place by the end of the 1930s. That they continued to employ it for the rest of their careers was not because it worked smoothly for them.

It's long been known that Fred and Manny disputed endlessly about their work, and the excerpts from their correspondence presented by Jon L. Breen in "The Queen Letters" (*Ellery Queen's Mystery Magazine*, February 2005) made it clear that when Manny told the *MD* interviewer that he and Fred have "been fighting each other for thirty-nine years" and Fred in an interview with the London *Sunday Express* compared his quarrels with Manny to those between Gilbert and Sullivan, neither man was exaggerating in the least. We now have a far more comprehensive account of their working relationship thanks to the recent publication of *Blood Relations* (Perfect Crime Books, 2012), edited by Joseph Goodrich and with a foreword by master TV mystery series creator William Link. The letters collected in this invaluable book offer literally a blow-by-blow account of the creation of three of the strongest Queen novels—*Ten Days' Wonder* (1948), *Cat of Many Tails* (1949) and *The Origin of Evil* (1951). Material specific to those novels will be covered in due course. Here however is the best place to consider the general aspects of the cousins' collaboration.

"We divided ourselves into rigid-boundaried 'zones' just because our differences of opinion on basic matters of both plot and writing were so strong that we found it impossible to reconcile. . . ." Manny wrote Fred on April 16, 1948. In practice, of course, it proved impossible to maintain those rigid boundaries. At times Manny felt compelled to add elements that would make Fred's sometimes outlandish plot notions more plausible. Fred often took such innovations as incursions on his turf. Manny's rejoinder is found in the same letter. "[I]n the way we work you have one tremendous advantage over me. When you start your work, and while you're doing your part of the work, *you are a completely free agent.* . . . [E]very time you do a novel outline you are presenting me with an accomplished fact. . . . You don't merely give me a basic idea. You don't merely give me a set of characters. You give me a basic idea worked out to the last detail, with a set of characters so completely delineated that you even indicate their type of dialogue. You give me alpha through omega. You give me, really, not an outline but a blueprint." He reiterates this complaint on November 3 of the same year. "Every time you sit down to plan a story you make final decisions that affect our income. Why have you rights that I do not? What am I, some miserable hack who sits at a machine waiting for the master to throw a blueprint down?"

Those blueprints were the work of an author with radically different literary imperatives from those of his partner. "I have a drive toward 'realism,'" Manny wrote on January 23, 1950, defining the word as "conformity to the facts and color of life and the world as we live in it. . . ." In Fred's plots, he said, "vastness and boldness of conception is nearly everything—the colossal idea, planned to stagger if not bowl over the reader. Since such ideas rarely if ever exist in life, they necessarily lead you, in working out the details of the story, into fantasy. . . . The bigger the conception, the more fantastic becomes the story. I then face this plot, with my compulsion toward reality, and the trouble begins." In an earlier letter (October 29, 1948) Fred had charged that in the preparation of every Queen novel a time comes when Manny begins "the process of (1) deflating the outline and (2) inflating the finished product." That was when the fur flew. Dannay on July 2, 1948: "Well, Man, if it is true that you do not like the new novel [i.e. the outline for *Cat of Many Tails*], the hell with it. It's okay with me. In fact, if you should happen to dislike [it] intensely, then send back the whole fucking outline to me, and that's that. All that will be lost is my time, my work, and my health." On August 4 of the same year, Manny described both himself and Fred as "ill-adjusted, emotional individuals. . . . [E]ach of us jealously guards his individual contribution to the work and . . . resents any encroachment on his work by the other." Three months later, on November 3, Manny wrote one of the bitterest passages in his correspondence. "Why am I writing to you? Why are you writing to me? We are two howling maniacs in a single cell, trying to tear each other to pieces. . . . We ought never to write a word to each other. We ought never to speak. I ought to take what you give me in silence, and you ought to take what I give you in silence, and spit our galls out in the privacy of our cans until someday, mercifully, we both drop dead and end the agony."

Personally, I see Fred as spiritual kin to the great Argentinian author Jorge Luis Borges (1899-1986), who was a Queen fan (almost certainly on Fred's side of the equation rather than Manny's) and some of whose best-known stories, including "The Garden of Forking Paths" and "Death and the Compass," are often set in the same kind of self-contained Cloud Cuckoo Lands as so many of Fred's plot synopses were. Manny's soul brother on the other hand was the character Joel McCrea played in Preston Sturges' *Sullivan's Travels* (1941), a Hollywood director who hates the hit comedies he's helmed and burns to create a Steinbeck-like "social consciousness" epic with the title *O Brother, Where Art Thou?* If ever there was a real-life Odd Couple, Fred and Manny were it, with the difference that their lacerations of each other aren't funny. The miracle is that they managed to stay together and produce so much excellent work for so many years. How did they do it?

One of the most surprising aspects of the letters collected in *Blood Relations* is that alongside the mutual lacerations are passages where each of these highly sensitive men empathizes with the other in times of trouble. "[W]e both keep misunderstanding each other," Fred tells Manny in November 1948, but "perhaps that really isn't too bad a thing, wearing as it is on our nerves and lives; it keeps both of us doing the best we possibly can, and . . . the resultant work—coming out the hard way—is, strangely enough, the better for it. . . . [W]e both have simply got to learn to trust each other more." Manny to Fred on February 24, 1950: "I can only imagine—and that inadequately—what all this [the birth of a son with brain damage, which we shall explore in later chapters] is doing to you, this unremitting worry, nervous drain, shock, etc. Keep up your strength. Don't give up hope. Grit your teeth. . . . This siege . . . would be too much for even the most stable individual. From somewhere you must find the strength to fight it." Passages like these confirm the truth of what Fred said after Manny's death: "We were cousins, but we were closer than brothers."

Turbulent as their brotherhood was, that's how they did it.

CHAPTER EIGHT

Ellery Conquers the Airwaves

As the Nineteen Thirties ended and the Forties began, the name Ellery Queen became better known than it ever had been in Period One or Period Two. The reason? Radio.

During the first weeks of *Author! Author!* on the Mutual network, George Zachary over at CBS was lining up the actors and support troops who would bring *The Adventures of Ellery Queen* to audible life. For the crucial role of Ellery he picked dulcet-toned Hugh Marlowe (1911-1982), who had played the dumb rich boy in Victor Schertzinger's Broadway musical comedy *Kiss the Boys Goodbye*. Inspector Richard Queen was portrayed by radio veteran Santos Ortega (1899-1976), whom Manny Lee once described as "one of the most deceptive [voice] doubles I've ever heard." The role of Sergeant Velie went to utility actor Howard Smith (1894-1968), who was replaced in November by gravel-voiced Ted De Corsia (1905-1973). For medical examiner Doc Prouty Zachary chose Robert Strauss (1913-1975), whose best-known part was as a homesick GI in the movie *Stalag 17* (1953). In order to provide the "love interest" that was supposed to attract the female audience, Zachary with the cousins' approval added a new member to the Queen radio family: Ellery's pert secretary, Nikki Porter. That part went to Marian Shockley (1908-1981), who had been a 1932 Wampas baby star in Hollywood and had debuted on Broadway with George M. Cohan in *Dear Old Darling* (1936). She and Zachary were married in October 1939, and Zachary made sure that Nikki was written out of the scripts during the weeks the newlyweds were off on their honeymoon. The first announcer for the series was Ken Roberts. During the show's first ten weeks its background music was composed and conducted by Bernard Herrmann (1911-1975), who accompanied Orson Welles to Hollywood a year later, wrote the score for Welles' classic film *Citizen Kane* (1941), and went on to compose the music for such Alfred Hitchcock masterpieces as *Vertigo* (1958) and *Psycho* (1960). As of this writing, anyone with access to the Web can hear three short samples of Herrmann's EQ music, two from "The Last Man Club" (June 25, 1939) and the third from "The Impossible Crime" (July 16, 1939), all performed on a synthesizer by David Ledsam. Just go to www.filmscorerundowns.net and click on "CBS Audio Clips." Two of the three clips lack the uniquely ominous sound that Herrmann was to become famous for, but the 31-second Cue 1 from "The Last Man Club" is instantly recognizable as his work.

George Zachary paralleled the Queen "Challenge to the Reader" device by stopping each week's drama after all the clues had been set forth so that a panel of guests who "represented" the home listening audience could engage in an unrehearsed debate as to Who Done It. At first these guest sleuths were drawn from the ranks of New York celebrities—writer Gelett Burgess, music critic Deems Taylor, playwright Lillian Hellman, photographer Margaret Bourke-White—but most of them turned out to be less than scintillating. One claimed that the murderer was his fellow guest detective, another spent five minutes arguing that the week's culprit must have been Ellery himself, and a third, whose regular job was as a producer for CBS, became so confused by the plot that all she could say was: "I'm an Ellery fan Queen." After a few months Zachary decided to replace the big-name guests with ordinary men and women, either members of the live studio audience at CBS or home listeners chosen on a write-in basis. But these folks didn't shine either, and the oscillation between celebrity guest sleuths and average-Joes-and-Janes continued through the show's life on the air.

The special guests weren't the only people in the CBS building who were trying to solve each Sunday evening puzzle. Zachary had decided to withhold the last scenes of each script from the actors until the final moments of the dress rehearsal, so that the one playing the murderer wouldn't blow the show by trying too hard to act innocent. By late in the year the regular cast had organized a pool, with the proceeds going to whoever identified the murderer. The most frequent winner was Ted De Corsia and the runner-up was Robert Strauss.

Zachary must have been one of New York's busiest men that summer of 1939. Not only was he producing and directing a 60-minute drama each week, but whenever a Queen script ran short he and his assistant, Charles Jackson (1903-1968), who was to become famous a few years later for his alcoholism novel *The Lost Weekend* (1944), had to insert more dialogue as needed. On top of all these chores Zachary functioned as story editor, taking special care to make sure that the Queen plot premises were sound. So week followed week and a new kind of radio drama was born and grew.

***

During much of 1939 Dannay and Lee must have spent almost every minute of their workdays writing 60-minute weekly scripts for *The Adventures of Ellery Queen*. Fred spoke of those hectic days when he visited the University of California's San Diego campus in 1977.

> Each week we received the magnificent sum of $25. Imagine doing a one-hour original drama each week for $25! And we didn't really keep the money, because at the end of each show we'd take the cast out for coffee and cake—that's all we could afford, coffee and danish pastry—and blew the $25 each week.

The cousins wrote and Zachary produced and directed a total of 34 hour-long radio dramas that CBS broadcast between June 1939 and February 1940. None are known to survive on audio but nine of the 60-minute scripts were published in book form in *The Adventure of the Murdered Moths* (2005), an indispensable volume for anyone interested in the cousins' radio work.

More than sixty years earlier, in 1942 and 1940 respectively, the first two episodes of the series had been recast by an anonymous hack into painfully infantile prose and published as Whitman Better Little Books, with the story on the left-hand pages and line-drawing illustrations on the right. (Decades later the two were reprinted in one volume without illustrations as *The Last Man Club,* Pyramid pb #R1835, 1968.) I am lucky enough to own a copy of one of the Whitman minibooks, inscribed to me by Fred Dannay. With some knowledge of dramatic radio and a bit of imagination, one can read the awful 1942 prose version ("Reaching the door, Ellery tried the handle. It gave! Opened! The door Peter Jordan always kept locked was—UNLOCKED!") and extrapolate backwards to the debut episode's lost audio original.

Frankly, "The Adventure of the Gum-Chewing Millionaire" (June 18, 1939; translated into story form as *The Murdered Millionaire,* Whitman 1942) doesn't appear to have been one of the best. The kickoff is intriguing enough as Ellery receives a friendly letter from a complete stranger asking him to recommend a nurse. Soon he's trying to solve the bludgeon murder of a crippled, gum-loving, will-changing old tyrant. His solution hinges on a scorecard from a baseball game supposedly played that very Sunday afternoon, June 18, 1939, between the Washington Senators and the St. Louis Browns. A few hours before air time, Zachary made a routine check and discovered to his horror that the game had been cancelled because of rain. But a frantic phone call to Washington satisfied him that the clue was still viable since several thousand fans had gone to the stadium before the game was called. Zachary's carefulness, however, didn't much improve the plot, which echoes *The Four of Hearts* (1938) in that no one seems to have had a motive for the crime. But this time Ellery handles the problem poorly, never considering the possibility, for example, that the killer might have been a person who mistakenly believed he'd benefit from the old man's will. And what turns out to be the real motive is lifted unconvincingly from the then current Queen novel *The Dragon's Teeth.* Ellery solves the case by determining that the murderer must have had a scorecard from the afternoon's Senators-Browns game and then deducing that only one person in the circle of suspects could have had that item; but since he forgot to establish that the killer must be among the people we've met in the story, his deduction proves nothing. The most interesting part of the play is its casual reference to how Nikki Porter became a member of the Queen household: she was a professional typist to whom Ellery had been taking his near-illegible manuscripts until she decided to do both herself and Ellery a favor by asking for a full-time job as his secretary so that he could dictate to her instead of scribbling.

For "The Adventure of the Last Man Club" (June 25, 1939) we

needn't rely on its translation into story form (*The Last Man Club*, Whitman 1940) since the original script is one of the nine 60-minute dramas included in the *Murdered Moths* collection. This one is a superior job on all counts—and the last one whose title I shall waste words prefacing with "The Adventure of . . . ." Ellery and Nikki witness a hit-and-run and are caught up by the victim's dying words into the affairs of a survivor-take-all group to which the dead man belonged. One of the script's main elements was red-green color-blindness, and Zachary made it his business to find out whether someone with this handicap could tell the difference between crème de menthe and a cherry liqueur. The clues are neat and subtle and Ellery's solution plays perfectly fair with the audience, although Queen fans might have recalled certain elements of the denouement from *The Greek Coffin Mystery* (1932) and "The House of Darkness" (1935). Misleading dying messages and death-plagued tontines were soon to become staple items in the Queen canon both on radio and in print.

"The Fallen Angel" (July 2, 1939) is not accessible on audio or in script form, but Manny Lee later reworked it into a short story of the same name, first published in *Ellery Queen's Mystery Magazine* (July 1951) and collected with eleven other transformed radio scripts in *Calendar of Crime* (1952). On a Fourth of July weekend Nikki pulls Ellery into the affairs of her girl friend, who recently married an aging tycoon and moved into the monstrous family mansion beside the East River and apparently into an affair with her husband's artistic younger brother. Then murder enters the picture, along with a few plot elements from "The Hollow Dragon" (1936). Ellery solves the crime by puncturing an incredibly chancy alibi gimmick that could have worked only at that time of year. The apparent triangle consisting of old husband, young wife and young artist would be revived many years later in the superb *Ten Days' Wonder* (1948).

In "Napoleon's Razor" (July 9, 1939), whose script is printed in the *Murdered Moths* volume, Ellery and Nikki are returning from California on a transcontinental train when a French historian asks the gentleman sleuth to find out which of the other passengers—an alcoholic salesman, a pair of newlyweds, an aging movie star, three characters calling themselves Smith, Jones and Brown—stole one of his most prized possessions, a razor given to Napoleon in 1815 by Empress Josephine. (In fact, as we learn from a footnote in *Murdered Moths*, the Bonapartes were divorced in 1809.) Then the traveling salesman is found stabbed to death in the professor's sleeping berth. One of the week's guest armchair detectives was playwright Lillian Hellman who, according to a write-up of the Queen series in *Time* (October 23, 1939), cracked the case instantly. Of course she had an edge over her fellow armchair guests in that she was the lover and protégée of Dashiell Hammett.

"The Impossible Crime" (July 16, 1939) deals with the stabbing of an escaped convict in the office of Nikki's doctor at a time when all the office doors were being watched. This was followed by "George Spelvin, Murderer" (July 23, 1939), in which Ellery and his entourage stop at a New England hotel where the cast members of a summer-stock theater are staying and quickly find themselves involved in the murder of a blackmailing actor. Learning that the weapon was a cane carried by a missing thespian named George Spelvin, Ellery warns his colleagues that "as ridiculous as it seems, everything is known about the murderer—and nothing!" The title hints at a connection with Queen's novel *The Scarlet Letters* (1953), in which the name George Spelvin (the traditional pseudonym adopted by an actor with both a bit part in a play and a featured role) crops up again, but nothing of the radio script seems to have been used in the book.

"The Bad Boy" (July 30, 1939), another of the nine hour-long scripts included in *Murdered Moths*, is set in an old brownstone overlooking Washington Square and furnished with several elements from *The Tragedy of Y* (1932) including a secret room, a vicious old matriarch and a precocious little boy. The challenge for Ellery and the listener is to solve the murder of hateful Sarah Brink, who was poisoned by arsenic in a serving of rabbit stew and found dead in her bed with several dozen live bunnies loose in the room. Among the clues is a top hat more or less borrowed from *The Roman Hat Mystery* (1929), although this time its owner is a vaudeville magician. Zachary as story editor checked out the claim in the script that rabbits are immune to arsenic but never made Fred and Manny explain how the one portion of stew could have been harmless and the other fatal, and never objected that a quick phone call to the police would have stopped the story in its tracks before the curtain rose.

The murder weapon in "The Flying Needle" (August 6, 1939) turned out to be an orchestra conductor's baton, hollowed out so that a poisoned needle could be blown through it. One afternoon before the air date, George Zachary spent several hours blowing needles through a soda straw to make sure the gimmick would work. "The Secret Partner" (August 27, 1939), which entangles Ellery and Nikki in a plot to smuggle diamonds from the Netherlands into the United States in shipments of tulip bulbs, was later adapted into a serialized comic book whose nine 4-page installments, given away at Gulf Oil stations on successive Sundays during May and June of 1940, are extremely rare and valuable today.

The script for "The Three Rs" (September 10, 1939) is another of the dozen which Manny Lee later rewrote as a short story, this one first published in *EQMM* for September 1946 and later collected in *Calendar of Crime.* As a new academic year begins and students and teachers all over the United States return more or less voluntarily to their classrooms, the administration of Barlowe College hires Ellery to locate one of its faculty, a Poe scholar who vanished in the Ozarks during the summer. The investigation turns up some intriguing clues but the solution sounds like a parody of genuine Queen and the final plot twist turns the show into a farce.

In "The Mother Goose Murders" (October 8, 1939) Ellery visits an old hotel to investigate a series of killings with nursery-rhyme motifs. Robert Strauss, taking a week off from his Doc Prouty role to play the mild-mannered proprietor Mr. Wiggins, turned out to be the killer. But the major significance of this play is that it may inadvertently have saved the Queen series from early cancellation. The high executives of CBS, Dannay recalled at the University of California in 1977, "did not believe that mysteries [meaning fair-play detective stories] would serve as good materials for radio in those days." And to make matters worse, the series had so far failed to attract a commercial sponsor and was still running as a "sustainer." But that evening a water hose burst in the transmitter cooling system of WBBM, the CBS affiliate station in Chicago, and forced the episode off the air nine minutes before the end of the hour. The station was besieged by thousands of angry phone calls from listeners demanding to be told the murderer's identity. Ad agency veteran that he was, Fred Dannay believed at first that this widely reported incident was a publicity stunt. He visited the CBS vice president who had insisted that fair-play detective stories would never make it on radio and asked him point blank: "Did you plant that incident in Chicago? If so it's one of the most brilliant moves you've ever made!" But the executive swore that it had really happened and, as both men saw at once, it demonstrated more convincingly than any poll that the Queen series was drawing a huge and avid audience. The cousins' pay was raised to $350 a week and sponsors soon began to make offers, although it wasn't until late April 1940 that Gulf Oil picked up the series and commissioned the EQ comic books that the company's filling stations gave away during May and June.

"The March of Death" (October 15, 1939) finds Ellery helping department-store magnate Samuel March locate his three scattered children. The tycoon's purpose, as Ellery only finds out after he's succeeded in the task, is to bring them all together (along with the wife of one son and the husband of a daughter) and tell them that he's disinheriting them in favor of his longtime companion. Before he can sign a new will he's stabbed to death, leaving a dying message—his own last name—carved on his desktop with the murder weapon. In the script as printed in the *Murdered Moths* volume, we don't learn until way too late that the first two letters of the name had been carved in capitals. I trust that as broadcast the clue was provided earlier.

In "The Haunted Cave" (October 22, 1939) Ellery is invited to a lodge in the Adirondacks where a serial strangler had operated a century earlier but soon finds himself sleuthing a new strangulation murder when a psychic investigator is found dead inside a cavern that no one else could have entered. This episode was adapted (not by the cousins) into a sort of short story of the same name, published in *Radio and Television Mirror* for May 1940, but thankfully the original script is in the *Murdered Moths* volume.

The Halloween episode "The Dead Cat" (October 29, 1939) was later recast by Manny into a real short story, first published in the October 1946 *EQMM* and later in *Calendar of Crime*. Almost immediately after the story appeared in *EQMM* it was mentioned in mystery writer/critic Anthony Boucher's weekly column for the San Francisco *Chronicle* (September 29, 1946). Queen, Boucher said, "has transformed a good routine radio plot into a first-rate short by adding elements of ironic subjective commentary impossible to radio." I have no way to judge the radio script, but the story version is a tightly plotted fair-play puzzle, in which Ellery and Nikki attend a Halloween party in cat costumes and stay to find out who cut a guest's throat in pitch darkness during a game of Murder. EQ fans might once again have been reminded of that oft-recycled 1935 short story "The House of Darkness," in which Ellery also had to figure out how a murder in a totally dark place was possible, but this time the problem is resolved in a substantially different way.

The script of "The Cellini Cup" (November 12, 1939) has never been published, but a heavily condensed summary in a semi-story arrangement appeared in *Radio Guide* (January 26, 1940) as "Here Is a Mystery" under the byline of Ellery Queen. It's a minor exploit that begins with an irate man telling Ellery that an art-gallery proprietor cheated him out of a priceless cup from the hand of the great Benvenuto. The next day Ellery and Nikki attend the auction at which the cup is to be sold and encounter various people with motives for wanting the item. That night the cup is stolen from the son of the art dealer, in total darkness and in the presence of Ellery and Nikki, but it takes Ellery no time at all to deduce who the thief was and how he vanished in the dark.

More interesting than the plot is an editorial sidebar to the *Radio Guide* story, reporting that the Queen radio series had inspired regular Sunday evening Whodunnit parties in living-rooms across the country, "where the armchair sleuths gather around the loudspeaker with loud shushes to hear the evidence and match wits with the personable and brilliant Ellery in reaching a solution to the mystery." George Zachary's dream of a detective series in which the listening audience would act as armchair sleuths had come true. Apparently this issue of *Radio Guide* came to the attention of Dannay and Lee, who had had nothing to do with the script's rendition into prose and promptly let the editors know it. The following week's issue contained an abject apology:

> In presenting this fictionization, our intent was to present an illustration of the program so that such of our readers as may not have heard this program would and could perceive the high interest it held out for listeners and would tune in. We indicated that this fictionization was written by Ellery Queen. It was not, and in fairness to the writers who are the real Ellery Queen, we want our readers to know this fact. In translating the drama of the broadcast into prose, our staff writer who did the fictionization undoubtedly lost some of the original qualities that have made the Ellery Queen novels the outstanding detective fiction of our day. For this, we are sorry, and we refer any reader who read that story to their many best-seller novels.

In November 1939 the Queen series experienced its first major cast change, with Howard Smith being replaced in the role of Sergeant Velie by Ted De Corsia, who was to keep the part for most of the program's long run. One of the first episodes featuring De Corsia was the Thanksgiving drama "The Telltale Bottle" (November 19, 1939), another of the dozen which Manny Lee later recast into a short story (this one published in *EQMM*, November 1946) destined eventually for *Calendar of Crime*.

The following week came "The Lost Child" (November 26, 1939), collected in *Murdered Moths*. In this edgiest of all the Queen radio scripts, Ellery becomes involved when a wealthy newspaper publisher's 8-year-old daughter is kidnaped. After endless emotionally harrowing hours, the father is murdered while delivering the $100,000 ransom as demanded, and then the dead body of the child is found too. Only a few years later, radio network censors would certainly have forbidden such a shocking script. It's also hard to believe that any sponsor would have allowed a drama about the murder of a child, but the Queen series was still being aired as a "sustainer" at the time.

"The Man Who Wanted To Be Murdered" (December 3, 1939) was published eight months later as a rather creditable short story (*Radio and Television Mirror*, August 1940), without a byline but billed as "An Ellery Queen Mystery." A wheelchair-bound old gambler deliberately tempts his brother, nephew, niece and doctor into trying to murder him when he executes a will dividing most of his estate among them if he dies within one week but leaving everything to charity if he lives longer. Simultaneously the old man makes a $25,000 bet that Ellery can't solve his murder—which sure enough takes place on the last day of the specified week. Ellery connects a Caruso aria, a missing sock, and a solid glass ball that was replaced by a thin glass bubble and comes up with a neat solution.

In "The Black Secret" (December 10, 1939) Ellery and Nikki go to bat for the staff of a rare-book emporium, all of whom were fired by the store's Scrooge-like principal owner not long before Christmas and after a series of first edition thefts. Working as clerks in the store in hope of catching the thief, they are on the spot when the owner is murdered, leaving a dying message which Ellery deciphers—as anyone can see from the script as printed in *Murdered Moths*—in his most ingenious manner.

The last play of the year was "The Scorpion's Thumb" (December 31, 1939), which was adapted into another story for *Radio and Television Mirror* (December 1940). At year's end Ellery is asked to look into an embezzlement from a Wall Street brokerage house, but then a partner in the firm dies of a poisoned cocktail during a New Year's Day party. Ellery's solution is fair and satisfying even if probably familiar to listeners who remembered "Man Bites Dog" from its appearance in *Blue Book* six months earlier.

Part one of "The Dying Scarecrow" (January 7, 1940) is set in July: Ellery, Nikki, the Inspector and Velie are driving through Midwestern farm country when they stop to take home movies of a picturesque scarecrow and find a badly knifed man inside the scarecrow outfit. The victim pulls through but remains unidentified and vanishes from the local hospital soon afterwards. Six months later Ellery and his entourage return to the area during a blizzard and discover the same man once again, this time dead as a doornail and concealed inside a snowman in a farmyard. The solution rests on some neat deductions from the absence of the traditional pipe from the snowman's mouth. This script too can be found among the *Murdered Moths*, as can that for "The Woman in Black" (January 14, 1940). Ellery investigates the legend of a ghost haunting a major English novelist on a visit to the U.S. and, though unable to prevent the eventual murder, solves it brilliantly.

By early 1940 Fred and Manny must have begun to feel the strain of coming up with a 60-minute radio script each week. The Queen series continued at hour length only for the first seven weeks of the new year. The last new hour-long episode was "Captain Kidd's Bedroom" (February 11, 1940), in which Ellery probes the murder of a retired explorer on his private island. Manny Lee later adapted the script into a short story ("The Needle's Eye," *EQMM*, August 1951) whose ultimate home was the *Calendar of Crime* collection. The episode that aired on February 18 was a rerun of "The Last Man Club." A week later the series was cut from sixty to thirty minutes and moved to the 8:00-8:30 p.m. time slot on CBS's Sunday schedule. At around the same time an obscure actor named Arthur Allen (1881-1947) took over the role of Doc Prouty from Robert Strauss.

Of the first nine half-hour *Adventures of Ellery Queen* the only one that made it into published form in the cousins' lifetime is "The Emperor's Dice" (March 31, 1940), which Manny Lee later adapted into a short story (*EQMM*, April 1951; collected in *Calendar of Crime*, 1952). The characters and atmosphere are standard old-dark-house stuff and Ellery's elucidation of the "dying message" sounds like another parody.

The following week's episode, "The Forgotten Men" (April 7, 1940), is the earliest of five 30-minute Queen scripts included in the *Murdered Moths* collection and perhaps the most "socially conscious" of the cousins' radio dramas. Ellery comes to the aid of four homeless men, prime suspects in the murder of another apparently homeless man who stole a diamond ring and hid it on the vacant lot where his comrades are living hand to mouth. The deductions at the climax are neat—although Ellery himself admits that they're possible only because the real murderer did something stupid—and even with the shorter running time there's plenty of vigorous advocacy for the down and out.

***

On April 28, 1940, *The Adventures of Ellery Queen* ceased being a "sustainer" and came under the sponsorship of the Gulf Oil Company. Its time slot was moved back an hour to 7:30-8:00 p.m. and the Doc Prouty character was dropped, but the rest of the continuing cast remained unchanged—Hugh Marlowe as Ellery, Santos Ortega as Inspector Queen, Ted De Corsia as Sergeant Velie, Marian Shockley as Nikki. Announcer Ken Roberts was replaced by Bert Parks (1914-1992), who is better remembered as host of the Miss America pageants than for his stint with the Queen show. In this format the series was broadcast over 66 CBS-affiliated stations for a total of 22 weeks. More than enough of these episodes have been preserved to form a representative cross-section. One is available on audio (albeit in a rerun of a few years later), two as unpublished scripts to which I've had access, eleven as scripts printed in early issues of *EQMM* or elsewhere, two (including one of the *EQMM* eleven) in the *Murdered Moths* collection.

The first of these sponsored adventures was "The Double Triangle" (April 28, 1940), whose script was included in that hardest-to-come-by of all Queen story collections, *The Case Book of Ellery Queen* (Bestseller pb #B59, 1945). Although not a top-drawer play, it ties together so many strands from earlier exploits that to the Queenphile it's a source of endless fascination. Ellery tries to locate the anonymous lover who's romancing the wife of a volatile young bookkeeper, but his efforts to keep the husband from murdering the lover culminate in his becoming a virtual eyewitness to the killing of the wife. The central clue depends on the ways in which a man puts away his clothes differently from a woman—the exact reverse of the situation in *The French Powder Mystery* (1930). The female who impersonates a male she wants to incriminate is derived from *The Dutch Shoe Mystery* (1931) and the triangular burn in the camel's-hair coat comes from the ripped coat in *The Devil To Pay* (1938). Fred and Manny were borrowing from themselves to the limits of their credit that week!

An awkward title is joined to a gorgeous plot in "The Man Who Could Double the Size of Diamonds" (May 5, 1940; script printed in *EQMM*, May 1943 and August 2005, and also in *Murdered Moths*). Ellery solves the murder of an eccentric scientist who claims to have discovered a chemical process for growing diamonds and simultaneously untangles the impossible theft of four such stones from a locked and heavily guarded vault. The culprit "devised a theft of such colossal simplicity that I was nearly taken in by the complicated props," Ellery remarks at the summing-up—words that fit the best Queen detective plots superbly.

The next few episodes were somewhat pedestrian but several survive in printed form. In "The Fire Bug" (May 12, 1940; script printed in *EQMM*, March 1943) Ellery investigates a series of suspicious blazes in his neighborhood, each of which destroyed a building owned by the same man. The fairness of his solution depends on how much high-school physics one remembers. In "The Honeymoon House" (May 19, 1940; script printed in *The Case Book of Ellery Queen*, 1945) love rivalries among the offspring of munitions manufacturers lead to a bride's murder on her wedding night and to a solution which Ellery admits is largely conjecture. In "The Mouse's Blood" (May 26, 1940; script printed in *EQMM*, September 1942, and in *The Fireside Mystery Book*, ed. Frank Owen, 1947) Ellery happens to be outside the house where a blackmailer is stabbed to death by one of the four athletes who were to have made payoffs to him that night, and he solves the murder by deducing which suspects are southpaws and which right-handed. "The Good Samaritan" (June 9, 1940; script printed in *EQMM*, November 1942) poses an odd problem as Ellery hunts the elusive benefactor who's been sending stolen $100 bills to the needy tenants in a certain tenement. He finds his man by neat reasoning but never satisfactorily explains the mechanics of the elaborate cover-up that the fellow engineered for himself. In "The Dark Cloud" (June 23, 1940; script printed in *Murdered Moths*, 2005) a game of charades played with the names of famous authors helps Ellery solve the riddle of the South African millionaire who was shot to death while dictating his will on his relatives' yacht.

Ellery's job in "The Blind Bullet" (June 30, 1940; script printed in *EQMM*, September 1943) is to protect a ruthless tycoon from an anonymous enemy who has threatened to kill the magnate at a precise minute on a precise day. Sound familiar, Queen fans? It's the situation Dannay and Lee later made the springboard for that flawed but fascinating novel *The King Is Dead* (1952). But in the radio play the threat is carried out in a pitch-black railroad tunnel under the noses of Ellery and his father, so that we're back to the murder-in-darkness gimmick that recurs so often in these adventures. Two weeks later Queen borrowed from himself once again in "The Frightened Star" (July 14, 1940; script printed in *EQMM*, Spring 1942), in which Ellery solves the locked-room death of a mysteriously "retired" Hollywood actress. The plot gimmick comes straight out of *The American Gun Mystery* (1934) and Ellery's main deduction presupposes listeners' familiarity with the workings of the Postal Savings System current in the early 1940s. Next came "The Treasure Hunt" (July 21, 1940), an adaptation of the 1935 short story of the same name (collected in *The New Adventures of Ellery Queen*, 1940) in which Ellery has to find a rope of pearls that one of a retired general's house guests stole from his daughter's bedroom and devises a treasure-hunting game as a psychological trap for the thief.

"The Black Sheep" (July 28, 1940) was never published but thanks to having a copy of the script I can describe it. A masked thief steals a $15,000 payroll from the owner of a mill in the village of Fallboro and the victim's surly stepson is arrested for the crime on circumstantial evidence. The boy's distraught mother appeals to Ellery for help, and soon not only EQ but the Inspector and Velie and Nikki are tramping through the quiet woods for clues. The play was repeated in 1944 as "The Robber of Fallboro" and recast several years later as a short story ("The Accused," *Today's Family*, February 1953; collected as "The Robber of Wrightsville" in *Queen's Bureau of Investigation*, 1955), in which a neater solution is grafted onto the identical plot.

I am lucky enough to have a copy also of the following week's script, "The Fatal Million" (August 4, 1940), in which Ellery hunts the impersonator who murdered the owner of a chain of roadside restaurants, posed as his victim during a secret sales transaction, and walked away with a suitcase containing a cool million in cash. The gimmick is rather routine and depends on the withholding from the listener of any information about the time the murder took place. Another play of this sort was next week's "The Invisible Clock" (August 11, 1940; script printed in *The Case Book of Ellery Queen*, 1945), in which a priceless ruby disappears during a society ball Ellery and Nikki are attending. The clue is a clock that is heard ticking where no clock exists and the solution revolves around a device called a radio nurse which I gather was well known to the 1940 audience.

Fred and Manny were never terribly convincing when they introduced elements from the world of law and lawyers into the Queen novels, and they fared no better when they wrote a law-based Queen radio play. "The Meanest Man in the World" (August 18, 1940; script printed in *EQMM*, July 1942) opens with the kind of situation that makes so many mysteries laughable to lawyers: Ellery and Nikki are empaneled side by side as jurors in the same murder trial. The destitute defendant, Will Keeler, seems to be the only one who could have plunged the paperknife into the back of skinflint Sylvester Gaul's neck, but Ellery reads the evidence differently, jumps out of the jury box, cross-examines witnesses himself, and extracts a confession in open court from the real murderer. The plot itself is rather interesting, although a bit similar to the second murder in *The Dutch Shoe Mystery* (1931), but the courtroom behavior is strictly from *Alice in Wonderland*.

In "Box 13" (September 1, 1940), which is a sort of ode to the cousins' favorite sport, a New York press agent arranges a reserved box at a major-league baseball game for Western movie star Chick Ames and several other people—like the star's nightclub-dancer wife and her oily Latin rumba partner—who want to see him bite the dust. In the box Ames agrees to sign some autographs for his juvenile fans. When he moistens the tip of the pencil with his tongue as is his habit, suddenly he's a corpse: one of the pencils he was handed had been coated with poison. Reluctantly Ellery leaves his own box seat to expose a gimmick somewhat similar to the one in the cousins' then recent baseball-murder story "Man Bites Dog" (1939). The 1944 rerun of this episode, retitled "The Foul Tip," is available on audio.

"The Disappearing Magician" (September 15, 1940; 1943 rerun under title of "The Vanishing Magician" available on audio) is one of the season's neatest episodes despite being crimeless. When the two-story

Chelsea brownstone owned in common by four decrepit ex-vaudevillians is threatened with mortgage foreclosure, Avanti the Magician tries to save the house for himself and his colleagues by issuing a challenge to Mr. Steele, a sharp businessman who has made a standing offer of $25,000 for any illusionist's trick he can't solve within 24 hours. Avanti claims that he can disappear from the brownstone after it has been minutely examined for secret compartments and while the place is surrounded by a small army of police. Inspector Queen generously supplies the bluecoat guards and the trick is miraculously pulled off. Ellery penetrates the gimmick but his social conscience leads him to refuse to reveal his solution until the 24 hours are up.

The final episode of the Queen series broadcast on CBS and sponsored by Gulf, the last to star Hugh Marlowe as Ellery and to feature Bert Parks as announcer, was "The Mark of Cain" (September 22, 1940; script printed in *The Pocket Mystery Reader*, ed. Lee Wright, Pocket Books pb #172, 1942). Ellery, Nikki, Sergeant Velie and Inspector Queen masquerade as servants in an attempt to prevent murder among the heirs of eccentric millionaire John Cain. After a full complement of clichés like the gloomy mansion with non-working lights and the enigmatic servant who prowls by night, a murder is indeed committed. It turns out that the killer knew four detectives were in the house, had no assurance that they wouldn't observe or interfere, yet went on to do in the victim for ridiculously weak motives. Ellery's solution rests on a creative variant of the ticket-book clue in *The Tragedy of X* (1932).

It had been a grueling fifteen months for everyone who had brought *The Adventures of Ellery Queen* to the air: Dannay and Lee, George Zachary, the regular cast of the show. To the end of his life Fred credited Hugh Marlowe, the first man to play Ellery on radio, with being the best interpreter of the role in that medium. In a letter of December 1947 to Anthony Boucher, Manny Lee registered a blistering dissent, describing Marlowe as "the greatest ham that ever strode the stage clad in imaginary buskins. . . . The only thing the guy has is an organ-like voice which gives old ladies in Jersey City contractions of the uterus, what's left of it; but it's combined with a brain composed of murky and mysterious mud crawling with all sorts of algae, and the combination is frustrating." Imagine how he must have fumed when Marlowe was chosen to reprise the role in the filmed television series *The New Adventures of Ellery Queen* (1955-56)!

If we are to believe an anecdote often told by Fred Dannay, Marlowe identified with Ellery so closely that at times during his tenure he lost track of the distinction between the character and himself. As Fred related (without mentioning Marlowe by name) in a 1947 reminiscence reprinted in *In The Queens' Parlor* (1957):

> One first-of-the-month [Manny and I] were shocked to receive a handful of statements from department stores and men's furnishing establishments for a large number of suits, shoes, and sundries, all charged to Ellery Queen. The curious fact was that we had never purchased any of the items listed. Naturally, we checked with the business firms in question, only to learn that a man calling himself Ellery Queen had opened the charge accounts and selected all the articles in person. Further investigation revealed that [Marlowe] had come to think of himself so realistically as Ellery Queen that he had stepped over the borderline of mere play acting and had become Ellery in the flesh. . . . [He] had no intention whatever to defraud [and] paid all the bills out of his own pocket. . . . But we have often wondered if the shirts he ordered were monogrammed and if the monogram was EQ.

CHAPTER NINE

Softcovers and Celluloid

THE QUEEN RADIO SHOW raised the profile of their detective hero to heights that Fred and Manny could only have dreamed of a few years earlier. One result of its success was that they were invited in on the ground floor of a new and revolutionary form of book publishing.

During the Thirties the price of a new hardcover mystery was $2.00. For those who couldn't afford that price—and millions couldn't during the Depression—the most popular whodunits often came out, a year or two after their original publication, in hardcover reprint editions, offered by publishers like Grosset & Dunlap for a buck apiece. Those who didn't want to wait that long for their favorites could simply visit their local drugstore, which usually housed a rental library where customers could borrow recent books for a few pennies a day. (A lousy deal for authors, who would be paid royalties on just a few copies, each of which might be read by dozens of rental library patrons, while those who ran the libraries would make a profit on every copy once rentals exceeded the $2.00 purchase price.) With the founding of Pocket Books, Inc. in 1939, readers were offered a new option: complete, unabridged, attractive paperbound copies of all sorts of titles for twenty-five cents each. This publishing revolution with its one reader/one copy business model was a great boon to readers, who began building paperback libraries at relatively little expense, and even more to authors, whose royalty checks got bigger as the many readers/one copy model of the rental libraries began to fall.

Among the first detective novelists to be published widely in the new paperback format was Ellery Queen. *The Chinese Orange Mystery* had come out in September 1939, a few months after the debut of the radio series, as Pocket Book #17. This was soon followed by *The French Powder Mystery* (#71, 1940), *The Roman Hat Mystery* (#77, 1940), *The Adventures of Ellery Queen* (#99, 1941), *The Siamese Twin Mystery* (#109, 1941), *The Tragedy of X* (#125, 1941), *The Spanish Cape Mystery* (#146, 1942), *The Greek Coffin Mystery* (#179, 1942), *The Dutch Shoe Mystery* (#202, 1943), *The Egyptian Cross Mystery* (#227, 1943). A softcover edition of *The American Gun Mystery* appeared in 1940 as #4 in the rival paperback series issued by the Dell publishing house. Within a few years every single book the cousins had written during Period One except *The Tragedy of Y, The Tragedy of Z* and *Drury Lane's Last Case* was available in the new format, and those titles plus the Period Two output followed soon afterwards. Meanwhile the cousins' hardcover publisher Stokes had put out new editions of the first two Drury Lane books, featuring new introductions by Fred Dannay and the byline of Ellery Queen rather than Barnaby Ross.

***

It was also thanks to his success as a radio detective that Ellery soon reappeared on the big screen. In 1940 Columbia launched a new series of movies, produced by Larry Darmour (1895-1942) and with a permanent cast consisting of Ralph Bellamy as Ellery, Charley Grapewin as the Inspector, James Burke as Sgt. Velie, and Margaret Lindsay as Nikki Porter, the romantic interest on the radio series. Critic Tom Tolnay rightly describes Bellamy's version of Ellery as "a disorganized thinker with a host of foibles."

The series kicked off with *Ellery Queen, Master Detective* (1940), directed by Kurt Neumann from a screenplay by Eric Taylor. The supporting cast included Michael Whalen (Dr. Jim Rogers), Marsha Hunt (Barbara Braun), Fred Niblo (John Braun), Charles Lane (Dr. Prouty), Ann Shoemaker (Lydia Braun), Marion Martin (Cornelia), Douglas Fowley (Rocky Taylor), Morgan Wallace (Zachary), Byron Foulger (Amos), Katherine DeMille (Valerie Norris), and Lee Phelps (Flynn).

Film historian Edward Connor gave high praise to the brief appearance of old-time film director Fred Niblo (best known for the silent version of *Ben-Hur*) as murder victim John Braun, but the soundest comment on the picture as a whole was that of the critic for *Variety*. "Despite a somewhat surprising ending, the story moves too slowly for sustained interest. . . . [T]he film is inauspicious as an introduction to a famous 'master detective.'"

Since the contract with the cousins permitted Columbia to exploit any element in their published work in connection with these films, the studio commissioned a "novelization" of the script, also titled *Ellery Queen, Master Detective*, which was ghost-written by Laurence Dwight Smith (1895-1952), published by Grosset & Dunlap as a tie-in with the movie and, for those who now eschew DVD, offers a reasonably accurate prose rendition of the film. Shortly after being told by his doctor that he's dying of cancer, John Braun, wealthy physical culture tycoon and domestic tyrant, is found in his locked study with his throat slit. The weapon, a jewel-studded paper knife, has vanished. The only other person in the room is a frightened young woman named Nikki Porter. Ellery happens on the scene, reads in her dark limpid eyes that she's innocent, and sets out first to hide her from his father—in the apartment the two Queens share!—and then to clear her by solving the impossible crime himself. Sound familiar? The plot has been yanked from *The Door Between* (1937), which is never mentioned in the screen credits. John Braun stands in for Karen Leith, Nikki for Eva MacClure, Dr. Jim Rogers for Dr. John MacClure, the jeweled paperknife for the jeweled half-scissors, Joseph's raven for the Loo-Choo jay—and Ellery Queen for Terry Ring, the self-styled tough PI who acts as nitwit romantic hero in the novel. The differences between *The Door Between* and these derivative works make them look even sillier. In the movie and its novelization the cancer motif comes at the beginning rather than the end, requiring the murderer to steal John Braun's body, while the police are on guard, not once but twice, getting away with the corpse both times thanks to the cops going conveniently blind at all the right moments. The film's and the novelization's account of how Ellery first met Nikki is completely at odds with the version in the first EQ radio play.

Bellamy, Grapewin, Lindsay and Burke returned in *Ellery Queen's Penthouse Mystery* (1941), which featured Anna May Wong (Lois Ling), Eduardo Ciannelli (Count Brett), Frank Albertson (Sanders), Ann Doran

(Sheila Cobb), Noel Madison (Gordon Cobb), Charles Lane (Doc Prouty), Russell Hicks (Walsh), Tom Dugan (McGrath), Mantan Moreland (Roy), and Theodor von Eltz (Jim Ritter). Once again Ellery is portrayed as a goofball and a klutz, as in the scene where, thinking Nikki is in danger, he draws his gun and attempts to ram down the penthouse door just as Velie is opening it from inside, with the result that the logical successor to Holmes flies headlong into the room and lands on his kiester and his gun goes off. This "flimsily fabricated affair" (as *Variety* called it) was directed by James Hogan from another Eric Taylor screenplay which according to the credits was based on a Queen story. In fact its source was "The Three Scratches" (December 17, 1939), a 60-minute radio script that is not accessible on audio or in print but only in the form of the novelization commissioned by Columbia and published by Grosset & Dunlap. In *The Penthouse Mystery* (1941), which takes place in August 1940, Nikki's friend Sheila Cobb asks Ellery to locate her ventriloquist father, who has vanished just after returning from a trip to war-torn China. Ellery soon finds Gordon Cobb but he's been strangled and stuffed into a trunk in the Cobb penthouse. Three other people in the same apartment hotel turn out to have come over from China on the same ship with Cobb, and it soon develops that Cobb secretly brought with him a fortune in Asian heirlooms, intended to be sold to aid the victim's of Japan's war with China. The treasure is being sought by its rightful owners, Japanese spies, and free-lance American crooks. When all the red herrings have been cleared off the plate, Ellery exposes the murderer through a neat piece of deduction which is absent from the movie and presumably comes from the radio play.

Ellery Queen and The Perfect Crime (1941) brought back the same four stars and screenwriter, with James Hogan once again directing. The supporting cast included Spring Byington (Carlotta Emerson), H.B. Warner (Raymond Garten), Douglass Dumbrille (John Mathews), John Beal (Walter Mathews), Linda Hayes (Marian Jardin), Sidney Blackmer (Rhodes), and Walter Kingsford (Henry Griswold). "Any amateur sleuth could solve it in the first reel," said *Variety*. Queen readers who skipped the film could tell from the Grosset & Dunlap novelization, published in 1942, that its basis was *The Devil To Pay* (1937). Ellery's friend Walter Mathews (Walter Spaeth) is in love with Marian Garten (Valerie Jardin), whose father Raymond (Rhys Jardin) has been ruined in the Chickawassi petroleum debacle (the Ohippi dam swindle) by Walter's uncle, John

Mathews (Solly Spaeth). Raymond must sell his beloved library to pay off creditors. Walter, who's wealthy in his own right, asks Ellery to purchase the library as a whole with Walter's money so it can be restored to his future father-in-law. That evening John Mathews is murdered under circumstances which point to either Walter or Raymond, each of whom is trying to shield the other. Also under suspicion are Carlotta Emerson (Winni Moon), the dead man's attorney Rhodes (Anatole Ruhig), and the Garten librarian Henry Griswold (Pink). The novelization offers a meticulous diagram of the premises that isn't in the novel and a noble reconstruction scene at the climax, but Ellery forgets to explain how he deduced the murderer's identity.

The movie series continued to grind on but without any more tie-in books. *Ellery Queen and the Murder Ring* (1941) was directed by Hogan from a homicide-in-the-hospital screenplay by Eric Taylor and Gertrude Purcell that was loosely based on *The Dutch Shoe Mystery* (1931). Bellamy, Lindsay, Grapewin and Burke were joined this time by Mona Barrie (Miss Tracy), Paul Hurst (Page), George Zucco (Dr. Janney), Blanche Yurka (Mrs. Stack), Tom Dugan (Thomas), and Leon Ames (John Stack). Of all the seven Columbia Queen films this one is by far the closest to an all-out slapstick comedy, with (in Tom Tolnay's words) "misplaced bodies, a cigar-smoking hood wheeling about on an operating table, a philosophizing hobo, and nearly everyone chasing up and down hospital wards with guns drawn and/or voices raised." In one scene Ellery "bounds out of his hospital room only half into his trousers, his foot stuck in a drawer, and barges head-on into a nurse guiding a food cart. . . . [He] ends up seated on the floor ranting, with spaghetti hanging from his ears." *Variety* called it "depressingly routine. . . . [There is] nothing to recommend the picture except the fact that it finally comes to an end."

For the last three of the Columbia septet, Lindsay, Grapewin and Burke continued respectively as Nikki, the Inspector and Velie. Perhaps it was the influence of Humphrey Bogart's performance as Sam Spade in the 1941 film version of *The Maltese Falcon*, but Ralph Bellamy was replaced by the tougher and more taciturn William Gargan (described by Tom Tolnay as "the most unromantic of all those who played EQ") and the slapstick was kept to a minimum. Hogan directed and Taylor scripted all three. *A Close Call for Ellery Queen* (1942), which has a blink-and-you-miss-it resemblance to *The Dragon's Teeth*, involves Ellery in a blackmail plot and a man's hunt for his two long-lost daughters. Ralph

Morgan, Kay Linaker, Edward Norris and Addison Richards were featured. According to the American Film Institute's reference catalogue, *A Desperate Chance for Ellery Queen* (1942) was based on the radio play "The Good Samaritan" (June 9, 1940; *EQMM*, November 1942), but in fact there's not the least resemblance between that script and the film, which brings the four leads to San Francisco for an incomprehensible plot about a missing man and a vanished $100,000. John Litel, Lillian Bond, Jack LaRue, Morgan Conway and Noel Madison had supporting roles. *Enemy Agents Meet Ellery Queen* (1942) supposedly came from *The Greek Coffin Mystery* but it would take a microscope to find any resemblance between that masterpiece of Golden Age detection and this hodgepodge about Nazi spies and a mummy case. The cast included Gale Sondergaard, Gilbert Roland and Sig Rumann. *Variety* called it "an undistinguished little thriller."

It was not the sheer awfulness of these pictures but the sudden death of series producer Larry Darmour at age 47 that brought the series to an end, unmourned by Queen fans and filmgoers alike. In 1970 Fred Dannay described the seven to British journalist Graham Lord as "each one more dreadful than the others." I know that's logically impossible, but Fred nailed it. Anyone who questions this verdict and has approximately eight hours to waste is welcome to check out the septet on DVD.

CHAPTER TEN

A Frantic Fruitful Time

L ATE IN NOVEMBER 1940, about two months after the Queen program
left radio, an auto accident left Fred Dannay with serious internal
injuries and several broken ribs and kept him hospitalized for weeks.
"Take care of yourself and leave everything to me," Manny wrote upon
his release. "From now on I shan't make important decisions without
getting your okay [which suggests that he was doing just that during
Fred's time in the hospital], but I don't want you to sit and fret about
details; you can do yourself and me the greatest amount of good by
nursing yourself back to health in a determined campaign of
recuperation." In mid-January 1941 Fred went to Florida for a month's
rest, but his close brush with death slowed him down hardly at all. By
the time of the accident he had built up his library of detective-crime
short story collections to the point where it was probably the finest in the
world. That collection became the basis for the projects that took up
much of the next fifteen months.

The first of these to come to fruition was a new mystery magazine,
issued—at first on a quarterly basis—by publisher Lawrence A. Spivak.
The premiere issue of *Ellery Queen's Mystery Magazine* (Fall 1941)
featured Dashiell Hammett, Margery Allingham, T.S. Stribling, Anthony
Abbot, Cornell Woolrich and, surprise surprise, Ellery Queen. Stories by

Agatha Christie, Geoffrey Household, Stuart Palmer, Vincent Starrett, Dorothy L. Sayers and Steve Fisher were prominent in the next issue (Winter 1941-42), while the third number (Spring 1942) included tales by R. Austin Freeman, Ben Hecht, Edgar Wallace, Jacques Futrelle and Michael Arlen. At first most of the stories Fred selected were reprints, but as early as the second issue he chose a Frederick Irving Anderson tale that had never seen print before, and the third included two stories from English authors that hadn't been published before in the United States. From the get-go Fred clearly intended *EQMM* to be a home for the most widely diverse stories and authors available. Old and new, from pulps and slicks, originals and reprints, hardboiled and cerebral, locked rooms and gang wars and women in jeopardy; stories by professionals and debutants, set in every corner of the earth and at every time including the remote past and the remote future. The only constant Fred demanded was quality. He personally edited every issue from Volume One Number One until shortly before his death more than forty years later.   Among the major decisions the cousins reached during the fifteen months they weren't burdened with the grind of turning out a new radio script every week was the decision to change publishers. The Frederick A. Stokes firm had issued every single Ellery Queen title since the debut of that byline on the spine of *The Roman Hat Mystery* back in 1929. Around the middle of 1941 the cousins switched their allegiance from Stokes to the more prestigious Boston-based firm of Little, Brown.

Before the move, however, they had contracted with Stokes to launch a new series of mystery novels, this one aimed at a juvenile audience and bylined "Ellery Queen, Jr." All of the first eight featured Djuna, the houseboy character from the early Queen novels, and shared a title pattern—*The (Color) (Animal) Mystery*—derived from the pattern Dannay and Lee had used from *The Roman Hat Mystery* (1929) through *The Spanish Cape Mystery* (1935). All of these juveniles were ghost-written. Fred had nothing to do with them but Manny seems to have edited and supervised them.

The series began with *The Black Dog Mystery* (1941). The author was Samuel Duff McCoy (1882-1964), a well known early 20th-century journalist whose papers are archived at his alma mater, Princeton University, and include many documents related to his work as Ellery Jr. As Samuel Duff he wrote "The Bow-Street Runner" (*Ellery Queen's Mystery Magazine*, November 1942), a historical whodunit—narrated in first person by a Cockney—which was one of the earliest original stories to appear in the magazine Fred founded in 1941. The next title in the Djuna series was also published by Stokes but a year or so after the cousins had moved to Little, Brown—which means that they must have had a two-book contract with the former house. *The Golden Eagle Mystery* (1942) was written by Frank Belknap Long (1901-1994), a specialist in pulp horror fiction. That was the last book with any kind of Queen connection to be published by the firm which had launched the cousins' career just as the stock market was crashing.

***

The first Queen title issued by Little, Brown was not a novel but an anthology, another offshoot of Fred Dannay's private library of detective-crime short story volumes. In *101 Years' Entertainment: The Great Detective Stories 1841-1941*, which remained in print for decades as a Modern Library Giant, Fred intended to "paint a whole picture of what the First Hundred Years have brought forth. . . ." Included in this thousand-page volume were stories by Poe, Chesterton and R. Austin Freeman and Melville Davisson Post, by Margery Allingham, Dorothy L. Sayers, John Dickson Carr, Agatha Christie and of course by Queen himself. Conan Doyle was represented not by a complete Sherlock Holmes story but by scenes from four separate tales, each one presenting one of the Master's most famous deductions. Of the American pulp tradition only Hammett appeared, and he with a story from the *American Magazine* rather than *Black Mask* as one might have expected. But aside from under-representing the distinctively American school, *101 Years'* is a near-perfect summation of short crime fiction from Poe down to its own time—or perhaps one should say from Poe to the event a few months after its publication that would turn America upside down: Pearl Harbor.

***

Late in 1941 the cousins decided to put their noses back against the radio grindstone and commit themselves once again to a script a week. Their highest priority became the return of Ellery Queen to the airwaves. The reason why they felt they had to go back to radio was discussed most fully by Fred Dannay during his Carroll College appearance in 1979.

One day we wrote the best book that we thought we had written up to that time. It was a book called *Calamity Town*, and it was submitted in the usual way to a national magazine, and it was turned down. And we couldn't understand it. So we set up a three-party telephone conversation, a telephone conference with the editor and our agent and Manny and me. And I asked the editor certain questions like: "Didn't you like the book?" And he said: "Oh, I liked the book very much, in fact it's the best story you've sent to us." So I said: "Why didn't you publish it, why didn't you accept it?" And he said: "I don't know." So I said, "May I probe?" And I said: "Is it possible that our price has risen to the point where it's too high for your budget?" And he said: "No." And I said: "Is it possible that you have too many stories in inventory and don't want to add to the inventory?" He said: "No." And I asked various other questions, and I finally wound up by saying: "Why are you rejecting this manuscript?" And his answer was . . . . : "I don't know."

So Manny and I walked out of our agent's office where the conference took place, and I think it was I who said to Manny: "We'd better find another basket for our eggs, because we can't keep all our eggs in the basket we thought we could keep them in. If you can be turned down with no reason apparent on the best book you've ever written, . . . then you've got to do something else."

The obvious contenders for the position of "something else" were the movies and radio. But their three stints as screenplay writers had been unsatisfactory, the pair of Ellery Queen movies in 1935-1936 had been wretched, and Columbia Pictures' then current EQ series was no better. They had had to work a lot harder in radio, but they'd had far greater input into that medium and more luck with the results. So they asked their agent to find them a new network and a new sponsor.

CHAPTER ELEVEN

Back to the Airwaves

T HE *ADVENTURES OF ELLERY QUEEN* returned to the air in January 1942, one month after Pearl Harbor, on NBC's Red Network and under the sponsorship of the Emerson Drug Company, makers of Bromo-Seltzer. On the west coast it was heard Thursdays from 12:30 to 1:00 a.m. Eastern War Time (which translates to 9:30-10:00 p.m. conventional Pacific time), and on the east coast from 7:30 to 8:00 p.m. Saturdays. The role of Ellery was taken over by reliable utility actor Carleton Young (1907-1971). The new announcer for the series was Ernest Chappell (1903-1983) and background music was supplied by organist Charles Paul. But Santos Ortega, Ted De Corsia and Marian Shockley were back as Inspector Queen, Sergeant Velie and Nikki Porter. George Zachary carried on as producer of the series, although others took over the director's chair. And of course Dannay and Lee were back with scripts that hewed to the same pattern as in 1939-1940. Indeed several episodes were simply 30-minute versions of hour-long dramas from the program's earliest months on the air. "A new plot every week knocked me out," Dannay admitted in the late 1970s. It's no wonder that the cousins borrowed liberally from themselves nor that some of their scripts were routine and mechanical. What is astonishing is that so many Queen dramas were so good. In the memories of fans in the Forties who became writers later, it was the best whodunit on the air.

One of those fans was Chris Steinbrunner (1933-1993), whose article "Challenges to the Listener" (*The Armchair Detective*, Summer 1979) conjures up the framework of the program.

> The audio memory machine clicks on. First the commercial, "the one and only talking train" rolling you into the show, hoarse and chugging voice-box locomotives: *"Fiight headache threeee ways! Bromo-Seltzer Bromo-Seltzer Bromo-Seltzer. . . ."* Then the smooth-voiced announcer (generally Ernest Chappell, who was also the velvet-mild spokesman for Pall Mall cigarettes, and whom Ellery with mischievous familiarity would always call "Chappie") introduced you to the "celebrated gentleman detective in person"—*Ellery Queen*. And Ellery "invited you to match wits with him as he relates another story of a crime he alone unraveled. Then, at the point where he is able to solve the mystery, he stops the play, gives you a chance to solve the mystery."

That point was signaled by Ellery's announcement: "Now, Dad, I know who killed So-And-So." Then both he and Nikki would step out of their roles—a device which, according to Dannay many years later, "added distinction and suspense, and broke some radio rules"—and Nikki would introduce the evening's guest armchair detectives, who tended to be government bureaucrats, media personalities or people with special knowledge bearing on the plot. Ellery would ask each guest who he or she thought was guilty, the sleuths would propound and defend their solutions, then Ellery would step back into character and explain his own deductions to Nikki and his father and the perpetually dumbfounded Sergeant Velie and the audience. Finally the Maestro (as Velie called him) would step outside his role again, congratulate the rare armchair guest who had come up with the right answer, and present all the guests with copies of the latest Queen novel or anthology plus a subscription to *EQMM*. Apparently they got cash too.

The first episode in the reconstituted Queen series was "The Song of Death" (January 8/10, 1942), in which Ellery visits a night club and becomes involved in the murder of a female FBI agent on the trail of counterfeiters. The following week's play, "The Invisible Clue" (January

15/17, 1942), has been preserved in Margaret Cuthbert's anthology *Adventures in Radio* (1945). A terrified man writes a letter asking Ellery to wake him up at seven o'clock the next morning. Thus the gentleman detective walks into the case of the unseen persecutor, which is reminiscent of G.K. Chesterton's famous Father Brown story "The Invisible Man" but without the overtones of GKC's religious philosophy. Ellery solves the puzzle appropriately enough through the invisible (i.e. negative) clue of the title, but I found it hard to believe that the victim wouldn't have thought of the answer himself while he was being exhaustively questioned. Anthony Boucher missed this episode when it was broadcast in 1942 but was ecstatic when he caught the rerun six years later. "I cannot think of a more pure specimen of [Fred] Dannay in all the Queen products," he wrote Manny Lee on January 20, 1948.

The topical episode for the third week in February was "George Washington's Dollar" (February 19/21, 1942), which Manny later adapted into the short story "The President's Half Disme" (*EQMM*, February 1947; collected in *Calendar of Crime*, 1952). Although the tale lacks any crime, it boasts an intellectual adversary worthy of Ellery's mettle, namely our first president.

In the 1940s the income tax returns of all Americans had to be filed by March 15, so it was fitting that the Queen exploit broadcast closest to that date was "The Income Tax Robbery" (March 12/14, 1942), later revised as the short story "The Ides of Michael Magoon" (*EQMM*, March 1947; collected in *Calendar of Crime*, 1952.) Ellery investigates the theft of a private eye's income tax records from his briefcase 48 hours or so before the filing deadline which balloons into a case of blackmail and murder. At least as of this writing, you can hear the episode on your computer just by googling "Ellery Queen" and the original title. What a marvelous age we live in!

In "The Black Syndicate" (April 2/4, 1942) Ellery is called in when the head of an export firm disappears after his four partners, following his instructions, have liquidated the business and sent him all the proceeds. Manny Lee happened to visit the NBC studio during the rehearsal of this episode and met Kaye Brinker (1914-1991), a young actress in the cast. "[S]he always played bad girls and divorcees on radio because she had a sexy alto voice," one of her sons wrote decades later, "and in the Thirties and Forties all the good girls were sopranos." She and Manny began dating almost at once.

Next week came the disappointing "Ellery Queen, Swindler" (April 9/11, 1942; script printed in the Queen-edited anthology *Rogues' Gallery,* 1945). With no conceivable motivation except that he's German, a respectable jeweler named Adolf Humperdinck bamboozles one of his employees out of $4,000. Ellery enlists the equally unmotivated aid of a M. Jallet, who as a good Frenchman needs no reason for combating an Adolf, and works out a jewel-switching maneuver to get the young man's money back.

In "The Millionaires' Club" (April 23/25, 1942), Ellery takes a hand when four members of a subgroup within a larger club of tycoons are menaced by a series of fatal "accidents." This episode was rerun at the end of 1944 as "The Inner Circle," the same title used when Manny adapted the script into a short story (*EQMM*, January 1947; collected in *Calendar of Crime*, 1952).

In "The Missing Child" (May 7/9, 1942) Ellery searches for a small boy who vanished shortly before the finalization of his parents' divorce. This script was the source of the later short story "Child Missing!" (*This Week*, July 8, 1951; collected in *Q.B.I.: Queen's Bureau of Investigation*, 1955).

Those who tuned in to the series during the last week in May heard the Memorial Day case of "The Old Men" (May 28/30, 1942), which Manny later adapted into the short story "The Gettysburg Bugle" (*EQMM*, May 1951, as "As Simple as ABC"; collected in *Calendar of Crime*, 1952). Ellery stumbles upon a Pennsylvania hamlet and into another tontine, whose last survivor is slated to enjoy a fabled Civil War treasure.

June being the traditional month for weddings, it was natural that the cousins would write a script entitled "The June Bride" (June 11/13, 1942) and equally natural that Manny would later turn the script into a short story ("The Medical Finger," *EQMM*, June 1951) to represent that month in *Calendar of Crime*. Ellery attends a wedding but puts on his detective hat when the lovely and wealthy young bride drops dead after the ceremony.

On July 4, 1942, Manny Lee married Kaye Brinker after a whirlwind three months' courtship. Not only was the ceremony unmarred by a murder but the marriage lasted until Manny's death in 1970. The wedding day was also the last day *The Adventures of Ellery Queen* was broadcast for the next three months, and the break gave Manny time for a honeymoon. He would not be able to take another vacation until six years later.

***

It was apparently during this hiatus that the cousins had lunch with a visitor from Washington which led to radical alterations in the shape of some segments of the radio series. Fred Dannay recounted the incident while visiting the University of California in 1977.

> One day, and it happened to be me, I got a call from someone who said that he represented the head of OWI. And the head of OWI, which was the Office of War Information during World War II, was at that time Elmer Davis. He asked if he could meet the two of us for lunch in New York; he had something important to tell us. So of course we went down.
>
> When we met him he said that they were having a problem with getting propaganda to the American people during wartime. There was a rule or a law at that time which said that if the United States government put on its own program it had to begin: "The United States Government Presents. . . ." And the moment you got to the word "Presents" everybody turned the dial, because they didn't want to—they wanted entertainment, they didn't want this kind of open propaganda. So he said that they would like to crack this problem, and that they had thought and thought, and that the two of us, my partner and me, were the answer.

Earlier in 1942 George Zachary had left the Queen series to work for the OWI, and it's likely that he initiated the proposal made by the man from Washington. Would Fred and Manny agree, without telling anyone at the network or the sponsor, to incorporate certain official propaganda motifs into some of their scripts so that "the message" would get across to unwary Americans in the guise of a detective story? They would retain complete control over their plots and the OWI would supply only the slogans. Fred and Manny said that they'd be happy to co-operate. It was completely improper but, considering the patriotic fervor of the time, understandable.

***

In October the Queen program returned to NBC's Red Network with Carleton Young, Santos Ortega, Ted De Corsia and Marian Shockley back in their respective roles as Ellery, Inspector Queen, Sergeant Velie and Nikki Porter. Ernest Chappell returned as announcer, Bromo-Seltzer continued as sponsor, and the 39 episodes of the 1942-43 season were broadcast in the same east coast and west coast time slots as before. The season's first drama, "The World Series Crime" (October 8/10, 1942), happens to survive on audio and provides a good example of how Dannay and Lee used a script as a vehicle for OWI propaganda. Three hours before the seventh game of the Series, the "Eagles" team hires Ellery to break the jinx on its powerhouse hitter, Sparky, by retrieving his lucky bat, Uncle Sam, which was stolen the morning after game three. Ellery succeeds just in time for Sparky's home run to lead the Eagles to victory and to demonstrate the OWI's slogan for the day: "You Can Always Trust Your Uncle Sam!" Ironically enough, in 1985 the Japanese publisher Gogaku Shunjusha printed the script as a booklet, with Japanese notes apparently aimed at helping youths in that country who were studying English.

Near the end of the year, in "The Yellow Ledger" (December 17/19, 1942), Ellery replaces a wounded FBI agent and deliberately walks into a trap while traveling to Washington with a ledger containing evidence against a Nazi spy ring. Long after the war Manny recast this play into the short story "The Black Ledger" (*This Week*, January 26, 1952; collected in *Q.B.I.: Queen's Bureau of Investigation*, 1955), with the Nazis replaced by a domestic crime syndicate.

In "The Singing Rat" (January 7/9, 1943; available on audio) Ellery investigates the disappearance from his father's office of a hollowed-out cigarette containing a document that incriminates four suspects. It's a glaringly artificial puzzle with a solution that could have occurred only to two men who had been chain smokers all their adult lives.

The next week's play turned out to be one of the finest in the entire Queen series. "Mr. Short and Mr. Long" (January 14/16, 1943; script printed in *The Misadventures of Sherlock Holmes*, ed. Ellery Queen, 1944, as "The Disappearance of Mr. James Phillimore" and, under its original title, in *The Adventure of the Murdered Moths*, 2005) is a superbly mounted impossible problem, inspired by Dr. Watson's famous cryptic reference to the man who returned to his house for an umbrella and was never seen again. Confined to bed, Ellery functions as his own armchair detective, devising all sorts of wonderful suggestions as to how Phillimore could have vanished from a house surrounded by police, before finally topping even the best of them with a magnificent analysis of how the trick was really worked.

Two weeks later came one of the baldest pieces of OWI propaganda that has survived from the Queen series. In "Tom, Dick and Harry" (January 28/30, 1943; script printed in *EQMM*, July 1943, as "The Murdered Ship") Ellery is summoned to Washington by "an extremely important official of the Government, who must remain anonymous." Whoever this bureaucrat is, he inspires in Ellery an all-but-religious awe. "An urgent summons from such a distinguished Government official as yourself, Sir—I can't imagine why I should be so honored." Nameless entrusts Ellery with a double mission: to find out how the slimy subs of the filthy Japs (it was politically incorrect to call our enemy anything else in those days) were able to ambush a heroic American convoy on the high seas, and why the captured enemy commander was carrying a note on him with the message "ELLERY Q." Accompanied by Nikki, his father and Velie, Ellery sets out on a cross-country journey to interview the families of every American killed in the ambush. After talking to thousands of people, he arbitrarily pieces together three little scraps of talk out of the millions of words he's heard, assumes that the countless Axis agents among us could do and had done likewise, and thereby demonstrates another OWI slogan: "The Slip of a Lip Can Sink a Ship." Literally!

> Official: "Yes, if people would only remember not to talk about anything but what they hear over the radio or read in their newspapers!"
>
> Inspector (quietly): "We're all prone to be offenders once in a while, Sir. But we mustn't be—ever."
>
> Nikki: "I'll make the resolution to keep my mouth shut—right now!"
>
> Velie: "That goes double."
>
> Ellery: "Amen."
>
> (The music comes up.)

When this script was reprinted in Leslie Charteris's anthology *The*

Saint's Choice, Volume 7: Radio Thrillers (1946), it was prefaced by a letter to Charteris from Manny Lee, explaining the genesis of this and similar Queen plays.

> This was a "command performance," so to speak, by the OWI, with whom we co-operated in the "loose talk" campaign. As a special assignment from Washington, it represents—we think—something superior in radio propaganda, inasmuch as it doesn't bat its audience over the head, but approaches the lesson through entertainment.
>
> This sort of program, serving a higher purpose than mere commercial entertainment, surely deserves being anthologized.

"All propaganda is lies," George Orwell wrote in his war diary, "even when one is telling the truth." If he had heard of these stern warnings to say nothing to anyone unless it's been released or approved by Big Brother, he might have thought that 1984 had come early.

In "The One-Legged Man" (February 25/27, 1943; script printed in *EQMM*, November 1943) Ellery visits a munitions plant on a mission for the nameless official of "Tom, Dick and Harry." The setting permits Dannay and Lee to push not one but two OWI slogans of the moment. One: "War Is Good."

> Inspector Queen: "See those cannon? Big babies!"
> Nikki: "Makes you feel all proud inside, Inspector."

Two: "Keep Your Mouth Shut." Throughout most of the play's first half Ellery and his cohorts systematically humiliate any plant worker who tells them a blessed thing.

> Ellery: "Miss Muller, do you know who I am? Any of us? . . . How do you know we can be trusted with this information? . . . You haven't any idea how we got into the plant."
> Inspector: "We might be carrying false credentials."
> Ellery: "The fact is, you've told us a lot of things some Axis agent would give a great deal to learn!"

Miss Muller (nervously): "I didn't say anything important. I'm just a secretary. . . ."

Velie: "It ain't your job to say what's important."

Nikki (gently): "You're working in a *war* plant, Miss Muller."

Ellery's assignment is to investigate some mysterious one-legged tracks in the snow within a sealed courtyard forming part of the plant, but the case becomes one of murder and sabotage when the head of the plant is incinerated by a booby-trapped pencil. Despite all the propaganda, purely as a deductive puzzle this is one of the better entries in the series.

Four weeks later came "The Circus Train" (March 25/27, 1943; available on audio), in which Ellery, Nikki, the Inspector and Velie find that their return reservations on the train from Chicago to New York have been commandeered by the Army. They manage to hitch rides in the passenger car of a circus train heading east, but while en route the show proprietor's skull is bashed in by the shoe of the circus giant and three $10,000 bills vanish from the speeding train. The denouement makes use of the two-solutions device so common in the Queen novels, but few will swallow the plot premise that the police would return the fatal shoe to its 8-foot-tall owner right after the murder.

In "Crime, Inc." (June 10/12, 1943; condensed version of script published as "The Crime Corporation" in *Story Digest*, November 1946) Ellery tries to deduce which of the surviving members of the so-called Secret Six who rule the city's organized criminals stabbed crime kingpin Oscar Wunsch in the back shortly after Wunsch had framed another member of the group as a squealer and had him executed. The problem is that all four suspects seem to have unbreakable alibis. At least for longtime Queen readers, Ellery's solution would have been familiar.

This middle year of the war was the peak of success for the Queen series. No doubt this was the reason why the November 22, 1943 issue of *Life* magazine included a lengthy profile of the cousins by journalist John Bainbridge, who reported their earnings as slightly more than $50,000 apiece per year. The vast bulk of that money came from the radio adventures, which were drawing more than fifteen million listeners every week. At the time Bainbridge interviewed them, Manny and Kaye Lee had moved into a charming old rented house at 5 Cannon St.,

Norwalk, Connecticut, where they lived with his two daughters by his first wife, Kaye's daughter by her first husband (who grew up to become the celebrated dancer and choreographer Anya Flesh, 1933-2008), and their own newborn daughter Christopher Rebecca Lee. Fred and Mary Dannay and their sons were still living in Great Neck, although Mary was severely ill from cancer and virtually bedridden in the Dannay home. Perhaps her absence as a force in Fred's life explains the bizarre outfit of loud sport blouse and bright corduroy trousers that he wore during the Bainbridge interview. He and Manny still met weekly at the 545 Fifth Avenue office which they rented for $45 a month under their joint pseudonym. And, thanks largely to radio, that name had become so well known that whenever Fred dropped in the mail an empty envelope addressed to "Ellery Queen, N.Y."—and he did this as a sort of private Gallup poll every time he took a trip out of town—he invariably found the envelope waiting for him the next time he visited the EQ office. Indeed the Queen name was so prestigious that, shortly before the Bainbridge interview, the New York *Journal-American* offered the cousins a fortune to go to the Bahamas and report on the sensational trial of Alfred de Marigny in the courts of Nassau for the murder of his wealthy American-born father-in-law Sir Harry Oakes. Their radio commitments and disinterest in true crime led them to turn down the paper's offer, which was then extended to and accepted by Erle Stanley Gardner, the creator of Perry Mason.

During the summer months of 1943 the Queen series aired thirteen reruns: a dozen from the 1940 season plus, during the appropriate week in late September, a rebroadcast of "The World Series Crime." This doesn't mean, of course, that Fred and Manny were able to take thirteen weeks off.

***

Even while the series was requiring a new 30-minute script every week, the cousins kept the Queen name visible in other media. Their next novel, which inaugurated the third and perhaps richest period in their work, was *Calamity Town* (1942). We know from Fred Dannay's comments during his Carroll College appearance that he and Manny had completed the book in 1941, before the radio series returned to the air. But the series was going full blast when the novel was published by Little, Brown, which would remain home to the Queen novels and story collections for a dozen years. Not only the new publisher but also the book's subtitle—"A Novel" rather than "A Problem in Deduction"—signaled that the cousins had taken a new turn. Ellery Queen is still the central character but he's dropped his pince-nez and polysyllables and is no longer a detached intellect resolving terrible events but a human being involved in and torn by them. In the third period the deductive puzzle merges with rounded characterization, superb writing (Manny's main contribution), and intellectual and imaginative patterns of a depth long believed both impossible and inappropriate in crime fiction.

On the afternoon of August 6, 1940, Ellery steps off the train at Wrightsville, a small tight-knit American community that with the outbreak of war in Europe has become a boomtown. He needs a place to stay where he can write his next novel but neither hotel rooms nor furnished houses are available—except Calamity House. Old John F. and Hermione Wright, heads of Wrightsville's founding family, had had the house built next door to their own home, planning to give the house as a wedding present to their daughter Nora and her fiancé, Jim Haight. But Jim had vanished from town the day before the wedding, and later a potential buyer had dropped dead of a heart attack in the house itself, and the place became known as a jinx. Ellery rents it, is quickly lionized by the Wrights, and finds himself seriously attracted to Pat, the family's youngest daughter, who is on-again-off-again in love with county prosecutor Carter Bradford. Then Jim Haight comes back to town and is reconciled with Nora Wright and they marry and move into the house built for them three years before. Little by little the marriage goes bad: threats, arguments, and the shadows of hints that slowly rise to near certainty that Jim is planning to kill his wife. Murder comes with the new year. At the traditional family party, one of the drinks with which the Wrights toast the beginning of 1941 is poisoned. The town's first homicide in twenty years tears apart the family and the community. The investigation, local reactions, the sensational trial and subsequent events are presented not as pieces of a puzzle (although a fine plot is hidden among them) but as horrible things happening to real people. Ellery is simply one of these people, powerless to affect events and contributing nothing until the final chapter.

Superficially *Calamity Town* might be taken as a sort of Norman Rockwell painting in prose, a simple-minded tribute to the goodness of an unspoiled American community. Actually Wrightsville is a fairly realistic American microcosm, with plenty of rot and inhumanity and strife alongside the grace and bucolic peace. The bad qualities aren't limited to the characters with black hats like bitterly jealous Frank Lloyd, or the kids who stone Jim Haight on the street, or Aunt Tabitha who turns on the Wright family in its crisis. The same qualities are evident, for example, in Hermione Wright herself, who made her divorced daughter Lola an outcast. No one here is overwhelmingly good and almost no one is overwhelmingly bad but some are clearly better than others, and better than most are the very few like Pat Wright, who gives totally of herself and expects nothing back.

Among the elements at the heart of *Calamity Town* are the rhythms of nature. *In the midst of life, death.* Nora Haight's illnesses occur on Thanksgiving and Christmas, death strikes with the New Year's toast, Jim is arrested on St. Valentine's day, Nora dies on Easter Sunday. *In the midst of death, life.* The child born of Nora's dead body lives. The old trees in the cemetery sprout every spring "with sly fertility," as if nourished by the dead in their graves, "as if death were a great joke." Out of the horror of the full truth, revealed by Ellery on Mother's Day, comes the possibility of happiness for two young people and a baby. Ellery's final explanation is counterpointed by quotations from Walt Whitman, the poet of nature's rhythms. The action of the novel covers nine months, the gestation cycle.

> He was looking at the old elms before the new Courthouse. The old was being reborn in multitudes of little green teeth on brown gums of branches; and the new already showed weather streaks in its granite, like varicose veins.

In conversations with me, Fred Dannay suggested that the strongest influence on *Calamity Town* was Edgar Lee Masters' *Spoon River Anthology* (1914-16), that sardonic free-verse classic in which the dead of a "typical American town" tell their own stories from their graves. Certainly both books share a similar bleak tone and a sense that everything changes, nothing lasts. I thought then and still think that a deeper influence on the novel was exerted by Thornton Wilder's play *Our Town* (1938), which has much in common with *Calamity Town* even though the play takes place at the beginning of the 20th century and has no crime elements. The physical description of Wrightsville often echoes the tour through Grover's Corners at the beginning of Wilder's first act, and both works evoke the flux of life and the sense that beneath the Norman Rockwellish existence of these small towns lie bottomless "ignorance and blindness." There are also some intriguing similarities between *Calamity Town* and Alfred Hitchcock's film *Suspicion* (1941). In both works a charming but mysterious male outsider marries a superficially unattractive young woman whose family is at the top of the pecking order of a closed small-town society, and we watch the corrosion of the marriage and become afraid that for financial reasons the husband is in process of murdering his wife. I don't think it's by chance that there are also resemblances between *Calamity Town* and Hitchcock's *Shadow of a Doubt* (1943), which was written in large part by none other than Thornton Wilder. The town in the film is something like Grover's Corners in *Our Town* but even more like Wrightsville. The film's Charlie (Teresa Wright) isn't like any character in *Our Town* but closely resembles *Calamity Town*'s Pat Wright, even to the point that the fathers of both young women are bankers. The "ignorance and blindness" beneath small-town placidity pervade Hitchcock's film—witness the idiot neighbor who keeps blatting about the corking good murder mystery he's just read, while a serial killer is only a few feet away—just as they pervade *Calamity Town*. A few years later Orson Welles got into the act with his film *The Stranger* (1946): another insular New England community, another newcomer who marries the daughter of the local aristocracy, another marriage corroding, another round of fear that husband will kill wife, another gallery of shrewd-seeming Yankee types blissfully ignorant of the horrific drama unfolding around them. Certainly *Calamity Town* is at the center of a network of influences that encompasses some of the finest creative works of the years just before and after its publication.

***

After such a powerful novel, what do you do for an encore? Dannay and Lee weren't sure that *Calamity Town* with its radical departures from earlier Queen novels would be a success and deliberately planned their next book as a return to the old manner, rich in convoluted plotting and deductive masterstrokes. Much of the work was probably done in the summer of 1942, during the three months the radio series was on hiatus, but there's reason to believe that part of the plot dates back to the novel Fred and Manny were working on in 1939 when they discovered that Agatha Christie's *And Then There Were None*, then being serialized in the *Saturday Evening Post*, had a similar plot. If nothing else, this would explain the absence of World War II home front ambiance from a novel published in the second full year America was at war. In *There Was an Old Woman* (1943) the cousins set out to merge a complex puzzle with the kind of way-out wacky mystery which more or less paralleled Hollywood's cycle of screwball comedies. Among the contributors to this subgenre in the Thirties and early Forties were Craig Rice, Richard Shattuck, and Phoebe Atwood Taylor as Alice Tilton, whose first novel under that byline had appeared in the debut issue of the cousins' *Mystery League* magazine. In an interview with *Look* decades later, Fred Dannay described this aspect of the Queen canon as "Ellery in Wonderland": You plunge the quintessential man of reason into a milieu as mad as the underside of Carroll's rabbit hole and see if he can forge some sort of order out of the chaos.

A chance meeting in a courtroom corridor entangles Ellery in the tentacles of the crackpot Potts dynasty, proprietors of the world's largest shoe empire. Matriarch of the clan is 70-year-old Cornelia Potts, a living gargoyle whose heart should have given out long ago but keeps beating. Squashed beneath the Potts shoes are her six children, three by each of her husbands. The older trio, fathered by long-vanished Bacchus Potts, wear their nuttiness on their sleeves. Horatio, a total dropout, lives in a gingerbread cottage full of children's toys and writes juvenile adventure stories and, in Ellery's words, is either the sanest or the looniest man alive. Louella is a wild-haired crackbrain scientist who lives in a turreted tower and is working feverishly on a formula for a plastic shoe that will put the family company out of business. Thurlow is a tubby, foul-tempered troglodyte who loves to file defamation suits against anyone who makes the slightest crack about the Pottses. Since Cornelia had forced her second husband to change his name to hers as a condition of the marriage, the younger three children are also surnamed Potts. Twin brothers Robert and Maclyn manage most of the shoe empire. Their sister Sheila is in love with Charley Paxton, the family lawyer, but refuses to marry him until Cornelia's heart finally stops.

When Thurlow gets miffed at the dismissal of one of his daily defamation suits and threatens personal vengeance on whoever next sullies the glorious Potts name, attorney Paxton enlists Ellery in a conspiracy to keep the tubby terror from killing somebody. That very evening Thurlow climaxes a business argument by challenging his half-brother Robert to a pistol duel at dawn beneath the huge sculptured shoe on the grounds of the Potts estate on Riverside Drive. Ellery substitutes blanks for the live ammunition but death strikes anyway, the first of several within the potty family. Among the clues that pile up as the deadly farce proceeds are two pairs of twin pistols (one hidden in a bird's nest), a plate of cold soup beside a corpse, and a misplaced reverse pencil impression of a signature. Ellery disrupts the climactic wedding ceremony with an impromptu solution which throws off fireworks of virtuoso reasoning but demands perhaps too much technical knowledge of us. Remember Manny Lee's remark that EQ novels are fair to the reader only if the reader is a genius? Anthony Boucher, reviewing the novel in the San Francisco *Chronicle* (March 28, 1943), said: "What it's most like is an E.Q. radio program in book length: the same freakish situation, grotesque characters, rapid movement, economical dialogue, low comedy relief. And the same consummate combination of devious trickery and absolute fairness that is the Queen trademark."

Certain plot motifs in *There Was an Old Woman* are intimately related to earlier and later Queen works. The killer who uses another person as a living murder weapon, and the long-missing family member who might be posing as someone else, will return far more satisfyingly twenty years later in *The Player on the Other Side*. The family of grotesques cursed with a sort of metaphysical syphilis leading to madness goes back to *The Tragedy of Y* and will reappear in various forms even in Queen's fourth and final period. The account of Ellery's first meeting with Nikki Porter contradicts all the other accounts, in the first Queen radio drama and Columbia's first Queen movie and the 1953 novel *The Scarlet Letters*, all of which also contradict each other.

The marriage of Mother Goose and murder goes back at least as far as S.S. Van Dine's *The Bishop Murder Case* (1929), and writers like Agatha Christie and Richard Sale had played with the motif before the cousins. But no one else piles on the black humor like Fred and Manny, for example in the stock-market maneuver scene where grieving Cornelia connives at making a tidy profit out of her son's death, or the board-of-directors sequence where Thurlow the incompetent twerp elects himself president of the Potts empire. There are several discussions of whether one or more of the family could be committed to an asylum, but the recurring objection is: They're not insane. Which is absurd in the light of what we've seen. That's the point. Mad is sane, sane is mad, and we've all fallen down the rabbit hole without knowing it. But side by side with this novel of the Absurd the cousins give us a convoluted formal deductive puzzle, for purposes of which the gargoyles of the Ellery in Wonderland scenes shed their grotesque qualities and take their places as figures in a typical solid Queen plot. Who could swallow the premise that dotty Thurlow could be the consummate actor he needs to be when the book goes "serious"? If I may cite an apt phrase from the novel itself, *There Was an Old Woman* is "too rich a mixture of sense and nonsense, a mixture too thoroughly mixed." Stated another way, there are some fine individual sequences in both parts of the book but it's at odds with itself at every step and never adds up to an integral whole.

***

During the period when Carleton Young was the Ellery of the airwaves, Fred Dannay not only devised a new radio plot every week and the plots of the new Queen novels just considered but also worked prodigiously as editor and anthologist and scholar of the genre he loved. With the May 1942 number *Ellery Queen's Mystery Magazine* speeded up its publication schedule, requiring Fred to put together a new issue every two months rather than four times a year. His never-ending work on the magazine didn't keep him from staying active wearing other hats. His scholarly book *The Detective Short Story* (1942) was a ground-breaking bibliographic study of short detective fiction collections in the century since Poe. On the anthology front he assembled *Sporting Blood* (1942), a book of twenty sports detective tales featuring Conan Doyle, Chesterton, Sayers, E.C. Bentley, Leslie Charteris and—with three different stories!— Queen himself. *The Female of The Species* (1943) was an even more generous package, weighing in at 420 pages devoted to the great women detectives and criminals. The contributors by and large were more contemporary than those in *Sporting Blood*. But Christie, Mary Roberts Rinehart, Mignon G. Eberhart, Roy Vickers, Stuart Palmer and Anthony Boucher were joined by a few old-timers like Fergus Hume and John Kendrick Bangs. Manny Lee, needless to say, was too busy turning Fred's synopses into radio scripts to work on any other projects.

CHAPTER TWELVE

A Man Named Smith

IN AUGUST 1943, while the Queen radio series was still on hiatus, Carleton Young signed a Hollywood contract and bowed out as Ellery. He was replaced by Sydney Smith (1909-1978), a seasoned professional in radio and the theatre who in the late 1930s had done live broadcasts of *Gang Busters* literally on the same evenings he was playing Laertes on the stage opposite Maurice Evans as Hamlet. In a letter he wrote me in 1977, Smith described how he got the Ellery Queen job.

> I was well enough established as a radio actor that I knew when they had auditions I would be called. Since I had always been a mystery fan in general and Ellery in particular (and also because the salary budgeted for the part was generous) I decided to do some research so I perhaps might have an edge. I read and reread all the [Queen] novels in order to establish a distinctive approach. I decided the intent was to create an American [Sherlock] Holmes. I took the novels in chronological order and discovered a change in [Ellery's] outward characteristics. . . . The later ones were not as fussy as the earlier. This gave [Ellery] more of a sophisticated manner than before.

Keeping that in mind I began to work on a characterization. As for the outward vocal characterization I adopted a Ronald Colman approach but with no attempt to ape an English intonation or accent. I was pleased when Manny [Lee] said I was an American Sherlock.

Good as Smith was in the role of Ellery Queen—and he was good enough to keep the part for more than three years, longer than any other actor in any medium—one suspects that listeners noticed the differences in voices. But it's unlikely that anyone was aware of the next change in the regular cast. Near the end of the summer reruns, Marian Shockley, whose husband George Zachary had transferred from the OWI to the Navy and by then was stationed in the Pacific, took two months' leave from the role of Nikki on her doctor's orders. Her stand-in was Helen Lewis, who had been her roommate six years earlier at the Rehearsal Club, a residence hall for hopeful actresses. Lewis's specialty was voice impersonations, and on the *March of Time* program she had mimicked everyone from the Queen of England to Eleanor Roosevelt to Ginger Rogers. During her two months as Nikki she made it a point to sound as much as possible like Shockley. It was with these changes in personnel—Sydney Smith as Ellery, Helen Lewis as Nikki, Santos Ortega and Ted De Corsia carrying on as Inspector Queen and Sergeant Velie—that the next cycle of EQ's audio exploits opened in October.

For the rest of 1943 and all of 1944 *The Adventures of Ellery Queen* was on the air every single week with no time off. Sydney Smith, Santos Ortega, Ted De Corsia and announcer Ernest Chappell continued in their accustomed parts through the long long stretch, but Helen Lewis left the role of Nikki after the first episode of November 1943 and Marian Shockley returned to the part the following week.

If the cousins fell behind schedule or if Fred failed to come up with a new idea in a given week, they had only two alternatives: either to condense a 60-minute drama from 1939-1940 into half-hour form, or to recycle one of the golden oldies from the first season of 30-minute plays. Research confirms that they exercised both options often.

Shall we take some instances of the first option first? "The Disaster Club" (January 6/8, 1944) is a condensed version of "The Last Man Club," second of the 60-minute episodes from 1939. "The Scarecrow and the Snowman" (January 20/22, 1944; available on audio) is a rewrite of

"The Dying Scarecrow" from early 1940, and stacks up very well against the first-run episodes of four years later. "Wanted: John Smith" (March 9/11, 1944) is based on "The Devil's Violin" from January 1940. "Dead Man's Cavern" (April 13/15, 1944; available on audio) comes from the October 1939 episode "The Haunted Cave," and "The Buried Treasure" (April 27/29, 1944) from "Captain Kidd's Bedroom" which was first aired in February 1940. "The Thief in the Dark" (May 4/6, 1944) was originally the hour-long episode "The Cellini Cup" from November 1939, and some of the scenes preserved in the Armed Forces Radio Service Asneak preview" of the 30-minute version contain dialogue identical to lines of "Cellini" as they were printed without permission in *Radio Guide* back in 1940. "The Great Chewing Gum Mystery" (May 25/27, 1944) was a condensation of the first Queen radio play, "The Gum-Chewing Millionaire." "The Murder Game" (June 1/3, 1944) comes from "The Dead Cat"; "The Dark Secret" (June 8/10, 1944) from "The Black Secret"; "The Corpse in Lower Five" (June 22/24, 1944) from "Napoleon's Razor"; "The College Crime" (September 14/16, 1944) from "The Three Rs." Of the 34 hour-long episodes broadcast between June 1939 and February 1940, at least 26 were recycled as half-hour episodes broadcast between January and November 1944.

The cousins' earliest exercise of their second option dates back to two episodes from the fall of 1943 which had been first heard in the summer of 1940: "The Frightened Star" (October 21/23, 1943; originally July 14, 1940) and "The Vanishing Magician" (November 4/6, 1943; originally "The Disappearing Magician," September 15, 1940). They did it again five more times in the months after D-Day: "The Egyptian Tomb" (July 6/8, 1944; originally "The Pharaoh's Curse," August 25, 1940); "The Man Who Wanted Cash" (August 17/19, 1944; originally "The Fatal Million," August 4, 1940); "The Mayor and the Corpse" (August 24/26, 1944; originally "The Picnic Murder," September 8, 1940); "The Robber of Fallboro" (September 21/23, 1944; originally "The Black Sheep," July 28, 1940); and "The Invisible Clock" (September 28/30, 1944; originally August 11, 1940). A later 30-minute episode was recycled right after Christmas: "The Inner Circle" (December 28/30, 1944; originally "The Millionaires' Club," April 23/25, 1942). Overworked as they were during this period of intense pressure, Fred and Manny coped by recycling as much of their earlier output as was humanly possible.

Of the genuinely new episodes that were heard during 1943-44, one of the finest was that audacious miracle problem "The Dauphin's Doll" (December 23/25, 1943), which was written by Manny Lee alone, without any input from Fred Dannay. Ellery, his father and dozens of the Inspector's men join forces to protect the titular doll and its diamond crown from the legendary thief Comus, who announces that he'll make the figure vanish while it's on exhibition at a major department store on the day before Christmas. Despite a gantlet of security arrangements Comus lives up to his boast, but Ellery's reasoning exposes the working of the miracle and nets both thief and loot as Christmas dawn floods the city. Manny later recast this script into the short story of the same name (*EQMM*, December 1948; collected in *Calendar of Crime*, 1952), which is equally dazzling.

At least in its 30-minute version, which is available on audio, "The Mischief Maker" (January 13/15, 1944; originally "The Anonymous Letters," January 21, 1940) is a routine exercise with Ellery trying to find out who's writing poison-pen letters to the residents of a single apartment building—the exact obverse of the situation in "The Good Samaritan" (June 9, 1940). The motivation for the letter-writing binge turns out to be ridiculous and Ellery's key deduction pedestrian.

Of the episodes broadcast in the spring and early summer of 1944, three were printed, albeit in condensed versions, in that impossibly rare volume *Chillers & Thrillers* (Street & Smith, 1945), a fragile 107-page paperback that forms Volume 18 of the "At Ease" series, distributed by the Special Services Division of the Army Service Forces. The scripts were adapted for live impromptu staging in GI recreation halls, without scenery or costumes or props. In lieu of the guest armchair detectives on the radio series, these versions called for a jury of audience members— always an odd number so as to avoid deadlocks. The earliest script offered was "The Glass Ball" (March 23/25, 1944), which was a 30-minute version of "The Man Who Wanted To Be Murdered" (December 3, 1939). You can compare the versions if you have a copy of *Radio and Television Mirror* for August 1940, which contains an adaptation (not by the cousins) of the longer version into a short story, and of the *Chillers & Thrillers* volume. On the other hand "The Blue Chip" (June 15/17, 1944), which was a 30-minute version of "The Wandering Corpse" (August 13, 1939), can be accessed only in *Chillers & Thrillers*. Last of the trio is "The Foul Tip" (July 13/15, 1944), which was first broadcast as "Box 13" (September 1, 1940) and is also available on audio.

In both "The Dark Secret" (June 8/10, 1944) and its 60-minute source "The Black Secret" (December 10, 1939) the tyrannical owner of a rare-book emporium fires all his help after the theft of some valuable first editions, and Ellery and Nikki apply for clerks' jobs in order to find the missing volumes and save the innocent employees' positions. It might be instructive to read the script of the earlier version in the *Murdered Moths* collection while listening to the few "sneak preview" scenes from the Armed Forces Radio Service which are all that survives of the later version.

Speaking of the armed forces, what ever happened to the cousins' commitment to lace a certain number of Queen scripts with OWI material? In "The Bullet-Proof Man" (November 18/20, 1943) Ellery investigates a murder among the bizarre tenants of a new office building that is not yet officially open and discovers that loose talk by soldiers (while drinking soda pop!) caused the deaths of American troops. "The Red Cross" (March 2/4, 1944) finds Nikki, as a volunteer for the Red Cross Home Services, entangling Ellery in the mystery of a pregnant military wife who disappeared shortly before she was to give birth. Fred and Manny also wrote one 15-minute script that was broadcast as a "special" under the overt sponsorship of OWI and was published that summer in *EQMM*. Like "Tom, Dick and Harry" and "The Bullet-Proof Man," "The Wounded Lieutenant" (available on audio; script published in *EQMM*, July 1944) is a diatribe against "loose talk." This time the military catastrophe takes place in the China-Burma-India theater and once again Ellery demonstrates that agents of the fiendishly clever enemy are ever waiting to overhear scraps of casual chatter and deduce from them the plans for D-Day or whatever.

Whether working with new scripts or with plays that originally had starred Hugh Marlowe or Carleton Young, Sydney Smith took to the part of Ellery like a cat to a mouse. Indeed, like Marlowe before him, he apparently convinced himself for a time that he was Ellery Queen in the flesh. NBC was keeping the identity of the actor who played Ellery a secret, and in newspaper stories dealing with the series he was usually photographed with his back to the camera. The network even booked him in his EQ persona as a guest on various NBC talk shows and elsewhere. One of these appearances was at Carnegie Hall, where "Ellery" was scheduled to lecture to a large group of children on the subject "Crime Does Not Pay." Anya, Kaye Brinker Lee's 10-year-old daughter by her first marriage, happened to be taking ballet lessons at one of the Carnegie Hall studios, and she and her mother were more than mildly surprised to read the placards on the building walls announcing that Ellery Queen was to make a public appearance. Kaye checked with Manny, who checked with Fred, and after Smith's lecture the cousins pointed out to him that he was not authorized to play Ellery anywhere but on the weekly radio program. As Fred described the incident in a 1947 memoir reprinted in *In the Queens' Parlor* (1957), Smith

> was both amazed and resentful. Why, he had done no harm—indeed, in his opinion he had done the real Ellery Queen a favor! Hadn't he been the instrument of considerable publicity? Hadn't he been photographed? How could the real Ellery Queen be offended? Why, we should actually be grateful! When we pointed out that there was one small error in his thinking—the small matter of the wrong person having been publicized and photographed—[Smith] woke with a start and half of the double image in his mind suddenly evaporated.

But the matter was no more than a tempest in a teapot, and Smith carried on as Ellery without further fuss.

***

The only Queen anthology published during this period was *The Misadventures of Sherlock Holmes* (1944), in which Fred Dannay brought together some 33 parodies, pastiches and variations on the sage of Baker Street, written by everyone from Mark Twain and O. Henry and Bret Harte to Agatha Christie and Vincent Starrett, with EQ himself represented by the radio play "Mr. Short and Mr. Long," here retitled "The Disappearance of Mr. James Phillimore." In pages v-ix of his introduction Fred drew a poignant picture of his boyhood in Elmira beside "the gentle Chemung" and of his introduction to Holmes at the feverish age of 12. The material, beginning with "This is one of the Queens speaking," unaccountably outraged Manny Lee and struck him as a betrayal of the Queen partnership. "Slowly but surely the nebulous substance of our fundamental conflict is clotting into recognizable shape. I am being driven by events, by myself, by you, into a corner. . . . [T]he trapped animal rarely has the capacity to sit down and 'reason things out' coolly. He blunders on toward his fate." And in a later letter: "[W]hereas once I stood in a position of relative equality to you, in the eyes of both of us as in the eyes of the world, I have gradually assumed a more and more inferior position, and that process . . . is only accelerating."

Misadventures not only temporarily poisoned relations between the cousins but led to a legal dispute with the Conan Doyle estate, which quickly forced the book off the market. Thereby hangs a tale, which Fred told me one evening over dinner. In *101 Years' Entertainment* Holmes had been represented not by a single story but by four separate deduction scenes, each taken from a different tale. But the Queen literary agent had secured permission from Conan Doyle's successors to reprint only the first of the four passages. Shortly after *Misadventures* was published, Fred discovered the oversight and brought it to the estate's attention. Conan Doyle's sons, who hated the new anthology but had no independent legal basis for taking action against it, threatened to sue over the *101 Years'* infringement unless *Misadventures* was withdrawn from circulation. Since the earlier title was by far the bigger seller of the two, Fred had no choice but to comply. I am the proud owner of a mint copy he gave me for Christmas 1968, the year we met—a copy inscribed of course by the editor. In all editions of *101 Years'* that postdate this fracas, an ancient Nick Carter story clearly in the public domain replaces the four Sherlockian deductions.

***

Fred had everything to do with *Misadventures* but no connection with *The Green Turtle Mystery* (1944), third in the "Ellery Queen, Jr." series and, like the second, ghost-written by pulp horror specialist Frank Belknap Long under Manny's supervision. Where he found the time to oversee that book while frantically trying to micromanage every episode of the weekly Queen radio series is as baffling a mystery as any solved by Djuna the houseboy sleuth.

CHAPTER THIRTEEN

New Blood on the Typewriter Keys

ON OCTOBER 5, 1944, *The Adventures of Ellery Queen* began its fifth season on the air in the same Saturday evening time slot on NBC and with the same continuing cast of Sydney Smith, Marian Shockley, Santos Ortega and Ted De Corsia. What was not known outside the inner circle of the production team was that Fred Dannay was no longer closely involved with the series as he had been from the start. By late 1944 his wife Mary was bedridden from cancer (which killed her in the early morning hours of July 4, 1945, the third anniversary of Manny's marriage to Kaye Brinker), and Fred had to make the welfare of his 11- and 5-year-old sons his highest priority. In the time he had left for work he wanted to concentrate on projects he found more congenial: editing *EQMM*, compiling hardcover anthologies of short mystery fiction, creating plots for new Ellery Queen novels. But he didn't want and, especially with two children to raise, couldn't afford to give up his share of the huge weekly checks that the radio series was generating.

To the creator of Ellery Queen the solution of the problem was simplicity itself. In the early years of the radio program Fred and Manny had authorized the publication of *Radio and Television Mirror* short stories and two Whitman Better Little Books, all based on Queen scripts but adapted into prose by uncredited others and issued under the Queen byline. Since 1941 various ghost writers working under Manny's supervision had been turning out juvenile mysteries as by Ellery Queen, Jr. If all those could be successfully subcontracted, why couldn't the creation of the detailed plot outlines that were Fred's contributions to the radio show? As long as the writers who took over the Dannay function were chosen with sufficient care, the listening audience wouldn't be able to tell the difference.

The first person picked for the role of plot creator was Tom Everitt, who may also have used the names John Tom or John Thomas Everitt. Even in the Google era nothing seems to be known about him beyond the titles of some (not necessarily all) of the episodes on which he worked with Manny Lee. We know that Everitt had replaced Fred Dannay by January 1945 at latest, but there is reason to believe that some of the EQ episodes broadcast on NBC in the last three months of 1944 also started out as Everitt synopses. Take, for example, "Cleopatra's Snake" (October 12/14, 1944). As a backstage observer at a live production of *Antony and Cleopatra* for experimental TV, Ellery becomes a key witness when the genuine poisonous snake being used in the death scene bites to death the actress playing Cleopatra. Or "The Glass Sword" (November 30/December 2, 1944), in which Ellery tackles the case of the circus sword swallower who died when the sword in his stomach broke while the lights were out. These strike me as way too outrageous to have come from the mind of Fred Dannay.

Other episodes from late 1944 are clearly based on synopses by Fred. In "The Booby Trap" (November 9/11, 1944) Ellery is dragooned into appearing as a guest on the radio quiz program *Life and Literature*, whose host Sid Sherman is a wizard at identifying literary quotations and allusions. After the show Sherman is murdered by a bomb inserted into a hollowed-out copy of *Alice in Wonderland* and planted in his study. Just before dying he manages to pull down four books from his shelves—one each by Shaw, Shakespeare, Walt Whitman and Ulysses S. Grant—and Ellery's challenge is to translate Sherman's last literary act into the name of his murderer. If that plot isn't pure Dannay, toads fly. But there's further proof. Many years later, in the short story "Enter Ellery Queen" (*Argosy*, June 1960; collected as "Mystery at the Library of Congress" in *Q.E.D.: Queen's Experiments in Detection*, 1968), the cousins recycled the same gimmick with a different plot.

We know from Manny Lee's correspondence that he had not made use of all the synopses Fred prepared before he stepped down but had squirreled away several for emergencies or in case his new plot provider should fail him. In due course he would adapt all of these into new EQ scripts, the final one being broadcast in August 1946.

The final episode aired during the last full year of the war was "The Inner Circle" (December 28/30, 1944), which as we've seen was a retitled rerun of a genuine Dannay-Lee script from two and a half years earlier. The Queen series then left the air for almost a month. When it returned it was not to NBC but to the CBS network where it had been born. Its new time slot was from 7:30 to 8:00 p.m. on Wednesdays, and Anacin took over from Bromo-Seltzer as sponsor. Sydney Smith, Santos Ortega and Ted De Corsia continued as Ellery, the Inspector and Sergeant Velie, but Marian Shockley retired from the role of Nikki and was replaced by Barbara Terrell. Don Hancock took over from Ernest Chappell as announcer, a new organist whose name is unknown sat down at the bench formerly occupied by Charles Paul, and new producers and directors were assigned to the show as well. With two brief summer vacations the series remained on CBS until mid-April of 1947.

A substantial excerpt from the first episode under the new regime has been preserved on audio as another of those "sneak previews" from the Armed Forces Radio Service. "The Diamond Fence" (January 24, 1945), written by Manny from a synopsis by Tom Everitt, involves the murder of a middleman for stolen gems and the disappearance of five diamond rings from the scene of the crime under impossible circumstances. The scenes that survive make it sound like a puzzler of the first water.

***

Calamity Town had proved itself by the time the cousins prepared to write their next novel, and another Wrightsville book seemed called for, but in order to provide that case they had to rewrite the town's history slightly. "Ain't never had a homicide in Wrightsville before," Chief of Police Dakin had remarked to Ellery in Chapter 14 of the first book about that community, "and I been Chief here for pretty near twenty years." But in *The Murderer Is a Fox* (1945), which was published in the spring of the year the war ended, Ellery probes a twelve-year-old Wrightsville murder. You do the math.

The time is the summer of 1944 and the problem grows out of the return of Captain Davy Fox to his home town. A dozen years earlier, Davy's mother had died after swallowing digitalis in a glass of grape juice. His father, the only person with opportunity to commit the crime, had been convicted of her murder and sentenced to life in prison. Ten-year-old Davy had then been raised by his Uncle Talbot and Aunt Emily, and their adopted daughter Linda became first a sister to Davy and later his wife. Davy's adolescence had been a nightmare of failed attempts to escape the stigma of his father's crime and the fear of his own "tainted blood" and "killer instinct." Then the war came, and two days after marrying Linda, Davy had been sent as a fighter pilot to the China-Burma-India theater where the blood of many stained him. Unsigned letters arrive from home, intimating that Linda has been unfaithful, and on his return to the States a nerve-shattered Davy finds himself wrestling with an uncontrollable compulsion to kill her. Remembering the trouble in the Wright family, Linda asks help from the man who had helped them. And Ellery concludes that the only way to release Davy from the trap in which the past holds him is to reopen the twelve-year-old murder case, to try to prove that Davy's father did not kill his mother, that he is not the son of a murderer.

Parts Two and Four, which deal with the investigation of Jessica Fox's death, might well have been subtitled The Detective As Historian. Ellery's meticulous reconstruction of the exact events of June 14, 1932 in the house of Bayard and Jessica Fox is carried out with the historian's intellectual tools and generates the same sense of excitement that spurs conscientious historians in their search for truth. Many authors seeking to merge the detective story and historical reconstruction have fallen into the trap of gifting all or most of the parties to the ancient crime with implausibly photographic memories. *The Murderer Is a Fox* skirts all the pitfalls, permits the witnesses to forget a great deal, and never tempts us to think that someone's recollection of events after twelve years seems too precise. Like many Queen novels since, this one culminates in a false or partial explanation followed by the true, final and stunning solution, although here as in *The Door Between* Ellery relies not on reasoning but on intuition in the manner of Georges Simenon's Maigret.

More vividly than any other Queen novel, *The Murderer Is a Fox* evokes the excitement of the quest for truth. Perhaps this is why Ellery's ultimate solution here is left completely unverifiable, for so is the truth historians seek, and that profession knows no counterpart to the murderer's confession in whodunits. Nothing else in the genre matches *Fox*'s depiction of historical thinking in action, and of the exhilaration Aristotle hinted at when he said "The activity of mind is life."

In his review for the San Francisco *Chronicle* (May 27, 1945), Anthony Boucher described *Fox* as a "[h]ighly satisfactory combination of [an] astonishing technical tour de force with [a] warmly human novel." Manny Lee on the other hand was bitterly disappointed with the book, although he never fully explained why. "We sweated over that one," he wrote to Boucher (May 24, 1945), "and some day . . . we'll relate the saga of its magazine adventures, which in some degree dictated—the hell; in large degree—dictated the book. Even its length and sequence. I know I had to cut gobs, and each cut was a slice out of my heart. And then the dirty bastards went and—But some other time." That other time never came. But even a mediocre historian can fill in the blanks in Manny's last sentence since *The Murderer Is a Fox* wasn't published in a magazine as a serial or condensation before its hardcover appearance. Was the subject of mentally disturbed combat veterans (whom we now describe as suffering from PTSD) deemed politically incorrect?

***

Beginning in the spring of 1945 and extending over the next few years, Manny and Boucher exchanged literally hundreds of letters. What was behind this torrent of correspondence?

After five and a half months during which the vast majority of EQ radio scripts were written by Manny from synopses by Tom Everitt, a new idea generator was brought in to provide plots for Ellery to unravel. It was Boucher, the well-known mystery writer and reviewer of whodunits for the San Francisco *Chronicle* (and later *The New York Times*), who took over this function and continued in it till the series went off the air. The selection was ideal. Boucher had started writing detective novels out of admiration for fair-play masters like the cousins, his character Fergus O'Breen had been conceived as a sort of West Coast Ellery Queen with an Irish brogue, and several Boucher short stories had already been published in *EQMM*. In addition, as shown by his comments in the *Chronicle*, he was a fan of the radio series. Beginning with "The Corpse of Mr. Entwhistle" (June 13, 1945), about 70 of the *Adventures of Ellery Queen* scripts were the joint work of Boucher, who was never credited, and Manny Lee.

Both Boucher and Fred Dannay were devotees and practitioners of the pure deductive problem that played eminently fair with the consumer, but their personalities were poles apart. Fred was an apolitical person, uninvolved in causes, at home in abstractions, a private man in almost every sense of the phrase. Boucher like Manny Lee was a public man, a political activist and a staunch liberal. Unlike either Fred or Manny, Boucher was deeply religious. When Fred was with the series his specialty had been the kind of script in which Ellery would confront three or four suspects with diagrammatic names and purely functional characterizations—Mr. Anson the attorney, Mr. Benson the ballplayer and Mr. Charleson the cheesemaker—and would deduce that only one of them possessed a trait which the murderer must have had. Boucher could conjure up this kind of storyline as well as Dannay but his tended to be more rooted in the real world and he devoted more care to rounded characterizations. And during the years of the Boucher-Lee regime, Ellery was portrayed less as the Celebrated Gentleman Detective and more as the Socially Concerned Citizen.

Boucher's file copies of 77 synopses, each one banged out in minuscule type on six or eight sheets of yellow paper, are preserved at Indiana University's Lilly Library, along with copies of most of the final scripts as fleshed out by Lee and of the Boucher-Lee correspondence. Reading this material is a fascinating experience akin to traveling backward in time. Boucher's synopses are almost like friendly letters, full of asides in which he explains to Manny where this or that plot notion came from or what movie actor Boucher had in mind in creating this or that suspect. Comparing any given synopsis with the final script reveals that Manny often made radical changes in Boucher's conceptions. Indeed several synopses weren't used at all.

On the other hand, some of the broadcast scripts whose origins remain unknown to this day may have been based on Boucher synopses that for some reason were never deposited at the Lilly. Born list-maker that he was, Boucher numbered most of the synopses he sent Manny Lee. The highest number he used was 77. Does this mean he wrote exactly 77 synopses, no more and no less? Hardly! The Lilly archives contain two separate and distinct synopses numbered 14 and none at all with the numbers 18, 21, 24 or 28. Does this mean Boucher never used these numbers? Perhaps. But as Ellery Queen himself might have asked, why would a systematic person like Boucher have skipped them? Isn't it just as likely that the Lilly either never received or misfiled the synopses to which he assigned those numbers? Close examination of Boucher's correspondence with Manny Lee confirms that four scripts with previously unknown origins were indeed based on Boucher synopses that somehow never made it to the Lilly. Does this mean that we know for sure that Boucher wrote exactly 78 synopses, no more and no less? Hardly! The Lilly also has three synopses numbered 13a, 15a and 17a. To how many other synopses might Boucher have assigned a number with a letter after it? Any script that can't be traced to a source might possibly have been based on a lost Boucher synopsis. All we can say for sure is that Boucher prepared at least 81 synopses, 77 of which are at the Lilly. My own view is that there are no unknown others but I've been wrong before.

Of the last ten episodes from the series' fifth season, eight were demonstrably based on Boucher synopses. The only one known to survive on audio is "Nick the Knife" (August 1, 1945), which is not only immensely exciting in its own right but historically crucial as a forerunner of perhaps the finest Queen novel of all, *Cat of Many Tails* (1949). A madman has slashed the wrists and faces of more than thirty beautiful women on the night streets of Manhattan. Finally a woman is attacked inside an ornamental maze with only one exit, which is being watched by Ellery and several policemen. But later events seem to prove beyond doubt that not one of the handful of suspects found in the maze could possibly be the slasher. Ellery resolves the dilemma magnificently, although most listeners probably fell into the trap for the overly clever that Tony and Manny cunningly built into the story. After Boucher and Lee's "The Time of Death" (August 15, 1945) the series went on hiatus for three weeks.

***

Early in the fall, the first season of peace in four years, Little, Brown published the next Queen anthology. For *Rogues' Gallery* (1945) Fred Dannay selected 32 stories dealing with the great criminals of modern fiction. Among the well-known mainstream authors included in the book were Arnold Bennett, O. Henry and Sinclair Lewis, while among the contributors known mainly or exclusively for crime fiction were H.C. Bailey, Leslie Charteris, Dashiell Hammett, Dorothy L. Sayers and Edgar Wallace. Fred also included two rare radio scripts, one by John Dickson Carr and the other by—well, can't you guess?

***

After its brief hiatus the Queen radio show came back for a sixth season that lasted a full 52 weeks, with no changes in sponsorship, network or time slot and only one newcomer in the regular cast, namely Gertrude Warner, who had replaced Barbara Terrell as Nikki four weeks before the end of the previous season. Boucher provided the plots for 36 of these episodes, Tom Everitt for four, newcomer Richard Manoff for two. At least five and possibly six new episodes were written by Lee based on synopses by Fred Dannay and held in reserve against emergencies after Fred left the series. The origins of three or perhaps four episodes remain unknown. One was a rerun from the war years.

How much Everitt and Manoff and the other synopsis writers (if any) were being paid remains unknown, but Boucher's compensation is clear from Manny Lee's letter of November 29, 1945: of the $2,000 being paid by the sponsor for each script, Manny was receiving roughly $1,000, Fred Dannay (who had dropped out of the series completely by this time) roughly $500, and Boucher roughly $500 for each of his synopses that Manny turned into a script. These are only approximations because Dannay and Lee were paying the agent commissions on Boucher's take out of their own shares.

The fourth episode of the season was "The Green House" (September 26, 1945). Both Lee's script and the untitled Boucher synopsis on which he based it are preserved at the Lilly. In both versions Ellery is kidnapped and taken to a mythical country to solve a crime for its dictator. Boucher in his synopsis pointed out to Lee that he named his imagined country San Pedro after the banana republic whose fugitive dictator figured in the Sherlock Holmes story "The Adventure of Wisteria Lodge" (1908). Lee kept Boucher's plot but changed the setting to a postage-stamp dictatorship in middle Europe that he called Serakia. The concept of Ellery being dragged off to solve a crime in an isolated fascist domain was recycled by Dannay and Lee a few years later in their novel *The King Is Dead* (1952).

In "The Kid Glove Killer" (October 10, 1945) Ellery's quarry is a masked criminal who committed murder in order to steal a box of kid gloves from a men's store. Boucher's version is entitled "The Criminous Commando" and deals with a masked thief who wears an outfit resembling that of a World War II commando and who is described differently by everyone who sees him.

In "The Message in Red" (November 7, 1945) a public stenographer, a manuscript reader for a publishing house and a French maid are all shot to death on the same night with the same gun, and Ellery soon realizes that someone is out to drop a certain incriminating document down the memory hole by killing everybody who's seen it. The "dying message" solution is rather tame but, being based on the fact that people tend to think in their native language in times of crisis, it hints at the multi-lingual Boucher. And sure enough, a document in the Boucher-Lee correspondence files confirms that Lee's script was based on Boucher's synopsis "The Calloused Maid," which is missing from the Lilly. Luckily the episode survives on audio.

"The Ape's Boss" (November 21, 1945) finds Ellery trying to identify the secret mastermind who's giving orders to Ape Loogan, the moronic front man for a gang whose crimes are terrorizing the city. Boucher's more topical synopsis, "The Reluctant Restaurateur," had the proprietor of Ellery's favorite restaurant blown up by a time bomb after telling the sleuth he's being forced to buy meat from a black market ring led by a mystery man. In these months just after the war, Lee seemed to be trying to eliminate as much wartime ambience as possible from Boucher's plots.

In "The Curious Thefts" (December 19, 1945; condensation of script published in *Story Digest*, September 1946) a well-known novelist whose marriage is collapsing comes to Ellery for help when his household is plagued by a rash of bizarre pilferings, culminating in murder. The solution presupposes a fairly intimate knowledge of the Bible like Boucher's own, but the title doesn't appear in the legal document I found at the Lilly, listing all of Boucher's contributions to the series through early 1946. A letter from Manny to Boucher, dated December 5, 1945, confirms that this was another of the scripts based on synopses by Fred Dannay that Manny had held back after Fred's departure in case of sudden emergencies. There are some intriguing similarities between "The Curious Thefts" and certain elements in Queen's powerful religious detective novel *Ten Days' Wonder* (1948).

Three episodes from the early months of 1946 nicely illustrate how Lee's final drafts altered Boucher's originals. "The Green Eye" (January 16, 1946) pits Ellery against an international criminal who, doubtless inspired by the stick figures habitually left behind by Simon Templar the Saint, leaves an eye drawn in green ink at the scene of each of his jewel robberies. For the most part Lee followed Boucher's synopsis, "The

Stormy Petrel," but in Boucher's version the criminal left bird drawings as his sign.

Much more radical changes can be seen in "Ellery Queen's Tragedy" (January 30, 1946). The Boucher synopsis at the root of this episode was entitled "Murder at *EQMM*" and had Ellery solve a murder in the offices of his own magazine, the victim being a Frenchman in New York to locate a fellow countryman who had had stories published in *EQMM*. By the time Lee had rewritten the story, it became that of two men who show up in New York claiming to be the famous French mystery writer for whom a fortune in wartime U.S. royalties is waiting. *EQMM* is left completely out of Manny Lee's version. Manny goes on to have the impostor shoot Inspector Queen and leave him near death, apparently because Santos Ortega was taking a leave of absence from the part and somehow or other had to be written out of the series for a while.

Manny was not an easy taskmaster, as witness his letter of January 30, 1946, criticizing "The Scarlet Ghosts," Boucher's latest synopsis. "When I actually got into it—in fact, the first draft was half-finished—I suddenly made the ghastly discovery that the 'solution' didn't solve a goddam thing. It had a hole big enough to take a nap in—and no way that I could see of stopping it up without chinks and crannies, although I spent two full days trying to do just that thing. . . . Finally I saw the handwriting on the wall and gave up. Behind schedule, harassed and biting my nails—I threw the whole damn thing out and invented brand-new material which affected the entire second half of the show and, of course, gave you a new solution entirely." Lee's script based on this synopsis was "The Living Dead" (February 13, 1946).

"The Phantom Shadow" (March 6, 1946) was based on a Boucher synopsis called "The Shadow of Murder" in which a woman visits Ellery and claims that while working late at night she witnessed a murder through the window of the lawyer's office across the street, although when the office was examined neither a corpse nor any signs of a struggle were found. Lee kept the basic plot, which is an obvious take-off on Cornell Woolrich's classic "Rear Window" (1942), but in his version the woman is Nikki, who witnesses the murder that wasn't while substituting on a night secretarial job for a girlfriend.

The only sixth-season episode known to be by Boucher and Lee and preserved on audio (in a repeat performance dating from two years later) is "The Armchair Detective" (March 27, 1946), a rare gem in which Ellery solves a poisoning that takes place on the Queen radio show itself. The idea obviously came to Boucher from Orson Welles' 1938 adaptation of *The War of the Worlds*, which convinced thousands of panicky listeners that Martians had invaded Earth. But the dying-message situation is a neat one indeed: first Ellery interprets the clue in the conventional way, then he gets fancy and works out a much more complex reading, whose possibility the killer has also seen and planted evidence to support.

"Mr. Warren's Profession" (June 5, 1946) is based on Boucher's synopsis "The Man Who Liked Bad Puns," in which Ellery probes the murder of a professional blackmailer who, just before dying, intoned "The safe . . . is safe" and shook a bell upside down. In Lee's script the blackmailer is addicted to making wordplays based on book titles and his dying message is wordless, consisting only of ringing a bell over and over in double peals.

In "Cokey and the Pizza" (June 19, 1946) Lee fairly closely follows Boucher's synopsis "The Perilous Pizza," in which Ellery tries to figure out how a fugitive gangster holed up in a room above an Italian restaurant is being supplied with cocaine. The titular dish was so unfamiliar to the 1946 radio audience that both the synopsis and the final script include a scene where Ellery explains to Nikki what pizza is while they watch one being made. In his synopsis Boucher even spelled the word phonetically, peet-za, so that it wouldn't be mispronounced over the airwaves!

The last of the scripts based on a Fred Dannay synopsis that Manny had been holding in reserve was "The Doomed Man" (August 28, 1946), in which Ellery uses a candlestick clue to clear a young man charged with the murder of his father. After that episode the series left the air for a vacation well-earned by everyone but perhaps most of all by Tony Boucher, whose radio commitments at their peak involved writing script synopses for the Queen program, the Basil Rathbone-Nigel Bruce *Sherlock Holmes* series, and *The Case Book of Gregory Hood*, a detective show in the Queen vein created by Boucher and Denis Green, who fleshed out each of Tony's *Holmes* and *Hood* synopses into a full script just as Manny Lee was doing on the EQ program. Being one of those rare people who lives joyously at 78 r.p.m. while the rest of the world revolves lazily at 33, Boucher thrived on that kind of life.

***

The beginning of the radio hiatus roughly coincided with the appearance of the next Queen anthology. By this time *EQMM* had been around for almost five years, publishing plenty of stories from which Fred Dannay could select the contents of *To the Queen's Taste* (1946), a gathering of 36 tales from the magazine's pioneer days. In assembling the book he relied heavily on his earlier anthology *Best Stories from Ellery Queen's Mystery Magazine* (1944), a volume of 23 tales which had been published by the Detective Book Club exclusively for its members. Twelve of the 23 *Best Stories* were recycled in *To the Queen's Taste* and another six of the authors appearing in *Best Stories* showed up in *To the Queen's Taste* with different tales. The remaining five *Best Stories* authors (including Margery Allingham, Anthony Boucher and Cornell Woolrich) don't appear in *Taste* at all. To put it another way, twelve of the 36 *Taste* tales come straight out of *Best Stories*, six are different tales by authors who had appeared in *Best Stories*, and the remaining 18 are direct from *EQMM*. Among the gems in *Taste* are "lost" stories by G.K. Chesterton and E.C. Bentley, first-rate contributions by Eric Ambler and James M. Cain and T.S. Stribling and Mark Twain, and S.J. Perelman's famous parody of Raymond Chandler. Writing in the San Francisco *Chronicle* (August 11, 1946), Tony Boucher called it "the essential book of the year for all permanent libraries of detection."

***

On October 9, 1946 the Queen series returned for a seventh season, this one lasting 27 weeks and with a much tighter budget. According to a letter from Manny to Boucher dated September 12, the total script allocation had been cut by one-third so that Manny would now receive $600 per script, Fred Dannay $300, and Boucher $450. But by now Boucher was so deeply involved with *Holmes, Hood* and countless additional projects that he found time to contribute only ten new synopses for Manny to expand into scripts. Tom Everitt provided 11, Richard Manoff four, pulp veteran Ken Crossen one, and one episode was a retitled Dannay-Lee rerun from the war era. Since Gertrude Warner had recently married and retired from radio, the producers needed a new Nikki Porter for the seventh season and, after auditioning more than forty actresses, hired Charlotte Keane.

Six weeks into the season a format change that had been under discussion for some time was implemented. Beginning with Manoff and

Lee's "The Prize Fighter's Birthday" (November 20, 1946) the guest armchair detectives in the studio were dropped and instead, at the point where Ellery issued his Challenge to the Listener, he placed a long-distance phone call to a pre-selected member of the home audience and invited him or her to deduce whodunit. The experiment was dropped after two and a half months and the series returned to celebrity armchair sleuths.

At some time late in 1946 or early in 1947 and perhaps simultaneous with the temporary abandonment of celebrity guests, the three longest-lived of the four regulars in the cast were replaced: Ted De Corsia as Sergeant Velie by Ed Latimer, Santos Ortega as Inspector Queen by Bill Smith, and Sydney Smith, who had played Ellery since the summer of 1943, by Richard Coogan, who was born in 1914 and is the last person alive to have portrayed the master sleuth in any medium. After "The Hunted House" (February 5, 1947) Coogan in turn was replaced by Lawrence Dobkin (1919-2002).

In "The Crooked Man" (March 12, 1947) Ellery frames himself for Nikki's murder in order to set a trap for a blackmailing private eye. The head of the blackmail ring eventually captures Ellery and taunts him with the clue that the key to the combination of the safe containing the crucial evidence may be found in the second verse of the nursery rhyme "Simple Simon." Lee changed the clue from the hint Ellery is given in Boucher's version—that the safe "is doubly guarded by magic numbers—the Bullet and the Beast"—because he thought it was both too difficult and likely to run into censorship problems. Why Manny thought so you will understand if you grasp Tony's clue.

***

The last months of 1946 saw publication of *The Red Chipmunk Mystery*, fourth in the "Ellery Queen, Jr." series. Like *The Black Dog Mystery* with which the series had begun, this one was written under Manny Lee's supervision by Samuel Duff McCoy. Around the same time the cousins' "adult book" publisher Little, Brown offered the first of what turned out to be a large number of volumes of *The Queen's Awards*, an annual anthology of the best new stories from *EQMM*, selected of course by Fred Dannay. Winner of the first prize was Manly Wade Wellman's "A Star for a Warrior," the first whodunit (a full quarter century before the debut of Tony Hillerman) to feature a Native

American detective. Among the winners of the six second prizes ($250 apiece) was William Faulkner's "An Error in Chemistry," the future Nobel laureate's only original contribution to *EQMM*. Faulkner lost no time deriding both the magazine and the prize. "What a commentary," he wrote his agent early in 1946. "In France I am the father of a literary movement. In Europe I am considered the best modern American and among the first of all writers. In America, I eke out a hack's motion picture wages by winning second prize in a manufactured mystery story contest." A true Southern gentleman, yes? Of the tales that won fourth prizes, the only one whose author remains a household name today was "Find the Woman," the first short story of Kenneth Millar, a young academic recently discharged from the Navy who a few years later changed his byline to Ross Macdonald. Reviewing the collection in the San Francisco *Chronicle* (November 24, 1946), Anthony Boucher promised every reader "the pleasure of several solid hours spent with the detective story at its best."

CHAPTER FOURTEEN

The Final Half Hours

DURING THE SECOND HALF of April 1947 and all of May the Queen series again left the air. On its return it was still sponsored by Anacin but in virtually every other respect—network affiliation, time slot, cast, geographic origin—the program underwent radical alterations. During the six-week break the Queen show, along with Manny and Kaye Lee and four of their children (three they had had together and one by Kaye's first marriage) moved from Connecticut to the San Fernando Valley so that Manny could oversee the revamped show. They had first considered relocating to the state that bills itself as the Land of Enchantment but soon changed their minds, as Manny explained in a letter to Boucher dated July 28 of that year:

> New Mexico offered almost literally nothing, and that at extremely high prices; . . . the only place we saw which was . . . within both our desires and our dreams—Santa Fe—lay 20 miles from Los Alamos—you could see the spot from the terrace across the canyon—and we were told . . . that "they often pop off little atomic bombs in the canyon for experimental purposes—it's like the Fourth of July—little ones that don't hurt." I said to Kaye: Let's get the hell out of here fast.

In a follow-up later of September 9, Manny made it clear to Boucher that the move to California had not gone smoothly.

> . . . [M]y books, which I had shipped via the post office from Connecticut, arrived in a state of utter ruin. 42 cartons, containing my entire library of some 1700 volumes, many of them very expensive, including my entire Queen library—literally pounded to a pulp. There is not a jacket left untorn, scarcely a book left unstained or unmarred in some way—my new Encyclopaedia Britannicas are bent, corners crushed, etc.—the limited-edition, very beautiful 15-volume set of the Bible which I got Kaye for Christmas three years ago—bound in leather with solid oak covers— utterly demolished—well, I won't exaggerate—but from a booklover's standpoint ruined—since 7 of the 14 books have gouges and big hunks of oak torn out of the covers, others have corners clipped, all are weather-stained, etc.— and those 14 books cost me $250!
>
> The shipment was insured to the limit of $200 per carton, but they cannot repay me for the Queen collection, as many of the damaged items are, as you well know, irreplaceable, such as the early first editions and foreign editions. I tell you, Tony, when I began to realize the extent of the damage I sat down in a corner and sobbed like a kid. This has taught me a very hard and bitter lesson about possessions.

Fred Dannay had no wish to accompany the series and return to supplying weekly plot skeletons. After Mary's death he had sold the Great Neck home and bought a house in Brooklyn, on Carroll Street, a few blocks from Ebbets Field. A sister of Mary's and her husband had moved in to care for Fred's sons. Fred lived and worked furiously in one upstairs room, coming down only for meals. This hiatus in his life lasted until mid-1947 when he married Hilda Wiesenthal (1917-1972), the daughter of a second cousin of Nazi hunter Simon Wiesenthal and the widow of Dr. Isadore Silverman, who had been killed during the Battle of the Bulge. In a letter of July 3 to Boucher, Manny Lee described his new cousin-in-law.

. . . She's a lovely, straightforward, candid person of very excellent education, exemplary character, refinement, and feminine dignity. She is, in fact, very much like Kaye in certain ways—Dan himself has remarked that. They even look something alike. She is a graduate of several universities, at the time she met Dan [she] was a speech teacher at Brooklyn University. Her level-headedness and poise, covering quite successfully a sensitive nature (in many ways much more sensitive than Dan's), give her a fine balance. She will make Dan a good wife and, as I told him, she will never stand for his taking her for granted. In fact, I told him she was much too good for him, to his annoyance; but it is true. I believe she will handle the two boys with good sense and understanding; she has made a wonderful start—she knows just what she is facing. She was married before, to a physician. When they were married about two years, I think, he went into the Army; and he was killed while with Patton's tank corps overseas. No children. Apparently she was much in love with him. Her name is Hilda (Dan calls her Bill) and you will be entirely taken with her, I know. Kaye and I are mad about her, and I think it's at least reasonably reciprocated.

After the wedding Fred and Hilda bought an unpretentious new colonial house in Larchmont, a quiet New York suburb about forty minutes by train from Manhattan. The house was on Byron Lane, in a tree-lined area of Larchmont where every street was named for one of the world's great poets, and there Fred at age 41 moved himself and his family and started life over.

***

Besides domestic matters like caring for his children and remarrying and relocating, what had Fred Dannay been doing with the time he had freed up by first drastically curtailing and then eliminating completely his radio commitments? Many of those hours he spent editing *EQMM*, which had become a monthly with the issue of January 1946, and the hardcover anthologies already noted. He also launched a series of original paperback collections of stories by individual authors.

Eight such collections of tales by Dashiell Hammett appeared between 1944 and 1952, the first few while Hammett was in the Aleutian Islands serving in the Army, and there were also volumes by Margery Allingham, John Dickson Carr, O. Henry, Stuart Palmer and Roy Vickers, almost all of them consisting of tales that had first appeared as originals or reprints in *EQMM*.

In the spring of 1946, soon after being discharged from the Army, Hammett settled on the East Coast and arranged with the Jefferson School of Social Science, an openly Marxist adult education institute located at 545 Sixth Avenue, to offer a course on mystery fiction aimed at writers and writer wannabees, each of whom paid a $10 fee for the privilege of submitting stories for Hammett to critique. Fred read the announcement of the course, which met on Thursday evenings between 6:45 and 8:15 p.m., and was impelled by curiosity to attend the first session, on May 2. Hammett invited him on the spot to co-teach the course and Fred agreed. The two titans of crime fiction followed up each weekly two-hour stint with "all-night bull-and-brandy sessions" which were probably held at the bar on nearby University Place that was one of Hammett's favorite watering places.

Among the students taking that course was Samm Sinclair Baker (1909-1997), who worked in advertising and submitted a typical hard-boiled tale in the Chandler manner. According to Baker years later, Hammett's critique wasn't terribly helpful: he simply said, "Brrr, that story is so tough it scares me." Fred Dannay offered more practical advice—"Take out every other wisecrack"—and in due course the tale sold to *Street & Smith's Detective Story Magazine*. Baker soon became a full-time writer, specializing in best-selling self-help books like *The Complete Scarsdale Medical Diet* (1978).

Also taking that course was Hazel Hills Berrien, who at the end of the May 16 session approached Fred and offered him a manuscript she had begun after the first class meeting two weeks earlier. Fred as always suggested certain changes—"in the character of the detective, in the plot construction, and in the title"—and eventually bought the story, which appeared as "The Unlocked Room" by Hazel Hills (*EQMM*, September 1946). Then as now, magazines appeared on newsstands some time before the publication month listed on their front covers, and the September *EQMM* had been available for a few weeks before August 31. That evening's episode of the popular ABC radio series *The Green Hornet* was called "Death in the Dark" and dealt with a civil servant accused of embezzlement who is found shot to death in a room with the door locked and the window bolted. Hazel Hills Berrien wrote ABC four days after the broadcast, admitting she hadn't heard the episode but claiming she'd been told by a friend that it "bore a peculiar resemblance to a recently published short story of mine." In this and several subsequent letters, each more threatening than the last, she demanded a copy of the script for the episode but refused to send ABC's lawyers a copy of her story. Eventually Fred heard of the dispute and, on October 11, wrote to Green Hornet creator George W. Trendle, promising a copy of September's *EQMM* and asking in return for a copy of the allegedly infringing script. Four days later, after reading "The Unlocked Room," Trendle replied to Fred, rejecting any allegation of plagiarism but saying: "Had Miss Hills handled the matter as diplomatically as you have, I think a copy of our script would have been in her hands long ago." The tempest in a teapot quickly blew away since the only similarity between story and script was that both involved a murder in a locked room with a gimmicked window. As far as I can determine, Hazel Hills never wrote another story. Certainly no more were published in *EQMM*.

***

The next Queen anthology with a pattern was assembled for Mystery Writers of America (MWA), an organization created in the last months of the war, with Fred Dannay among its founding members. The editors of any number of previous crime-fiction anthologies had made life easy for themselves by asking each of two dozen or so well-known authors to select from among his or her own output a tale of detection or espionage or whatever. In compiling *Murder By Experts* (Ziff-Davis, 1947) Fred made infinitely more work for himself by canvassing the membership of MWA (which was much smaller at the time than later) and soliciting each member's choice of five or six favorite short mysteries by others. That delicate aesthete Helen McCloy chose a tale by hard-boiled author Brett Halliday, who was her husband at the time, and atheistic Leslie Charteris selected one of Chesterton's Father Brown stories. Locked-room enthusiast Clayton Rawson opted for a sealed chamber exercise by John Dickson Carr, and Baynard Kendrick, creator of the foremost blind detective, for a story by Ernest Bramah about the genre's first sightless sleuth. The tasks of collating all the selections, eliminating the overfamiliar, and cajoling each of twenty MWA members to write an introduction to the story he or she had selected, fell upon Fred—judging from his exhausted comments on the project, like a ton of bricks. Tony Boucher's *Chronicle* review (June 19, 1947) called the book "a volume you cannot possibly afford to miss."

Later that year Little, Brown published the second volume of *The Queen's Awards* (1947). First prize this time went to H.F. Heard's "The President of the United States, Detective." Many readers including Boucher thought that story was really a science-fiction tale inappropriate for *EQMM* and would have preferred that the first prize go to the "Special Award" winner, "The House in Goblin Wood" by Carter Dickson (John Dickson Carr), the first and only short story about Dickson's bald fat sleuth Sir Henry Merrivale. Among the second and third prize winners were Roy Vickers, Hugh Pentecost, Michael Innes, Leslie Charteris, Helen McCloy, Edmund Crispin and Stuart Palmer. The volume closed with three stories by newcomers, including "The Widow's Walk" by Jack Finney, who would become one of the stars of the s-f and fantasy worlds, and "The Nine Mile Walk" by Harry Kemelman, future author of the best-selling "Rabbi" detective novel series. The only reason Tony Boucher didn't give this anthology a glowing review is that he had left the *Chronicle* a few months before its publication and hadn't yet been hired by *The New York Times*.

***

By the beginning of the Queen radio series' eighth and final season, the Ellery of the airwaves had morphed into a liberal very much like Boucher and Manny Lee. At the start of each episode Ellery would solemnly intone: "I dedicate this program to the fight against crime—not only crimes of violence and crimes of dishonesty, but also crimes of intolerance, discrimination and bad citizenship—crimes against America." A similar speech concluded each adventure. "This is Ellery Queen saying goodnight till next week, and enlisting all Americans every night, and every day, in the fight against bad citizenship, bigotry and discrimination—the crimes which are weakening America."

At a time when legally mandated segregation was still proudly being practiced in many states of the Union, and when the game of baseball that Fred and Manny loved was being torn apart over whether one black man should be allowed to play on a major league team, these were brave words indeed in a mass medium notorious for its timidity. But Manny's motivation for writing them was also rooted in survival instincts. The radio whodunit had come under attack from various self-anointed social critics who claimed the genre glorified crime, and several series had already been canceled. "I am trying to work out a new opening for Queen," Manny wrote Boucher on April 7, 1947, "and a new gimmick, which will attune E.Q. more closely to 'the forces of law and order.' (SHIT!) And of course I am going to try to make every possible Queen show on NBC this summer some sort of 'crusade,' or some damn thing, so that they won't have any possible kick coming about how we're an evil influence on the kiddies." Replying on April 26 to Boucher's question what the apolitical Dannay would think of the format change, Lee said: "I frankly haven't thought much about it."

With the episode broadcast June 1, 1947 the series returned to the NBC network where it had been a staple item from 1942 through 1944. Lawrence Dobkin, Bill Smith and Charlotte Keane contined respectively as Ellery, Inspector Queen and Nikki, but Ed Latimer as Sergeant Velie was replaced by George Matthews. Don Hancock kept his job as announcer but musical duties were taken over by organist Chet Kingsbury. The series was heard from 6:30 to 7:00 p.m. on Sunday, the evening on which it had first been aired back in 1939. It lasted this way for exactly two performances, one a rerun, then left the air again. Manny expressed his outrage in a letter to Boucher dated June 8.

> To have gone off CBS for six weeks, to go back on the air on another network, another day, another time *for two weeks* . . . and then go off again for seven weeks, returning at the beginning of AUGUST . . . is all too incredible to moon over for very long. This makes radio history, I'm told.

When the series resurfaced on August 3 it was in the same time slot as during its two-week June run but Ed Latimer had reclaimed the part of Sergeant Velie from George Matthews.

The Queen program's new social conscience wasn't confined to introductory and closing remarks but also permeated many of the scripts broadcast from the summer of 1947 until the series left the air for good. Manny based the scripts for six of the first eight episodes on synopses by

Tom Everitt and two on outlines by Boucher, but with either collaborator the liberal tone came forth loud and clear. In a letter to Boucher dated May 2, 1947, Manny reveals that his wife Kaye came up with the title for his latest script based on a Boucher synopsis and goes on: "I think I can say that it is the most important script I have done in eight years of this kind of labor." "Murder for Americans" (July 17, 1947) takes place in an upstate New York community that is being flooded by hate pamphlets attacking Jews, Catholics and blacks. While visiting the city Ellery is asked by a 10-year-old Jewish girl to find her vanished friend, the daughter of an Irish cop. The hate literature turns out to be the work of a white businessman looking to buy up a certain neighborhood cheap by turning its people against each other but the script is careful to give the villain a black accomplice so that Ellery can point out: "Virtue and vice co-exist in all races. No race has a monopoly on either."

Working with outlines by others had no effect on Manny's social conscience. In "Number 31" (September 7, 1947; available on audio), written from a synopsis by Tom Everitt, Ellery tries to crack the secret of international mystery man George Arcaris's success at smuggling diamonds into the Port of New York and to comfort a wonderfully dignified black woman by solving the murder of her son, the servant for a wealthy man-about-town. The cases seem unconnected until Ellery discovers the number 31 popping up in both.

After Boucher and Lee's "The Man Who Squared the Circle" (September 21, 1947) the series once again went on hiatus, returning late in November as a "sustainer," the way it had been during its first months of life back in 1939-40. Most likely the liberal slant of the scripts had given the people at Anacin a headache. As if the loss of sponsor weren't enough to contend with, every regular performer in the series except for Larry Dobkin was fired and replaced during the hiatus. Herb Butterfield took over as Inspector Queen, Alan Reed as Sergeant Velie, Virginia Gregg as Nikki, Paul Masterson as the announcer and Rex Koury at the organ. After a few months the role of Nikki was taken over by Kaye Brinker, who outside the studio was Mrs. Manfred B. Lee. As Manny explained in a letter to Boucher dated January 9, 1948:

> The girl I had [Virginia Gregg] got herself messed up
> with the movies and, finding it impossible to keep her at
> rehearsal, [I] had to fire her. This left the part open. It

suddenly occurred to me that I had a better actress in my bed than any other guy in Hollywood and I offered the part to Kaye. She accepted, not without personal misgivings, since she's the epitome of the inferiority complex, but I know—she has already demonstrated in one show—that she will bring the character a warmth and womanliness—not to mention an ability to act—which it has always needed and never received. Things are so rugged with us financially that Kaye had, even before this came up, decided to go back to work, at least for a few months or until things straighten out a bit for us. . . . It's both a sad and a proud day for me, Tony. . . . sad because I have to accept my wife's financial help when I had always prided myself on my ability to earn a living; proud because I have a wife who, at great personal sacrifice, and against everything she really wants in life, is willing to jump in and help.

A letter of February 4 to Boucher made it clear that Manny had made a wise move.

> . . . Kaye is working out so superbly, she has brought so much warmth, believability, and humanity to the role of Nikki that I think you should bear it in mind in planning future stories. . . . Nikki is no longer the wide-eyed ingénue as Kaye plays her. She's a likable, regular-gal woman; and she can handle any situation you provide for her. Kaye and Larry [Dobkin] work together like a charm, as you may have noticed recently. Their scenes together are a delight and need virtually no direction. They have that beautiful thing, harmony of timing, that makes every interchange a delight.

Manny continued to alter Boucher's plots as and when he pleased. "The Saga of Ruffy Rux" (November 27, 1947) pits Ellery against a gangster who talks like Elmer Fudd and has a habit of constantly jingling the two silver dollars he carries in his pocket for luck. The gangster in Boucher's synopsis had a different speech defect (as witness his title

"Louie the Lisp") and the plot is infinitely wilder, with both Inspector Queen and Sergeant Velie getting seriously wounded and Ellery being kidnapped and replaced by a double.

***

Discharged from the Navy with a Bronze Star after the war, George Zachary had resumed his career as a producer-director in radio. His marriage to Marian Shockley had broken up soon after his return to civilian life. During the 1947-48 season as producer of NBC's Sunday afternoon series *The Ford Theater*, he decided to reassemble the regular cast of the Queen series for most of its first fifteen months—Hugh Marlowe as Ellery, Santos Ortega as Inspector Queen, Ted De Corsia (who hadn't been in the original cast) as Sergeant Velie—and to restage one of the earliest EQ dramas. The survival of "The Bad Boy" (January 4, 1948) on audio allows us to hear a 60-minute Queen radio play more or less as listeners in 1939 heard it, although without the theorizing of the guest armchair detectives and with substantial revision of the original script. In a December 1947 letter to Boucher, Manny said that upon hearing of Zachary's rebroadcast plan "I asked George to send me the script. It confirmed some of my worst fears, and I spent about 36 hours more or less consecutively rewriting it. Gad, some of the dialogue!" Zachary didn't mind Manny revising the script but ignored his objections to Hugh Marlowe playing Ellery. "I wrote George to please, please try to take the stuffing out of Marlowe's shirt and make him sound—I know it can be done only approximately—like a human being." On January 6, two days after the program was broadcast, Boucher wrote Manny.

> I had a fine time with the Ford EQ—very agreeable return to the past, and wonderful to hear De Corsia and Ortega again. . . . [My son] Larry (aged 7), who usually evinces no interest in the radio, settled down seriously and thought it was wonderful, ending up with embarrassing queries as to whether I could write a show that good. We are wondering a little as to whether or not he was disappointed when the boy turned out not to have poisoned his family.

***

Returning to the 30-minute Queen series on ABC, one of the most unusual scripts from the eighth season was Boucher and Lee's "The Private Eye" (January 22, 1948), a rather feeble parody-diatribe aimed at the hardboiled detective programs that by 1948 were saturating the airwaves. Ellery's nemesis in this episode is a fascistic meathead named Cam Clubb, who bullies Nikki into leaving Ellery and going to work for him.

> Clubb (easily): "Sure I'm tough, Nikki. It's a tough world. Take these chivalry boys, like your former boss."
> Nikki (demurely): "My *present* boss. . . ."
> Clubb: "He lives back in the time of King Arthur. Gentleman Detective! The Deductive Method! That's for old maids—of *both* sexes."
> Nikki: "And what's *your* method, Mr. Clubb? . . ."
> Clubb: "My method? Get the jump. Blast first. Unfair play. If I have to kick a man's teeth in, I kick a man's teeth in. If I have to break a pig's nose, I break a pig's nose."
> Nikki: "Pig?"
> Clubb: "Dame."

Remembering that Mickey Spillane's sadistic private eye had debuted only a few months earlier in *I, the Jury* (1947), one might conclude that Cam Clubb was intended as a lampoon of Mike Hammer—until one reads more of the script and learns that Boucher and Lee are attacking not just the sociopath excesses of Spillane but the legitimate hardboiled tradition typified by Dashiell Hammett's Sam Spade, whose radio exploits were on opposite Ellery's at this time.

> Nikki: "You know Cam Clubb's name as well as you know your own. After all, he's a competitor of yours."
> Ellery: "Clubb—a competitor? Don't be funny! Why, the fellow's no more than a paid thug. . . ."
> Nikki: "Ellery—"
> Ellery: "Oh, don't feel bound by any loyalty to *me*, Nikki. If you want to live in a Dashiell Hammett novel. . . ."
> Nikki: "I've been seeing Cam because—well, he *is* a fascinating sort of monster."

Ellery: "So was Hermann Goering!"

Nikki: "Enormous vitality—the kind of strength a woman can't help noticing—"

Ellery: "You can find the same thing at the gorilla's cage in the zoo."

Nikki: "When I'm with him I—almost begin to feel he's right. We do live in a world where only toughness works."

Ellery: "Then let's all go back to the jungle, shall we? Please, Nikki. I'll listen to your half-baked, second-hand Nietzscheisms some other time."

Eventually the outrage morphs into a detective plot in which Ellery and Clubb apply their diverse methods of sleuthing to the murder of a statesman in exile from a mythical Balkan country. Both of them identify the right person as the killer but Boucher and Lee leave no doubt about who did it the right way. "He was guessing, Nikki," Ellery says. "I wasn't." Then he says to his rival: "The trouble with your method, Clubb, aside from the fact that it's inhuman and degrading, is that it doesn't prove anything. Also—it's . . . going to cost you your private detective's license."

After this episode a final wave of changes washed over the series. Its time slot was moved to Thursday evenings, 8:30 to 9:00 p.m., and Howard Culver replaced Larry Dobkin as Ellery for the final 18 episodes, eight new scripts written by Lee from Boucher synopses and ten reruns.

"The Three Frogs" (April 29, 1948; available on audio) is another tale of social concern, the subject this time being juvenile delinquency. Nikki finds an implausible young tough hiding in her apartment and bravely sets out to reform him—a project that meshes with Ellery's hunt for a Faginesque hidden mastermind known as the Frog who has organized a youth gang for criminal purposes. The crucial deductions require expert knowledge of bubble-gum chewing procedure but take a back seat to a sermon against racial bigotry. Ellery and Sergeant Velie are trying to figure out which of their suspects is the Frog.

Velie: "Hey, wait a minute. Frog! The Frenchman! That's a slang word for Frenchman!"

Ellery: "Yes, and as nasty a word, Sergeant, as kike,

nigger, wop, Polack or any of the other insulting terms some people use to assert their purely imaginary superiority over their fellow citizens."

Velie: "Aww, I didn't mean it that way, Maestro."

But even at trail's end not every Queen episode was a vehicle for social messages, and indeed the next week's adventure, "One Diamond" (May 6, 1948; available on audio), is a "pure" Boucher-Lee detective story in which Ellery solves the murder-by-hanging of germophobe millionaire Mark Gallows and the puzzle of the killer who wasn't able to steal the fabulous Gallows Diamond because he couldn't read a simple map correctly. It's a clever tale, although not too hard for the listener to solve ahead of Ellery.

The last new episode of the series was Boucher and Lee's "Misery Mike" (May 20, 1948). The title character, who in the synopsis is called Miserere Mike, reflects both Boucher's function in the Queen series and his love of opera: Mike's nickname comes from his penchant for playing the Miserere from *Il Trovatore* on the accordion and he earns his living dreaming up new ideas for rackets as Boucher earned his conjuring up plot outlines. Listeners the following week were treated to yet another rerun, at the end of which *The Adventures of Ellery Queen* left network radio for good.

Manny explained the axing of the series in a letter to Boucher dated May 5, 1948. "I have very few details. I was told (this happened very suddenly) that the reason is 'the time situation'—in other words, they have sold our time out from under us for a commercial [series], apparently, and have nowhere else to put us, commensurate with the cost of putting the show on. This is the second time this has happened; that we've built up a time spot for ABC and they've sold it—for some other show. Exactly what I was afraid of when the deal was first set up, exactly what happened. . . . I am as thoroughly disgusted with the chicanery of mortal man as ever in my life and I could wish for a sign from heaven or anywhere else that man is not the lowest form of animation in the whole of creation."

Eventually ABC gave a fuller explanation for its dropping of the series to an executive of the advertising agency that was handling the program. He in turn informed Fred, who on June 24 wrote Manny. ABC, he said, "had to drop some shows" and "conducted a sort of survey . . .

on mystery shows to determine which should be kept on the air. . . ." The survey convinced the network that all the mystery shows that "the listeners kept coming back to" had "two essential characteristics. . . ." The first of these was that "there must be a central character. . . ." On that basis ABC dropped its anthology series *The Clock*. The second essential feature was that the protagonist "must be alive, must have the human-being qualities that make listeners feel they are participating in the adventures of a real person, one they know and like. . . ." Compared to the main characters in series like *The Fat Man, Mr. and Mrs. North* and *Mr. District Attorney*, Ellery was considered "weak, colorless, deliberately understated. . . ." Unsurprisingly, Fred blamed Manny, or more precisely the changes Manny instituted after Fred had dropped out of the series. The episodes based on Dannay synopses, he claimed, had a "sincerity, integrity, purity . . . that the last couple of years of Queen shows did not have. . . ." The later and more "socially conscious" episodes "had—to my mind—a certain phoniness and a certain hybrid quality. . . . I always found it phony to hear the Queen show start with a high-sounding opening about good citizenship, the fight against bigotry, . . . and then seldom hear this theme actually borne out by the plots." Manny despised the artificial concoctions of the Dannay period and had no qualms about telling Fred so. "The plots you worked out for the earlier Queen shows were largely mathematical puzzles. . . ," he wrote on June 30. "The emphasis was placed on problem and cerebration." Manny's later scripts, he claimed, were "a synthesis of persons, relations, and events rather than a puzzle-in-logic." Now he knew what Fred thought about the overt liberal flavor of those scripts. An odd couple indeed!

***

Here, where we take leave of Ellery's various radio incarnations, is the appropriate place to summarize the later lives of the people most closely associated with the series.

As radio declined and television began to grow, George Zachary changed media, working on the production of early TV series like NBC's comedy *The Life of Riley*. Eventually he and his second wife relocated to Sarasota, Florida where in May 1964, at age 52, he died of a heart attack.

Hugh Marlowe continued acting both on the stage (for example, opposite Gertrude Lawrence in *Lady in the Dark*) and in movies (including key roles in *Twelve O'clock High*, 1949, with Gregory Peck and in *All About Eve,*1950, with Bette Davis). In 1955-56 he played Ellery in the 32-episode syndicated telefilm series *The New Adventures of Ellery Queen* and also gave a fine performance on the other side of the law as a suave, corrupt district attorney's investigator in *Illegal* (1955), starring Edward G. Robinson. His best-known role in later life was as the patriarch of the principal family in NBC-TV's daytime serial *Another World*. On May 2, 1982, at age 71, he died of a heart attack in his Manhattan home.

In 1946 Marian Shockley married radio actor Clayton "Bud" Collyer, best known as the star of the long-running *Superman* series but also active in a variety of soap operas and game shows. She appeared with Collyer in series like *Road of Life* and *The Guiding Light* and moved into TV with him in the early Fifties. In the late 1960s they were living in Greenwich, Connecticut but after Collyer's death in 1969 Shockley moved to Westlake Village, California where she served on the board of a local adoption agency. She died on December 14, 1981.

Both during and after his years as Inspector Queen, Santos Ortega starred in other radio detective series of the 1940s including *Perry Mason, Nero Wolfe* and *Charlie Chan*. In 1956 he signed to play Grandpa Hughes in the new CBS-TV daytime serial *As the World Turns* and was still in the part twenty years later when, at age 76, he took a brief trip to Florida and suddenly died there.

Ted De Corsia, who was Sergeant Velie on the Queen series for most of its duration, was promoted to the top of the police ladder when he took over the role of Commissioner Weston in *The Shadow*. In the late Forties he made the transition to movie acting with his performances as heavies in two memorable *films noir* of 1948: Orson Welles' *The Lady from Shanghai* and Jules Dassin's *The Naked City*. During the 1949-50 season he starred as a Scotland Yard inspector in the CBS radio series *Pursuit*. During the Fifties and Sixties he enjoyed a prolific career in both movies and TV. He died in 1973.

Sydney Smith's post-EQ years were filled with acting assignments on the stage, in radio and for early television. Later he moved to the West Coast and was featured in several movies such as *No Time for Sergeants* (1958) with Andy Griffith and *Some Came Running* (1958) with Frank Sinatra. He wasn't proud of his film period, which he described in a letter to me as the time when he "toiled among the whores." Returning to school, he earned a Master's degree when he was over 50 and began a new career as Associate Professor of Theatre at Northern Illinois University. He retired in 1976 and moved to Washington, where he acted off and on with the Seattle Rep until his death in March 1978.

Richard Coogan, who replaced Smith as Ellery Queen but lasted only a few months in the part, was one of the first radio actors to leave that medium and make his mark on television. Children whose parents bought their first set soon after World War II may remember him as star of the live sci-fi series *Captain Video* during its first season (1949-50). Later he starred as Marshal Matt Wayne on *The Californians* (1957-59). As of this writing he is 98 years old.

After radio's golden age, Larry Dobkin continued to act on TV, usually playing ethnics, but devoted most of his time to directing. Among the dozens of series to which he contributed episodes are *The Rifleman, 77 Sunset Strip, The Donna Reed Show, Barnaby Jones* and *The Waltons*. He died on October 28, 2002, at age 83. His ashes were scattered at sea.

As radio slowly died, Anthony Boucher spent progressively less time writing mystery stories and scripts and more time reviewing the mystery fiction of others, a sideline he'd started in 1941 for the San Francisco *Chronicle*. Ten years later he landed the most prestigious crime reviewing position in the United States, the proprietorship of *The New York Times Book Review*'s "Criminals at Large" column. His *Times* work is generally considered the finest body of mystery criticism there is. He continued as *Times* reviewer, while simultaneously turning out a mountain of other editorial and critical work, until April 1968 when at the unbearably early age of 56 he died of lung cancer.

One by one the lights go out, the lives go out, the memories fade to black. Ellery Queen's first radio adventure was broadcast four years before I was born, and I was five when the series was cancelled. I never heard a single episode "live" yet, thanks to the miracle of audio and the easier-to-take-for-granted miracle of print, I can almost believe that I listened to it every week. *The Adventures of Ellery Queen* was part of the golden age of a very special medium which deeply affected the lives of those who were instructed and entertained by it and also decisively shaped many of the subsequent Queen novels and stories.

To which we now return.

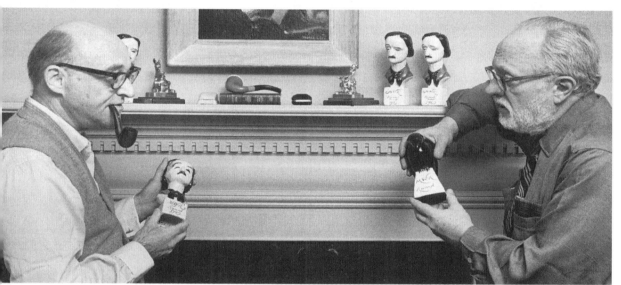

Old masters Frederic Dannay and Manfred B. Lee in 1967 with Mystery Writers of America awards.

Daniel Nathan (left) at age 3 in 1909 and Manford Lepofsky, probably age 5 in 1910, cousins who later became Frederic Dannay and Manfred B. Lee. Lepofsky was nine months the older. Both were from Brooklyn's Brownsville district, but Dannay recalled a joyous "Tom Sawyer childhood" after the family moved to upstate Elmira, N.Y. Below, Manford and Daniel duriing a Lepofsky family visit to Elmira in 1912.

Danny Nathan, future mystery writer, and
the house in Elmira, N.Y. (all 1915).

Layering the mystery, Lee and Dannay hid the identity of Ellery Queen early in the author's career. Manny Lee donned a mask on the cover of *The American Gun Mystery* (1933). They also adopted another pseudonym, Barnaby Ross, for four novels featuring retired actor Drury Lane published in 1932-33.

Dannay and Lee were well established mystery writers when they visited the Poe House in Philadelphia in 1941. By the end of that decade their novels had grown from almost pure puzzles of logic to complex portraits of American life and social ills.

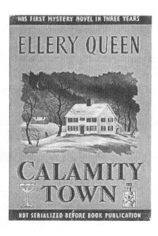

Ellery Queen takes to the air. Dannay and Lee consider a script for *The Adventures of Ellery Queen* radio series, which ran from 1939 to 1948. For several seasons Dannay provided plots and Lee turned out scripts at a starting rate of $25 an episode. By 1945 the pressures of Dannay's family life forced the cousins to hire a series of other writers to create plots.

Sometime critic, sometime collaborator Anthony Boucher reviewed many Ellery Queen titles favorably for *The New York Times,* including paperbacks that Dannay and Lee had little hand in writing. Wearing another hat Boucher earlier had provided plots that Lee turned into scripts for episodes of the Ellery Queen radio adventures. Boucher also contributed short stories and critical writing to *Ellery Queen's Mystery Magazine* under Dannay's editorship

Hugh Marlowe and Marian Shockley were the first Ellery and Nikki when *The Adventures of Ellery Queen* hit the airwaves. A number of actors filled the roles during the series' several incarnations. Later Marlowe returned as Ellery on TV.

Manfred B. Lee (above) in 1947 or '48 with his second wife, Kaye Brinker, whom he married in 1942. Above right, the couple in 1965 with a granddaughter. Manny Lee in his study in Roxbury, Connecticut, around 1960 (right). And (bottom) Fred Dannay and Manny Lee in Dannay's study.

On the big screen Donald Cook (above left) was the first actor to portray Ellery Queen in *The Spanish Cape Mystery* (1935). In 1936, *The Mandarin Mystery* starred Eddie Quillan (above right). Ralph Bellamy and Margaret Lindsay were Ellery and Nikki in four films in 1940-41: *Ellery Queen, Master Detective; Ellery Queen's Penthouse Mystery, Ellery Queen and the Perfect Crime,* and *Ellery Queen and the Murder Ring.* When William Gargan took over the lead, Lindsay stayed aboard for three installments in 1942: *A Close Call for Ellery Queen* (bottom), *A Desperate Chance for Ellery Queen,* and *Enemy Agents Meet Ellery Queen.* All seven films also featured Charley Grapewin as Inspector Queen and James Burke as Sergeant Velie. Dannay described the pictures as "each one more dreadful than the others."

Ellery on TV. Among the many actors who played Ellery on television were suave Lee Bowman (top left), who took the role in the first series in the early 1950s after Richard Hart's death, and George Nader (top right) in the late '50s. Peter Lawford (center) was a hip British swinger in a 1971 TV movie. Jim Hutton (right), in the mid-'70s, reminded Dannay of a young version of himself.

Silent partners. When Dannay and Lee agreed to have ghost writers turn out paperbacks under the "Ellery Queen" byline, literary agent Scott Meredith found writers who would work for a flat fee. Talmage Powell (top right) was a veteran of the mystery field, as was Edward D. Hoch (bottom right). But other "ghosts" included three notables from the science fiction world: (left, top to bottom) Jack Vance, who had written mysteries as John Holbrook Vance, Avram Davidson, and Theodore Sturgeon.

Clockwise from top left: an undated photo of Fred Dannay; the second Mrs. Dannay, Hilda Wiesenthal ("lovely, straightforward, candid," said Lee); the Dannays and the Lees at an awards ceremony in 1968; Dannay and Lee at a Mystery Writers of America event in 1970, with a new crime fan.

Photos courtesy of The Frederic Dannay Literary Property Trust.

Fred Dannay in 1973, the year after Hilda's death.

Dannay receives an honorary Ph.D. from Carroll College in 1979.

CHAPTER FIFTEEN

When God Died and the Cat Came

T HE FIRST QUEEN VOLUME published after the cancellation of the radio series was *20ᵗʰ Century Detective Stories* (World, 1948), an anthology edited by Fred Dannay for the "Living Library" series. Included were a number of generally obscure tales by Chesterton, Hammett, Christie, Carr, Boucher and others, plus the first version of "Queen's Quorum," a 60-page bibliographic/critical guide to short detective fiction. That Boucher at this point was no longer writing for the San Francisco *Chronicle* and had not yet come aboard at *The New York Times Book Review* probably explains why he said nothing about it in print.

With *The Brown Fox Mystery* (1948), written by Samuel Duff McCoy under Manny's supervision and published in September, Little, Brown took over the "Ellery Queen, Jr." series, which would be continued under its aegis until the cousins moved all their operations to another house six years later.

Not long after that juvenile came the third volume of *The Queen's Awards* (1948). Top prize this year went to "Justice Has No Number" by Alfredo Segre, an Italian author who apparently dropped out of the genre soon after this coup. Also included were fine stories by Clayton Rawson, Philip MacDonald and Helen McCloy, but perhaps the most interesting tales in the book were by newcomers. "The Specialty of the

House" launched the stellar career of Stanley Ellin, one of the supreme masters of the short crime story, and "The Garden of Forking Paths," translated and brought to Fred Dannay's attention by the multilingual Anthony Boucher, introduced American readers to one of the greatest South American authors of the 20th century, Argentinean Jorge Luis Borges.

But by far the most interesting and controversial Queen book of the year—and one might almost say of any year—was the cousins' next novel.

***

"In the beginning it was without form, a darkness that kept shifting like dancers." With that echo from Genesis I:2 we return a third time to Wrightsville in *Ten Days' Wonder* (1948). Howard Van Horn, sculptor son of a multimillionaire, comes in desperation to Ellery after a series of amnesic blackouts that began on the night of his father Diedrich's marriage to the beautiful Sally whom Diedrich had raised from childhood. Psychiatrists have failed to free Howard from his obsessive fear that he has done or will do something horrible during a blackout. Ellery agrees to stay at the Van Horn mansion in Wrightsville and watch over this tormented young man but before long he finds himself drawn into the hopeless trap in which Howard and Sally are caught. He reluctantly agrees to act as their go-between with an anonymous blackmailer and comes close to being jailed for grand theft. A missing necklace, a midnight chase through a storm-tossed graveyard and a night-prowling religious fanatic combine with less theatrical elements to sustain the sense of menace among a cast of (excluding Ellery himself) only four central characters. In the final quarter of the novel there is a murder, followed by Ellery's virtuoso reconstruction of the crime, capped by an even more thunderous solution, revealed by Ellery to no one but the murderer, who will remind some of Drury Lane, others of Iago, and a great many of the biblical God. Beneath the mind-boggling plot *Ten Days' Wonder* is an audacious attempt to recreate the cosmic drama of Western culture since the Enlightenment: the penetration through a facade of infinite knowledge and love to the sadistic beast beneath, the demand of reason and decency for God's death.

The reader is warned: *Ten Days' Wonder* is one of the very few Queen novels whose solution simply must be revealed by anyone who wants to discuss the book seriously. Its entire structure turns out to revolve around the breaking of the Ten Commandments. Diedrich Van

Horn, having learned that his young wife has been committing adultery with his adopted son, manipulates events so that Howard will be made either to break or to seem to break the other nine commandments, culminating in the violation of "Thou shalt not kill." Diedrich's plan is to murder Sally in such a way that (1) Howard will believe he killed her during one of his blackouts and (2) Ellery will uncover the Ten Commandments element but will conclude that the violator in each case has been Howard. Throughout the novel Diedrich is clothed in the attributes of deity—great power, apparently limitless goodness, awesome knowledge—but the climax exposes him as a monstrously evil being with an infallible ability to manipulate others. At the end of the final thunderous dialogue between Ellery and Diedrich, the humane man of reason demands the death of God.

As far back as 1932 the cousins had created their first Iago figure who wound up killing others and finally himself: Drury Lane. And there had been intimations of a war between more-than-human powers within the detective-story framework in that magnificent short novel "The Lamp of God" (1935). *Ten Days' Wonder* is more ambitious, integrating symbolic allegory with psychology, showing how the influence of Diedrich's sadistic hell-preaching father and the boy's childhood immersion in the vengeful god his father worshiped turned Diedrich into the same kind of god, simultaneously embodying and mocking the proverb "Like father like son" and the teaching that man was made in God's image. But with all the psychological detail and despite all the cousins' skill at explaining, it's almost impossible for readers to accept Diedrich as simply Iago to the nth power. But the whole structure of the book and all its religious imagery presuppose that we won't accept it and force us willy-nilly into theology or, more precisely, theomachy.

Fred Dannay told me that it took him several years to perfect *Ten Days' Wonder*'s structure, but his letter to Manny Lee of October 18, 1947, to which his 59-page synopsis was attached, tells a slightly different story. "It represents, after the abandonment of my first attempt [which must have been what he had in mind when he told me of the years he'd been working on it], two months of solid, grueling work, with the fluorescent lights in my study on many a night. I hit a peak one night by working until three a.m. . . . [T]his is the first sustained full-length job I've done in a long time, and I did it under harrowing circumstances—ill health, rustiness, self-doubts." From then until the end of the month the cousins wrangled over the synopsis in telephone conversations and long letters. Manny objected that Howard Van Horn oscillated between being "a pretty decent sort" and being "a rat with a ridiculous sense . . . of injury" with the result that readers, who needed to empathize with Howard's plight, would "drop him like a hot potato. . . ." He also claimed that most of the incidents leading up to the climax were commonplace. Fred defended his decisions zealously as usual. "The Ten Commandments theme, in my opinion, is sensational material, spectacular to the point of verging on fantasy. If anything, it is too sensational." If that theme "were surrounded by equally spectacular material," the result "would become fantastic, even bizarre." That, he says, is why he surrounded the leitmotif "with seemingly commonplace events. . . ." As for Howard, "for all [his] decency . . . there is a chink in his armor. He has these blackouts, which have produced a phobia in him and a guilt complex." He is "a decent guy who is forced, or thinks he is forced, to do indecent things. . . ." The wrangling went on even after Manny agreed to "do the novel substantially along the lines of the present outline. . . ." By mid-April 1948 he had sent his final draft to Larchmont and was defending himself against Fred's furious objections to certain themes he had interpolated. From Manny's perspective the Howard of Fred's outline was not admirable or sympathetic but a "weakling." Therefore, Manny explained, he had added a whole psychological dimension of his own, portraying Howard as "dominated from childhood by his father," turning the young man into "a confused, manipulated poor human who might have been strong and admirable if he hadn't been raised by a man who didn't insist on dominating those he loved." Why didn't he explain to Fred what he wanted to do before he did it? "We would have got into an argument, probably bitter, . . . and then we would have been—as always—hung up." Yes, he had handed Fred a *fait accompli*, but that's precisely what Fred has handed Manny with every new novel synopsis. "You give me, really, not an outline but a blueprint."

Anthony Boucher hated the novel, writing Manny on October 7, 1948, after its publication, and calling it "the first unquestionable failure in the Queen collaboration. . . . I've never read such a tissue of nonsense as that Decalogic business either in its first interpretation or in its second." Later in the same letter he described the novel's "abstract inhuman gimmickry" as "more outrageous than anything else I can recall." In his undated reply letter Manny told Boucher of the "months of bitter correspondence" with Fred that ensued after he'd read the synopsis. "What was left to me . . . was to try to smother the enormous ridiculousness of it all under the cloak of sheer rhetoric. . . . [E]very last morsel of psychological interpretation in the finish is my own; there was none in the original. The whole thread of the father-image and its ramifications I set into the fabric. Arousing, I might add, the most vehement response of all from Dan [i.e. Fred]. . . ."

What made the situation especially troubling to Boucher was that Fred had just hired him to conduct a review column in *EQMM*. On his next trip east, late in October, he visited Dannay in Larchmont and, in the presence of fellow mystery writer John Dickson Carr, who lived in nearby Mamaroneck, spoke of the dilemma in which he found himself. On November 1, in a letter to Manny, Fred described the meeting. "He . . . disliked the book enormously (I think it offended his deep sense of religiousness and theological purity, though he won't admit it). . . . [He] asked me what I should do. . . . Did Boucher expect me to say: Give [it] a good review or else[?] Did he even expect me to say: Forget the book rather than pan it[?] . . . I told Boucher that the review column was his, without strings . . . to write what he damned pleased. . . . [I]t was actually a supreme insult on Boucher's part even to ask me what he should do. . . ."

In his first bi-monthly column for *EQMM* (February 1949) he was much kinder to *Ten Days' Wonder* than he'd been in private, complaining only that it was "based on motivations so implausible that the at best tenuous relationship between the whodunit and life seemed, to me at least, totally severed. . . . [But] Queen has rarely written more solidly nor plotted more intricately (though the two don't always jibe); and . . . I'm ashamed of myself for quibbling." After the August 1949 issue Boucher's column was canceled, apparently because publisher Lawrence Spivak thought the magazine was printing too much nonfiction.

***

Soon after Fred and his second wife had settled into the suburban life in Larchmont, tragedy invaded their existence when, in 1948, Hilda Dannay gave birth to their first and only child. As Fred remembered during the Carroll College interview 31 years later:

[Stephen] was born prematurely at seven months and

weighing less than two pounds. He was the miracle baby of Doctors Hospital in New York City. We didn't realize for about a year that he—that the boy had had brain damage at birth. And the brain damage was so severe that the child, who had an absolutely angelic face, never walked and never talked. . . . I was aware long before my wife that one of these days the tragedy would be capped by the death of that child. Actually he lived till he was six years old."

The short unhappy life of Stephen Dannay is documented in the correspondence collected in *Blood Relations*. Manny on April 16, 1947: "We are just delighted with your news about the baby. . . . It's fantastically soon for him to be coming home from hospital, considering his start. He sounds like a strong, determined youngster, and Kaye and I have been rooting for him like anything since you phoned that night." Fred on June 24: "Steve will be circumcised July 3rd—the earliest date we could get an operating room in a New York hospital! No one but the doctors (2) and the rabbi will be permitted in the room, and we will take Steve home the same day. He went on regular cow's milk today!" Manny on June 30: "Bravo to Steve. He's really made it. Hope everything goes all right at the circumcision. No reason why it shouldn't." Fred on July 3: "Bill and I were up at six this morning to bring Steve to the hospital. . . . [We waited] a solid hour in the hospital waiting-room for word from the doctors that everything is all right, and [I hear] the little guy cry[ing] in pain at home now. . . ." Manny on the 7th: "For heaven's sake don't you and Hilda generate the psychology . . . that he's 'different' from other babies—except in the most normal sense." Fred on the 8th: "Steve is having a hard time of it. The circumcision has disrupted his habits— eating, sleeping, everything. He still suffers pain, and while the healing is noticeable, it is a slow process. We think the kid lost weight this week. . . . He sure takes after me—always-the-hard way." The doctor came to see the baby that night. Fred on July 9: "It will be a week tomorrow since the circumcision, yet Steve is not yet back to normal. . . . He cries considerably more than usual, so it is possible he still has bouts of pain. . . . He's a most interesting little guy, partly because in some ways he is his full age and in other ways he's only a month or so old. . . . He's very high strung—a bundle of nerves, the doctor says. (Hell, he's my son, isn't he?—stubborn and hair-trigger). The least change seems to affect him, and he undoubtedly has my nervous stomach." Fred again, on August 3: "Steve is teething, and of course he picked the hottest spell—the kid just does everything the hard way. Hereditary, no doubt." Flash forward to February 20, 1950, when Fred tells Manny that on Christmas 1949 "the doctors told us that they did not expect Steve to live more than a month or so. That was our Christmas present. It is now well over a month, and Steve has actually improved. . . . He has been getting insulin injections for about a month. . . . Bill [Hilda Dannay] gives the injections" although "there is hardly any flesh on Steve into which the needle can be plunged. . . . [H]e is more alert, more active, less nervous, sleeps better, and generally looks better. . . . The doctors refuse to commit themselves. The truth is, they do not know what is precisely the matter with Steve, except that they are all agreed that it is something in the brain."

On February 24 Manny offers Fred "my fervent hope that Stevie is on his way to a healthier state." The last reference to Steve comes in Fred's letter of March 9: "[H]e has gained weight (all that he lost since the hospital and more); he is standing up again; his personality is improved—he is much more his old happier self. Bill and I are elated, even though we force ourselves to go easy with our hopes. . . . The doctors are flabbergasted, and don't know what to think. It might be the insulin, which we are continuing to give him twice a day. Whatever it is, we hope for the best."

Those hopes were dashed. Steve died in 1954. It is to him that we owe the pervasive birth-death themes in several Queen novels, beginning with *Cat of Many Tails* (1949), perhaps the finest in all the canon, which grew out of an anecdote told to Fred by one of the infant's doctors over dinner in a hospital cafeteria.

The opening introduces us to a new Ellery, a man somewhat akin to *Calamity Town*'s Aunt Tabitha, who ran out on the Wright family in its time of need, and to escapist Horatio Potts in *There Was an Old Woman*, in the sense that he's renounced his habit of intervening in others' lives. "Just let me be. . . . I've given all that up. I'm not interested any longer." Racked with guilt over his responsibility for others' deaths and perhaps over his deicide victory in the Van Horn tragedy, he has detached himself, performed an inner emigration. It's a scorching Manhattan summer a few years after the end of World War II, and the reminders of Hiroshima, the Nazi death camps, the Cold War, the division of Vienna, the first Arab-Israeli conflict, the anti-Communist witch hunts and the threat of nuclear annihilation generate an atmosphere thick with impending holocaust. At one point Ellery wakes up in the midst of a crisis and asks: "What is it? War?" But the world and national news headlines are dwarfed by local headlines that convey the same message of mortality. A serial killer is loose in the city. Six people strangled in less than three months, each victim totally different from fellow victims in ethnic roots, economic worth, social position, neighborhood of residence and every other way. The faceless bachelor from the Gramercy Park district, the aging prostitute living above Times Square, the struggling shoe salesman from Chelsea, the madcap heiress who loved the subways, the bitter paralytic of East 102nd Street, the black girl from Harlem and the later victims of the Cat share only the cord of Indian tussah silk knotted about each one's neck. The bait of involvement is dangled before Ellery again with all its pain and risk and once again he snaps at it, immersing himself in the Cat hunt until like his father and the police commissioner and the mayor and everyone else he's ready to drop in his tracks from the exhaustion and frustration of strategy conferences, press releases, radio addresses, coordination among agencies, liaison with psychiatrists, confrontations with neighborhood self-defense committees, endless reviewing of files and plodding up blind alleys until, suddenly and beyond human expectation, the obvious yet subtle link connecting all the victims and making sense of the carnage leaps into sight. Once again the apparent solution is topped by another and, as in *Ten Days' Wonder*, Ellery is left shattered.

Also as in the previous novel, the murder method is strangulation, the "player on the other side" is compared to a god, and Ellery's failure to comprehend costs lives. In *Cat of Many Tails*, however, he learns wisdom, receiving instruction from a father figure in key scenes at the beginning, middle and end. His first mentor is Inspector Queen, who spurs him to involve himself again. Then, after the carnage of the Cat riots, he is visited in a dream by the titan Prometheus, in Greek mythology the father of civilization. Finally he visits the Viennese psychiatrist Dr. Bela Seligmann, the "grandfather of the tribe," who has seen all the terrors in the world and the human heart.

The last line of the novel, the "great and true" lesson Seligmann asks Ellery to remember, is a quotation from the Bible: "There is one God; and there is none other but he." (Mark 12: 32) What is this homily doing in a dark horrific book that was written by two agnostic Jews and clearly takes place in a godless universe? Were Fred and Manny trying to finagle Boucher into writing a favorable review? It's important to remember that the quotation and the speaker are not Christian but Jewish. Jesus has just recited Judaism's fundamental article of faith, the so-called Sh'ma; and his Jewish interlocutor replies: "Thou hast said the truth, for there is one God and there is no other but he." Equally important to note is that, in context, Seligmann's message can be paraphrased in completely secular terms. If you take part in the world, he tells Ellery, you will be hurt yourself and you will hurt others. This is humankind's experience and fate. Only one with the attributes traditionally ascribed to God can escape tragedy. Nevertheless you must go back into the world and struggle to make it better. "You have failed before, you will fail again. This is the nature and the role of man." At the point of decision between fire and ice, Ellery is urged to commit and to care. But Seligmann paradoxically has performed the inner emigration that he talks Ellery out of. "I do not read newspapers since the war begins. That is for people who like to suffer. I, I do not like to suffer. I have surrendered myself to eternity. For me there is today this room, tomorrow cremation, unless the authorities cannot agree to allow it, in which case they may stuff me and place me in the clock tower of the *Rathaus* and I shall keep reminding them of the time."

Much of *Cat of Many Tails* supports Seligmann's detachment. New York City and its people are evoked with affectionless clinical repugnance, especially in the riot scenes and the acid little Christmas-shopping sequence but one way or another in every presentation of people in sizable groups. Yet despite their fastidious contempt for humanity in the abstract, the cousins infuse life into countless individual men and women (although millionaire reporter Jimmy McKell is such a glaringly artificial character he singes one's eyeballs). Even the Cat's victims, who are never seen alive but are resurrected, as it were, in the words of others, become as real as the living people, each one carefully distinguished and presented not as a statistic but as a person. From the interweaving of victims and survivors and bystanders and investigators, from the vivid pictures of where and how each one lives and what he or she thinks and hopes and fears, there emerges a portrait of the city as a living character itself. The novel encompasses countless aspects of urban life from the racial turmoil to the struggle against the heat, from the chaos of a full-scale riot to the simple delights of radio programs like *The Shadow* and *Stella Dallas*. It's the most abundant book in the canon, offering permanent testimony to the potential of mystery fiction.

The disputes that accompanied the creation of this masterpiece are vividly documented in *Blood Relations*. The first issue they fought out was over whether an obstetrician would deliver his own children as Fred's plot required. Finally they agreed that the practice was uncommon but not illegal or unethical. Next came disagreement over the book's title. Ardent Lewis Carroll fan that he was, Dannay's first choice was *Off With His Head!*, although much later he proposed an alternate, a line from the traditional Passover song "Chad Gadya": *And the Cat Came*. Finally they settled on *Cat of Many Tails*. Manny tussled with Fred over the length of the book, over whether it was appropriate or a disgusting exercise in what we now call political correctness to have the murder of a Jew or a Negro be the catalyst for Ellery's involvement, over whether there was any chance of serialization in a major magazine like *Cosmopolitan*, over how much space should be devoted to capturing the ambience of New York City in 1949, the bones of contention go on and on. What a miracle that there ever was a final version!

Despite the Biblical quotation at the climax, Tony Boucher again had problems with the book. "Thank God I can talk frankly to you," he wrote Manny on September 20, 1949, "as I cannot to Fred. . . . The psychological novelist conceives his case history and works out his action from it. [Fred] designs a plot and a plot-trick and then tries to imagine a case-history that will fit." His public comments in the October 9 *Times Book Review* were milder: "What you will most remember the novel for is its descriptive passages and atmospheric preoccupations. If the human characters still betray a touch of the bloodlessness of the Van Dine era, the City of New York comes magnificently to life."

***

Less than a month later Little, Brown published the *Queen's Awards* volume for the year. The author line-up was predictably stellar, with first prize again going to a European story—Georges Simenon's "Blessed Are the Meek," translated by Boucher—and authors like Nicholas Blake, Stanley Ellin, Edmund Crispin, Fredric Brown, Helen McCloy, Clayton Rawson and Leslie Charteris weighing in with excellent tales. Boucher's comments were ecstatic as usual, at least when he was discussing a

Queen anthology. "If the detective short story is today as literate and imaginative as it has been ever since Poe," he wrote in the *Times Book Review* (November 20, 1949), "the reason is very largely the driving resolution of editor Queen." Then, after a few good-natured quibbles: "I seek flaws only because perfection is intolerable. Here is the detective short story at its best."

CHAPTER SIXTEEN

Of Calendars and Kings

T HE NEXT QUEEN NOVEL was less intense than the two masterpieces that had preceded it but just as distinctively Queenian. The title *Double, Double* (1950) comes from the witches' incantation in *Macbeth* but refers to Ellery's observation that reality is Janus-faced, that each set of events can be interpreted in two ways. Like *There Was an Old Woman* (1943), this novel centers around a children's rhyme, and the relations between Ellery and the female lead and the murderer are similar in both books. But while *Woman* had a Theater of the Absurd milieu tied to a "straight" puzzle, in *Double* the setting is idyllic Wrightsville while the weight of the Absurd is borne by the plot. Ellery is sent a series of clippings from the Wrightsville *Record*, detailing the "natural" death of an old miser who was discovered to have died rich and the "suicide" of a local manufacturer who was discovered to have died broke. Three days later comes another clipping, this one describing the disappearance and presumed death of old Tom Anderson, the alcoholic intellectual who had quoted Whitman in counterpoint to Ellery's solution in *Calamity Town*. The next day Anderson's daughter Rima visits 87th Street and asks Ellery to find out why and by whom her father was killed. Ellery instantly falls for his beautiful flower-child client and returns to Wrightsville, where he becomes involved in the lives of a crotchety and terrified old doctor, a *nouveau riche* attorney, a bitchy female newspaper publisher, and a philosophical gardener whose employers have a habit of dying in droves. The bodies continue to pile up after Ellery's arrival, and the facts are so equivocal that he can't satisfy himself even that all the deaths are connected, let alone that they're murders. Eventually he stumbles across the connecting link between the dead men and the harbinger of further deaths: an old children's counting jingle.

The key to Ellery's exposure of the person who killed so as to make a rhyme come alive is an analysis of motive: the murderer, in the best tradition of the sorcerer's apprentice, followed the words of the jingle up to a certain predetermined point, then was horrified to find the jingle forcing the culprit to conform more killings to it. "Think of it in terms of lunacy," Ellery advises, "and it at once becomes reasonable." Since we're reading a formal deductive puzzle, we can never share the murderer's horror as the pattern takes on its own life. But there are a few glimpses of this missing dimension now and then, as when Dr. Dodd says: "With all our sulfas and atomic bombs and electronic microscopes and two hundred inch telescope lenses, we don't begin to know the powers that fill the universe. All we can do is wait and try not to be too afraid." Rima the proto-hippie confounds Ellery at every turn in the early chapters, showing up his "wisdom" with her "foolishness," but as the book progresses she becomes dull and girdled and conventional like the silent majority around her, so that despite the hint at the end that Ellery may come back for her, it's just as well he didn't bother. Wrightsville of course is evoked superbly, so that we feel an almost personal sense of loss at the casually dropped news that John F. Wright and Doc Willoughby have died since Ellery's last visit. But the sense of place is spoiled by too much overdone satire on the theme of the noble old-timers vs. the slimy arrivistes and also by an analogous literary attack on Mickey Spillane and his imitators, who in Queen's view relate to the classic tradition of mystery fiction precisely as Malvina Prentiss and the other Snopesian interlopers relate to the indigenous solid American Wrightsvillians.

Anthony Boucher criticized *Double, Double* in a letter to Manny Lee (July 8, 1950). "It seems a perfectly good valid straight novel until you get to the end & discover that the mechanical gimmickry means forced violation of all the psychology of the characters up to that point successfully created. I frankly did not believe a word of the solution or motivation. . . . [and] that has been the reaction of every one I know who's read it." His comments in the *Times Book Review* (July 9, 1950) were a bit more conciliatory, describing Wrightsville as "one of the most real and believable towns in fiction" but complaining that the mystery is "resolved by one of the more unlikely motives on record."

***

Later that year came the 1950 volume of *The Queen's Awards*. Winning the first prize was John Dickson Carr's "The Gentleman from Paris," with strong competition from Stanley Ellin's "The Orderly World of Mr. Appleby" and fine contributions by Margery Allingham, Philip MacDonald and John D. MacDonald. In the *Times Book Review* (November 26, 1950) Boucher described all the tales in the volume as "fresh and unhackneyed, . . . delightful in themselves and especially delightful as departures from formula." The book as a whole he called "the one indispensable anthology of the year, and the perfect refutation to all charges that the detective story is stagnant or exhausted."

At the very end of the year Little, Brown published the last "patterned" anthology Fred Dannay would assemble for more than fifteen years, a book that clearly was close to his heart. In his editorial capacity, and drawing on his early years with an advertising agency, he never missed an opportunity to hawk the literary merits of the whodunit, to the point where John Hersey, the author of *A Bell For Adano* and *Hiroshima*, once accused him of "adopting a highly promotional tone in favor of the profession." Manny Lee on the other hand dismissed Fred's views on the genre as (in the immortal words of Edmund Wilson) a farrago of balderdash, and said as much in one of his most revealing letters to Boucher (April 26, 1947).

> I chafed for years under the glossy artificial brittle manufactures put out under the Queen name—little edifices of taffy offered to a world hungry for substantial fare—all under the name of "escape literature." Fred's enthusiasms for the short detective story historically, the little puffings of chest, etc. and the making out of detective stories what they never were and can never be, have always left me dissatisfied, and a little ashamed. I admit he has done a wonderful job of selling, and in the selling has

quite managed to obfuscate the truth—which is that the majority of the vast literature of detection, short and long, is hogwash, illiterate and mechanistically mystic in a world crying for art to grapple with reality. . . .

Isn't this precisely how Joel McCrea's character in *Sullivan's Travels* felt about the commercial comedy films he had directed? One can easily imagine Manny's reaction to *The Literature of Crime* (1950), in which Fred brought together 26 short detective, mystery or crime stories by literary luminaries like Dickens, Hemingway and Faulkner, Sinclair Lewis and John Steinbeck, Ring Lardner and James Thurber, Robert Louis Stevenson and Somerset Maugham. There's an odd tone to this anthology, as if Fred were trying to refute snobs like Edmund Wilson, who proclaimed themselves too sophisticated to waste their time on mystery fiction, by the absurd argument that one mystery apiece (mystery in the broadest sense) by two dozen literati somehow guaranteed the genre's respectability. But most of the stories are first-rate and offer much food for thought about just what mystery fiction is.

***

Almost simultaneously with the publication of *Double, Double*, civil war broke out in divided Korea, the U.S. quickly intervened in the conflict, and the likelihood that the "police action" would escalate into universal nuclear war seemed to increase daily. The war was still in its early stages while the cousins were working on their next novel but its grim reflections on human nature must seem darkly apt considering how many hundreds of thousands were senselessly killed and maimed on that obscure peninsula over the next few years. *The Origin of Evil* (1951) opens in mid-June 1950, shortly before the outbreak of the war. Ellery has returned to gay gaudy goofy Hollywood to work on a novel but finds that the place has changed. The movie industry on which its economy had rested has been all but wiped out by that new toy of the middle class, the TV set, and munitions factories and retirement communities are filling up the economic vacuum. Ellery's work on the novel is interrupted by lovely 19-year-old Laurel Hill and her claim that her foster father, a wealthy jeweler, was literally frightened to death two weeks earlier upon finding a dead dog lying on his doorstep. Laurel contends that Leander Hill's partner, a foul-tempered invalid named

Roger Priam, has also been receiving strange warnings but is keeping his mouth shut about them. At this point, though not by coincidence, Roger Priam's lush and exotic wife Delia shows up to ask Ellery's help, confirming that something strange is happening to her husband. Ellery becomes entangled in the bizarre Priam menage—which includes an enigmatic secretary, a wandering philatelist and a young man who lives in a treehouse—as the senseless warnings keep appearing. Partway through the investigation the war begins and the novel then moves on three fronts: the intensification of the mass slaughter, the deepening of Ellery's involvement with the Hill and Priam households, and the continued arrival of objects like a mess of dead frogs, an empty wallet and a portfolio of worthless stock certificates. Eventually Ellery discovers the pattern and once more his first solution is capped by a second, even more breathtaking, and tying plot and theme together neatly.

This is both the best of the Queen Hollywood novels and one of the cousins' finest books of the Fifties. It's full of familiar Queen elements like murder by psychological shock (as in *The Door Between*), a killer who uses another person as a living weapon (as in *Ten Days' Wonder*), the solution within a solution, the "negative clue" device, and the series of seemingly absurd events connected by a hidden logic (as in *Ten Days' Wonder, Cat of Many Tails* and *Double, Double*). The religious motifs from *Ten Days' Wonder* return with the appearance of not one but two Diedrich-like manipulators, each playing upon the other, one referred to as "the invisible god" and the other as "the god of events." If there's a flaw in the structure, it's that Ellery enters unexpectedly and by accident into a plot that requires the presence of a master detective to unravel certain complexities the murderer wants discovered.

The novel's larger subject is stated in its title, the answer to whose implicit question is, in two words, human nature. As in *Cat of Many Tails*, Ellery in a key scene receives instruction. Near the end of Chapter VII he approaches Collier, the old retired naturalist-adventurer, and asks him bluntly: "Have you any idea what this is all about?" Collier replies:

> "I'll tell you what this is all about, Mr. Queen. . . . It's about corruption and wickedness. It's about greed and selfishness and guilt and violence and hatred and lack of self-control. It's about black secrets and black hearts, cruelty, confusion, fear. It's about not making the best of

things, not being satisfied with what you have, and always wanting what you haven't. It's about envy and suspicion and malice and lust and nosiness and drunkenness and unholy excitement and a thirst for hot running blood. It's about man. . . ."

Jungle imagery recurs every few pages, and all the major characters except Ellery and his nemesis are likened again and again to various animals. The killer's adopted name and his plot are grounded in Darwinian biology with its themes of the endless struggle for survival and "nature red in tooth and claw." The player on the other side turns out to be literally "the old Adam," who is not only unbeaten at the end of the novel but has become Ellery's intimate and familiar — a fitting development when we recall our hero's moralistic outrage and contempt upon learning of Delia's sexual habits despite his clear desire to have her himself. None of us can call another animal. The same nature stains us all. "People mean trouble. . . . There's too much trouble in this world."

Judging from *Blood Relations*, the disputes between Fred and Manny over this book seem to have been fewer and conducted at a lower decibel level than their warfare over *Ten Days' Wonder* and *Cat of Many Tails*. Manny questioned dozens of small points in Fred's synopsis but his major objection was that it "painted an exaggerated, distorted picture of Hollywood" and contained too many characters marked by "eccentricity or goofiness. . . ." He insisted, and finally convinced Fred, that Inspector Queen had no real function in the novel. With great vehemence he challenged Ellery's sexual attraction to Delia Priam, who from Manny's rather puritanical point of view was a pervert. At one point Fred warned Manny not to change any of the characters' names, and explained why in a letter of January 27, 1950. Leander Hill is supposed to evoke Neanderthal; Roger and Delia Priam are Primates; Crowe Macgowan conjures up Cro-Magnon. "Okay, so I'm having fun." I suspect that the number of readers who caught the joke could be counted on the fingers of one hand.

In a letter to Tony Boucher (February 13, 1951) Manny said: "I particularly had fun doing it because I was able to vent . . . a little of what spleen I have left on 'God's Country' — in a nice clean slick way, of course. . . ." The problem with the book is that its grim view of humankind is at odds with its treatment of the Korean conflict and impending nuclear holocaust. Here the war is not one more monument to the race's power hunger and blood lust, it's a case of the Commies from the North attacking their peaceful democratic neighbors to the South. The threat of World War III turns out to be a hoax, a publicity gimmick intended to get movie roles for a young actor—who fittingly winds up volunteering for the crusade against evil in Korea. *The Origin of Evil* owes much to Manny's fervid anti-Communism but it's also a product of the time, when the blacklist and HUAC and Senator Joe McCarthy ruled and political incorrectness could ruin one's career in days. In any event it's an excellent detective novel, praised by Boucher (April 8, 1951) as "one of the best of the twenty-five Queens. . . . [a] grandly fantastic, even improbable, but compellingly constructed murder problem."

***

Back in 1948, Fred Dannay had published the 60-page essay "Queen's Quorum" in his anthology *20th Century Detective Stories*. Three years later he expanded the essay into *Queen's Quorum* (1951), in which he identified and evaluated the 106 "cornerstone volumes" of short crime fiction. Boucher (September 30, 1951) treated the book with the seriousness it deserved. Among the elements he objected to were the "historical distortion" resulting from Fred's "treating the detective short story as a thing in itself quite apart from the novel. . . ," and to the use of a "chronological order dependent upon book publication" so that, for example, Fred's own groundbreaking Dashiell Hammett collections are considered as works of the Forties rather than of the Twenties and early Thirties when Hammett's stories were first published in *Black Mask* and other magazines. Boucher also found "a certain capriciousness" in Fred's definitions of a crime story and a short story, leading to the absurdity that a tale of 40,000 words gets classified as short. But after such "minor sniping" Boucher went on to praise the volume as "indispensable to the literary student and to the book collector, and an entertaining source of curious information for the general reader."

Six weeks later, Boucher in his weekly column (November 11, 1951) found the latest annual *Queen's Awards* anthology "disappointing," but "only by the high standards which earlier volumes have set." He particular admired the tales by Charlotte Armstrong, A.H.Z. Carr, Roy Vickers and Oliver La Farge but also pointed out "several weak items . . . which hardly seem of prize-winning caliber." Clearly the leading critic of the genre was not about to give any book a free pass just because it had the Queen name on its spine.

***

Fred Dannay, the editorial half of the Queen partnership, had long contended that a first-rate mystery anthology needed a central concept or theme, but the early Queen short story collections like *Adventures* and *New Adventures* had been themeless. Soon after dropping out of radio work, Fred decided that the next collection should have a theme, and Manny in whatever moments weren't consumed by airwaves crises began adapting various of his radio scripts based on Fred's synopses into short stories, published in *EQMM* beginning in 1946 and collected as *Calendar of Crime* (1952), one story for each month of the year and centering on an event associated with that month. The first six had been written close together and published in consecutive issues of *EQMM* (September 1946-March 1947) with one exception. There was no story in the December 1946 issue, I suspect because Manny was having a hard time writing a satisfactory prose version of the "Dauphin's Doll" radio script (December 23/25, 1943), which he had written alone, without benefit of a Dannay synopsis, and therefore must have been uniquely fond of. On July 29, 1948, Fred told Manny that the story was "too long for [its] own good" and "is almost buried under the whimsy." Manny replied that he "would rather have the story excluded from the magazine altogether rather than trimmed or edited. . . ."

He went on to give Fred an overall appraisal of the calendar stories. "I like them immensely, I had a lot of fun doing them. . . ." On the other hand, Manny's letters to Boucher suggest that the project gave him all the pleasure of having his teeth pulled without anesthesia. Writing on October 16, 1946, he called the New Year's Day story he had just finished "by all odds the most difficult job I've ever had, as there was utterly nothing in the yarn, and the background was as barren as an old lady after a hysterectomy. It's a poor story, and I did it reluctantly." Late in 1948 he cursed the stories collectively as "little clods of deodorized crap magicked into a sort of alien dessert for connoisseurs." But he kept writing them, finishing the last five in a rush so that they could appear consecutively in *EQMM* (April-August 1951) before their collection in book form. Boucher (January 20, 1952) described the stories as "deliberately artificial intricacies" garbed "in very real and even touching Americana."

181

For my money the dozen stories in this collection range in quality from magnificent to indifferent. Manny hated "The Inner Circle" (*EQMM*, January 1947; originally "The Millionaires' Club," April 23/25, 1942), but I love it. One of the last survivors of the Januarians, the 1913 graduating class of Eastern University, visits Ellery shortly before the annual New Year's day class meeting and tells him of a survivor-take-all tontine among an "inner circle" of graduates, three of whom have died recently. It's a beautifully mounted puzzle with a solution neatly deduced from a word-association clue and a huge cast of vividly drawn Old Grads. There's no crime in "The President's Half Disme" (*EQMM*, February 1947; originally "George Washington's Dollar," February 19/21, 1942) as Ellery searches for a rare coin believed to have been buried by Washington on a remote Pennsylvania farm in 1791. The story hangs on multiple coincidence and the answer is perhaps too easy to work out but the overall effect is delightful.

The calendar reference in "The Ides of Michael Magoon" (*EQMM*, March 1947; originally "The Income Tax Robbery," March 12/14, 1942) refers to the income tax, which until 1955 fell due on March 15. A middle-aged, overweight, asthmatic, near-sighted and none-too-bright private eye reports to Ellery that someone stole all his tax records from his briefcase 48 hours or so before the filing deadline, but the oddball theft soon balloons into a case of blackmail and murder, which Ellery resolves surprisingly and with full fairness to the reader. Which is more than can be said for "The Emperor's Dice" (*EQMM*, April 1951; originally March 31, 1940), which reeks with standard old-dark-house characters and atmosphere as Ellery probes the apparent ten-year-old murder of a millionaire collector of gambling devices. The elucidation of the "dying message" is so absurd it sounds like a parody, and the final surprise (which anyone who figures out the story's connection with its month can guess in an instant) is infuriating.

In "The Gettysburg Bugle" (*EQMM*, May 1951, as "As Simple as ABC"; originally "The Old Men," May 28/30, 1942) Ellery stumbles upon a tiny Pennsylvania hamlet and a case involving yet another dwindling tontine, with the survivor slated to enjoy a fabled Civil War treasure. The solution to the series of Memorial Day deaths among the town's Union Army veterans is neat and satisfying but takes a back seat to the depiction of small-town patriotic solidarity. The background of "The Medical Finger" (*EQMM*, June 1951; originally "The June Bride," June

11/13, 1942) is a wedding, but the lovely and wealthy young bride drops dead seven minutes after the ceremony, prime suspect being a violent-tempered old flame who had threatened to kill her rather than see her marry someone else. This time Ellery has almost nothing to do, and his deductions fail to eliminate the other suspects and come too late.

Ellery enters the July adventure of "The Fallen Angel" (*EQMM*, July 1951; originally July 2, 1939) thanks to Nikki Porter's girlfriend, who recently married an aging laxatives tycoon and moved into his monstrous family mansion and apparently into a romance with her husband's brother, a young artist. Ellery solves the resultant murder by penetrating an alibi gimmick which integrates the story with its month but never covers up the flaw that if he'd been even a few minutes late for his appointment the scheme would have literally gone up in smoke. There's no connection with its month in "The Needle's Eye" (*EQMM*, August 1951; originally "Captain Kidd's Bedroom," February 11, 1940) beyond the fact that it takes place in August. A retired explorer, on whose private island Captain Kidd is rumored to have buried part of his treasure, asks Ellery to investigate his niece's new husband, but the digging becomes literal after his client is murdered. The crucial clue is neatly handled and the treatment of pirate lore nostalgic.

"The Three Rs" (*EQMM*, September 1946; originally September 10, 1939) finds Ellery retained by the administration of Barlowe College to locate one of its faculty, a Poe scholar who vanished in the Ozarks over the summer. He finds some intriguing clues—like the skeleton with two missing fingers—but the way he assembles the pieces turns the story into a parody and a farce. In "The Dead Cat" (*EQMM*, October 1946; originally October 29, 1939) Ellery and Nikki attend a Halloween party in cat costumes and stay to find out who cut the throat of one of the guests in total darkness during a game of Murder. It's never explained how the killer anticipated that someone would suggest the game, but otherwise this is a tightly plotted fair-play puzzle with yet another variation on the theme going back to the 1935 short story "The House of Darkness."

The Thanksgiving story "The Telltale Bottle" (*EQMM*, November 1946; originally November 19, 1939) opens with Ellery and Nikki delivering holiday food baskets to the poor. They soon blunder into a cocaine-pushing operation and murder, but the mess is resolved so incomprehensibly that the last six paragraphs literally make no sense.

Luckily the collection climaxes with by far the finest of the dozen. In "The Dauphin's Doll" (*EQMM*, December 1948; originally December 23/25, 1943) Ellery and his father and dozens of the Inspector's men join forces to protect the doll and its 49-carat diamond crown from the legendary thief Comus, who has boasted that he'll steal the figure while it's on exhibition at a major department store on the day before Christmas. The crime is pulled off brilliantly but solved even more brilliantly, and Manny Lee spices the clues with all sorts of learned digressions and a sardonic evocation of the Christmas rush that presages the more sustained treatment of the same subject in *Cat of Many Tails*. No collection of short whodunits could end more satisfyingly.

***

The international politics that formed a small part of the background of *The Origin of Evil* dominates the stage in the next Queen novel, *The King Is Dead* (1952). Ellery and his father are spirited away from Manhattan and escorted by armed guards to the secret island empire of weapons tycoon Kane "King" Bendigo, perhaps the most powerful person on earth, whose lust for and abuse of power have been responsible for billions of deaths and maimings. The King has been receiving anonymous death threats from someone in his entourage and his Prime Minister and brother, Abel Bendigo, has drafted the Queens to find the culprit. Among the members of the royal family are King's wife Karla, an international beauty of royal blood, and his second brother Judah, a saintly ineffectual lush whose caches of Segonzac VSOP cognac are strewn all over the island. The messages continue to reach Bendigo, each one more precise about the exact moment the king is to die. As the hour approaches, even after the potential assassin's identity has become known, the tension continues to mount until finally a man points an empty gun at a solid wall and pulls the trigger, while in a sealed room on the other side of a corridor filled with guards, the King falls. Ellery eventually unravels this superb locked-room problem but the truth avails him nothing and he's unable to influence the course of events.

Detection buffs who are at home in *Citizen Kane* (1941) might enjoy spotting the similarities between Orson Welles' Charles Foster Kane and Kane Bendigo other than their names. Here are a few for starters. Both men are ruthless and lust for power. Both appear with a full head of hair at one point and bald at another. Both live on isolated baroque estates, the Italian marble fireplace in the Bendigo reception room echoing the huge one before which Kane's wife in the movie did her jigsaw puzzles. The investigation into the childhood and young manhood of the dying titan is central to both works. If *Citizen Kane* is clearly the major cinematic source for *The King Is Dead*, Queen's evocation of mounting suspense as the hour of a predicted but seemingly impossible death comes nearer owes just as much to Cornell Woolrich's powerful novel *Night Has a Thousand Eyes* (1945, as by George Hopley). In effect Fred and Manny purged Woolrich's book of all its preternatural elements but maintained the suspense at a Woolrich level, adding a lovely locked-room puzzle with a naturalistic solution that is childishly simple but obscured by superb misdirection and completely fair to the reader. Boucher (May 18, 1952) described the novel as "one of [Queen's] noblest puzzles. . . , with a gratifyingly simple explanation" but questioned "just how seriously one is intended to take the whole concoction. . . ."

This strikes me as his gentle way of pointing out the many flaws in the book when considered as more than a brilliant puzzle. Would any sane person devise such a bizarre way of getting rid of an enemy as we find here? The same end could have been accomplished so much more easily by doing what actually is done before the beginning of Chapter XVII! And who can accept the climactic "reformation" of Abel Bendigo? "Do you think I can believe that?" Inspector Queen rightly asks. "That the leopard can change his spots? You were in it up to your neck for twenty-seven years." Who can buy the explanation of King Bendigo's fear of water, which is central to the novel? Can a total revolution be accomplished just by assassinating the one man at the top? How in the world will the successful insurgents be able to use a multi-billion-dollar armaments empire as a force for good? "The King is dead, long live the King," Ellery says on the last page. "Now who keeps an eye on the incumbent?" Judah Bendigo replies calmly: "I do." Here the novel ends, but I suggest there should be one final line: "And who will keep an eye on you?" Ellery asked.

That someone had better is strongly suggested by Judah's words to his brother King. "In the world we live in, munitions are unfortunately necessary, and someone has to manufacture them. But to you the implements of war are not a necessary evil, made for the protection of a decent society trying to survive in a wolves' world. They're a means of getting astronomical profits and the power that goes with them." If only

King would believe his own propaganda about the free world and godless totalitarianism while carrying on business as usual, Judah's conscience would seem to be satisfied. Aren't the values of this impotent Dostoevskian saint too wobbly to bear the weight the novel places on them?

The King Is Dead fares better when considered as another adventure of Ellery in Wonderland. Like the Potts estate in *There Was an Old Woman*, Bendigo Island is a private universe with its own paradoxical laws and behavior patterns. Cain seems to save Abel's life, then Abel kills him. The treason of Judas is a holy act. Virtually every event in the book, even the central confrontation between Kane and Judah in Chapter IX, is an intricately staged performance played for the Queens' benefit. Didn't we learn back in the Sixties that theatre and revolution were interchangeable? *There Was an Old Woman* failed to integrate a serious puzzle plot with a topsy-turvy milieu, and *The King Is Dead* fails to make an organic whole out of a locked-room puzzle, a psychological study, and a fable about fascism and revolution. At least the suspense and misdirection and the central clue are of the highest order.

***

The years these books were appearing coincided with the emergence of Ellery in the medium that had taken over radio's place as America's favorite form of home entertainment. Producers Norman and Irving Pincus bought the television rights to the character early in 1950 and assembled the team whose job was to create a 30-minute live episode every week. Fred and Manny had no desire to grind out weekly scripts for the new medium, so the brothers put together a coterie of freelance writers like Ethel Frank, Henry Misrock, Betty Loring and John C. Gibbs, whose efforts were overseen by story editor Eugene Burr and the producers. Brought in to direct these live dramas was Donald Richardson (1918-1996), who went on to helm episodes of countless TV series including *I Remember Mama, Dupont Play of the Week, The Defenders, Lost in Space*, and *The Virginian*.

The role of Ellery went to darkly handsome Richard Hart, who was born in Providence, Rhode Island in 1914 and became a soccer star at Brown University, from which he graduated in 1936. After some stage experience in New England, he moved to New York City and landed his first Broadway part in *Pillar to Post* (1943). His brooding good looks captured Hollywood's attention and won him three juicy parts at MGM, respectively opposite Greer Garson, Lana Turner, and Barbara Stanwyck, in *Desire Me* (1947), *Green Dolphin Street* (1947), and *B.F.'s Daughter* (1948). At the dawn of live TV he appeared in several New York-based productions, notably as Marc Antony in Shakespeare's *Julius Caesar*. Then came the offer from the Pincus brothers to solve small-screen murders on a weekly basis. For the role of Inspector Richard Queen the brothers recruited Florenz Ames, a peppery little rooster who had been appearing on the Broadway stage since 1917.

On October 19, 1950, *The Adventures of Ellery Queen* debuted on the short-lived DuMont network, occupying the Thursday evening time slot from 9:00 to 9:30 p.m. The debut episode, "The Bad Boy," was based on one of the 60-minute scripts Fred and Manny had written for the Queen radio series back in 1939. A week later Hart and Ames solved the case of "The Mad Tea-Party," based on the 1934 tale which Fred Dannay till the end of his life ranked as his personal favorite among all the Ellery Queen short stories. Of the eleven episodes broadcast during 1950, at least seven were adapted (not by Fred and Manny) from genuine Queen short stories or radio plays. "The Hanging Acrobat" (December 21, 1950), in which Ellery probes the backstage murder of a trapeze star, survives on kinescope, and differs hugely from its source.

Less than two weeks later, Richard Hart's career came to a sudden end. On Tuesday, January 2, 1951, during rehearsal for the following Thursday's broadcast, he suffered a heart attack and died soon afterward in New York's French Hospital. On 24 hours' notice he was replaced by Lee Bowman (1914-1979), whose roles in various Columbia films—notably opposite Jean Arthur in *The Impatient Years* (1944) and Rita Hayworth in *Cover Girl* (1944)—had earned him a reputation as a reliable leading man. With his urban accent and streetwise manner, Bowman's EQ was markedly different from that of the suave sophisticated Hart. But the new image kept audiences tuned in for just short of two years, during which all the scripts were originals by the Pincuses' stable of writers. Included in the casts of various episodes were Judith Evelyn, Eva Gabor, Dennis Hoey (Inspector Lestrade from the Basil Rathbone-Nigel Bruce Sherlock Holmes films), and Anne Marno (later and better known as Anne Bancroft). A photo-story version of one Bowman segment, "The Twilight Zone" (September 13, 1951), was published in *TV Show* magazine for January 1952 and can be downloaded from your computer, and at least four others with Bowman, plus one with Hart, survive on kinescope and are also accessible on the Web. All five of the Bowmans manifest zero interest in clues, deductions and fair play with the viewer, and for all the resemblance he bore to the character Fred and Manny had created, the detective in these dramas might as well have been named John Smith. Nevertheless the series was highly regarded, winning a *TV Guide* award as the best mystery program of 1950-51.

What was it like to work on the show? The only Queen scripter who found success in other media was Helene Hanff (1916-1997), whose charming book *84, Charing Cross Road* (1970) was later adapted into a Broadway play and a 1987 movie, starring Anne Bancroft and Anthony Hopkins. Hanff liked to set crime in an artsy milieu and she had Ellery solve murders at a ballet school, a ballet performance, an opera, a summer theater, an art gallery, and during a production of *The Mikado*. In a letter dated September 15, 1951 and included in *84, Charing Cross Road*, she wrote:

> I'm stuck on 95th Street writing the TV "Adventures of Ellery Queen." Did I tell you we're not allowed to use a lipstick-stained cigarette for a clue? We're sponsored by the Bayuk Cigar Co. and we're not allowed to mention the word "cigarette." We can have ashtrays on the set, but they can't have any cigarette butts in them. They can't have cigar butts either, they're not pretty. All an ashtray can have in it is a wrapped, unsmoked Bayuk cigar.

The series stayed in its Thursday evening slot (except for an 8-week summer hiatus) until early December 1951, then moved to the ABC network and was seen Sundays from 7:30 to 8:00 p.m., sponsored by the auto manufacturer Kaiser-Frazer, under whose auspices the sleuths and suspects began smoking up a cigarette storm. After thirteen weeks the show left the air for a month, returning to ABC in mid-April 1952 in the 9:00 p.m. Wednesday time slot with a new sponsor, Phillies cigars. The Pincus brothers continued to produce, Donald Richardson to do most of the directing, the same stable of writers to turn out the weekly scripts, and Bowman and Ames to play the Queens. After the final episode (November 26, 1952) the time slot was taken over by local basketball games.

***

With the fall came the seventh annual *Queen's Awards* volume. Boucher (November 7, 1952) complained mildly that of its sixteen tales "at most five can, under the most liberal interpretation, be labeled as detective stories." But that, he suggested, was an asset of the book, not a defect. "Queen [meaning Fred] is maturing from a technical detective specialist into a purveyor of pure fiction—and with his editorial ability, this may prove a very healthy development for the American short story."

CHAPTER SEVENTEEN

Gold, Scarlet and Glass

W
E HAVE SEEN that it was Fred Dannay's brain-damaged child Stephen who inspired *Cat of Many Tails* (1949). The year before he died, the boy inspired a second novel, the only one his father wrote without a collaborator.

The Golden Summer (1953) was published under Fred's birth name Daniel Nathan, although the editors of the annual Book Review Digest volume must have been in on the secret since its summary of reviews for the book appears under the Dannay name. Fred wrote this memoir as a kind of therapy against his son's impending death, a nostalgic reenactment of his own vanished childhood and an exorcism of his anguished middle life. The scene is Elmira in the summer of 1915 and the storyline deals with the business adventures of 10-year-old Danny Nathan, a skinny bespectacled weakling who's shrewd and nimble-witted enough to talk himself out of any spot and to manipulate his playmates to his own advantage. Most of the novel consists of a series of unrelated "business adventures" in each of which Danny winds up with a few coins net profit. He displays the ghost of Long John Silver for a two-cent admission fee, raffles off a damaged copy of the brand-new Sherlock Holmes novel *The Valley of Fear* (although in real life Fred didn't discover that book until 1917 and the volume he actually raffled off was

190

L. Frank Baum's *The Scarecrow of Oz*), organizes the Great Lollapaloosa Bi-Plane Company, and even adds a dime to his hoard through a splendiferous one-upmanship contest with his city cousin "Telford." *The Golden Summer* is at root a book-length *double entendre*: the season of innocent security and peace, the season when Danny tricked his contemporaries out of $4.73. Most reviewers found this duality to be a basic flaw: we're supposed to delight in Danny's adventures as if he were another Tom Sawyer or Penrod while we see he's just a money-hungry young con artist. But Fred's brutally honest self-portrait provides the key to countless features of the Ellery Queen world, including the image of Ellery I as the weak-eyed young genius who dominates his environment by the force of his mind and perhaps the Iagoesque quality of so many of the murderers exposed by Ellery in all his incarnations. The book also includes the only specimens of Fred's poetry published in his lifetime.

Commercially *The Golden Summer* was a thumping failure. Three years after its publication, Fred made a last desperate attempt to stir up some interest in the book, devising a stratagem worthy of little Danny himself. He reprinted three chapters of the novel in *EQMM* (June, August and October 1956), each chapter prefaced with a page of ecstatic commentary on the book as a whole by Anthony Boucher, Stanley Ellin and James Yaffe. The texts were revised to keep readers from suspecting the identity of Daniel Nathan, so that Ellery Herman the shoemaker, for example, morphs into Old Man Herman. Among the stories in the October 1956 issue was "Tough Break" by one Ryam Beck. The true author was Douglas Dannay, Fred's oldest son. Mary Beck had been the maiden name of Doug's mother, Fred's first wife.

***

In the years following World War II, the genre Fred and Manny loved was moving slowly but inexorably "from the detective story to the crime novel," and the next Queen novel was part of that move—up to a point. In *The Scarlet Letters* (1953), published on the heels of *The Golden Summer*, the cousins challenged themselves to create a complex milieu and breathe life into a very small cast of characters and generate an atmosphere of intense urgency while withholding all criminous elements until the last two chapters. The story revolves around Dirk Lawrence, a morbid, childhood-haunted, insanely jealous novelist, and his older wife Martha, a wealthy amateur Broadway producer and a born martyr to

Dirk's rages. After four years, as Dirk constantly accuses Martha of sleeping around and takes drunken swings at her suspected lovers, the marriage comes apart. Martha goes for help to her childhood friend Nikki Porter, who drafts Ellery into trying to reach the roots of Dirk's phobia. But is it phobia? Ellery soon discovers that Martha has been and is making alphabetically coded assignations, in hotel rooms and elsewhere, with an aging but still studly former Broadway matinee idol. He now faces a three-headed task: to find out what's behind Martha's actions, to keep Dirk from learning of the affair, and to pull the sexual blackmailer's fangs. These non-violent non-deductive events occupy roughly 75% of the novel, but then come a bloody double shooting, a splendid dying message, a murder trial, and Ellery's exposure of some stupendous double-dealing.

Those who know their Queen will find any number of links between *The Scarlet Letters* and earlier Period Three novels. For another war veteran whose father apparently killed his mother and who himself becomes intensely jealous of his wife, see *The Murderer Is a Fox* (1945). For another tiny cast of characters and another Iagoesque killer shaped by his father, see *Ten Days' Wonder* (1948). What is most unexpected in *The Scarlet Letters* is not the plot but the milieu. The cousins convincingly evoke the world of theatre people and Broadway columnists and swank night spots through a wealth of small details, referring to the then wildly popular game of Canasta and to TV shows like *The Stork Club* and Sid Caesar's Saturday night variety hour. The first three-quarters of *The Scarlet Letters* are full of mainstream excellences of setting and character, but once the time comes to introduce murder and the traditional apparatus of the whodunit, things fall apart. Ellery's solution is based on gossamer and speculative reasoning unworthy of Holmes' logical successor and raises all sorts of legal problems that the cousins evade. (Wouldn't you love to know what happened back in the courtroom when Judge Levy returned to the bench after Ellery's lecture?) Even worse is that once we learn the truth, we see that we've been misled unforgivably in the body of the book, that the true relationship between Martha and her apparent clandestine lover Van Harrison makes nonsense of all her observed and reported behavior. The entire murder plan depends on Ellery and Nikki learning certain facts prior to the crime but the murderer does nothing to point them towards those facts, which Ellery uncovers by sheer luck. Some of the killer's moves, like deliberately blocking Martha from her most public meeting with Harrison, are in retrospect appallingly stupid. The excellent prose and social observation and depiction of time and place surely deserved a stronger plot than this. It wasn't the first Queen novel whose novelistic and deductive elements collided and smashed each other up and it wouldn't be the last. Boucher in the *Times Book Review* (May 10, 1953) passed over most of these flaws. "Motivations seem sometimes to arise from plot-necessities rather than character, but the whole is, as one has come to expect from Queen, something different."

***

Six months later, upon the publication of 1953's *Queen's Awards* volume, Boucher went ecstatic, calling fourteen of its sixteen stories "extraordinary and outstanding" and singling out the contributions of Steve Frazee, Roy Vickers, A.H.Z. Carr, Stanley Ellin, Charlotte Armstrong and Dorothy Salisbury Davis. "[T]his is the best (as well as the largest) volume . . . in some years, and as fine a collection of the literature of crime as one is apt to encounter anywhere." Without mentioning Fred Dannay by name, Boucher praised him for publishing "literate, intelligent, sensitive fiction, on a par with much of the best 'serious' short-story writing—and sometimes a notch above, if one considers plot a virtue rather than a blemish."

***

By this point in the 1950s the reign of cultural terror spurred by Senator Joe McCarthy and HUAC and their ilk had been raging for several years. Thousands of Americans were labeled pinkoes or Communist sympathizers and fired from their jobs, blacklisted, jailed (like Fred's friend Dashiell Hammett, who served six months), or deported. Absurd categories like "Fifth Amendment Communist" and "guilt by association" became commonplace. Trials and hearings to determine whether one was "subversive" were held on a grand scale. The theatre, film and literature were extremely hard hit. This atmosphere of terror is captured vividly in the next Queen novel, *The Glass Village* (1954). Originally Ellery was to have been the protagonist of this powerful book, but while the writing was under way Fred and Manny changed their minds and decided—wisely, as it turned out—to make this their first stand-alone novel.

The setting is the back-country hamlet of Shinn Corners, a once thriving New England factory town reduced to a population of 36, all but a few of them embittered puritanical bigots. The single part-time resident, who keeps one foot in Shinn Corners and the other in the more enlightened world outside, is Superior Court Judge Lewis Shinn. The judge is spending a week in the village where he was born, bonding with his nephew Johnny, a war veteran who had witnessed Hiroshima and was sexually mutilated in Korea and calls himself "a vegetable" and "the missing link between the flora and the fauna." He never became a Communist because he found Marxism too optimistic a philosophy for him to accept. Judge Shinn still claims to believe in the patriotic formulas of grammar-school civics class — "Communism, hydrogen bombs, nerve gas, McCarthyism, and ex-majors of Army Intelligence to the contrary notwithstanding" — but admits that his faith is being shaken. "As we get poorer, we get more frightened; the more frightened we get, the narrower and meaner and bitterer and less secure we are." He goes out of his way to point out to Johnny the many evils America has inflicted on other peoples but, parroting one of the silliest commonplaces of the Fifties, he insists that those who act on their beliefs, "rightly or wrongly," are better than those who believe in nothing. Adolf Eichmann as the moral superior of Bertrand Russell. Yeah, right. Luckily the focus of *The Glass Village* is not on the Judge but on Johnny and his slow journey back to the human race.

What precipitates his return is the bludgeoning to death of 91-year-old primitive painter Fanny Adams in her studio one rainy afternoon. A foreign-looking tramp who had passed through the village shortly before the murder is instantly tagged as the perpetrator, hunted down, beaten and almost lynched by the outraged citizens of Shinn Corners, who refuse to turn over their prey to the state police and insist on trying him themselves. One of the grimmest aspects of the novel is that the common purpose of lynching another human being does forge a true sense of community in the village, with neighbor helping neighbor, sharing chores and meals. To avert a gun battle between the locals and the police, Judge Shinn gets permission from the governor to preside over a mock murder trial, a proceeding aswarm with legal gaffes, designed to placate the townspeople for now and be reversed by an appellate court later. Among the jurors is Johnny Shinn. Ten of the other jurors admit under oath that they're already certain the tramp is guilty. The bailiff, the court reporter, most of the jurors and even the judge testify for the prosecution. Judge Shinn takes over as prosecutor while the prosecutor testifies against the defendant. Defense counsel fails to object to gross violations of his client's rights but fights loudly over the admissibility of trivia. The judge bangs the darning egg he's using as a gavel and hands down legal rulings he knows are dead wrong. We might well call *The Glass Village* a study in due process on the other side of the rabbit hole. It's also one of the finest Queen novels of the Fifties, replete with bizarre clues and inspired misdirection and even a sort of dying message. Most of the characters are vicious morons whose sadism and bigotry during the capture of Kowalczyk make Johnny vomit. "Take a vote!" snarls Merton Isbel in the jury room. ". . . Ye think to balk the will of the majority? Vote guilty!" Rebecca Hemus, cheated of a victim, cries: "It's a conspiracy, that's what it is!" Her son Tommy screams "You a Commie-lover?" at whoever disagrees with him, Commie being the equivalent of nigger in a community whose harsh climate killed off all the slaves long ago. Small wonder that, near the end of the novel, Johnny reflects that "man was a chaos without rhyme or reason; that he blundered about like a maddened animal in the delicate balance of the world, smashing and disrupting, eager only for his own destruction." As in *The Origin Of Evil*, the root of all evil is not any political or economic system, it's us. What the events have taught Johnny is that to be human does not require him to believe in or hope for anything but only to care—a lesson very close to the wisdom of Dr. Seligmann in *Cat of Many Tails*.

The one major flaw in the novel is that it requires a crucial scene— Johnny convincing his fellow jurors not to lynch Kowalczyk yet and claiming he can prove someone else committed the murder—but Fred and Manny dodged the task of writing it. It would have been next to impossible to write a credible scene showing Johnny or anyone else persuading this gallery of grotesque fools not to go ahead with their blood sport, but the way the cousins evaded the problem—simply by stopping the jury-room action and shifting forward to the swamp—is a clear case of foul play on the reader. Aside from this lapse, however, *The Glass Village* is a magnificent novel, rich in plot and character and atmosphere and social commentary like nothing else in the Queen canon. The *Times Book Review* gave it the prestige of coverage by mainstream critic Lewis Nichols rather than in Boucher's column as usual. Certainly no Queen novel more richly deserved that honor.

***

The next time Boucher discussed Queen was that fall, upon the release of the ninth *Queen's Awards* anthology. In his review (October 24, 1954) he applauded Athe preponderance of strict detective stories (unusual in this annual series)" and gave special praise to Margaret Millar, Philip MacDonald and first-prize winner Roy Vickers.

***

Instead of the usual Queen novel the following year came *Q.B.I.: Queen's Bureau Of Investigation* (1955), another collection of short stories, most of them very short indeed. "Personally," Boucher wrote (January 2, 1955), "I find them too brief for comfort—pared down to little more than statement-and-answer of (in most cases) a not exactly startling gimmick. But they're neat and professional, and often colorfully amusing in what background the brevity permits." Most of the tales had first appeared in *This Week* and were reprinted in *EQMM* either before or after their appearance in this collection. In a letter to Boucher dated February 6, 1951, Manny had complained that *This Week*'s editors "steadily mangle [them] in editing." Some—probably more than I've identified—had roots in Queen radio plays from the Forties.

The collection opens with two competent but unspectacular tales. In "Money Talks" (*This Week*, April 2, 1950; *EQMM*, August 1952, as "The Sound of Blackmail") Ellery determines which of Mrs. Alfredo's boarders is trying to blackmail her over the illegitimacy of her daughter. In "A Matter of Seconds" (*This Week*, August 9, 1953; *EQMM*, January 1957) he is chosen to deliver the $100,000 ransom for a boxer kidnapped from his Colorado training camp just before the big fight but saves the money and the day by making a deduction which unless you're a devotee of pugilism is bound to seem esoteric.

"The Three Widows" (*This Week*, January 29, 1950, as "Murder Without Clues"; *EQMM*, January 1952) is a neat little puzzle in which Ellery solves the locked-room poisoning of wealthy Sarah Hood, while the equally scrumptious "My Queer Dean!" (*This Week*, March 8, 1953; *EQMM*, November 1956) concerns a priceless copy of the essays of Francis Bacon, the theft of $19,000 from a university administration building, and the outrageous spoonerisms of Dean Matthew Arnold Hope, which enable Ellery to make sense of the case. In "Driver's Seat" (*This Week*, March 25, 1951, as "Lady, You're Dead!"; *EQMM*, November

1955) Ellery faces a problem in elimination, deducing which of the three surviving Brothers brothers stabbed the fourth Brothers brother's widow to death in the middle of a teeming rainstorm.

"A Lump of Sugar" (*This Week*, July 9, 1950, as "The Mystery of the 3 Dawn Riders"; *EQMM*, February 1953) is a reworking of the Vienna anecdote Drury Lane told in Act III Scene 3 of *The Tragedy of X* (1932). The reason why the victim's last act was to clutch some sugar from a nearby table is different in the two versions but more ingenious in the later.

In one respect "Cold Money" (*This Week*, March 20, 1952; *EQMM*, January 1956) was influenced by Cornell Woolrich, whose superb novelet "Mystery in Room 913" had been reprinted in the December 1949 issue of *EQMM*. With fiendish neatness Ellery locates a vanishing $62,000 payroll and solves the murder of an ex-convict who had holed up in another Room 913. The earliest version of this story had been the EQ radio play "The Man Who Waited" (March 20, 1946), written by Manny from one of the Fred Dannay synopses he had squirreled away for emergencies after Fred left the series. Also based on a radio play was "The Myna Birds" (*This Week*, December 28, 1952; *EQMM*, September 1956, as "Cut, Cut, Cut!"), in which Ellery solves the murder of a bird-loving millionairess by analyzing what her myna said upon her death. The birds don't appear in the original radio version, "The 52nd Card" (January 29/31, 1942). The Woolrich influence returns in "A Question of Honor" (*This Week*, September 13, 1953; *EQMM*, May 1958), in which Ellery proves that the "suicide" of a visiting Scotland Yard man and Shakespeare scholar was murder. Woolrich's "Murder with a U," based on a similar gimmick, had been collected in book form in 1952.

The collection's only tale of true short-story length is "The Robber of Wrightsville" (*Today's Family*, February 1953; *EQMM*, December 1954, as "The Accused"), which was based on the radio play "The Black Sheep" (July 28, 1940). The prose version is set in Queen's favorite small town and brings back one major and two minor characters from *Ten Days' Wonder*: Wolfert Van Horn, Delbert Hood (the bellhop whom Ellery had paid to watch the door of Room 1010 in the Hollis Hotel) and Jeep Jorking (the policeman who was guarding Howard Van Horn shortly before his death). Ellery returns to Wrightsville on a skiing trip but gets sidetracked into clearing Delbert on an armed robbery charge and reconciling him with his stepfather, who was the robber's victim.

Ellery's problem in "Double Your Money" (*This Week*, September 30, 1951, as "The Vanishing Wizard"; *EQMM*, September 1955) is to find out how a clever confidence man disappeared from a locked and guarded office seven stories above the street, and the answer is both simple and satisfying. Less so is "Miser's Gold" (*This Week*, June 18, 1950, as "Love Hunts a Hidden Treasure"; *EQMM*, April 1954), where he has to interpret the last words of a miserly book-loving pawnbroker and determine where in his crammed-full shop the man hid $4,000,000 in cash.

Among all the Queen short-shorts my personal favorite is "Snowball in July" (*This Week*, August 31, 1952, as "The Phantom Train"; *EQMM*, July 1956), which was based on the radio play "The Train That Vanished" (November 25/27, 1943). One sizzling summer morning an entire train apparently vanishes on a straight stretch of track between two upstate New York whistlestops six minutes apart. The answer is blindingly obvious but concealed by stunning misdirection. On the other hand it's only by an uninspired and lucky bluff that in "The Witch of Times Square" (*This Week*, November 5, 1950; *EQMM*, May 1953) Ellery figures out which of two claimants to a fortune is the real John Gaard. The story isn't based on a radio play but incorporates some of the climax of "The Lost Child" (November 26, 1939) and corrects a mistake in genetics on which the radio play had hinged. "The Gamblers' Club" (*This Week*, January 7, 1951; *EQMM*, March 1955) is a con-game tale involving an anonymous dispenser of accurate stock-market tips, not too difficult for Ellery to solve but neatly mounted and satisfying.

The only short-short in the collection not originally published in *This Week* is "GI Story" (*EQMM*, August 1954). Again Ellery returns to Wrightsville for a skiing trip and gets sidetracked into a mystery. One of wealthy merchant Clint Fosdick's stepsons—known as Wash, Linc and Woody, two of them military veterans and the third presently serving—poisoned him for the inheritance. The murdered man's last act was to write the letters GI. It's a superb little tale, one of Queen's finest at this length.

The perpetrator of the impossible in "The Black Ledger" (*This Week*, January 26, 1952, as "The Mysterious Black Ledger"; *EQMM*, December 1955) is Ellery himself, with the detective role played by a narcotics kingpin whose empire will collapse if the ledger gets safely to Washington. Ellery is captured on the Capitol Limited, stripped and searched over and over, but pulls off the miracle with the aplomb of a Houdini, even giving us a subtle pointer to the document's location. In the earliest version of this tale, the radio play "The Yellow Ledger" (December 17/19, 1942), the villains had been a Nazi spy ring.

The collection closes with "Child Missing!" (*This Week*, July 8, 1951, as "Kidnaped!"; *EQMM*, June 1958), which had first seen life as the radio play "The Missing Child" (May 7/9, 1942). Ellery solves the disappearance of 7-year-old Billy Harper five weeks after the separation of his wealthy parents by determining why the subsequent ransom note demanded payment under physically impossible conditions. His solution is breathtakingly simple and brings the collection to an end on a note of gentle humor.

***

Ellery had not been seen on television since the live Queen series had gone off the air in 1952. Three years later the Pincus brothers, who had produced that program, formed a small independent company they called Norvin Productions and put their previous show on film as the syndicated series *The New Adventures of Ellery Queen* (1955-56), a misleading title indeed since at least half of its 32 episodes were based on scripts from the Lee Bowman era of the live program. Signed for the role of Ellery was Hugh Marlowe, the first actor to have played the part on radio and in Fred Dannay's opinion the finest, although Manny Lee loudly dissented from that view. Florenz Ames from the live Queen series returned as the Inspector. Most of the episodes were directed by old B-movie hands like Ray Nazarro and Harold Schuster, and among the actors who appeared in one or more segments were Elisha Cook, Jr., Sherry Jackson and Brian Keith. As in the live series, detection was conspicuous by its absence. Though still gifted with a beautiful voice, Marlowe's Ellery bore little resemblance to the master sleuth loved by readers—and by listeners when he'd played the same part on radio.

***

With almost no exceptions, every Ellery Queen anthology since *101 Years' Entertainment* (1941) and every Queen novel and story collection since *Calamity Town* (1942) had been published by Little, Brown. Between *The Brown Fox Mystery* (1948) and *The Blue Herring Mystery* (1954), all written under Manny's supervision by Samuel Duff McCoy, even the "Ellery Queen, Jr." books had been Little, Brown titles. For reasons I haven't been able to determine, that regime came to an end late in 1955 with the tenth *Queen's Awards* volume. Boucher (December 18, 1955) wrote that the book "contains few true detective stories but a number of impressive studies in the psychology and sociology of crime." First prize that year went to Stanley Ellin's "The Moment of Decision," which Boucher called "as insoluble a challenge story as has appeared since [Frank R. Stockton's] 'The Lady Or the Tiger'."

CHAPTER EIGHTEEN

Third Period Twilight

IN THE MIDDLE 1950S, when the American family was being idealized on TV series like *Father Knows Best* and *Leave It to Beaver*, what was life like in the Dannay and Lee families?

Fred and Hilda had settled into the house on Byron Lane in Larchmont which would be the Dannay home until Fred's death. Their son, brain-damaged Stephen, had died in 1954 at age six. The boy's parents were still raising Fred's sons by his first marriage. When not plotting the next Queen novel or short story, Fred spent long hours editing the next *EQMM* issue or the next anthology of stories from the magazine. According to a brief profile in *Coronet* (February 1956) he did much of his manuscript reading in bed.

With the decline and fall of dramatic radio, Manny and Kaye Lee had returned from the west coast and made their new home in suburban Connecticut, first in Westport, later on a 63-acre estate in Roxbury which they bought in 1951. According to one of Manny's letters to Tony Boucher (December 4, 1951), the purchase price was an amazingly cheap $35,000. The main house, on South Street, was huge and painted white and dated back to 1792. The Lees quickly discovered that the bare oak planking of the upstairs dressing room had been defaced by a coat of gray deck paint and, in the words of their son Rand, who was a baby at the time, "stripped it together inch by inch, marveling at the blockheadedness of anyone who could not comprehend the glory of old oak." That was the room where, twenty years later, Manny died.

By 1954 he and Kaye were raising a total of eight children: the five they had had together, Kaye's daughter by her first marriage, and Manny's two daughters by *his* first marriage, who joined the household in 1951 when they were in their late teens. Manny had been a boy of the tough Brownsville streets but took to the life of a country gentleman as if to the manor born, buying a station wagon for the family, keeping chickens and cows, helping make butter and pasteurized milk for home consumption, planning a garden, declaring his property a game preserve, relaxing with his collection of around 4,000 classical music records, adding to the stamps and medals he had amassed over the years.

Both Manny and Kaye were animal lovers, and their son Rand has put together a catalogue of the non-humans who shared the Roxbury property. The house was "filled with Chesapeake Bay retrievers. . . ." There was also a toucan they called Mr. Kipling who shouted Kip-kip-ka-KIP from his flight cage eighteen hours a day. When Kaye went into the cage to change his food and water, the bird "would sit on his perch and run her hair through his beak over and over, uttering low moans." Then there were "several cows" and "an Indian pony named Patsy" and a coop full of chickens and "a longtailed black and white magpie named Billy who used to call the dogs and laugh at them when they came running" and "a wild garter snake that used to crawl into Mother's lap and fall asleep there when she was weeding in the garden" and some parakeets and canaries and a pair of lovebirds and some sheep, "including a ram who butted Mother halfway across the yard one morning. . . ."

Manny's workroom was about a hundred yards from the main house's kitchen door, a small converted cottage that had been a schoolhouse in the Revolutionary War era. The most vivid description of this period in his life we also owe to Rand.

> At home, I knew him as a pot-bellied, tee-shirted, smoke-enveloped, irritable hater of parties, whose idea of Hell was having to make the journey into New York to meet with his publisher, or [Fred], or attend some MWA

dinner. He worked four hours a day in his study and spent much of the rest of the time doing crossword puzzles, driving to New Milford, or watching TV news and sports broadcasts, upon which he commented loudly with the transplanted New Yorker's love-hate for the Mets and the liberal's contempt for the stupidity and racism of Man. He ate voraciously, jealously guarding his stashes of refrigerated citrus salad and lox. Though he left the running of house, children, dogs, cats, birds, and gardens to my mother, he occasionally cooked for pleasure, and to this day I have never eaten beef and vegetable soup to compare with his: I used to marvel at the textures of the vegetables floating in the dark broth, and the thin golden sheen of the fat that haloed each morsel.

For many of the vivid details with which he fleshed out the Queen novels and stories he drew on family and friends. "My mother would use pet words and mannerisms that would frequently appear in his books," said Christopher Rebecca Lee, Manny's oldest daughter with Kaye. "When I was a teenager it would wreck it for me. I'd be reading about this glamorous woman and then out would come one of my mother's phrases." The noise level of Manny's collaborations with Fred remained deafening as ever. Rand Lee was an ear-witness to some of the fights. "Often I would pick up the phone, hoping the line was free, and put down the receiver moments later with Dad's and Fred's arguing voices still ringing in my ears. On one occasion, Dad threw down a plot outline and exclaimed, 'He gives me the most ridiculous characters to work with and expects me to make them realistic!'"

Judging from his letters to Boucher, Manny had been a classic Type A personality during the radio years, which probably shortened his life. With that time of insanely high pressure behind him, he remained productive but managed to slow down and relax as most workaholics are never able to do. "Dad didn't act like a famous author," Rand recalled. "He watched baseball on TV in his shorts and T-shirt; he hated parties and had to be blackmailed into wearing a tie." At one of those parties, at the house of his neighbor the novelist William Styron, he was cornered by a fanatical Queen devotee and fell asleep in a chair while she gushed at him. When he gave a talk at the local school, his daughter

Christopher's fifth-grade teacher was dumbfounded to discover that "Ellery Queen" was not the prototype WASP hunk she had always imagined but a short stocky Jew wearing overalls and red socks. Manny took an increasingly active role in Roxbury's civic life, serving in 1957-58 as Justice of the Peace, later beating his playwright neighbor Arthur Miller in an election for a seat on the Library Board.

***

Ellery had not appeared as protagonist of a novel since 1953's *The Scarlet Letters*. As if to suggest that the cousins were trying to wean themselves from their series characters, he was also absent from their next short novel and their next full-length novel after *The Glass Village*.

"Terror Town" (*Argosy*, August 1956) introduces us to the deftly sketched New England hamlet of Northfield, which might almost be Wrightsville passing under an alias. The town is being plagued by a series of violent crimes, all taking place at the muddy gravesite where the first body, that of a farmer's son, had been discovered. The off-and-on romance between librarian Susan Marsh and deputy sheriff Linc Pearce slowly merges into the killings, to which the town reacts just as vilely as had New York City in *Cat of Many Tails* and Shinn Corners in *The Glass Village*. The solution, which is reached without deductions, exposes a murderer with delusions of divinity recalling *Ten Days' Wonder*. The crucial facts about passage of title to a certain automobile are kept from the reader too long, and I can't quite believe that the police couldn't tell what killed the first victim, but otherwise this is a good solid novelet, adapted seven years later into an equally good hour-long telefilm.

***

After the *Queen's Bureau of Investigation* collection Fred and Manny switched publishers from Little, Brown to Simon & Schuster, whose imprint was on the final novels of their third period. *Inspector Queen's Own Case* (1956) resembles *The Glass Village* only in that Ellery is again absent, and that his absence results in an excellent novel that would have been impossible had he been a character. The theme this time is gerontology, the process of growing old—a theme possibly related to the fact that both Fred and Manny had recently turned fifty. We open with Richard Queen involuntarily separated from the NYPD, having reached the mandatory retirement age of 63. Ellery is traveling in Europe for the summer and Richard is visiting his old compadre Abe Pearl, now chief of police in the sleepy hamlet of Taugus, Connecticut. Feeling glum, useless, slipsliding into senescence, Richard happens to meet 49-year-old Jessie Sherwood, a trained nurse employed by millionaires Alton and Sarah Humffrey to care for their newly adopted baby. From this point forward we witness the ripening of Richard's and Jessie's relationship, which is evoked in all its ups and downs with delicate witchery. The event most responsible for bringing them together is the suffocation of two-month-old Michael Stiles Humffrey one summer night. Chief Pearl and the coroner's jury and the Humffreys themselves agree that the death was accidental but Jessie is certain that the baby was murdered. Richard takes up the quest with her—partly because he has nothing else to do, partly because he wants to see more of Jessie, hoping against hope that he isn't making himself look ridiculous to her, and perhaps partly because he believes her—and tries to prove that the dirty handprint she is convinced she saw on the pillow that smothered the baby (although it wasn't there when the police arrived) is more than a figment of her overwrought imagination. The trail leads to a shady lawyer, a fading nightclub singer, a walled sanitarium, a plush park Avenue apartment, and to more deaths, these indubitably murders. Although the solution is completely fair and deducible by the reader, it isn't deduced by anyone in the book but merely discovered.

The gerontology motif appears in several other aspects of the novel besides the relationship between Richard and Jessie. Every significant character with two exceptions is well past his or her prime, and even one of the exceptions, Connie Coy, is beginning to age. (The other exception is the baby, who provides deliberate contrast.) When Richard needs help on the case he goes to five police retirees, all feeling useless and delighted at the chance to see action again. They call themselves the 87th Street Irregulars after the Baker Street Irregulars in the Sherlock Holmes stories, who of course were a group of young boys. The plot owes much to the traditional Gothic romance—female outsider comes to lonely mansion to work for gaunt and wealthy master, claims that an apparent accidental death was murder but can get no one to believe her, prowls about mansion by night and is trapped by killer and rescued at last minute by ardent swain—but with the switch that all the characters are in their middle years or older.

As usual in third-period Queen, there are echoes from earlier works. The true/false confession stems from *The Siamese Twin Mystery* (1933), the Humffreys function much like the Cazalises in *Cat of Many Tails* (1949), the construction and fortuitous timing of the Connie Coy murder recall the death of Margo Cole in *The Dragon's Teeth* (1939). But all these elements are reworked and integrated into the new framework, turning *Inspector Queen's Own Case* into a superbly written story of vividly drawn characters and an excellent mystery as well. Boucher (September 30, 1956) called it "a quiet, gentle novel" and its gerontology theme "developed . . . with tenderness and understanding."

Two months later Simon & Schuster published the eleventh volume of best stories from *EQMM*, the overall title changed to *Ellery Queen's Awards*. Boucher's review (November 25, 1956) questioned whether the $1,500 first prize might not more fittingly have gone to the contributions by Stanley Ellin, David Alexander or Veronica Parker Johns rather than to the actual winner, A.H.Z. Carr's "The Black Kitten," but lavished praise on the book as a whole. "[H]ardly any anthology chosen from assorted sources can equal this collection from a single magazine."

***

There was no new Queen novel the following year, but late that spring Simon & Schuster issued *In The Queens' Parlor* (1957), an assortment of *EQMM* editorial shoptalk including a number of the informative introductions with which Fred Dannay for years had been prefacing the tales he printed or reprinted in *EQMM*. Boucher (May 26, 1957) did all he could to boost the volume, calling its material "somewhat shapeless, occasionally incomplete without the story meant to be introduced . . . , but wholly captivating to any prowler of mystery by-paths. . . ." If it had sold decently, Fred told me, there would have been a sequel. But sales were miserable, as almost anyone could have predicted, and thousands of words of his criminous commentary remain buried in issues of *EQMM* dating roughly from 1946 to 1955.

The twelfth volume of the series now called *Ellery Queen's Awards* came out in the fall. This time Boucher was more critical than usual, referring to it (October 6, 1957) as "the least distinguished of these annual collections . . . with a tiresome insistence on the theme of juvenile delinquency." But he did have high praise for five of its sixteen stories including contributions by Avram Davidson, Charlotte Armstrong, Dorothy Salisbury Davis and Stanley Ellin.

***

The previous Queen novel, *Inspector Queen's Own Case*, had been subtitled: November Song by Ellery Queen. The obvious inference was that with December the canon would end, and in fact the next Queen novel was not only set in December but published as *The Finishing Stroke* (1958). The opening sequence takes us back to 1905, the year Fred and Manny were born, and deals with the last days of publisher John Sebastian, whose son is born in the middle of an ice storm. Most of the novel, however, unfolds between Christmas Eve of 1929 and Epiphany of 1930. A cocksure young literatus named Ellery Queen has just published his first book, *The Roman Hat Mystery*. (Remember T.S. Eliot's "In my end is my beginning"?) Arthur B. Craig, Sebastian's ex-partner, has invited Ellery and a number of other guests—including a composer, an actress, a doctor, a lawyer, a clergyman and a publisher—to his estate for a 12-day house party, at the end of which his ward, John Sebastian, Jr., is to come into his father's fortune and marry the fashion designer he loves. The festive mood begins to dissolve when a costumed Santa Claus distributes gifts and then vanishes. Then all sorts of bizarre objects start to pop up, each addressed to John Sebastian and accompanied by a piece of doggerel derived from the traditional English carol "The Twelve Days of Christmas." The first gift, a sandalwood ox, is followed by a toy house, a tiny lead camel, and so on. An unidentified body is discovered in the Craig library, more weird gifts turn up, John Sebastian begins to act like a schizophrenic, blackmail and a love quadrangle and a second murder enter the picture. Ellery is unable to shed any light until 28 years later, when chance again throws the case in his path and he sees the truth.

The characters of *The Finishing Stroke* are little more than line drawings, the prose is direct and unadorned, and the extremely simple plot abounds in hoary clichés like the snowbound house party, the thirteenth guest, murder with an antique dagger in the lordly mansion's library, a séance, identical twins, and mysterious clues dropped by an unseen hand. The cousins deliberately chose overfamiliar elements so as to reduce the genre to its barest fundamentals. Everything is stylized, reflexive, nostalgic, elegiac—in a word that ties together much of the book's matter and manner, abecedarian. At the end of the novel both Arthur Craig and Inspector Queen have reached the last of Shakespeare's seven ages of man, "Sans teeth, sans eyes, sans taste, sans everything." After that what can come but the end, which is also the beginning? The letters "ABC" are repeated in the book's last line.

As usual the plot resounds with echoes from earlier Queen novels and stories. For an assortment of seemingly unrelated objects showing up at an isolated house party, see "The Mad Tea-Party" (1934). Ellery's irrelevant attempts to connect each suspect with the number 12 parallels the long and equally irrelevant game of Who Is Backward in *The Chinese Orange Mystery* (1934). The Iagoesque adversary with an uncanny ability to manipulate others' thinking goes back to *The Greek Coffin Mystery* (1932) and *Ten Days' Wonder* (1948) and several other Queen novels, but that kind of character simply can't be convincing in the *eine kleine Nachtkriminalroman* ambience of *The Finishing Stroke*. The plot couldn't have happened but for John Sebastian's idiotic and unmotivated keeping quiet about his brother, even after the murder. But John's behavior is a model of lucidity next to that of his brother, who had neither the motive nor the requisite knowledge to make the two blackmail attempts that the novel credits to him.

At the beginning of Chapter VI one of the characters mentions an All-American halfback who's about to play his last college game and who acquits himself "with valedictory brilliance." During a discussion of popular musicians in Chapter VIII, Ellen Craig remarks: "They play standard works familiar to everybody, and they play them beautifully." These are clear hints that Fred and Manny wanted to end their career as novelists on a note of quiet mastery. Boucher (February 16, 1958) made it clear that in his view they had succeeded admirably, recalling with nostalgia the Golden Age of pure detective fiction, "a preposterous yet wondrous world in which murderers plotted patterns of complex magnificence and detectives challenged the reader to a duel of wits. . . ." He went on to describe *The Finishing Stroke* as "wildly imaginative yet sternly disciplined, complete with startling surprises, shrewdly placed deadfalls for the clever, and even the formal Challenge to the Reader. . . . [T]he novel's true setting is Cloudcuckooland, its true time Nevernever—and how good it is to be back there and then!" I would love to be able to share Boucher's enthusiasm, but I still feel that Fred and Manny deserved a more perfect "December Song."

CHAPTER NINETEEN

At Random

THE COUSINS' LIVES after the publication of *The Finishing Stroke* give clear signs that they had retired from fiction writing but not from life. Fred Dannay sold his huge library of detective short story collections to the University of Texas and wound up spending two semesters on its Austin campus as a professor of creative writing. He never thought of turning over his *EQMM* editorial work to anyone else and in fact arranged a contest, with publication in the magazine the grand prize, for the best story submitted by one of his students. The name Ellery Queen continued to appear almost as frequently as if Fred and Manny were still doing everything they'd been doing before, but the only aspects of the Queen franchise which continued as in the past were the monthly issues of the magazine and the annual Best from *EQMM* volume, which in the fall of 1958 moved from Simon & Schuster to Random House and the aegis of legendary editor Lee Wright (1902-1986), who among other coups had purchased Anthony Boucher's first detective novel and the first suspense novels by Cornell Woolrich.

Soon after the cousins' retirement a new and ambitious attempt was made to turn their character into a star of the small screen. *The Further Adventures Of Ellery Queen* (1958-1959) was broadcast on the NBC network, live and (if you were one of the handful who owned a color set) in color, under the supervision of Albert McCleery, one of the top producers of Fifties teledrama. For the first twenty weeks Ellery was played by George Nader (1920-2002), a hunk of beefcake in the Tony Curtis mold, who had starred in Universal features like *Man Afraid* (1957) and *Flood Tide* (1958) and, in the Sixties, relocated to Germany where he played FBI agent Jerry Cotton in a series of ersatz James Bond flicks. McCleery admitted in a *TV Guide* interview that he'd never read a Queen novel or story but claimed that his ignorance was irrelevant because "of all the Queen material, we can use only four of the novels." In fact he used six. "We're going to spend money for scripts and actors," he continued, "not costly props and sets." But the acting turned out to be adequate at best and most of the scripts abominable. Six of the first eight segments were very freely adapted from Queen novels. The debut episode, "The Glass Village" (September 26, 1958) was surprisingly good—with Johnny Shinn, the lead character in the stand-alone novel of the same name, replaced by Ellery as Fred and Manny had originally intended—but the other five were awful. The remaining fourteen episodes with Nader in the lead were based on mystery novels by a wide assortment of American writers including Harold Q. Masur, William P. McGivern, Hillary Waugh, John Roeburt (who was story editor for the series), and Edgar Box, the mystery-writing pseudonym of Gore Vidal. Shoehorning Ellery into these scripts as a substitute for radically different detectives like Masur's Scott Jordan and Box's Peter Sargeant did little to improve the show's quality.

After twenty weeks Nader left the series and was replaced by Lee Philips (1927-1999), who played Ellery as a man of awareness and compassion, much closer to the character from the Queen novels of the Forties and Fifties. The series switched from live performances to videotape and the policy of adapting miscellaneous mystery novels was scrapped in favor of original scripts. The first of Philips' dozen episodes, "Shadow of the Past" (February 27, 1959), struck me at the time as superb, so much so that I wondered whether the author of the teleplay, one Sam Dann, might have been a disguised Fred Dannay. (It wasn't.) But despite the fine actors who consistently appeared in the series— Conrad Nagel, Ruth Warrick, Alexander Scourby, Martin Balsam, Judith Evelyn, Wayne Morris, Glenda Farrell, Leueen MacGrath, Hurd Hatfield and Morey Amsterdam, to name a few—none of the subsequent eleven matched the premiere in quality. The final episode, "This Murder Comes to You Live" (June 5, 1959), was written by Ben Hecht, who also played Alonzo Christian, a flamboyant poet murdered on a live TV talk show with Ellery in the studio. Featured in the cast were Geraldine Fitzgerald, Ray Walston and Buster Crabbe.

***

If the TV series was a disappointment, the annual *EQMM* anthologies continued to draw high praise. The thirteenth in the series, which was also the first to be published by Random House and the first not to be built around a prize contest, sported the grandiose title *Ellery Queen's Thirteenth Annual: A Selection of New Stories from Ellery Queen's Mystery Magazine* (1958), and coincidentally (or was it?) contained thirteen stories—by Stanley Ellin, Robert Bloch, Agatha Christie and John Dickson Carr, among others. Boucher (November 2, 1958) called it "one of the best of the annuals. . . . It's clear that, even without prizes, Queen's taste and editorial skill and the prestige of his magazine will attract the best crime stories now being written." The following year's volume bore the simpler title *Ellery Queen's 14th Mystery Annual* and contained fifteen stories by, among others, Stanley Ellin, John Collier, Ray Bradbury, Agatha Christie, Hugh Pentecost, Somerset Maugham, Craig Rice, Margery Allingham, Cornell Woolrich, and one of the students in Fred's University of Texas creative writing class. Boucher's comments (October 4, 1959) were again ecstatic. "I can't recall that ever before, in reviewing an anthology, I have felt compelled to mention every story in it. . . . This fourteenth volume is, friends, a beauty even by Queen standards—and there are no higher." As for *Ellery Queen's 15th Mystery Annual* (1960), his comments (October 2, 1960) were briefer than usual, but he maintained that the volume "upholds the dizzyingly high standards of this series. . . ." and singled out a "subtle study in the origin of evil" by Stanley Ellin, "an entertaining scrap of juvenilia" by a 13-year-old F. Scott Fitzgerald, and "possibly the funniest and most adroit of all parody-pastiches of Sherlock Holmes," the first in a long series by Robert L. Fish. *Ellery Queen's 16th Mystery Annual* (1961), which contained 22 tales, was also very much to Boucher's taste. In his review (September 10, 1961) he called it "one of the best volumes of short stories I've ever read in the crime field—and I'm not sure I needed to add those last four words. . . . [T]he whole book has about it a happy air of freshness, as if editor, authors and reader were all discovering for the first time the wonders of the short story of crime."

At this point someone, probably either Fred Dannay or Lee Wright or both, decided that including the number of each year's volume of *EQMM* stories served no commercial purpose. The following year's collection of 21 tales was simply called *To Be Read Before Midnight* (1962). Judging from his review (October 7, 1962), Boucher was especially fond of the contribution by Avram Davidson, which had won an Edgar award from MWA as best story of its year just a few months before.

The following year the old numbering was back but as part of a stand-alone title, *Ellery Queen's Mystery Mix No. 18* (1963), published about two months before the Kennedy assassination. For this one volume Fred revived the traditional contest that had been dropped a few years earlier and immediately awarded the first prize to a story by Cornell Woolrich that he'd bought for $250 back in 1958 and had been holding in reserve ever since. Thanks to the flood of suspense-packed novels and stories he'd published between 1934 and 1948, Woolrich was a living legend, widely recognized as the Hitchcock of the written word, but he had written very little since the late Forties, and Fred hoped that the prize check for $1,150, which Woolrich received in January 1962, would encourage him to resume his career in earnest. "One Drop of Blood" appeared in *EQMM* for April 1962, and Boucher in his review of the *Mystery Mix* anthology (September 29, 1963) voiced agreement with Fred's decision, calling the Woolrich tale "a powerful inverted detective story which seems to me the best thing [he] has done in many years. . . ." He did fault Fred as contest conductor for making a "quite unfortunate choice" for best first story of the year, but with his hard-wired kindness he declined to name the author, and so shall I.

Ellery Queen's Double Dozen (1964) contained an unusually generous 24 stories plus, as Boucher pointed out (September 6, 1964), "a larger sampling of Queen's [meaning Fred's] interesting editorial commentaries than has been the case in recent years." Among the authors whose contributions he especially liked were Stanley Ellin, John D. MacDonald and relative newcomer Edward D. Hoch (1930-2008), who would have a story in every issue of the magazine from 1973 until his death 35 years later.

The final Best-of-*EQMM* anthology published by Random House was *Ellery Queen's 20th Anniversary Annual* (1965), which fittingly contained exactly twenty tales including gems by Dorothy Salisbury Davis, Michael Gilbert and Lawrence Treat. Boucher (September 5, 1965) called the book "one of the best in the whole dazzling series. . . . The 20th anniversary is china, and Queen's contributors have matched the highest standards of Spode or Wedgwood."

***

During his long sabbatical from fiction writing, Fred decided that the back files of *EQMM* could provide material for a second annual anthology, this one a generous assortment of originals and reprints from the magazine's 20-year history, issued in paperback by Davis Publications, which also put out the magazine each month. Never averse to softcover originals, Boucher reviewed these volumes too. In his *Times* column (October 25, 1959) he publicly hoped that *Ellery Queen's 1960 Anthology* would "become (as its title should indicate) an annual event." A year later he praised the 1961 anthology for its "scope and variety" and for its inclusion of "long novelettes" by Georges Simenon and Hugh Pentecost. He was even fonder of *Ellery Queen's 1962 Anthology* because, as he said (November 12, 1961), "the primary emphasis is upon the simon-pure detective story, and sixteen of the twenty-three stories feature a detective at work—and in a dozen cases a familiar and respected series detective. . . . [T]he contents page is a roster of the great names in fictional detection . . . plus a smattering of Big Names from other fields" like Ray Bradbury, Arthur Miller and Sinclair Lewis.

On the publication of *Ellery Queen's 1963 Anthology*, which offered 150,000 words by 19 authors for a mere $1, he complained mildly (October 7, 1962) that "not a few stories . . . have seen print in books and even in other anthologies. . . ." Some of the tales in these thick paperback volumes may have been overfamiliar, but Fred decided to increase production from one to two books a year. Boucher was not disappointed by the 1963 mid-year edition of *EQA*, offering special kudos to "strong novelettes by Carr, Gardner and Stout" and "a superb pair of contrasting short stories by T.S. Stribling and Melville Davisson Post. . . ."

Ellery Queen's 1964 Anthology offered what Boucher (October 20, 1963) called "a startling bargain. . . .": nineteen short stories and novelettes "of remarkably high quality." Among the tales included in the 1964 mid-year anthology were works by Rex Stout, John Dickson Carr, Roy Vickers, Philip MacDonald and, to quote Boucher (March 22, 1964), "an extraordinary and brilliant essay in logical fantasy by, of all people, George Bernard Shaw. You can't find a better use for a buck."

Ellery Queen's 1965 Anthology was the first of these paperbacks to have a central theme of sorts: each author represented was a past president of MWA. "A unique anthology," Boucher said (October 18, 1964) "and, despite a few unavoidable weak spots, an excellent one." His review of the next mid-year volume (April 4, 1965) singled out a Nero Wolfe novelette by Rex Stout, stories by Stanley Ellin and Cornell Woolrich, and a "neglected classic of murder and detection" by, of all people, Edith Wharton. But he drew the line when Fred began recycling yet again some stories that had already been printed or reprinted in both *EQMM* and one of these paperback anthologies. In his review (December 27, 1964) of *Ellery Queen's 12* (Dell pb #259, 1964) he called the book "a random assembly of" stories "you're pretty sure to have read . . . before." That he didn't bother to list even a single author suggests his growing exasperation. In his review (December 12, 1965) of *Ellery Queen's Lethal Black Book* (Dell pb #2261, 1965), he dismissed this sequel volume as "a shapeless regathering of stories all of which had appeared recently in other Queen paperback anthologies." At this point the Dell series came to an abrupt and unmourned end.

***

After a few years' sabbatical from fiction writing, Fred Dannay decided that it was time to start creating more plot synopses for Manny Lee to expand into Ellery Queen novels but found himself stymied as he had never been before. During the hiatus years Manny had developed some kind of writer's block and was unable to work on any more collaborations with his cousin. As we know from his letters to Boucher, he'd been "chafing for years under the glossy artificial brittle manufactures put out under the Queen name. . . ." To his daughter Christopher he called himself "a literary prostitute." Random House editor Lee Wright empathized with his frustration and offered him a contract committing Random to publish, sight unseen, any novel he might write alone. Manny started *Welcome to Bugsville*, which his son Rand called "a humorous work about our family's legion of pets. . . ," but abandoned the manuscript after a few pages and never sent Wright that or anything else.

Manny's paralysis, of course, left Fred paralyzed too. Unlike his cousin, he had written a novel on his own (*The Golden Summer*), but he must not have felt capable of writing an Ellery Queen book solo. The only solution was to enlist another author or authors to carry on Manny's function of fleshing out Fred's lengthy synopses into novels. The Scott Meredith literary agency, which represented the Queen output, found two appropriate replacements for Manny, neither well known in the mystery field but both with high reputations in science fiction.

The Player on the Other Side (1963) was written by Theodore Sturgeon (1918-1985) from Fred's outline, with both Fred and Manny fine-tuning Sturgeon's version before publication. The setting is York Square, an isolated pocket of the past that is in New York City but not of it. At each corner of the square is a castle and in its center a diamond-shaped park. The castle on the southwest corner is inhabited by Robert York, a cold precise philatelist; the one on the northwest corner by Emily York, a white-haired and determined social worker; the building on the southeast corner by Myra York, a gentle but mentally unbalanced lush; that on the northeast corner by aging womanizer Percival York. All four cousins are required to live in York Square by the terms of Nathaniel York, Sr.'s will, which provides that after ten years' residence they'll inherit his millions in equal shares, with the share of any cousin who dies during the residence period to be divided among the survivors. That's right, our old friend the tontine again. Walt, a weak-brained and robot-like handyman, serves as caretaker for all the cousins, three of whom also share the same housekeeper. Robert employs a young intellectual to help with his stamp collecting and Myra engages a lovely young woman as her nurse and companion. Along with Nathaniel York, Jr., the long-dead (or is he?) son of the founder of the empire, these are the characters at the heart of the novel when murder and madness strike.

We know from the start the murderer's identity. The person sending a paper polygon stamped with a cryptic initial to each of the cousins before killing them is the caretaker Walt. But this zombie is a simple soldier following orders, carrying out the detailed written instructions of an Iago figure who is using him as a living murder weapon. The unknown's signature is Y.

When we first see Ellery, he's suffering from writer's block, obviously a reference to Manny's problem but with a different cause, one that at least in part explains the isolated settings of novels like *The King Is Dead* and *The Finishing Stroke*. He himself, the quintessential man of reason, and the rationalistic kind of detective story that had been his career (and his creators'), have become implausible and obsolete thanks to the rise of technology and forensic science, not to mention the immense success of more naturalistic police procedural mysteries like TV's *Dragnet* and Ed McBain's 87th Precinct series. Fred's solution, here and in later Queen novels of this fourth period, was to set Ellery down in one milieu after another that is as remote from external reality as the inside of an egg and as stylized as a chessboard, which is the unifying image in *The Player on the Other Side*, the four castles being in the exact positions of the rooks, or castles, at the start of a game. In *Cat of Many Tails* (1949) Richard Queen had prodded his son out of guilt-haunted detachment by dangling before him the bait of involvement with the real world, but in *Player* the Inspector prods him out of the real world and onto the chessboard of York Square. As the murders continue and Ellery several times comes achingly close to the part of the truth we readers have known from the beginning, the complex patterns of the web become bit by bit more intelligible until they coalesce in the encounter with Y, the player on the other side.

Boucher must have known that another author had replaced Manny in the Queen collaboration as Boucher himself in the Forties had replaced Fred, but in the *Times Book Review* (September 22, 1963) he found the solution "as startling as it is fair and faultlessly clued" and the book as a whole "gratifyingly authentic Queen. . . ." In view of his all but brotherly friendship with Manny, it must have hurt him deeply to be compelled by honesty to suggest in print that Manny was not indispensable. Of course no one but a handful of insiders could have understood. *Player* is a superb novel but, like *Ten Days' Wonder*, it can't be discussed seriously without the revelation of a key element. Y—or, as he also signs himself, JHWH—turns out to be not just a human being but Yahweh, Jehovah, the stern and vengeful father. The primal Y. God. As in *The Tragedy of Y* (1932) we have once again a morally irresponsible murderer whose acts are under the control of Y, indeed of a father and a York. As in *Ten Days' Wonder*, the climactic moment has Ellery witness God's death. If the earlier book turned inside out the old teaching that man was made in God's image, this one inverts the maxim that God manifests himself in the meek and humble of heart. If there's any inspiration for *Player* beyond earlier Queen novels, it's clearly Alfred Hitchcock's *Psycho* (1960). "I think we're all in our private traps," Tony Perkins as Norman Bates tells Janet Leigh before the shower scene. "Clamped in them. And none of us can ever get out. We scratch and claw, but only at the air, only at each other, and for all of it we never budge an inch. . . . I was born in mine." The film is about being trapped in the past, the novel deals with manipulating and being manipulated, but the former is a paradigm of the human condition in the one as the latter is in the other. "One is played upon, not player."

***

For reasons still unclear, Theodore Sturgeon never worked with Fred on another Queen novel. Performing Manny's function the next time was Avram Davidson (1923-1993), another star of science fiction, several of whose non-s.f. stories had first appeared in *EQMM*. Fred told me that *And on the Eighth Day* (1964) was inspired by his reading about the Dead Sea Scrolls. Having known him, I suspect his source was Edmund Wilson's series of articles in *The New Yorker*. The novel is set in the spring of 1944, one of the bloodiest years of World War II. Having spent the last four months in Hollywood writing scripts for Army training films, Ellery has reached the point of collapse from sheer exhaustion and is sent home. Driving across the western desert, he loses his way and comes upon what amounts to a lost race, a religious-socialist community that has created a sort of Eden in the wilderness. On hearing Ellery's name, the Teacher of the community prostrates himself in awe, for the Sacred Book had foretold that this man would come, and that great trouble would come with him, and that a second visitor greater than the first would follow him. Unsure whether he's dreaming or awake, Ellery enters the Valley of Quenan, where all property is held in common, no crime or violence has taken place in fifty years, the word war is not in the vocabulary, no one is alienated from their labor, and natural harmony connects humankind and the earth. In a phrase, Eden before the Fall. But the fall seems imminent. On the second night of Ellery's stay, someone tampers with the Teacher's key to the Sanquetum, the forbidden room in the Holy Congregation House which none but the Teacher may enter. The tampering recurs the following night. The next afternoon Storicai the storesman is found bludgeoned to death in the Holy Congregation House. Murder in Eden, and Ellery, the only person in the valley who knows anything about crime, must identify the murderer.

The structure of *And on the Eighth Day* is kept very simple since the first violent act in a civilization can hardly be made to happen under locked-room conditions. The plot is not terribly interesting and in some respects incredible, for instance the matter of those fingerprints on the hammer. But here more than in any other Queen novel the plot is a pretext for something deeper. What that something is can easily be misconstrued as a one-for-one allegory of the passion, death and resurrection of Jesus as related in the Gospels. And, up to a point, the Teacher with his last supper and trial and his taking upon himself and suffering and dying for the sins of the community is meant to evoke Jesus. At the same time, judging from the manner of his death, he's Socrates; and judging from the fact that instead of a physical resurrection his spirit is reincarnated in another, he's a Buddhist or Hindu figure too. If Ellery stands for John the Baptist, the forerunner of the Greater who is to follow, he's also both Moses—based on the encounter with the flaming bush and the trek through the desert to the promised land—and Pilate, the prosecutor of the Teacher. The Crownsil of Twelve simultaneously evokes the Apostles, and the Sanhedrin, the body which condemned the Teacher, and perhaps organized Christianity since greed for temporal power and material wealth lead it to betray its Teacher's simple message of peace and love. The exception that proves the rule of multi-functionality is Storicai, whose name is an anagram of Iscariot and whose acts are easily identified with the Biblical Judas. All sorts of secular resonances—Cortez and Montezuma, Churchill, Bernard Shaw and Amy Lowell, to name a few—are included in order to create a sense of "the recurrence of the great and the famous across the shifting planes of space-time." This sense of historical awe parallels the sense of religious awe, the intuition of the presence of the numinous, which is the novel's central thrust. "It is too much . . .—too much, too much, too much; it's more than reason can bear. . . . Too much, an infinite complexity beyond the grasp of man. Acknowledge. Acknowledge and depart."

Unique as this is among the Queen novels, it's still packed with themes and devices we've seen in the canon before. First there's the isolated milieu, discussed above in connection with *The Player on the Other Side*. Then there are the false solution followed by the true one, and the enchantment with "the lovely past" as in *The Finishing Stroke*, and the distrust of human nature even in Eden as in *The Origin of Evil*. Finally we must note the pervasiveness of a condition which in any other atmosphere but the numinous one of this novel we'd have to call manipulatedness. *And on the Eighth Day* uses the detective-story form, which is based on the power of reason to order chaos and comprehend truth, in a manner calculated to undercut our faith in reason. It's not an intellectually exciting detective novel but attempts to reach higher beyond the genre than perhaps any other detective novel.

After reading the book twice, a month apart, and giving it a great deal of thought, Boucher frankly didn't know what to make of it, and said so in his review (March 29, 1964). "Queen is attempting a good deal more than a mystery here—indeed something in the nature of a Mystery. . . ." Thanks to "this serious, sincere, almost mystical element," he went on, the novel at times "seems daringly and movingly right" and at other times "it seems to fall lamentably close to bathos and parody."

***

The following year's early months saw publication of *Queens Full* (1965), a mixed bag of two short novels, one short story and a pair of short-shorts. Two of the five were first published in the years Manny Lee was suffering from writer's block, and it remains unknown who expanded Fred Dannay's synopses for those into finished products. Could it have been Anthony Boucher? Could he at different times have performed both the Dannay function and the Lee function for the cousins?

"The Death of Don Juan" (*Argosy*, May 1962; *EQMM*, August 1964) is set in Wrightsville and deals with the attempt of the town's amateur theatrical company to stage a creaky old turn-of-the-century melodrama. (In his student days Boucher had worked in Little Theater, and on his first date with the woman who was to become his wife, the couple went to a creaky old-time melodrama. Coincidence, or a clue to the identity of Fred's collaborator?) When the once-famous alcoholic wreck slated for the leading role of Don Juan breaks his wrist and ribs shortly before opening night and another has-been is rushed in as a replacement, the scene is set for offstage murder, complete with dying message. Ellery is in the opening-night audience and hears the crucial last words himself, but it's only after eliminating some red herrings through a dental test of his own design (shades of *The Dragon's Teeth*!) that he construes the message rightly and exposes a fairly obvious murderer. The satiric opportunities latent in the material are mostly wasted, and Wrightsville's new and hostile police chief Anse Newby is a pale shadow of old Chief Dakin. This short novel is trim and competent but lacks anything one could either fault or get excited about.

"E = Murder" (*This Week*, August 14, 1960; *EQMM*, May 1961) recycles the gimmick but not the plot of the Dannay-Lee radio play "The Booby Trap" (November 9/11, 1944). In this version Ellery's lecture at Bethesda University is interrupted by the murder of a noted physicist working on a top-secret project in a limited-access tower. Both Dr. Agon's dying message and Ellery's reading of it are pretty far-fetched, but so much is packed into the tale's eight pages that we're too busy sorting out possibilities to object.

In "The Wrightsville Heirs" (*Better Living*, January-February 1956; *EQMM*, November 1957), which with its soft lights and sloppy thinking was clearly designed for the women's slick magazine market, wealthy Bella Bluefield Livingston dies suspiciously soon after announcing that she's about to disinherit her three dissolute stepchildren and leave her fortune to her paid companion. Chief Dakin, not yet retired as in "The Death of Don Juan," summons Ellery to help find out which of the trio smothered the old lady to death. The answer is based on moronic reasoning, a ridiculous trap that proves nothing, and a colossally misinformed notion of how estates are administered, adding up to one of the worst Queen short stories of Period Three. The date of original publication makes it clear, however, that its expansion from Fred's synopsis was by Manny Lee.

The same is true of "Diamonds in Paradise" (*EQMM*, September 1954), a neat vignette in which Ellery untangles the last words of an unlucky gem-snatcher and recovers a pair of emeralds for a Broadway sex goddess without ever leaving the Queen apartment. Both the original version of this short-short and its much revised book version betray the influence of Damon Runyon.

"The Case Against Carroll" (*Argosy*, September 1958; *EQMM*, September 1960), also completed before Manny developed writer's block, is a gem of character interplay, moral ambiguity and leashed tension, second only to "The Lamp of God" among the Queen short novels. Attorney John Carroll is charged with the murder of his brutal partner Meredith Hunt, who was on the verge of ruining him. Swearing that he has a perfect alibi but can't prove it, he begs Ellery for help. In the death-house climax, which echoes *The Tragedy of Z* (1933), Ellery seems to do an act of terrible evil in order to accomplish some small good.

Boucher (April 4, 1965) was extremely kind to the three longer stories in the collection, which he called Ain the best Queen tradition of formal detection and elaborate gimmickry, with beautifully tricky examples of deceptive fair play." The two short-shorts he wrote off as "rather strained and verging on self-parody." Rarely has a Boucher review of one book been both too harsh and too gentle at the same time!

***

Later the same year came *The Fourth Side of the Triangle* (1965), expanded from Fred's synopsis by Avram Davidson. This novel is set in the present but its people and attitudes seem to date back to whodunits of the early 1920s, with Ellery incapacitated and offstage much of the time and coming a cropper when he finally does some detective work. As in *Ten Days' Wonder* there are very few central characters and most are concentrated in one family. Ashton McKell, last in a long line of merchant princes, and his wife Lutetia, a vague and submissive scatterbrain whose patrician existence has been sheltered beyond credibility, somehow managed to produce a son. Dane McKell is a handsome and headstrong young man with little talent but great ambition to be a novelist. When Lutetia tells Dane that Ashton has admitted an affair with another woman, the son decides to track down his father's lover and take his place in her bed so that dad will return to passionless fidelity. Dane's motives, which he only partly understands, recall Oedipus and Iago and Freud—and also Drury Lane. As a son he desires to supplant his father sexually, and symbolically to castrate him, but as a budding author he wants to intervene in a real-life drama and manipulate persons rather than fictitious characters. He shadows his father to a rendezvous in the McKells' own apartment building, takes steps to meet the lovely fashion designer who lives in the penthouse and begins his own campaign of sexual conquest which is cut short by murder within the four-sided triangle. With both legs broken in a skiing accident, Ellery is reduced to sitting or lying on the sidelines and making suggestions as the investigation leads to a first, then a second, finally a projected third murder trial. When he has healed and is ready to name the murderer, surprise and humiliation are waiting for him.

What's wrong with this novel? Plenty. The plot requires idiot procedure by the police and some whopping memory lapses by several characters, and its structure soon becomes mechanical and predictable. Inspector Queen's men turn up first all the evidence pointing to A, then all the pointers to B, then to C, conveniently missing every clue against B until the end of A's trial and all the clues pointing to C until the end of B's. The milieu is impossibly upper-upper, and incidental ethnic characters like the Irishwoman and the bartender speak in yes-sor-me-name-is-O'Rarke dialect. The false-solution-followed-by-the-truth device can be seen coming long before it arrives. The legal aspects would leave most lawyers laughing uproariously. Boucher's review (November 14, 1965) erred once more on the side of kindness. "As a novel of character [it] is rarely convincing, but as an exercise in the mechanics and form of the detective story it is impressive."

***

Not too long after *The Fourth Side of the Triangle* was published, the Queen operation broke ties with Random House and moved to the less prestigious New American Library. When I interviewed Random editor Lee Wright in 1979, she still vividly remembered the reason why. "He left Random House literally because Bennett Cerf didn't invite him to lunch. His feelings were hurt. . . . I said: 'Fred, Bennett isn't your editor. I am. You're sort of insulting me. My attention isn't enough for you, it has to be the head of the house, is what you're saying.'" That was Fred: hypersensitive to any suggestion that mystery writers were second-class literary citizens. Manny meanwhile had come to hate the genre and his own role in it. That he and Fred could have collaborated successfully even once, let alone for thirty years or so before the onset of his writer's block, is nothing short of a miracle.

***

Between November 1965 and February 1967 Ellery returned to radio, though in name only, in a syndicated package of 520 "Minute Mysteries." Neither Fred nor Manny had anything to do with the project beyond endorsing checks from the Cincinnati-based Creative Marketing and Communications Corporation for the use of their character, who was played by Bill Owen. A typical 60-second segment (my own pastiche, not a transcript) would sound like this.

> Friend: "Congratulate me, Ellery. What a deal I just
> made! Here, look at what I bought this morning. An

ancient Roman coin in mint condition. And it only cost me ten thousand dollars!"

Ellery: "Hmmmm. . . . According to these Roman numerals on the coin, it was minted in 37 B.C. Come on, let's find a policeman and visit that dealer's shop before he can cash your check. The coin's a fake."

Friend (flabbergasted): "Why—How do you know that, Ellery?"

Anyone who can't figure out needs to go back to third grade. These silly vignettes are reported to have caused outbreaks of giggles among personnel of the stations that aired them, but they could still be heard around the country at odd moments of the broadcast day until the early 1980s. When the licenses to air these programs were terminated, the Creative Marketing geniuses bleeped out Ellery's name from the audio masters and substituted "John Q."

CHAPTER TWENTY

An Intrusion of Ghosts

URING THE LONG HIATUS between Ellery's hardcover adventures in detection, something new began to appear under the Queen byline: original paperback novels, signed as by Queen but without Ellery and the other familiar characters dating back to 1929—indeed without series characters at all—or the Queen hallmarks of deductive fireworks and fairness to the reader, or Manny Lee's vivid and moving way with words. How did these paperbacks come to be? What connection if any did the cousins have with them? Are any of them worth reading in their own right? Almost forty years ago, when I was working on *Royal Bloodline: Ellery Queen, Author and Detective* (1974), Fred told me the whole story behind the paperback project but asked me to leave it out of my book. Since it was clear from what he told me that the softcovers really didn't belong in a discussion of Queen the author and Ellery the character, I agreed. But anyone who had learned from the Queen novels to read with care, and noticed the text's silence about almost thirty novels published as by Queen and the scrupulous listing of every one of those titles in the checklist at the end of my book, should have been able to figure out the truth.

For a number of years before 1960, the cousins had been represented by the Scott Meredith literary agency. As Fred explained to me, the paperbacks were launched when the Meredith people came up with a scheme to expand Queen's readership beyond the slowly fading genre of formal detective fiction and into the booming field of original softcover crime novels without detection. Contingent on the cousins' approval, Meredith arranged with Pocket Books editor Bucklin Moon for publication of a cycle of non-series paperback suspensers, to be ghost-written by other Meredith clients for a flat fee of around $2,000 per book and published under the Queen name, with all royalties split by Fred and Manny after the agency took its commission. Manny, who had a wife and eight children to support and was still suffering from writer's block, favored the idea. Fred was violently opposed but felt that his cousin's financial and creative problems left him little choice but to go along, especially since Manny had saved the Queen radio series by carrying on with Boucher and other plot suppliers when the death of Fred's first wife left him unable to perform that function. The manuscripts written by the various ghosts were submitted to Manny, who edited them more or less as Fred edited (and sometimes heavily revised) the stories he bought for *EQMM*. But Fred refused to read any of the books that were published under this scheme and, as we'll see, terminated the arrangement soon after Manny's death.

For the first five of the twelve years which saw the publication of ghosted paperback originals under the Queen byline, Pocket Books was their exclusive U.S. publisher. None of the fifteen softcover novels that came out during this period featured Ellery—or any other series character either—and the greater a particular reader's familiarity with genuine Queen, the more likely he or she was puzzled by this strange turn in what were advertised and sold as new books by Dannay and Lee. Even though Manny did touch up the manuscripts before their publication, none of them bears the least stylistic resemblance to his authentic work. For both Fred and Manny—the one an ardent advocate of authors' rights, the other a committed liberal and champion of the underdog—it must have been a humiliating experience to be involved with a project that took economic advantage of fellow mystery writers in need of ready cash. And there may also have been some legal risk. If the truth came out, might not some readers who had been misled sue for consumer fraud? In the U.S. these ghosted paperbacks looked quite different from the genuine Queen hardcovers, but Queen's English publisher Victor Gollancz increased the likelihood of consumer deception by issuing the ghosted books as hardcovers, with the same yellow dust-jackets as the true-blue Queens. Legal and ethical questions aside, the scheme was all but predestined to confuse and disappoint thousands of EQ fans since none of the actual authors of these paperbacks were at home in the Queen type of detective fiction and few of them could have been expected, for no credit and no royalties but only a flat fee, to turn out fine work in their own traditions. Amazingly enough, six of the fifteen Pocket Books titles proved excellent anyway.

The first author to pass as Queen on America's newsstands was Stephen Marlowe (1928-2008), a specialist in original paperback thrillers best known for his series about globe-trotting PI Chester Drum. *Dead Man's Tale* (Pocket Books pb #6117, 1961) is a plodding episodic account of a hunt across central Europe for a missing Czech war hero who's been named heir to an American racketeer's estate. The hunters of course are aiming not to tell the Czech of his good fortune but to kill him so that the money will gravitate to more suitable pockets. Marlowe had been living overseas for a while but his evocations of Holland, Switzerland, Vienna and Prague seem to come straight out of a guidebook. With its uninspired writing, bone-thin plot and characters so flatly drawn that their violent deaths couldn't matter less, it's no wonder that Boucher (December 24, 1961) tried his best to alert consumers without disclosing the truth he must have known. "Loyal Queen fans should perhaps be warned that *Dead Man's Tale* . . . bears no resemblance to any other book by Ellery Queen. No problem in deduction, no familiar characters, no off-trail erudition, no complexity of plot. . . . Possibly the maestro is trying to appeal to a new set of readers, who may find this a readable if hardly urgent chase-thriller, pursuing . . . improbable objectives." Stephen Marlowe went back to writing Chester Drum capers under his own name and never ghosted for Queen again.

The next Meredith client to take a stab at being Queen lasted much longer in the role and produced, at least some of the time, far better books. Richard Deming (1915-1983) began his career in the hardboiled mystery pulps of the Forties and turned out hundreds of short stories and dozens of paperback novels over four decades as a professional writer. In addition to his own byline he used the pseudonyms Max Franklin (mainly for movie and TV tie-in books) and Emily Moor (for Gothics). As if keeping these bylines going weren't work enough, he also wrote a total of ten softcover originals as Ellery Queen. "I am not overly proud of the EQ books," he said to me in a 1972 letter. "Manny Lee absolutely refused to share any subsidiary rights on these, so they were all written for a flat fee. Since it would have killed me to have one of them sell movie rights, I deliberately made them just barely acceptable, which is really harder than writing your best. On top of that, although the books were completely original with me, Lee did some rewriting. . . . Lee's style did not greatly impress me."

Despite Deming's claim that he wasn't trying hard on the ghosted Queens, his first contribution to the cycle is a shining example of the trimly understated detective novel. In *Death Spins the Platter* (Pocket Books pb #6126, 1962), reporter Jim Layton joins forces with the LAPD's one-eyed Detective Sergeant Trimble to solve the ice-pick murder of a local TV disk jockey who had just been exposed as a taker of payola. Suspects include the widow (with whom Layton begins to fall in love), the mistress, fellow payolees fearing exposure, and—since suicide remains a possibility—the dead man himself. Deming handles the social context of the early Sixties and the emotional crises of the characters as deftly as the plot. Boucher (August 26, 1962) called this second Queen-bylined paperback "a simple and straightforward whodunit" that was "a good deal better than his first, if still without a hint of the pyrotechnic intricacy of hardcover Queen."

Number three of the first fifteen was the work of Talmage Powell (1920-2000), another prolific veteran of pulps and paperback originals, who is fondly remembered for the *noir* suspense novel *The Smasher* (1959) and the five-book series about Tampa PI Ed Rivers. Powell ghosted four titles under the Queen name. "The deals were set by the Scott Meredith agency and then offered," he said in 1993, "on the assumption I would accept. It was a difficult situation." Powell and Manny Lee "got on okay for a long while; then one day [Manny] went off like an ignited package of Chinese firecrackers. My response was to complete the work in progress on the fourth book and quit, even though I empathized with Manny's state of health and career situation which must have been very galling to him. The book editors gave the Lee knuckles a rap, and efforts were made to have me continue, including an offer of a thousand dollars increase in the up-front money on each book. Jack Scovil at the Meredith agency phoned, apparently assumed that that would turn the trick, and when it didn't, he went uptight and vented a couple of pettishly mean remarks, whereupon I hung him up. Scott told everybody else to shut up, accepted my decision in a business-like way, and I continued as a client. . . ."

Writing as Ellery Queen, Powell actually turned out what Deming claimed to have done: minimally acceptable hackwork far below his best books under his own name. *Murder With a Past* (Pocket Books pb #4700, 1963) is a short, slow, dully competent little exercise in small-town intrigue and homicide, with the motel-room murder of a sex blackmailer leading builder Dave Tully to some uneasy suspicions about the former life of the vanished chief suspect: his own wife. One or two halfway decent clues are the only oases in this desert of flat writing, people and plot.

Among the early entries in the saga it was the even-numbered ones that were worth watching for. In Richard Deming's *Wife Or Death* (Pocket Books pb #4703, 1963), small-town newspaper publisher Jim Denton tries to cover up the apparent fact that his nymphomaniac wife has run off with another man, then finds himself prime suspect when her body is found in the woods and has to figure out which of her lovers was also her murderer simply in order to prove that he himself was not. Deming combines high craftsmanship and storytelling skill with sensitive treatment of relationships, including some neat vignettes of puritanical bitchiness. Boucher (December 8, 1963) called the story "familiar enough . . . but tightly plotted and told, with a credible picture of a small town."

The next ghosted EQ title was the work of Henry Kane (1908- 1988), a prolific writer best known for his long series of novels and stories about New York "private richard" Peter Chambers, who narrates his adventures in an eccentric style connoisseurs have dubbed High Kanese. No trace of that style, or of any individuality whatever, can be discerned in *Kill As Directed* (Pocket Books pb #4704, 1963), a routine time-waster in which a money-hungry young doctor is suckered into performing medical services for an aging, obese narcotics racketeer and sexual services for the gangster's greedy young wife. The tangle culminates in an ersatz James M. Cain murder plan that for sheer dullness is rivaled only by the book's prose and characterizations. Boucher (October 20, 1963) jointly reviewed *Murder With a Past* and this title but may have gotten the two confused, saying: "The second is mildly competent in plotting and conciseness (as the first emphatically is not)." Transpose the two numerical words and you have my sentiments exactly.

The ghostly baton then passed to Fletcher Flora (1914-1968), a mid-level hardboiled writer whose work appeared regularly in paperback original lines and magazines like *Manhunt.* In *The Golden Goose* (Pocket Books pb #4705, 1964) Flora tried his hand at another type of mystery but without much success. The title refers to rascally boozer Slater O'Shea, whose bourbon someone spiked with a lethal dose of insulin substitute despite the fact that the sly old man's will terminates his freeloading relatives' mooching privileges on his death. All the relatives are fugitives from the nut factory except for lovely Princess O'Shea, who tries to solve the mystery—an enterprise in which she manages to stay a hundred pages behind the dimmest-witted reader. Except for a few moments that vaguely evoke the wacky-murder farces of Forties writers like Richard Shattuck, this book is, if I may borrow one of its own lines, a cold potato sandwich.

Although he's still never admitted it publicly, science-fiction specialist Jack Vance (1916-   ), who also wrote a few whodunits under his full name John Holbrook Vance, is the author of *The Four Johns* (Pocket Books pb #4706, 1964). The title refers to an overly flirtatious young woman's quartet of suitors, who become the chief suspects when she disappears. A university teaching assistant turns amateur sleuth when the lady's body is found in the trunk of his car and he realizes that someone's trying to frame him. Of his detective skills the less said the better. The plot and main characters are in retrospect incredible but the pre-uprising Berkeley milieu and some nicely observed university hangers-on rescue this quickie from total forgettability. Boucher (May 17, 1964) simultaneously reviewed *The Golden Goose* and this title: although "still a few notches below Queen's hardcover level they are detective puzzles, with some reasonably adroit misdirection and nicely handled double-twist endings." I would not have been quite so kind myself.

In his second try behind the Queen byline, Fletcher Flora turned out the finest and most genuinely Queen-like in the first cycle of fifteen ghosted paperbacks. *Blow Hot, Blow Cold* (Pocket Books pb #45007, 1964), which according to Boucher's glowing review (January 24, 1965) "even has some similarity to hardcover Queen," also offers character sketches of four middle-class married couples in suburban Kansas City that are handled just as skillfully as the murder plot. When the bitchy nymphomaniac on the block and her long-suffering husband both die on the same sweltering summer night, Lt. Gus Masters rejects the obvious theory of man-kills-wife-and-then-self and exposes a complex manipulation of evidence with iron logic worthy of the one and only Ellery. Here is a flavorful treat for fans of mainstream fiction and whodunit addicts alike.

The next Meredith client to come aboard the Queen bandwagon was Charles Runyon (1928-), who had authored several paperback original crime novels for Fawcett Gold Medal and dozens of stories for *Manhunt* and other hardboiled magazines. In *The Last Score* (Pocket Books pb #50486, 1964), which Boucher (January 24, 1965) rightly called "a straight-out adventure thriller," tough tourist guide Reid Rance is hired to chaperon a wealthy teen-age sexpot on a journey through Mexico. When the girl is kidnapped and held for ransom, our macho protagonist doesn't bother to notify the local authorities but launches a one-man war against the abductors. The background is vividly evoked, the descriptions of a marijuana "high" ring true, and despite some implausibilities in the slender storyline this is a model of the men's-magazine adventure novel. "Good violent excitement," said Boucher, "tightly told."

Talmage Powell returned for a second stint behind the Queen byline in *Beware the Young Stranger* (Pocket Books pb #50489, 1965), a suspenser of no particular urgency or distinction about a diplomat-big game hunter's search for his missing daughter and the desperate young fugitive from a murder charge who ran off with her. Flat writing, uncompelling characters and predictable solution add up to a tepid bore that, despite his loyalty to Queen, Anthony Boucher didn't bother to review.

Echoes of the action pulps where Richard Deming learned his craft resound through his third ghosted Queen. *The Copper Frame* (Pocket Books pb #50940, 1965) is about a small upstate New York town which a syndicate boss wants to take over and turn into a hotspot. Young acting police chief Ted Saxon goes on the warpath after his father is murdered and he himself gets framed on a rape charge and suspended from office. A well-evoked chase through a snowstorm is the highlight in this adequate but unexciting job which Boucher (August 15, 1965) called "better than many of Ellery Queen's paperback originals: a transparently plotted but moderately lively and readable story. . . ."

Jack Vance's first foray into Queen's shoes was nothing special but his second, *A Room To Die In* (Pocket Books pb #50492, 1965), turned out to be a jewel of the first water. A young San Francisco schoolteacher finds herself teamed with a Marin County sheriff's detective as they investigate the locked-room death of the woman's father and the effect of his death on the estate of his also recently deceased second wife. Boucher's review (September 12, 1965) was mixed. "*A Room To Die In* . . . at least resembles hardcover Queen novels in presenting a bona-fide puzzle: a locked room, no less, and a clever one. But the writing is flat and the construction surprisingly amateurish." Certainly the motivation for the murder and some of the killer's subsequent ploys are not too well thought out, but with its superbly constructed puzzle and the tricky but fair clue that leads to its solution, this novel comes much closer than the vast majority of the Queen paperbacks to true-blue EQ.

Charles Runyon brought another macho action yarn under the Queen umbrella in *The Killer Touch* (Pocket Books pb #50494, 1965). A tough Florida cop, tormented by a wound and his guilt at killing a teen-ager in line of duty, comes to a tropical island resort where a gang of thieves headed by a doom-haunted sadistic intellectual has just moved in after pulling off a diamond robbery. The writing is vivid, the incidents lurid, the climax rushed, and Runyon crams in enough torture scenes, sex teasing and carnage to satisfy the most rabid, although Boucher was apparently turned off by the bloodletting and chose not to review this one.

Fletcher Flora came back for his third Queen softcover and second attempt at a mystery with chuckles in *The Devil's Cook* (Pocket Books pb #50495, 1966). The student and junior-faculty residents of a small apartment house in a university town find themselves in a thickening stew when the house sexpot suddenly vanishes, and suave Captain Bartholdi investigates the possibility that she was murdered either by her cuckolded professor husband or one of her lovers or a woman on whose man the victim had been poaching. It's an implausible tale, poorly plotted and characterized and written in a repulsively arch style that's a lot less humorous than it tries to be. For some reason (perhaps because he was a gourmet chef himself) Boucher loved this entry, describing it (June 19, 1966) as "far and away better than most of the Ellery Queen paperback originals: a good conservative straight whodunit about a Midwest college town, with a well-clued puzzle, an attractive (and quite non-procedural) police detective, and a promising recipe for Students' Ragout as the focus of the murder-problem."

Fifteenth and last in the initial package of ghosted Queens was Jack Vance's *The Madman Theory* (Pocket Books pb #50496, 1966), a theory that Detective Inspector Omar Collins of the Fresno sheriff's office refuses to buy as the answer to a shotgun killing among a group of Sierra backpackers. When the killer tries to cover his tracks by committing more murders, Collins doggedly sticks to the trail in this stolid California quasi-procedural. The murder gimmick requires God to be sitting in the killer's lap, but a marvelous and totally irrelevant model-railroad reproduction of the land of Oz provides a bright spot in this run-of-the-mill effort. Did Vance know that the Oz books were among Fred Dannay's favorites and did he share Fred's love? And why did Boucher choose to leave this last of the Pocket Books titles unreviewed?

***

During the years these fifteen titles were coming out, Pocket Books was also using another Dannay-Lee byline, Barnaby Ross, for six paperback historical novels: *Quintin Chivas* (1961), *The Scrolls of Lysis* (1962), *The Duke of Chaos* (1964), *The Cree from Minataree* (1964), *Strange Kinship* (1965), and *The Passionate Queen* (1966). All six were written by Don Tracy (1905-1976), the author of a number of thrillers and historicals under his own name including several published by Pocket Books. Whether Manny Lee supervised these as he had all the ghosted Queen books is uncertain. He and Fred must have received some money under this arrangement. But why did the publisher bother to pay them anything? It can't be coincidence that, during the same years Pocket was issuing ghosted paperbacks as by Ellery Queen, it was also putting out another line of softcovers under another Dannay-Lee byline. But apparently Pocket never made the slightest attempt to lure potential readers into identifying the byline on the six historicals with the byline on the four Drury Lane detective novels of 1932-33. What would have been the point? But if there was no point, why not just publish all six as historical adventures by Don Tracy, without the Barnaby Ross byline and without having to pay Fred and Manny for its use? Perhaps someday the business correspondence dealing with these books will be unearthed and allow us to understand a sequence of events which on their face make no sense.

Even if I understood how these books came about I wouldn't care to explore them. Years ago I made myself read one. Never again!

***

During the 1960s Ellery the character did not appear on the TV screen, but Queen's stand-alone short novel "Terror Town" (*Argosy*, August 1956; collected in *The Tragedy of Errors*, 1999), which dealt with a series of violent deaths on the exact same spot near a New England hamlet, was adapted for *The Alfred Hitchcock Hour* as "Terror in Northfield" (October 11, 1963). Harvey Hart directed from a script by Leigh Brackett which moved the action to a small town in California and, dropping most of the detection in Queen's version, stressed suspense, as did Bernard Herrmann's excellent music score. Dick York, Jacqueline Scott and R.G. Armstrong respectively played the puzzled deputy sheriff, the menaced local librarian and the mad farmer.

***

One of the minor but financially rewarding jobs Manny Lee performed for the Queen partnership dates back at least to 1952, when the editors of *American Weekly* began supplying him with research files on various true-crime cases. These he transformed into short essays with titles like "The Red Herring Murder" and "The Firebug Murders." At least 94 of these appeared in *American Weekly* between late 1952 and mid-1959 and at least two more in *Official Detective* in 1960 and 1961. Twenty of these were published as the paperback original *Ellery Queen's International Casebook* (Dell pb #2260, 1964). Boucher's review (May 24, 1964) was deadly. The tales, he said, "lie somewhere in the borderland between short stories and fact-crime essays. They are presumably (and sometimes recognizably) based on fact, but all gussied up with fiction-like trimmings (including Ellery's conferences with policemen all over the globe) and remarkably vague on dates and details." Two years later a different paperback publisher offered a sequel volume, *The Woman in the Case* (Bantam pb #F3160, 1966), which Boucher chose not to review. Finally there existed not one but two books which Manny had written on his own. But were they worth writing?

CHAPTER TWENTY-ONE

The Ghosts Multiply

W HEN SCOTT MEREDITH'S DEAL with Pocket Books had run its course, he moved the ghosted Queens to two other publishers at the same time, with Dell taking over the nonseries titles along the lines of the original fifteen while Popular Library contracted to publish something new in the Meredith package but borrowed from the genuine Queen canon: a series with a consistent title-pattern and continuing characters. Who initially dreamed up one-eyed NYPD Captain Tim Corrigan and his Jewish PI pal Chuck Baer is anyone's guess; they may even have been Manny Lee's idea. The series lasted for six books and, thanks to Richard Deming, improved prodigiously as it went along.

Talmage Powell opened the proceedings with *Where Is Bianca?* (Popular Library pb #50C477, 1966), in which a woman's body is found in a New York sewer with the face eaten away by rats and three different people make conflicting identifications of the corpse. The hunt for her identity and killer leads Corrigan and Baer into the off-Broadway theatrical milieu, which Powell sees as the exclusive province of degenerates and phonies. This routinely readable item is neither circumstantially convincing enough for a good police procedural nor intellectually involving enough for a good detective novel, but a deduction from the absence of andirons in a fireplace is almost worthy of

Ellery himself. Boucher (May 22, 1966) called it "a straightforward whodunit" with "good New York theater background, but flat writing and weak plotting."

Powell followed up this entry with *Who Spies, Who Kills?* (Popular Library pb #60C2111, 1966). Captain Tim and the bullish Baer have a messy problem in more ways than one when an East German defector with a politically hot reel of film to sell is dropped out of a nineteenth floor hotel window into Manhattan traffic. As the sleuths follow the trail to the spoiled members of a newsmagazine dynasty, Corrigan sets a world record for reasoning by baseless hunches. It was while Powell was working on this one that he had his bitter dispute with Manny Lee and resolved to quit playing Queen's ghost. The book is so flatly written and characterized, so abysmally structured and padded, so rabidly right-wing in its politics that I suspect Powell was going out of his way to get Lee irked. And not only Lee: Boucher's review (August 7, 1966) dismissed the second Corrigan novel as "hasty and just barely competent in plot and telling. . . ."

Powell's replacement at the uncredited helm of the series was old reliable Richard Deming, who wrote all four of the remaining Corrigan titles beginning with *Why So Dead?* (Popular Library pb #60C2122, 1966). During a reception at a posh Manhattan hotel, an oil-rich sultan is blown apart by a bomb at the precise moment that his most valuable ruby is stolen from a display case in the same room. The storytelling is perfunctory and the characters from stock but it's a minimally acceptable time-killer, described by Boucher (September 11, 1966) as "pretty flat in writing and plotting, but offer[ing] more color than previous Corrigan cases. . . ."

Deming's *How Goes the Murder?* (Popular Library pb #60-2168, 1967) is the third consecutive title in the series that deals with death in a large New York hotel. Corrigan and his beefy buddy Baer happen to be in the building during a political rally when the liberal candidate for state senator is assassinated right after a confrontation with a fascist hate group. Investigation soon unearths other suspects including the conservative candidate for the same seat, his sex-bomb wife and her muscle-bound lover. The situation is intriguing and the police work in the hotel sounds authentic but the story soon deteriorates into a standard pattern with a predictable least likely suspect at trail's end. "You can't quite say the book is bad," wrote Boucher (April 9, 1967); "but it wholly lacks distinction in its flat writing, its simple plotting and its unsubtle politics." This was the last EQ paperback he ever mentioned in print, and he may never have known that the fifth and sixth titles in the Corrigan series were dramatic improvements on those he had reviewed.

Deming's *Which Way To Die?* (Popular Library pb #60C2235, 1967) is head and shoulders above the earlier Corrigans thanks to a stronger situation, plot and characters than the series had seen so far. On a technicality the New York courts release two young psychos who, in the tradition of Leopold and Loeb, killed a young woman to see if they could get away with it. Soon Captain Tim and his pal from the private sector find themselves the killers' bodyguards, protecting them against the vengeance threatened by the dead girl's Mafioso father and her football-hero fiancé. Then, in a seemingly impregnable penthouse hideaway, one of the young sociopaths is murdered. The story's legal aspects are inexpertly handled, the killer's identity stands out like W.C. Fields' nose and the murder gimmick is too easily traceable to its source, but this one is a huge advance on the first four in the sextet.

Deming's *What's in the Dark?* (Popular Library #60-2269, 1968), sixth and last of the series, is also by far the finest. A philandering accountant is murdered in his office on the 21st floor of a high-rise tower a few minutes before the great East Coast power failure in the fall of 1965. When the lights go out, Corrigan and Baer are stranded on an island in the sky with the corpse still on the floor, an array of suspects trapped with them, and no chance of technical help from the NYPD. As the long night drags on, the killer strikes again. Deming exploits this fascinating premise to the hilt and caps it with a surprise solution marked by strict fairness to the reader, so that one might almost believe it was the work of Dannay and Lee.

***

Meanwhile the stand-alone entries in the package were being published by Dell but apparently without much success, for the line was dropped after three titles, two dispensable and the third and last an action classic. Richard Deming kicked off the trio with *Losers, Weepers* (Dell pb #5034, 1966), in which a young Los Angeles draftsman, plagued by mounting debts and a money-mad wife, accidentally winds up with $100,000 in payoff money from a gangster and is beset on three fronts at once: by the thugs who want the money back, some independent operators looking for a share of it, and his wife who's determined to keep all of it. A few bits of police procedure help raise this mediocre item barely above dead-level competence. "The story," said Boucher (August 7, 1966), ". . . is not unfamiliar; but the narrative is reasonably bright and moves at a fine, fast pace."

Deming's follow-up effort, *Shoot the Scene* (Dell pb #7845, 1966), has no merit as a mystery but is unique among the ghosted Queen paperbacks in that half the time it doesn't pretend to be a mystery at all. Instead it's a dreary and labored comedy of sexual politics on a Hollywood movie set, featuring a harassed screenwriter who's frantically dodging the come-hithers of a tempestuous nymphomaniac star. The book's mediocre criminous half is sparked by the kidnapping of the director's wife and the murder of his double during the ransom process. With its uniformly flat characters and style and a blatantly obvious villain, it's no wonder that Boucher dismissed this title in silence.

Charles Runyon contributed his third and last novel to the series with *Kiss and Kill* (Dell pb #4567, 1969), a tornado-paced fable of pursuit and menace complete with sex, sadism, machismo and a psychopathic monster. When a young Chicago housewife vanishes after returning from a solo tour of Mexico, her distraught husband and a local PI take up the trail and soon discover that everyone else on that tour has either disappeared or suffered a violent death. About halfway through the book the action shifts to south of the border where Runyon had spent many years, and the two urban male protagonists, joined by a woman photographer from St. Louis, become instant experts at guerrilla warfare against professional killers. But neither this implausible development nor the recycling of tough guy fiction's most overused climactic "surprise" diminishes the pure headlong storytelling drive that makes Runyon's ultimate men's-mag adventure impossible to put down unfinished.

***

The last gasps of the ghosted Queens were exhaled by Lancer Books, a much smaller and less prestigious paperback publisher that took over the package more or less where Popular Library had left off, only without any further Tim Corrigan exploits. Not that the characters in the Lancer entries were any improvement.

The publisher's first Queen title was *A Study in Terror* (Lancer pb #73-469, 1966), a prose version of the British film of the same name, which was directed by James Hill from a screenplay by Donald and Derek Ford, starring John Neville as Sherlock Holmes and Donald Houston as Dr. Watson. The film is set in garish gas-lit London and lovingly evokes the Holmes-Watson menage but bogs down in an impossible-to-keep-straight plot pitting the sage of Baker Street against none other than Jack the Ripper. The film was distributed in the U.S. by Columbia Pictures, which commissioned a "novelization" of the screenplay. When John Dickson Carr turned down the assignment on grounds of poor health, the contract was offered to Queen. Unlike every other paperback original discussed in this chapter, Fred and Manny actually wrote some of this one—to be precise, the framing chapters in which Ellery receives an anonymous package containing a manuscript purportedly by Dr. Watson. Racing to meet a deadline, Ellery manages to squeeze in time to read the material—and to make deductions from it that are more intriguing than almost anything in the manuscript itself—and then attempts to trace the sender. The inner story, supposedly by Watson and describing Holmes' duel with the Ripper, was written by science-fiction specialist Paul W. Fairman (1916-1977). It differs significantly from the screenplay and, as Erik Routley pointed out in *The Puritan Pleasures of the Detective Story* (1972), both narrative and dialogue suffer from Americanisms. Holmes and Watson follow the Ripper's trail to the demesne of a demented duke and the chill shadows of a combination hostel and mortuary in the Whitechapel slums, not to mention countless pubs and abattoirs and brothels. Can you imagine Conan Doyle's Holmes and Watson conversing casually with some half-clad ladies of the evening? The plot is plagued by numerous loose ends and unplugged holes and allows Holmes far too much lucky guesswork. "Fun," said Boucher in his *Times* review (July 17, 1966), "but not nearly what S.H. plus E.Q. could have added up to."

***

Guess Who's Coming To Kill You? (Lancer pb #73C802, 1968) unaccountably continues the title format of the Tim Corrigan series, but its hero is an unsubtle copy of all the superspy clones who cluttered popular fiction in the heyday of the early James Bond movies and TV series like *The Man from U.N.C.L.E.* Peter Brook, operative for an agency known as FACE, impervious to torture and irresistible to women like every other secret agent of his breed, is ordered to Tokyo to orchestrate a

KGBigwig's defection. There he encounters the usual mix of murder, pursuit, pain, bureaucratic doubledealing and fun in bed. Our side plays rough but theirs much rougher in this professionally paced and plotted, unexcitingly readable caper written by Walt Sheldon (1917-1996), a specialist in paperback thrillers with Asian settings.

Any thoughts of continuing Brook as a character and international intrigue as a fake-Queen genre were quickly scuttled in favor of a series with domestic settings and some tentative stabs at detection, featuring Mike McCall (The Troubleshooter), a sort of personal investigator for the liberal governor of an unnamed state. The first of the McCall trio was written by Gil Brewer (1922-1983), one of the original Fawcett Gold Medal paperback novelists in the Fifties. Being a Queen ghost apparently didn't come easy to him. "I had a letter from Gil," said his friend Talmage Powell, "asking how I had gotten through four EQ books. Gil said he'd just completed an umpteenth revised outline of 80 pages." All the revisions didn't help *The Campus Murders* (Lancer pb #74-527, 1969), in which McCall is sent to seething Tisquanto State College to investigate the disappearance of a student who happens to be the daughter of the governor's political rival. The murders start right after McCall arrives and force him to play detective, a role for which he displays minimal talent. The plotting is routine, the writing careless, the characters too numerous and hard to keep straight, and the evocation of campus unrest in the late Sixties is liberal in perspective but not well integrated into the storyline. I give it a D.

Richard Deming earned a B or C+ for his swan song as EQ. In *The Black Hearts Murder* (Lancer pb #74640-075, 1970), the governor dispatches McCall to an industrial city where a black militant organization, a racist police department and an upcoming mayoral election with opposing black and white candidates have polarized tensions almost to the point of race war. Deming fills pages with the Troubleshooter's sexual conquests and several debates on race relations (with the blacks and white liberals scoring most of the points) until the obligatory murder. Although the mystery plot is rather simple and the climax awkwardly staged, this is a briskly readable adventure and a healthy primer on the causes of the then current black rage.

***

The next publisher of Queen in hardcover after Fred Dannay broke ties with Random House was New American Library. The arrangement lasted for just six books—two novels, one story collection and three annual anthologies—but marked Manny Lee's return to his traditional role of fleshing out Fred's synopses.

The first of the NAL Queen novels is a work of simon-pure detection with Ellery squarely at center stage—a combination unseen in the canon since *The Player on the Other Side*, of which *Face to Face* (1967) is something of a mirror image. In *Player* the physical murderer was known from the outset and the problem was to locate the manipulator who was using him as a weapon, while in *Face* the Iago figure's identity is clear at once and the task is to identify *his* living weapon. Ellery returns from England on a New Year's morning accompanied by a new acquaintance, Scottish PI Harry Burke, and the two detectives find an urgent call for help waiting at the Queen apartment. Actress Roberta West tells them that seven months ago her lover, the notorious philanderer Count Carlos Armando, had asked her to murder his wealthy and much older wife for him. She had turned him down and run out of his life for good, she says. Now, seven months later, Mrs. Armando—better known as the once-famous radio singer Glory Guild—has been shot to death at a time when her husband has a perfect alibi, having been with Roberta in her own apartment at the time of the murder. Armando must have persuaded one of the other women in his life to do the job, but the only clue is Glory Guild's cryptic dying message, the single word FACE. Ellery and Burke unearth a small army of Armando's female friends, a long-lost niece, a will that says too much and a panhandler who knows too much, but the developing relationships among the main characters are even more crucial to the plot, which culminates in an exceptionally fine and fair bamboozlement of the reader.

As usual in fourth period Queen, the echo effect is deafening. The Iago element of course had been a Queen hallmark for decades. The murder trial that hinges on the defendant's having forgotten the single fact that will save his or her skin comes straight out of *The Fourth Side of the Triangle* but is handled a bit more plausibly here. The sexual blackmailer and the jaded gossip columnist are rooted in *The Scarlet Letters*. The climactic counterpoint between the Episcopal marriage ceremony and the murderer's exposure will be recalled from *There Was an Old Woman*. And devotees of the earliest Queen novels will easily remember where they first heard of the Roman Theater and Judge J.J. McCue.

The identity of the woman who pulled the trigger for Armando is a stunning surprise, but the most memorable aspect of *Face to Face* is the treatment of her in human terms. After Ellery's brilliant but bloodlessly mechanical explanation she takes center stage, insists that she really had fallen in love and hoped for a new life after having been used by Armando and left with nothing. Now her new life too is rubble. Of course, to some extent she allowed Armando to use her, but it's stressed with equal force that she was a tool in his hands, and was on the point of a lasting relationship when Ellery smashed her. This sense of moral ambiguity, which probably stems from Hitchcock's treatment of the Kim Novak character in *Vertigo* (1958), strikes me as the most fully human aspect of anything in fourth-period Queen. Boucher (April 9, 1967) called the novel "a fine fantastic farrago" marked by "technically faultless construction" and an "admirable final twist. . . ."

***

Between *Face to Face* and the next Queen novel came the last worthwhile Queen short story. In "Wedding Anniversary" (*EQMM*, September 1967) Ellery returns to Wrightsville just in time to witness the poisoning of his kindly host, jeweler Ernst Bauenfel, and to solve the puzzle of his death through another Wonderlandesque dying message analysis. If the plot evokes memories of the early EQ radio play "The Last Man Club," the early scenes leading up to Bauenfel's death are among the most touchingly beautiful pages in late Queen, and signal strongly, as did the final pages of *Face to Face*, that Manny Lee was back.

***

The House of Brass (1968) was intended as a sequel to *Inspector Queen's Own Case* (1956) but was expanded from Fred's synopsis to book length by Avram Davidson and therefore must predate Manny's recovery from writer's block. Returning to West 87th Street from their honeymoon, ex-Inspector Queen and his bride, the former Jessie Sherwood, discover a mysterious letter addressed to Jessie, inviting her for an extended visit to the ancestral seat of the Brass family, enclosing a $100 bill for traveling expenses and half of a $1,000 bill for bait. The letter is signed by Hendrik Brass, patriarch of a family of wealthy jewel merchants and a complete stranger to both Richard and Jessie, but curiosity draws them upstate to the village of Phillipskill and the grotesque mansion of the title. The house is filled with brass-plated brica-brac and with several miscellaneous guests who've received similar invitations. Waiting upon the guests is Hugo, a manservant built along the general lines of Frankenstein's monster. In due time the blind old schemer, Hendrik Brass himself, reveals that he's brought this motley group together to observe them and eventually to choose from among them the heir or heirs to his $6,000,000 fortune. Anyone who recognizes the source of this plot in Ben Jonson's *Volpone,* and remembers the low opinion of human nature expressed in *The Origin of Evil* and *The Glass Village* and other Queen novels, will not be surprised when the specter of greed rears its head among the guests. A murder attempt is followed by a successful killing and, with the publicity-hungry village police chief clearly out of his depth, Richard takes up the case unofficially with the help of Jessie and his old ex-police buddies in the 87th Street Irregulars. Ellery enters the proceedings late, baits a trap reminiscent of Sidney Toler in the worst Charlie Chan flicks, and snares the killer.

Clearly *Inspector Queen's Own Case* and *The House of Brass* run on their own separate and independent time track. Richard Queen was 63 years old when he met and fell in love with Jessie Sherwood in the earlier novel. In *The Finishing Stroke* (1958) he was over eighty and Jessie had been dropped down the memory hole. In previous Queen novels of the Sixties he held fast at just under retirement age and remained unwed. *The House of Brass* finds them at the exact same ages as in *Inspector Queen's Own Case* but Jessie never appears again. *Brass* nevertheless resounds with echoes from all over the Queen canon. For the isolated house-party ambience, see *The Finishing Stroke.* Ellery's last-minute solution bails out his father just as Richard had bailed out his son in *The Fourth Side of the Triangle.* For the obsessive animal imagery and the concern with the depravity of human nature, see *The Origin of Evil.* The figure of "Hard" Boyle, a.k.a. Vaughn J. Vaughn, reminds us of the satire on tough PIs in *Double, Double.* And haven't we seen earlier instances of a false solution followed by the true one?

As an attempt to update *Volpone* this novel fails miserably. Too many of its characters are immune from the disease of acquisitiveness that is the supposed target, and the greed of those who don't wear white hats is so stylized and artificial that it neither convinces nor repels. As a detective novel *Brass* suffers from overfamiliar devices like the isolated house party, the will-manipulating old tyrant, the enigmatic servant, the missing heir, the atmospheric storm. Even worse is the fallacious, baseless and often witless nature of the reasoning. The Inspector's deductions in Chapters 11 and 13, Ellery's in Chapter 15 and Dr. Thornton's in Chapter 8 are usually wrong and illogical even when right, the only exception being Richard's truly inspired hunch about the torn $1,000 bills. Boucher in the *Times* (March 17, 1968) praised the novel's "grand elaborate prestidigitation . . ." and offered only the mildest criticism. "[I]f I have a few trifling reservations about the plot, I found they could be easily forgotten in the warm charm of the retired policeman and his Jessie." Six weeks later the finest critic the mystery field has ever seen died of cancer at the age of fifty-six.

***

The last Queen titles published by New American Library were a short story collection and the annual best-of-*EQMM* anthology. *Q.E.D.: Queen's Experiments in Detection* (1968) brought together most of the as yet uncollected shorter fiction of the Fifties and Sixties: some good stories, some not so good, and one that must be called great. "Mum Is the Word" (*EQMM*, April 1966), the only short novel in the volume, stands dead center in the classic tradition with a Wrightsville setting, an isolated houseful of suspects, a missing million-dollar pendant and, of course, an impenetrable dying message. Retired flower seed tycoon Godfrey Mumford, a fanatic devotee of the chrysanthemum, announces some drastic financial retrenchments to his expectant heirs, suffers a severe stroke, and is stabbed to death in his bed with his own letter-opener, writing the letters MUM on a bedside pad before breathing his last. Ellery as usual happens to be in Wrightsville and is brought in by Chief Newby. His solution is uninspired and the murderer's motivation incredible. Some plot elements are lifted bodily from previous Queen stories—the Englishwoman and the sleeping pills in the hot milk first appeared in "Eve of the Wedding," also in this collection—and others are totally off the wall. Would you believe no hospital room or even a private nurse can be found for a seriously ill multimillionaire? But Ellery's analysis of the possible meanings of "Mum" and his explication of "doubleness" are outrageously fantastic in Fred's beloved Wonderland vein.

Next come four "Contemporary Problems in Deduction," a set of stories exploring characteristic urban problems like juvenile delinquency and poverty. In "Object Lesson" (*This Week*, September 11, 1955, as "The

Blackboard Gangsters"; *EQMM*, April 1958) Ellery visits the local high school to give a talk on crime and winds up having to solve one—petty theft from the teacher's desk—before the end of the period. This he does neatly, but the story is just too slight to bear the heavy sociological weight the cousins try to impose on it. In "No Parking" (*This Week*, March 18, 1956, as "Terror in a Penthouse"; *EQMM*, February 1958) a Broadway actress who disappointed several suitors is shot to death during a fierce rainstorm, but Ellery's solution is weak and unconvincing. "No Place to Live" (*This Week*, June 10, 1956, as "The Man They All Hated"; *EQMM*, March 1958) concerns murder in an apartment full of unauthorized subtenants. The plot centers on a GI just back from Europe who carries around $3,000 in cash amid a veritable nest of vipers, doesn't bother to tell his bride about the money, and forgets to tell the police where he'd kept the bills hidden before they were stolen. One sensible act on his part would have frozen the tale in its tracks. By far the best of the quartet is "Miracles Do Happen" (*EQMM*, July 1957), in which Ellery and his father investigate the murder of a usurer who was calling in his loans. The story vaguely recalls the 1941 EQ radio play "The Meanest Man in the World" but the solution is skillful and fair and the picture of urban lower-middle-class life more convincing than the portrayals of the social problems in the other three stories.

The next eight stories are headed "Q.B.I.: Queen's Bureau of Investigation," and most of them are abstract and artificial embodiments of what Fred liked to call "fun and games." First of the octet is the earliest Queen short-short, "The Lonely Bride" (*This Week*, December 4, 1949, as "The Lady Couldn't Explain"; *EQMM*, December 1951), which confronts Ellery with the problem of locating $20,000 hidden "in a book" in an apartment where there are no books. He solves the problem adroitly but leaves unsolved how the story's dim-witted thief could have found the money at all. In "Mystery at the Library of Congress" (*Argosy*, June 1960, as "Enter Ellery Queen"; *EQMM*, February 1963) the problem is to crack a book-title code used by a ring of narcotics smugglers whose leisure reading apparently included *The French Powder Mystery*, and anyone who glances at contemporary photographs of Fred and Manny may anticipate the solution. With "Dead Ringer" (*Diners' Club Magazine*, March 1965; *EQMM*, October 1966) we return to the dying message gambit. Why did the spy posing as a tobacconist use his last moments to pull off the shelf an empty canister labeled MIX C? File the kooky answer under Fun & Games, and right alongside it the solutions to "The Broken T" (*This Week*, July 27, 1963, as "Mystery in Neon Red"; *EQMM*, May 1966), which concerns a vanishing neon sign, and to "Half a Clue" (*This Week*, August 25, 1963, as "Half a Clue to Murder"; *EQMM*, August 1966), in which Ellery solves the poisoning of a druggist literally as the body hits the floor. "Eve of the Wedding" (*EQMM*, August 1955, as "Bride in Danger") is set in Wrightsville, where Ellery is invited to a wedding which comes close to getting canceled when the bride starts receiving anonymous threatening letters. Denouement and reasoning make little sense but the people are far more real than in most of this collection's tales. The challenge in "Last Man to Die" (*This Week*, November 3, 1963; *EQMM*, January 1967) is to determine which of two ancient butlers, last survivors of a tontine, died first, and not only the neat solution but every word of this superbly fashioned little puzzle entitles it to classic status. But "Payoff" (*Cavalier*, August 1964, as "Crime Syndicate Payoff"; *EQMM*, July 1966) is dismissible as another Fun & Games caper and a pale imitation of the name gimmick in "The Inner Circle."

The next two stories are headed "The Puzzle Club," which is a tiny coterie of enthusiasts who meet regularly to propound riddles to each other. This series, which continued in some later stories that remained uncollected until long after both cousins' deaths, was in effect a fiction version of their old *Author! Author!* radio show, although here the object is to construct not a rational beginning for the puzzle but an ending. In "The Little Spy" (*Cavalier*, January 1965; *EQMM*, September 1966) the group invites Ellery to become a member, posing for him by way of initiation rite a problem in elimination. By what means on or in his person was the secret agent trying to get the plans out of the country? "The President Regrets" (*Diners' Club Magazine*, September 1965; *EQMM*, July 1967) tells of a later meeting which LBJ is prevented from attending by affairs of state. Ellery improvises for the club a riddle billed as of presidential caliber, but it's just another name game coupled with a replay of the multi-suitored actress problem in the same collection's "No Parking."

"Historical Detective Story" is the heading of "Abraham Lincoln's Clue" (*MD*, June 1965; *EQMM*, March 1967), in which Ellery tracks a lost first edition of *The Gift: 1845*, containing Poe's "The Purloined Letter" and autographed by both Poe and Abraham Lincoln. This near-perfect story catches the pure essence of Queen, uniting such passions of the cousins as bibliophily, philately, history, the art of the riddle, and Poe and Lincoln scholarship. Since this and several of the other stories in the collection were first published in magazines during the years of Manny's writer's block, who actually worked with Fred on them remains a mystery.

***

During the short period when New American Library was the major Queen publisher, the firm also issued the annual Best-of-*EQMM* anthologies. *Ellery Queen's Crime Carousel* (1966) was the twenty-first volume in the series and, not coincidentally, offered 21 stories. "[T]he gems," said Boucher (October 30, 1966), ". . . are as usual magnificently cut and polished." His special favorite was "a masterpiece of condensed plotting by Christianna Brand," but he also praised the contributions by Julian Symons, Charlotte Armstrong and Holly Roth. There were 22 stories in *Ellery Queen's All-Star Lineup* (1967) and Boucher's review (July 2, 1967) shows that he loved all of them but especially those by John Creasey, James Yaffe, Charlotte Armstrong, Ursula Curtiss, James Powell and—I am not making this up—William Shakespeare. He surely would have heaped the same kind of praise on *Ellery Queen's Mystery Parade* (1968) but died a few months before it was published.

Not long after the *All-Star Line-Up* volume, New American Library published *Ellery Queen's Poetic Justice* (1967), the last of Fred Dannay's many patterned anthologies, this one containing 23 crime tales by distinguished poets from Chaucer through Byron and Poe and Whitman to contemporaries like Robert Graves and Dylan Thomas. Clearly this was one of the anthologies closest to Fred's heart, and in his Introduction he insisted on the affinity between the poetic and the deductive mind, which isn't odd at all when one remembers that he'd been writing poetry himself for much of his life. "[T]he reader is fascinated half by the story and half by the poet," said Boucher (October 8, 1967), complaining only that Poet Laureate C. Day Lewis, also known as crime novelist Nicholas Blake, was inexplicably omitted.

Boucher's reviews of the semi-annual paperbound volumes continued to be raves. Of *Ellery Queen's 1966 Anthology* he wrote (November 14, 1965) that "among its 19 entries . . . there are no weak spots." The 1966 mid-year volume, he said (March 20, 1966), "highlights one of the best and most characteristic of Cornell Woolrich's tales of everyday terror and a short-short by Edmund Crispin which presents one of the most beautiful subtle clues in detective literature. . . . You can't go wrong." His review (October 30, 1966) of *Ellery Queen's 1967 Anthology* suggests that he most admired two short novels by Ross Macdonald and Rex Stout, respectively highlighting Lew Archer and Nero Wolfe. From the 1967 mid-year volume his review (April 9, 1967) singled out "a grand short novel by John Dickson Carr, a historic find by Abraham Lincoln, a notable novelette by Christianna Brand" and "a gem" of a short story by Patricia Highsmith. Of the 22 stories in *Ellery Queen's 1968 Anthology* his favorites, judging by his comments (October 8, 1967), were the short novels by Helen McCloy and Roy Vickers, the stories by Ronald Knox and Harry Kemelman, "and a short-short by Richard M. Gordon [that] has one of the cleverest gimmicks of the past decade." The 1968 mid-year volume contained twenty stories of which his review (April 7, 1968) mentioned eight, including "a fine Cornell Woolrich" from *EQMM*'s Volume I No. 1. "Very few . . . are weak." Those were the last words discussing Queen in any capacity that he lived to write.

CHAPTER TWENTY-TWO

Death Comes to the Cousins

T HE BUSINESS RELATIONSHIP between the cousins and the Stokes publishing firm had lasted from 1929 until early 1942 and their connection with Little, Brown from then till well into 1955. Since that date their publishing contracts had been for relatively short periods, and their time at New American Library was the shortest yet. In 1969 they moved from NAL to the Chicago-based World publishing house, which put out the next Queen novel, intended to celebrate the 40th anniversary of the Dannay-Lee partnership.

Its dust-jacket billed *Cop Out* (1969) as "Different From Any Detective Story Ellery Queen Has Ever Written." A strange phrase indeed! Why "Any Detective Story" rather than "Any Other Detective Story"? Under a grammatical microscope the words mean literally that Fred and Manny were not the authors of the book. Could this be one of those subtle clues Fred adored? More likely it was just an editorial gaffe, but *Cop Out* was in fact so different from all earlier genuine Queen novels that many readers doubted that the cousins had written it. I wouldn't have believed it myself except that Fred Dannay looked me in the eye and told me unequivocally that he and Manny and no others had conceived and written the entire book. Manny's personal involvement was confirmed by his son Rand Lee after both cousins had died. "Dad," he remembered, "rode around all night on patrol" with cops from New Milford, the county seat, and "the authenticity shows. . . ." In essence *Cop Out* is a swift-paced hard-nosed paperback original that somehow wound up in hardcover. Did Fred and Manny intend readers of this book to think that the ghosted paperback originals published under the Queen byline since 1961 were also genuine Queen novels? If so, they must have been floored when the exact opposite happened and readers came to suspect that this genuine work of Dannay and Lee had been ghosted like the paperbacks.

The scene is New Bradford, Taugus County, Connecticut, and the storyline is simplicity itself. We open on the nighttime theft of a $24,000 payroll from the Aztec Paper Products Company, staged by a vicious trio unlike any other criminals in the Queen canon: the loutish sadistic ape Hinch, little Furia who believes he's the brains of the outfit, and Goldie, a cheap New Bradford-born tramp who does the real thinking for all three. The crime is discovered unexpectedly soon and a state police cordon on the major highways traps the trio inside the New Bradford area. Goldie decides that they should leave the loot with local cop Wes Malone and take the Malones' daughter as security for the money. Wes comes home late that evening to find his wife and child held at gunpoint by the trio, all wearing bear masks. The rest of the book consists of several rounds of cat-and-mouse, with many sudden reversals of fortune and endless agonies of suspense and conflicts of loyalty and sex and violence.

If *Cop Out* had been a softcover original by Day Keene or Harry Whittington or Jim Thompson or any other well-known paperback crime novelist, one might have balked a bit at its pretentious pseudo-cinematic prose but could otherwise have enjoyed it on its own terms. But the name Ellery Queen on the cover arouses a complex spectrum of expectations, all of which are frustrated by this novel with its credibly evil gangsters, its knowledgeable details of police routine, its voyeurism and fellatio and excremental allusions and a finger-search up a female suspect's vagina. There are a few recognizably Queen elements — the allegorical character-names, the manipulation theme (in a minor key), the county-name Taugus which harks back to *Inspector Queen's Own Case* — but everything else in the book could have been done by almost any solid practitioner of the paperback crime novel. Fred told me more than once that the objective in *Cop Out* was to do something utterly and completely different from anything he and Manny had ever done before. In this they succeeded beyond their wildest dreams.

***

Just as *The House of Brass* had taken up where *Inspector Queen's Own Case* had taken off, the next Queen novel opens where the last had closed. At the end of *Face to Face* Ellery was at JFK Airport watching a BOAC jet take Harry Burke away, and he's still there on the first page of *The Last Woman in His Life* (1970). In the airport restaurant a few minutes later, he and his father happen upon two of Ellery's Harvard classmates, the often-married jet-setting millionaire John Levering Benedict III and his attorney and buddy Al Marsh. Johnny invites the exhausted Queens to rest up at his 600-acre sylvan retreat, which happens to lie between Wrightsville and the "glass village" of Shinn Corners. Ellery finds that Wrightsville has changed for the worse but still considers it "a viable Shangri-La"—until Johnny and his three rapacious ex-wives and Al Marsh converge on the property for a showdown financial conference. Foreseeing trouble, Johnny executes a quick holographic will (though in fact such wills were not valid in any New England state, nor even in New York except for testators in the military). After each wife suddenly and simultaneously loses an article of clothing, Johnny is bludgeoned to death in his bedroom and all three articles—a wig, an evening gown and a pair of gloves—are found near the body along with (what else in a Queen novel?) a dying message. Chief Anse Newby asks the Queens to help locate both the murderer and also the mysterious "Laura," Johnny's true love, to secure whose future he was about to reduce his bequests to his three exes from a million to a piddling hundred thousand dollars apiece: the last woman in his life.

The long middle section of the novel is precisely what *The House of Brass* should have been but wasn't, a sardonic portrait of greed-driven power plays by various potential heirs to a fortune. Audrey the third-rate actress, Marcia the tough-talking showgirl, Sanford Effing the legal leech who sniffs a fat fee, Foxy Faulks the cheap gambler with large ideas, several hundred opportunists trying to pass themselves off as the missing Laura, all are consumed by money madness. The only exception is Leslie Carpenter, the self-effacing little social worker without the guts to fight for the fortune on behalf of the poor on whom she'd spend it.

Like *Ten Days' Wonder*, this novel can't be discussed seriously without giving away the solution, but since it's one of the least well kept secrets in the Queen canon, I reveal it without qualms. Al Marsh is a closeted homosexual and has come on to Johnny, whom he loves, but killed his furious and contemptuous client in a rage of fright when Johnny rejected and threatened to out him. Could any reader be so blind as not to have figured this out from the blatantly unsubtle dying message, or the variations on sex-confusion scattered throughout the book, or that terrible pun about "one of Ellery's queerest cases," not to mention the dinner scene in Marsh's apartment, which makes the truth so obvious it hurts? A number of crime novels with graphic gay themes had been published in the Sixties, notably Roderick Thorp's *The Detective* (1966) and George Baxt's Pharaoh Love trilogy, but Fred and Manny assumed, perhaps not too wrongly, that Queen readers' acquaintance with the gay world was limited to standard insults like faggot, fairy and fruit. (Ellery's Wonderlandesque analysis fails to explain why Johnny didn't use one of those words to identify his murderer.) For the sake of these readers, Ellery was made to deliver a ludicrous lecture to his father on the ABCs of homosexuality, a subject with which I should think a 30-year NYPD veteran would have been sufficiently conversant. In fact father and son had already exchanged some remarks on the subject in *Cat of Many Tails* (1949) and *The Scarlet Letters* (1953). Clearly Fred and Manny meant well, and tried to present Marsh's love for Johnny as one of the few decent elements in the novel, but they went about the book so clumsily and with such a flimsy knowledge base that I can't imagine the staunchest Queenian defending the book today.

As usual, the cousins lifted a huge number of *Last Woman*'s elements from earlier Queen fiction. Ellery's momentary compulsion to "drop out" in the first scenes echoes the opening of *Cat of Many Tails*. The two figures on the wedding cake date back to "The Lonely Bride" (1949), first of the EQ short-shorts. The negative clue in Johnny's wardrobe harks back to *The King Is Dead*, and the murderer's use of his victim's clothes to *The Spanish Cape Mystery*. In fourth-period Queen, self-borrowings come with the territory.

***

In the late 1960s Manny Lee suffered a series of heart attacks and, on doctor's orders, took off a great deal of weight. It didn't save him. On the night of Friday, April 2, 1971, he had another attack in the bedroom of his home and died in the ambulance on the way to the Waterbury hospital.

He and I had been corresponding for a while but I had met him only once, just before the 1970 Mystery Writers of America dinner which was the last public function he and Fred attended together. We had arranged to meet "under the clock" in the lounge of the Biltmore Hotel where the dinner was being held. When we were introduced to each other, a young man who happened to be sitting nearby jumped up at the sound of his name and ran over and pumped his hand and whooped: "Manfred B. Lee! I think you're the greatest writer that ever lived!" To which Manny replied, peering owlishly at the intruder: "That doesn't say much for your taste, does it?" For me that was Manny in a nutshell—genial, earthy, frank and unpretentious. I would have given much to have known him better.

***

Manny never lived to see a copy of the last Ellery Queen novel. *A Fine and Private Place* (1971) continues the tendency of Period Four novels to be built around a leitmotif. In *The Player on the Other Side* it was a chess game, in *The House of Brass* it was greed for worthless things, in *The Last Woman in His Life* it was gender confusion. This time the leitmotif is the number nine. Nino Importuna was born on the ninth day of the ninth month of 1899, whose digits add up to 27, which totals—and is divisible both by and into—well, go figure. With his younger brothers Julio and Marco he resides on the top floors of the 9-story building at 99 East 99th Street and from there controls the vast Importuna industrial conglomerate, valued at half a billion dollars. The squat, bestial, 9-obsessed entrepreneur forces a young woman one-third his age into marrying him on the ninth day of the ninth month of 1962, whose digits add up to 18—which totals, and is divisible both by and into, that number again—and rewrites his will so that on their fifth anniversary she'll become his sole legatee. Virginia Whyte Importuna falls in love with Peter Ennis, her husband's much younger confidential secretary, and exactly nine months before that fifth anniversary the seed of death is sown. As the anniversary approaches, a murderer apparently as 9-obsessed as Nino makes his first strike and Ellery comes on the scene.

A Fine and Private Place is brim-full of Queen signature ingredients—the self-enclosed chessboard milieu, the satanic manipulator, the adversary's mocking notes to the investigators, the false solution followed by the true—but they all pale beside the countless variations on nineness. Most obvious of these are the allusions to pregnancy, the growth of a fetus and childbirth: the entire crime, the murderer's brainchild, is conceived and developed like a human baby. Perhaps the most subtle variation is that, beginning and ending with the same three words—words that happen to connote fatherhood—the novel is shaped into a figure that curls back on itself, a 9 of sorts, a fetus of sorts.

As always in late Queen, the echo phenomenon is conspicuous. The Importuna *famiglia* in some respects evokes the Van Horns in *Ten Days' Wonder*, in others the Bendigos in *The King Is Dead*. Nino's matrimonial finances recall Glory Guild's "arrangement" in *Face to Face*. The rug and desk clues of the first murder hark back respectively to the *Egyptian Cross* and *Dutch Shoe* mysteries, and the note-scattering murderer to *The Finishing Stroke*. And as usual in late Queen, there are cracks in the foundation. Fred devised a brilliant way around the old rule that the murderer must be a major character and not a walk-on part, but the result is that there are literally no suspects on whom the wary reader can fasten and only one person who could possibly be the killer. That person's master plan requires of Ellery and his father at certain key points a huge amount respectively of stupidity and failure to communicate—qualities with which each obligingly comes through at all the proper moments. If Richard had done the natural thing and told Ellery about the New Milford motel, or if Ellery had read all the reports on the case, or stopped to think that his initial solution entailed a killer who for no reason gave away the crucial clue, the Iago figure's trap would have sprung on empty air. Raymond Chandler said it best: This murderer has God sitting in his lap.

***

The most ambitious theatrical feature based on a Queen novel, and the only one helmed by a prestigious director, was *Ten Days' Wonder*, directed in English by Claude Chabrol (1930-2010) in the fall of 1970 but not released in New York until April 1972. The screenplay by Paul Gardner and Eugene Archer was based on an adaptation of the 1948 Queen novel by Chabrol's frequent collaborator Paul Gegauff. The role corresponding to Diedrich in the novel was played by Orson Welles, with Anthony Perkins and Marlene Jobert as the characters based respectively on Howard and Sally. Ellery's functions are performed by Michel Piccoli in the role of philosophy professor Paul Regis, in whose classes Perkins lost his religious faith and to whom Perkins comes for help in learning the cause of his strange blackouts as Howard came to Ellery in the novel. Chabrol moves the action from Wrightsville, U.S.A. to an 80-room baronial estate in Alsace but preserves almost the entire Queen plot structure intact.

Reviews, at least in the U.S., were almost uniformly awful. "[T]ension and insight are subordinated to sorry stylistic flamboyance," wrote Jay Cocks in *Time* (May 15, 1972). "Chabrol's camera swoops almost like a dizzy flamingo, descending from great altitudes to light on such still lifes as a garden, a pond or two naked lovers entwined in the green leaves." What a shame that this often visually lavish film is slow, boring, full of pretentious symbolism and almost completely dehumanized except for Piccoli's character, whose somber and humane rationality is as close to the "real" Ellery as the cinema ever got. In the novel the symbolic meanings became apparent only near the end and grew out of a wealth of realistic social and psychological details (mainly contributed by Manny Lee), but Chabrol sets his film in an abstract chessboard universe and forces us to endure its heavy-handed symbolism for 100 minutes. When I saw it in New York soon after its release, the theater was all but empty. It's now available on DVD, but even Queen fans might wish to rent it before deciding whether it's worth buying.

***

The World firm continued as Queen's hardcover publisher after Manny Lee's death, but not for long. In addition to the three final Queen novels, the company released one special anthology, *The Golden 13* (1971), which brought together a baker's dozen of first prize winners from *EQMM*'s annual contest, plus four of Fred's annual Best of volumes: *Ellery Queen's Murder Menu* (1969), *Ellery Queen's Grand Slam* (1970), *Ellery Queen's Headliners* (1971) and *Ellery Queen's Mystery Bag* (1972). That no such anthology came out in 1973 was due to Queen being between publishers at the time. Random House took over the anthology series with *Ellery Queen's Crookbook* (1974), and I am proud to record that my own first story can be found there. Davis Publications, which put out *EQMM* every month, continued as publisher of the semi-annual paperbound anthologies. And the Pyramid paperback house offered four much skimpier softcovers consisting of stories culled directly from the semi-annuals: *Murder—In Spades!* (#T2036, 1969); *Shoot the Works!* (#T2129, 1969), *Mystery Jackpot* (#T2207, 1970), and *Best Bets* (#N2775, 1972). If recycling is an environmentalist virtue, truly Fred was an ecological saint in those years.

***

After Manny's death Fred took over exclusive control of the Ellery Queen property. One of his first acts in that capacity was to terminate the ghosted paperbacks which he believed had debased the value of the identity he and Manny had created as young men. One more Troubleshooter novel, however, was still due under the contract with Lancer, and it was Fred's obligation to deliver it. Slated to do the writing was Edward D. Hoch (1930-2008), a prolific and masterful author of short stories in the Queen tradition of clues and deductions and fair play with the reader. In an interview with journalist John Kowalski (*The Armchair Detective*, Spring 1990), Hoch explained how he'd become involved. "I had told Fred, at one time, that I'd be interested in doing one of them. The agent that was handling the whole thing contacted me, and I submitted an outline to Manny Lee. He replied about it the very day he died. I've still got the letter, dated the day he died. Fred said he wanted me to continue with it since it was Manny's last project. Fred did fairly extensive editing on it. That was the only one of the books Fred edited. . . ."

In Hoch's *The Blue Movie Murders* (Lancer pb #75277-095, 1972) a Women's Lib crusade against pornographic films coincides with the murder of a Hollywood mogul and leads the governor to send Mike McCall to the small city in his state that is reputed to be the Mecca of sex flick production, with the dual mission of placating the libbers and locating the killers. The liberal speechifying in earlier McCall adventures is replaced this time with plot complications, and although a few peripheral matters don't ring true, Hoch's involuted, fairly and subtly clued, legitimately surprising story brings the long line of EQ paperbacks to a noble conclusion.

***

Manny's death saved him from having to watch the next TV incarnation of Ellery, which might well have given him another heart attack. Early in the 1970s Universal Pictures made plans to return the character to America's living rooms. The 2-hour pilot *Ellery Queen: Don't Look Behind You*, based on *Cat of Many Tails* (1949), was broadcast as an

NBC TV movie on November 19, 1971. Peter Lawford played Ellery as a mod Londonesque swinger with silver-streaked hair down to the eyebrows and a veddy British accent, while Harry Morgan with his Brooklyn twang was cast as Richard Queen: not Ellery's father but, in the cockeyed hope of explaining their incongruous accents, his uncle! Featured in the cast were E.G. Marshall (Dr. Edward Cazalis), Skye Aubrey (Christy), Stefanie Powers (Celeste Phillips), and Coleen Gray (Mrs. Cazalis). The script, credited to one Ted Leighton, was actually written by Richard Levinson and William Link, who at age 20 had made their debut as authors with "Whistle While You Work" (*EQMM*, November 1954). They went to Hollywood and soon established themselves as one of the top scriptwriting teams for TV mystery series, but they remained staunch Queen fans. As wage slaves at Universal they had minimal control over their work, and the final version of *Don't Look Behind You* was so awful that they refused to have their names on it. "If you ever see the name Ted Leighton on the screen," Link advised recently, "I caution you to switch to another channel." Director Barry Shear reduced the novel's rich characterizations to cardboard and added several routine action-suspense sequences without counterparts in the novel. I suspect that no writer or director could have successfully updated by twenty years a novel, perhaps the finest in the Queen canon, which was so inextricably rooted in the late Forties, but at least the bare bones of the plot were not broken and the budget was higher than for any Queen-based film before. Fred Dannay told me that on the whole he liked it. Its popularity persuaded NBC executives to launch a prime-time EQ series but it was dumped at the last minute in favor of *McMillan and Wife*, starring Rock Hudson and Susan Saint James as a sort of Seventies Nick-and-Nora couple.

***

At first Fred planned to continue the Queen novels, either alone or with a new partner. But then on the heels of Manny's death a new tragedy invaded Fred's life. In 1972, twenty-seven years after his first wife Mary had died of cancer, his second wife Hilda did likewise. And with her death Fred himself began dying by inches. Each time I visited him during the next few years he seemed to have shrunk in his chair a little more. Photographs of him taken in 1973 show the empty, devastated face of a man waiting for the dark to claim him. The only thing that kept him functioning, he told me, was the inexorable work schedule demanded of him by the magazine. I couldn't help feeling that his days were numbered.

And then he met the third woman in his life. At a dinner party he happened to be introduced to Rose Koppel, a recently widowed artist who worked at Manhattan's Ethical Culture School. In November 1975 they were married, and Rose literally saved her 70-year-old husband's life. He had always been a private person, so much so that after almost thirty years in the house on Byron Lane many of his closest neighbors had no idea what he did for a living. Rose de-privatized him as no other person before her had succeeded in doing and made it possible for him to enjoy his role as elder statesman of mystery fiction that time and the deaths of most of his contemporaries had bestowed on him.

***

In the years since the failure of the *Don't Look Behind You* telefilm, Richard Levinson and William Link had become one of the most successful producer-writer teams in TV history, thanks mainly to having created the long-running *Columbo* series, starring Peter Falk. They were still fond of EQ and decided to write another pilot. *Ellery Queen: Too Many Suspects* (March 23, 1975) was directed by David Greene and based on *The Fourth Side of the Triangle* (1965), which Levinson and Link backdated to the 1940s while preserving its structure intact and even in some ways improving on it. Fashion designer Monica Grey is murdered in her penthouse, pulling out the plug of her TV set and clock as a cryptic dying message (an element not in the novel). Chief suspects are her Thursday-evening lover, financier Carson McKell (Ray Milland), and McKell's jealous wife (Kim Hunter) and hot-tempered son (Monte Markham), each of whom in turn is charged with and then cleared of the murder. Ellery uses anagram clues to uncover a fourth theory and then, after issuing a Queenlike "Challenge to the Viewer," turns the dying message into the keystone of a fifth and final solution. David Wayne (1914-1995) was properly crusty as Inspector Queen but Jim Hutton (1934-1979) portrayed Ellery not as a dynamo of intellectual excitement and detached compassion but rather as a nearsighted young stumblebum, forever misplacing his glasses and bumping into people and objects as if he were a live-action Mr. Magoo. Clearly the Levinson-Link version of Ellery owed all too much to the immortal Lieutenant Columbo.

Queen purists weren't happy with the decision to turn Ellery into a diffident sloucher, but it was Hutton's pleasantly vacuous performance that sold the series, and in the fall of 1975 *Ellery Queen* returned to prime time on NBC after seventeen years' absence. The series consisted of 22 60-minute episodes, set in the late 1940s like the pilot. Each segment boasted big-name guest stars: Joan Collins, Ray Walston, Farley Granger, Barbara Rush and Guy Lombardo just in the first episode. The night that episode was broadcast, Fred Dannay happened to be home alone. "When I saw [Hutton] on the screen," he said later in an interview with *Playboy*, "I had the most curious reaction. I had the feeling I was seeing myself, years and years ago." The series featured a satisfying number of attempts to play fair with the viewer and several delightful continuing characters like Simon Brimmer (John Hillerman), the pompous radio supersleuth with an infallible genius for coming up with the wrong solutions to murders outside the studio. After the first seven episodes Jim Hutton shed his klutziness and began to play Ellery as a more human detective. All but one of the 22 segments were from original scripts. The single exception was "The Mad Tea-Party" (October 30, 1975), which for my money is the finest filmed Queen ever. Director James Sheldon and scriptwriter Peter S. Fischer were faithful to the plot of the classic 1934 short story but changed the names of several suspects so as to evoke some famous Golden Age mystery writers—Spencer Lockridge, Howard Biggers, Mrs. Allingham—and managed to improve on the original tale by providing a rationale for its single logical loophole.

Fred Dannay told me that the series drew as many as twenty million viewers a week. But the networks were unimpressed by such numbers and Ellery was taken off the air after a single season. The entire series including the pilot telefilm is now available on DVD.

***

The Queen TV program was only the beginning of Fred's late-blooming career as a media personality. During the next few years he was regularly in the public eye—guest lectures at the University of California, two appearances on TV's *Dick Cavett Show*, superstar treatment at the International Crime Writers' Congress held in New York early in 1978 (at which Fred and Rose were seen dancing cheek-to-cheek at 3:00 a.m.), interviews with *Playboy* and *People* and dozens of other periodicals, testimonial dinners celebrating the fiftieth anniversary of the publication of *The Roman Hat Mystery*, an honorary doctoral degree from Carroll College, a lavish trip to Tokyo for the premiere of a Japanese movie based on *Calamity Town* and to Stockholm for the 1981 International Crime Writers' Congress—so that it was a miracle he accomplished any work at all. He gave up the idea of breaking in a new collaborator and writing more Ellery Queen novels, saying that it would be disloyal to Manny's memory, but continued to edit both *EQMM* and a prodigious number of hardcover and paperback anthologies. After he turned 75 his health began to deteriorate and he was forced to curtail more and more of his work. He was hospitalized twice and then, late in the summer of 1982, a third time. That Labor Day weekend his heart stopped.

For me his death meant not only the end of a great tradition in detective fiction and of an exciting and fruitful editor-writer interaction but also the end of an infinitely precious friendship. Many of our viewpoints and interests were different but our feeling for the literature of crime brought us together and gave birth to our feeling for each other. We shared heartbreak and triumph, happy times and sad. But for me the best times were when we'd talk, hour after hour, about the writers who had preceded Fred and those who were his contemporaries and those who were coming up after him and, as I got older, some who were coming up after me. I never felt so much a part of a living tradition as I did on those occasions. He was the closest to a grandfather I've known. Without him I would never have written a word of fiction worth reading. Now the excitement of his presence lives only in memories.

CHAPTER TWENTY-THREE

End Time for Ellery

FRED DANNAY HAD COMPLETED his synopsis for the next Ellery Queen novel and sent it to Manny before his cousin's death. No one has ever expanded this document to novel length and no one ever will, but it's been published, and gives us an opportunity to see and evaluate for ourselves the kind of raw material with which Manny had worked for decades.

The Tragedy of Errors opens on Monday, April 3, 1967, in a castle known as Elsinore on a hilltop overlooking Hollywood. A violent quarrel is taking place between 65-year-old Morna Richmond, a superstar of silent screen who had invested wisely after talking pictures had ruined her career, and her decades-younger paramour Buck Burnshaw, a failed actor in cheap Westerns. At the climax of their battle over his affair with ex-starlet Cherry O'Hare, Buck comes very close to strangling Morna. Two days later, in the office of her lawyer Ted Curtis, Morna signs a will, making sure that neither Curtis nor the witnesses can see how she fills in the blank space where the name of the person to whom she's leaving her estate belongs. One copy of this will she leaves with Curtis, the other she takes with her. Soon afterwards, Buck steals the latter copy of the will from Morna's wall safe and leaves it with Cherry O'Hare.

On the morning of April 24 a servant finds Morna shot to death. Buck phones Dr. Rago, the psychiatrist on whom she was dependent, and the police. Ellery is in Hollywood and soaked in Shakespeare, being on assignment to turn *Othello* into a contemporary detective film. When the squeal comes in he happens to be chatting with Lieutenant Perez of LAPD Homicide, who invites him to accompany the police to Elsinore. Evidence against Buck Burnshaw piles up, notably a tiny BB shot pellet clutched in Morna's hand, which the sleuths interpret as (what else?) a dying message. The one copy of her will has of course vanished from her wall safe—which has a special dial consisting of the letters of the alphabet and a combination made up of four of those letters—and the other copy is discovered to have vanished from her lawyer's office. Buck is arrested and put on trial, but the case against him collapses when Ellery finds a suicide note in Morna's indisputable handwriting, dated the day of her death, in a copy of the complete works of Shakespeare in her bedroom. Acquitted and therefore safe forever from being retried, Buck then reveals that Morna actually wrote the suicide note back in 1961, and that he himself had added a tiny horizontal stroke to turn the 1 in the year date into a 7. Why did he frame himself for her murder? So that he'd inherit her fortune under her will, which he then produces. To whom did she leave everything she possessed? *To whoever murdered her*. In many a Queen story or radio play, the validity of such a wacko will would have gone unquestioned. Here however Ellery knows enough law to point out what Buck never understood: that Morna's will is invalid and unenforceable as against public policy, so that Buck killed her for nothing. Since Morna had no known blood relatives, the issue of who will inherit her estate now arises. Just when it seems that her fortune will go to the state of California by the process known as escheat, a forgotten old shoot-em-up actor named Reed Harmon enters the picture with proof that back in 1930 he and Morna were secretly married. The marriage only lasted ten days but was never dissolved, which means that Harmon as her surviving spouse will take the estate. Complications continue to abound—including a suicide, another murder, and a young black playwright who hovers around the fringes of the plot with his motorcycle—until Ellery identifies seven characteristics that Morna's murderer must have and names one of the characters as the culprit. Then as so often before he discovers something he's overlooked and offers a second and more flabbergasting solution that finally reveals the murderer, perhaps the most Iagoesque of all the many Iago figures in the Queen canon.

Manny's death aborted the expansion of this Shakespeare-saturated synopsis into a novel, but Fred's raw material offers us a fascinating look at precisely how his mind worked. Accompanying his synopsis was an undated covering letter to Manny which has also been published, and makes clear that for Fred the subject of the book was to be "the insanity of today's world." Sane is mad, mad is sane. Fred never let me read the synopsis in his lifetime but told me of its leitmotif and added that it had come to him from reading some of the work of psychiatrist R.D. Laing, who believed that some of the sanest people alive were in mental hospitals. In fact, as I discovered when his sons invited me to read it after his death, it had even deeper roots in *There Was an Old Woman*(1943).

***

Around the time of Manny's death, Davis Publications advertised in the *Times* for a new managing editor at *EQMM*. One of the applicants was Eleanor Sullivan (1929-1991). "[W]hile I had strong experience in editing trade books, especially fiction, I had no magazine experience whatsoever, and my knowledge of mystery fiction, as I candidly admitted, was limited." Both Fred and publisher Joel Davis were impressed with her. In later years she decided that what led them to hire her was her answer to Fred's question: "How good are you at taking instructions?" Her reply: "I went to parochial school." For her first two years as managing editor, Fred from his home in Larchmont made countless phone calls to her at *EQMM*'s New York office, patiently and painstakingly instructing her, in effect giving her a one-on-one tutorial in the history of the genre and the mechanics of magazine production.

Fred did all his work at home. He never went to New York on business and never met most of the people who worked on the magazine. Every afternoon Eleanor Sullivan would make up a package containing the day's submissions (except those that were hopeless), attach comments to each story, and mail the parcel to Byron Lane. Fred would read each story but wouldn't read the comments until he'd formed his own opinion. When a story needed changes, he'd discuss them with the author over the phone or in letters, usually handwritten. This was the daily routine whose end product was an issue of *EQMM* every month for decades. In 1980, when Fred turned seventy-five, he stepped down from active editorship. Upon his death two years later, Sullivan took over as editor-in-chief in every sense of the term. She continued in that role until her own death of brain cancer in 1991. Since then Janet Hutchings has served as editor-in-chief. The magazine is now in its early seventies, and it's still the finest periodical of its kind ever published.

***

Until the late 1960s, those years of torment and ferment, it was the consensus among academics that subjects like movies and vintage radio and TV and science-fiction and Westerns—and mysteries—had no intellectual significance and no place in any self-respecting college curriculum. In my own college years, which roughly coincided with the Kennedy presidency, there wasn't a single course on any of those subjects in the entire curriculum. I vividly recall one of my professors bewailing the fact that William Faulkner had been forced by a Philistine reading public to support himself by writing for the movies. Carolyn Heilbrun, a young professor of English at Columbia University, had begun writing mystery novels but had to do it under a pseudonym (Amanda Cross) because, as she explained years later, she would never have gotten tenure if her colleagues had known of her sideline.

That was the academic environment when Ray B. Browne (1922-2009) came into the picture. With a Ph.D. in English and Folklore and twenty years of university teaching under his belt, he moved from Purdue to Ohio's Bowling Green State University and, with the support of the administration, launched the movement that made it academically respectable to teach and study popular culture—a term he is said to have invented. He and the cadre of young doctoral candidates he gathered around him as the Vietnam war raged literally reshaped the American academic ambience. It was now okay for professors to study and write about movies and radio and TV and science fiction and Westerns and, yes, about mystery fiction. I was one of those professors. I published all sorts of material in the *Journal of Popular Culture*, which Ray had launched soon after arriving at Bowling Green, and gave presentations at annual meetings of the Popular Culture Association, which Ray had founded a few years later. It was Bowling Green's Popular Press which published my first non-fiction book, *Royal Bloodline: Ellery Queen, Author And Detective* (1974), for which I received an Edgar from Mystery Writers of America. Other publishers launched all sorts of popular culture reference book projects. Every one of them which dealt with mystery fiction included an entry of substantial length on Queen. (Those in *20ᵗʰ Century Crime and Mystery Writers*, which survives into the new century as the *St. James Guide to Crime and Mystery Writers*, and in *Mystery and Suspense Writers: The Literature of Crime, Detection and Espionage*, are by me). Specialized magazines like *The Armchair Detective* featured countless discussions of the contributions Fred and Manny had made to a now respectable form of literature. Manny, who was a college graduate with hopes of becoming a literature professor, largely shared the consensus of pre-1960s academics that the genre was trash and would have been appalled had he lived to see this development. Fred, who never went to college and therefore perhaps overvalued attention to the genre by intellectuals, had been preaching for years (to the choir) about the importance of mystery fiction and became ecstatic when it gained academic respect.

There were no more books about Queen until the year Fred died. I had remained interested in the subject and, thanks to Ray Stanich (1927-1992), a tireless researcher into the golden age of American radio, I had come into possession of much more information about the EQ radio series than was available to me when I was working on *Royal Bloodline*. That information formed the core of my book *The Sound Of Detection: Ellery Queen's Adventures in Radio* (1982). A hugely expanded second edition, on which I was assisted by Martin Grams, Jr., came out in 2002, and I hope to have an even more detailed edition ready before too long.

A few years after the first edition of that book came out, I was asked by another publisher to put together a collection of the finest Queen short stories. For *The Best of Ellery Queen* (1985) I chose three from *Adventures* (1934), two from *New Adventures* (1940), two from *Calendar of Crime* (1952), four short-shorts from the *Q.B.I.* volume (1955), three from the *Q.E.D.* assemblage (1968), and the previously uncollected "Wedding Anniversary" (1967). I still believe I chose wisely.

***

It wasn't until the tail end of the century that another significant Queen book appeared. *The Tragedy of Errors* (1999) contained Fred's synopsis for the novel that Manny didn't live to expand and 22 "essays and reminiscences" about the cousins by various authors and editors and members of the Dannay and Lee families. On the fiction side, the volume brought together all the as yet uncollected shorter work, most notably "Terror Town" (1956). All the other uncollected tales were trifles from Queen's final period. In "Uncle from Australia" (*Diners' Club Magazine*, June 1965; *EQMM*, November 1967) Ellery interprets the dying words of the cockney-accented huncle from down hunder and determines which of his three greedy relatives skewered him for the inheritance. The victim probably couldn't have known the truth himself, and almost every reader will see it literally as soon as the words are spoken. Next come three Puzzle Club anecdotes, challenging Ellery to solve imaginary riddles devised by other club members. All appeared in famous magazines that paid handsomely, one being published shortly before and two soon after Manny Lee's death. In "The Three Students" (*Playboy*, March 1971) Ellery must decide which of the trio—handily named Adams, Barnes and Carver—stole a valuable ring from the university president's desk. The key to the answer is a fact so specialized that the tale must seem child's play to those who know it and gibberish to those who don't. "The Odd Man" (*Playboy*, June 1971) requires Ellery to tell his Puzzle Club confreres which of their three imagined suspects is a secret criminal when he has no information about the trio except their names and occupations. And in "The Honest Swindler" (*Saturday Evening Post*, Summer 1971) he must explain how an old prospector could have spent five years on a fruitless uranium hunt and still have returned every penny of his backers' money.

Was that the end of the saga? Had the ghost of Long John Silver been exhibited for the last time? Not quite. Four years after Manny died, the *National Inquirer* tabloid paper offered Fred the lordly sum of $5,000 for a Christmas story about Ellery. Fred wanted the money but didn't feel up to creating the story on his own. He phoned his most reliable *EQMM* contributor, Edward D. Hoch, who was then appearing in every issue, and offered him $500 to write the tale, which Fred would edit before sending it to the *Inquirer*. "I decided the story should contain a dying message," Hoch wrote a quarter century later in an introduction for *The Tragedy of Errors*. "The Children's Zoo at Central Park seemed the perfect setting, with a reindeer display for the holidays." "The Reindeer Clue" (*National Inquirer*, December 25, 1975), the last tale about Ellery published under the Queen byline, is far superior to the "fun and games" short-shorts of the cousins' last active years and on a par with the best tales of that length in the *Q.B.I.* collection.

**

The centenary of both Fred's and Manny's birth, in 2005, led to a flurry of new material. *EQMM* celebrated the entire year by running an essay on some aspect of Queen in each monthly issue. Columbia University, the repository of the Dannay papers, hosted a one-day EQ symposium which drew the attention of *The New York Times*. And the small publishing house of Crippen & Landru, which had issued *The Tragedy Of Errors* in 1999, celebrated the centenary with *The Adventure Of The Murdered Moths* (2005), a generous assortment of some of the finest EQ radio dramas: nine scripts from the first season (1939-40), when each show ran 60 minutes, and five 30-minute scripts from later years.

Seven years later, with the publication of much of the Dannay-Lee correspondence in *Blood Relations*, edited by Joseph Goodrich (Perfect Crime Books, 2012), every Queen devotee was given a ringside seat at the brutal verbal duels Fred and Manny fought during the period when some of the finest third-period Queen novels were being plotted and written. Almost all the material from their letters that I quote here comes from this fascinating book.

**

When the author dies, the work dies. That is almost always the reality, and certainly it's the rule in genre fiction. There are always a few exceptions, like Agatha Christie and Louis L'Amour, but those authors are *rarae aves*. I took it for granted that Ellery Queen was one (or two) of them. I never thought I'd live to see the falling off into near oblivion of what had been a household name for more than a decade before I was born and for at least the first thirty years of my life. Why did this happen? Mystery author and reviewer Jon L. Breen wrote a notable piece for *The Weekly Standard* (October 10, 2005; collected in *A Shot Rang Out*, 2009) both celebrating the cousins' centenary and attempting to account for why their work had been so completely forgotten. He offered five reasons. (1) Hardboiled or *noir* detective fiction has become so closely identified with male authors like Hammett and Chandler, and classic formal detective puzzles (now called cozies) so closely linked to women authors like Christie and Sayers, that the great masters (as opposed to mistresses) of Golden Age detection—like John Dickson Carr and the cousins Queen—have fallen between the cultural cracks. (2) Perhaps the Queen prose style has fallen out of favor and become a barrier to today's readers. (3) There seems to be a "general critical prejudice against literary collaboration." (4) The farming out of so much of the EQ product to ghosts in the 1960s was "disastrous in its effect on the Queen reputation." (5) "Ellery Queen has fallen from public attention because our respect for intelligence, our cultural literacy, and our attention span are all in steep decline."

This analysis strikes me as unarguably correct. But will Queen remain forgotten? In Japan and to a certain extent in Italy, the name is still meaningful. Might it become so again here? Fred Dannay and I discussed this in his last years, and since his death I've had similar discussions with the editors of the magazine he founded. I am no oracle, but it seems to me that EQ's return, if it happens at all, will not be driven by the print medium in which Fred and Manny worked. Perhaps, as I once suggested to Fred back when Columbo was king, a high-quality series of TV movies might be the answer. Perhaps the computer or e-books or the smartphone or some high-tech device no one has yet imagined will return Queen to the public eye. Whatever the future holds for the authors and characters and novels and stories that meant so much to me and to countless others going back to the early 1930s, it's good to have had them as part of my life.

APPENDIX

EQMM: The Dannay Years

BETWEEN LATE SEPTEMBER 1940 and early January 1942 *The Adventures of Ellery Queen* was not on radio and Fred and Manny had some time on their hands. By the beginning of this 15-month hiatus Fred had built up his library of detective-crime short fiction to the point where it was probably the finest in the world. His collection became the basis for *Ellery Queen's Mystery Magazine*, which continues today, more than 70 years later.

For most of the later 1920s, and until around 1931 when he and Manny became full-time writers, Fred had held a job writing copy for an advertising agency. Throughout his career in the mystery field, he never ceased to think about ways of promoting the product. It was almost certainly his idea, which he sold to publisher Lawrence A. Spivak, to launch *EQMM* with a media event. Since Poe had created the detective genre in 1841 with "The Murders in the Rue Morgue," the event was billed as a Detective Story Centennial Luncheon, held at the Waldorf-Astoria on September 25, 1941 and broadcast over a coast-to-coast radio hookup, with dozens of current celebrities and even a few mystery writers among the invited guests.

In the beginning the magazine was a quarterly. The premiere issue (Fall 1941), saddle-stitched and with cover art by George Salter, ran 128 pages and featured stories by Dashiell Hammett, Margery Allingham, T.S. Stribling, Anthony Abbot, Cornell Woolrich and, surprise surprise, Ellery Queen. All were reprints (although Allingham's tale was new to the U.S.). Stories by Agatha Christie, Geoffrey Household, Stuart Palmer, Vincent Starrett, Dorothy L. Sayers and Steve Fisher were prominent in the next issue (Winter 1941-42), while the third number (Spring 1942) included tales by R. Austin Freeman, Ben Hecht, Edgar Wallace, Jacques Futrelle and Michael Arlen, plus a script from the EQ radio series, the first of ten printed in the magazine during the war years. Most of *EQMM*'s earliest stories were reprints, but the second issue offered a Frederick Irving Anderson tale never published before, and the third included two stories by English authors (R. Austin Freeman and Michael Arlen) that were new to American readers. From the get-go Fred intended the magazine to be a home for the most widely diverse stories and authors available. Old and new, from pulps and slicks, originals and reprints, hardboiled and cerebral, locked rooms and gang wars and women in peril, set in every corner of the earth. The only constant he demanded was quality.

With its fourth issue (May 1942) the magazine became a bi-monthly, increasing Fred's workload from four issues a year to six. With the return of the Queen radio show to the airwaves in January 1942, he once again had to devise a new plot synopsis every week for Manny to expand into script form. And with the United States plunged into World War II, he faced problems he couldn't have anticipated when the magazine had debuted. One of these was paper shortages. The first issue had been printed on book-quality paper, but the second and many later wartime issues used stock of much poorer quality which long ago turned brown and brittle like issues of *Black Mask* and other pulps from the same period. Another problem was that countless potential contributors to *EQMM* were putting their writing careers on hold and joining the military. However much Fred might have preferred new stories for the magazine, the war situation forced him to rely heavily on reprints. The best known author who had new stories regularly in the wartime *EQMM* was Anthony Boucher (1911-1968), a lifelong asthmatic who was 4-F in the draft. Both Boucher and his alcoholic sleuth Nick Noble debuted in the September 1942 issue, and two months later the magazine published the first short story by Georges Simenon to appear in the U.S., translated by the multi-lingual Boucher. The November 1942 issue also included a historical whodunit written in Cockney dialect by ex-journalist Samuel Duff McCoy (1882-1964), who ghosted several of the juvenile mysteries published as by "Ellery Queen, Jr." If McCoy was too old for military service, another author who debuted in the wartime *EQMM* was too young: 16-year-old James Yaffe (1927-), whose first story appeared in the July 1943 issue. In the Fifties Yaffe contributed countless teleplays to the Golden Age of live TV drama and also created a memorable series for *EQMM* about "Mom," the mother of a young Jewish homicide cop who solves crime puzzles for her son during their Friday-night suppers. Yaffe is the earliest *EQMM* debutant alive today.

In his introduction to the first issue of *EQMM* Fred had described the magazine as a "book," a sort of quarterly anthology of mystery stories, and accordingly the first nine issues had contained one column of print per page as books did. With the tenth issue (May 1943) the magazine adopted double-column format, which it retained for several decades.

Fred had always written a brief introduction to each story in the magazine, but late in 1944 his remarks became longer, chattier, almost like mini-essays. A reader endowed with Ellery's intellect might have deduced that Fred was devoting more time to the magazine than before, but only a tiny inner circle knew the truth. Fred's first wife, Mary Beck Dannay, had been diagnosed with cancer (which took her life on July 4, 1945), and he was no longer able to supply Manny with the plot synopses that were needed week in and week out for the radio series. (From the spring of 1945 until the series left the air more than three years later, more than 70 of Manny's scripts were based, as we've seen, on synopses by Boucher.) With a dying wife and two young sons to raise, Fred needed to devote whatever work time he had available to projects he found more congenial, like the magazine. Soon his introductions in a given issue of *EQMM* took up more words and space than a complete short story might.

Despite so many authors in uniform, Fred could boast in the May 1945 issue that seven new detective series had been launched in *EQMM* since Pearl Harbor. Only two are likely to be remembered today: Boucher's Nick Noble, whose nine cases are included in *Exeunt Murderers* (1983), and Lillian de la Torre's Dr. Sam: Johnson, whose adventures—narrated of course by James Boswell—fill four collections. With its last bi-monthly issue (November 1945), published soon after the

Japanese surrender, the foundational period in *EQMM*'s history came to an end.

***

Page 2 of that final bi-monthly issue announced a short story contest, offering a $2,000 first prize and six second prizes of $500 each. The deadline for submitting stories was December 3, 1945, about two months after the November issue hit the newsstands. The contest judges were author Christopher Morley, whodunit historian Howard Haycraft, and Fred Dannay himself. The annual competition would continue for the next twelve years and become a hallmark of the magazine's most fruitful period. But I date that period's beginning here for other reasons too. Not only were authors returning to their civilian careers behind typewriters, but those who wrote crime fiction had a professional organization to come home to. Mystery Writers of America (MWA), created early in 1945, was small at first but grew rapidly as the United States settled into peacetime again. No longer facing wartime paper shortages, and with increasing numbers of authors back in civilian life, the magazine became a monthly with the January 1946 issue. One month later Fred inaugurated "Speaking of Crime," a column of commentary and book reviews conducted by his fellow contest judge Howard Haycraft, whose *Murder for Pleasure* (1941) remains the definitive history of the genre from Poe to Pearl Harbor.

Aside from Haycraft's column, the monthly *EQMM* looked much like its earlier bi-monthly incarnation. Reprints of pulp classics by Hammett and Woolrich, radio scripts by John Dickson Carr, tales previously published only in England by authors like Agatha Christie and Margery Allingham and Roy Vickers, and new stories by the likes of Lillian de la Torre and Miriam Allen De Ford and Stuart Palmer made up the bulk of each issue both before and after New Year's 1946. But almost every month offered something new as well, for example Manly Wade Wellman's "A Star for a Warrior" (April 1946), the first mystery with a Native American protagonist and the first-prize winner in the first annual contest. The June 1946 issue presented "An Error in Chemistry" by William Faulkner, who would soon be hailed as the 20th century's foremost American novelist, and "Find the Woman" by returning Navy veteran Kenneth Millar, who as Ross Macdonald would soon be hailed as the successor to Hammett and Chandler in private-eye fiction. What a double-header! The September 1946 issue brought the first of a series of new stories by and about Ellery Queen himself, each based on a Queen radio play and centering on a month of the year, all twelve collected as *Calendar of Crime* (1952). "The Nine Mile Walk" (April 1947) was the first story by Harry Kemelman, who in the Sixties would write the best-selling series of mystery novels about Rabbi David Small. The July 1947 issue included the first story by Jack Finney, a future star of fantasy and science-fiction.

Fred's next innovation was to print one much longer story in most issues of *EQMM*, beginning with "The Third Bullet" (January 1948), a radically condensed version of John Dickson Carr's 1937 short novel, which wasn't reissued uncut until 1991. Novelettes by Rex Stout, Erle Stanley Gardner and Lawrence G. Blochman among others appeared later that year, all reprints. With the February 1948 issue the magazine's page count rose from 128 to 144 and its newsstand price to 35 cents. Stanley Ellin's "The Specialty of the House" (May 1948) was the first story by perhaps the finest of all the authors who became *EQMM* regulars. Students of African American literature hail the July 1948 issue since it contained Hughes Allison's "Corollary," the first serious crime story set in the black ghetto. The August 1948 number was billed as an International Issue, each of its fourteen stories coming from a different nation, with Argentina represented by Jorge Luis Borges' "The Garden of Forking Paths," the first English-language publication by perhaps the foremost Latin American author ever. It was Boucher who brought this story to Fred's attention and translated it to boot. With the February 1949 issue, the first to be bound like other digest-sized periodicals rather than saddle-stitched, Boucher took over "Speaking of Crime" from Howard Haycraft but left after four bi-monthly columns. Many of that year's issues continued to reprint novelettes by authors like Hammett and Woolrich.

Among the notable stories at the opening of the new decade were John Dickson Carr's "The Gentleman from Paris" (April 1950), first-prize winner in that year's contest, and Stanley Ellin's "The Orderly World of Mr. Appleby" (May 1950). The November 1950 issue presented A.H.Z. Carr's "The Trial of John Nobody" and Philip MacDonald's "Love Lies Bleeding," perhaps the first serious crime story about (all but) openly gay characters. Hollywood quickly made movies from the stories by the two unrelated Carrs, and likewise from Charlotte Armstrong's "The Enemy" (May 1951).

The April 1951 "Once-in-a-Lifetime Issue" contained just eight stories, their authors ranked by a Gallup Poll as the best mystery writers of all time. Fred designed this issue to the specifications of prestidigitator Richard Himber, to serve as a prop in one of Himber's magic tricks. After copies were handed out, Himber would ask a member of the audience to turn to the first page of any story and add the digits of that page number, so that page 53 would yield an 8, page 94 a 13, and so on. When the subject identified the eighth or thirteenth word on that page, whatever the number might be, Himber would instantly identify the word. How could he do that? Because Fred had doctored the texts of the issue's eight stories so that the same word, "problems," was on the first page of each in its appropriate spot. Obviously the trick could only be used once in each performance or the audience would catch on.

The June 1951 issue launched a new feature, the Detective Directory, excerpting reviews of mystery novels from major publications like the *Times* and *Saturday Review*. The last of the twelve Queen stories soon to be collected as *Calendar of Crime* appeared in the August 1951 issue, and the final number of that year included the earliest of the Queen short-shorts that had been appearing in *This Week* magazine since 1949. Meanwhile reprinted novelettes kept coming, by Christie and Stout and Erle Stanley Gardner among others.

The June 1952 issue offered the first of James Yaffe's "Mom" tales, and in November the first *EQMM* story of Dorothy Salisbury Davis. Yaffe and Davis, respectively 85 and 96 years old as I write, are perhaps the last surviving authors who helped shape the magazine in the Fifties. Crime novelist Margaret Millar, the wife of Ross Macdonald, made her debut in the magazine with "The Couple Next Door" (July 1954). "Whistle While You Work" (November 1954) launched the careers of two 20-year-old high-school classmates who were to become the foremost names in TV mystery: Richard Levinson and William Link.

In 1953, soon after the legendary hardboiled pulp *Black Mask* went under, publisher Lawrence Spivak bought the rights to the name and incorporated it into the *EQMM* masthead. Fred of course had been publishing new and old stories in the *Black Mask* vein since Day One, but the magazine's commitment to that vein was now formalized. It was probably not *Black Mask* but the newly founded *Playboy* that led to so many scantily clad women appearing in *EQMM* cover art around this time. Objections were heard from subscribers and also from at least one contributor, English novelist Phyllis Bentley, who wrote Fred in March and April 1954: "The cover illustrations reveal so much naked femininity that one really hardly likes to be seen with the magazine in one's hand! . . . I have covered them in brown paper before reading them! I simply could not bear either to see or to touch pictures of that kind." In October 1955 it was announced that special non-pictorial covers would be used on all copies of the magazine sent to subscribers.

If any period in *EQMM*'s history demonstrate Fred Dannay's bent for publicity, it's the mid-Fifties. "Alibi on the Steve Allen Show" (May 1956) was written to order by O.H. Leslie (Henry Slesar) as a tie-in with Allen's TV program, and Stuart Palmer's "You Bet Your Life" (May 1957) was a tie-in with the TV quiz show hosted by Groucho Marx. The June, August and October 1956 issues contained chapters from Daniel Nathan's *The Golden Summer* (1953), a novel set in 1915 and all but unnoticed on its first publication. Anthony Boucher, James Yaffe and Stanley Ellin contributed glowing prefaces, one to each installment. What no one mentioned was that Daniel Nathan was Fred Dannay, trying to drum up interest in the most personal novel he ever wrote and the only one written without Manny Lee's collaboration. (Among the other stories in the October 1956 issue was "Tough Break" by Ryam Beck, who was actually Fred's oldest son, Douglas Dannay, using a byline taken from his dead mother's name.) In the September 1956 issue Fred announced a contest to find a fitting name for an untitled story by Lawrence G. Blochman. Who but someone with deep roots in the advertising game could have devised this jingle?

> We've got a block, man—
> Need a title with sock, man,
> So send in a flock, man
> FOR THE STORY BY BLOCH-MAN....

Beginning with that September issue, the 35-cent newsstand price of an issue purchased not 144 pages of reading matter but 138, and with the January 1957 number the page count dropped to 130. Luckily there was still space for Anthony Boucher's "Best Mysteries of the Month" column, which lasted from the November 1957 issue until just before Boucher's death of lung cancer in the spring of 1968.

***

Boucher's column was perhaps the last innovation before the transition from *EQMM*'s fruitful second period to its third and final phase under Fred's editorship. An early foretaste of changing times was that Fred's long informative enthusiastic introductions to just about every new story and every reprint in every issue became noticeably shorter and more perfunctory. With the February 1958 issue Davis Publications bought the magazine from Lawrence Spivak's Mercury Publications, and George Salter's long run as principal cover artist ended with the March issue.

"Death in the Harbor" (December 1962) was the first *EQMM* story by Edward D. Hoch (1930-2008), who in a few years became by far the most prolific contributor to the magazine, a total of over 500 stories including one in every issue of the magazine from the May 1973 issue until several months after his death. Hoch was a devotee of the Ellery Queen novels and a godsend to *EQMM* since many of his stories were the sort of fair-play deductive puzzles that Fred Dannay loved and found in such short supply as the puzzle-spinners of his own generation died off. Several of Hoch's most popular series characters—like the espionage detective Rand (whose name Fred changed from Randolph so it would subliminally evoke James Bond), and the professional purloiner of valueless objects Nick Velvet, and the New England physician-sleuth Dr. Sam Hawthorne—appeared exclusively in *EQMM*.

By early 1963 Fred was growing desperate. "[I]t is so hard to keep up the basic quality," he wrote to Boucher on February 7. "[T]he boys and girls have virtually given up the short story. I am at my wits' end for the future. . . ." At that time he had seen only a few stories by Ed Hoch and had no idea that the most reliable of all *EQMM* authors was already under his editorial roof. Perhaps his desperation accounts for some decisions that he wouldn't have dreamed of making in *EQMM*'s earlier phases. Too much of what he reprinted in the Sixties was easily available elsewhere, like Christie's early Poirot stories and Rex Stout's Nero Wolfe novelettes, not to mention exploits of Ellery Queen himself. Every 1965 issue from March to December contained a story from the *Calendar of Crime* collection that had first appeared in the magazine decades earlier and, like the Christie and Stout reprints, were readily accessible elsewhere. (The remaining two *Calendar* tales were recycled in January and February 1968). All too many of the new stories he ran were parodies or pastiches (or both) of big-name authors or characters, including EQ himself. Perhaps the best of the parodists was Robert L. Fish, whose hilarious Schlock Homes stories began with "The Adventure of the Ascot Tie" (February 1960) and continued for years alongside Fish's mainstream crime novels. With the March 1963 issue the magazine's page count rose to 162 per issue and its newsstand price 50 cents, with another ten-cent increase exactly five years later. With the January 1969 issue John Dickson Carr with his "Jury Box" column took over for the late Anthony Boucher.

The stories reprinted during *EQMM*'s third phase were often overfamiliar but the percentage of first-rate new tales was high as ever. Cornell Woolrich, whose powerful pulp suspense fiction Fred had reprinted in more than sixty issues dating back to Volume 1 Number 1, began sending new stories to *EQMM* in 1958 and continued until his death ten years later. Among his contributions to the magazine were two of the most powerful *noir* stories ever written: "For the Rest of Her Life" (May 1968), later filmed by German director Rainer Werner Fassbinder, and the posthumously published "New York Blues" (December 1970), a perfect summation of this dark angel's literary career.

Other authors of Woolrich's and Fred's generation, whose stories had often appeared as *EQMM* reprints in earlier decades—Michael Gilbert and Thomas Walsh, to name two—also began sending him their latest work. Their contemporaries Lawrence Treat and Christianna Brand, who had rarely if ever appeared in the magazine before, launched two wonderful series of new stories in *EQMM*, Treat's in the police-procedural vein and Brand's rich in deductive puzzlement. Among the younger writers who began their careers elsewhere but appeared in the magazine during Phase Three and rose high in the field were Jack Ritchie, Joe Gores, Donald E. Westlake, Clark Howard, John Lutz, Lawrence Block and Bill Pronzini. In *EQMM*'s third phase ten winners of the annual MWA Edgar award for best short story were tales Fred had published, including Lawrence Treat's "H as in Homicide" (March 1964), Joe Gores' "Goodbye, Pops" (December 1969), Thomas Walsh's "Chance After Chance" (November 1977), Clark Howard's "Horn Man" (July 1980), and Jack Ritchie's "The Absence of Emily" (January 1981).

Fred's insistence on publishing in each issue of *EQMM* at least one story by someone who had never contributed to the genre before was one of his wisest policies and brightened the magazine's third phase by launching the careers of countless writers who blossomed under his editorial guidance: Robert L. Fish, Josh Pachter, Jon L. Breen, and perhaps, in a small way, me.

With the January 1969 issue Fred's close friend John Dickson Carr had taken over from the late Anthony Boucher as conductor of *EQMM's* monthly review column. But Carr's poor health and lack of interest in current crime novels caused problems. His "Jury Box" column for October 1976 was his last, and he died of cancer in February 1977. Jon L. Breen had assumed the reviewing function by then, and with one hiatus hung onto it until 2011 when he retired.

With the September 1970 issue the *EQMM* masthead bore a new name: Eleanor Sullivan, Managing Editor. She had had no previous magazine experience and knew little about mystery fiction but Fred found her very impressive. "How good are you at taking instructions?" he asked her. "I went to parochial school," she replied. Later she attributed her being hired to that answer. Fred did all his work from his home in Larchmont. During her first years as managing editor he made countless phone calls to her at *EQMM's* New York office, patiently giving her a private tutorial on the history of the genre and the mechanics of magazine production, in effect training her to be his eventual successor. Every afternoon she would make up a package containing the day's submissions (except those that were hopeless), attach comments to each story, and mail the parcel to Fred's house. Fred would read each story but wouldn't read the comments until he'd formed his own opinion, which he would then share with her over the phone. Occasionally Sullivan would include a short story of her own under a pseudonym, and if Fred liked it and told her he'd buy it, she would reveal—no doubt chortling in her joy—that she was the author. She had to use a different name on each story she submitted to Fred but all that were published appeared under a single byline, Lika Van Ness,

In 1980, having reached age 75, Fred relinquished most of the magazine's editorial functions but continued to appear on the masthead as "Editor." He died over the Labor Day weekend of 1982. The January 1983 *EQMM*, printed not long after his death, is the first whose masthead omits his name entirely and lists Sullivan as "Editor."

It was the end of perhaps the most exciting and fruitful magazine-editing career in the mystery genre. But thanks to Fred's forty years of intense labor, the magazine still stood tall.

APPENDIX

At Work and Play With Fred Dannay

ON THE NIGHT of Friday, September 3, 1982, six and a half weeks short of his seventy-seventh birthday, the life of Frederic Dannay ended. Even so many years later, each time I realize he's gone I feel an emptiness.

For the millions of readers who loved the adventures of Ellery Queen which he wrote in collaboration with his cousin Manfred B. Lee, Fred's death meant the end of a noble tradition in mystery fiction: the tradition of the detective as towering intellect, the tradition whose last surviving giants were Rex Stout and Fred himself. I was one of those readers. I discovered Ellery Queen in my early teens, the formative years when the heroes a person adopts can last a lifetime. I can still see myself sitting in a creaky old rocking chair in front of my grandmother's house during the heat of the 1957 summer, lost in ecstasy as I wandered with Ellery through the labyrinths of *The Greek Coffin Mystery*. Through my high school and college years I found and devoured in haphazard order all the other Queen classics: *The Egyptian Cross Mystery, The Tragedy of X, The Tragedy of Y, Calamity Town* and the unforgettable *Cat of Many Tails*. Fred wrote no fiction after Manny Lee's death in 1971, but while he lived there was always the hope that he would. When Fred died, Ellery Queen died irrevocably with him.

For the writers who appeared regularly in *Ellery Queen's Mystery Magazine*, which Fred founded in the fall of 1941 and actively edited for almost forty years, his death meant the end of the most exciting and fruitful of professional relationships. He wasn't easy on his contributors. He made them work and rework stories until every detail had taken its place in a harmonious mosaic, and thereby taught them more about the storyteller's art than any course or textbook could possibly teach. I was one of those writers. Our first meeting was in 1968, soon after I'd begun work on my book *Royal Bloodline: Ellery Queen, Author and Detective* (1974). I can still see myself stepping off the New Haven Railroad commuter train at Larchmont station and shaking hands for the first time with Fred and his wife Hilda and riding in their car to the Dannay home on Byron Lane. Fred was not just co-operative but flattered that somebody was actually writing a book about Queen, and over the next few years he helped me in countless ways. It was only after we'd come to know each other well that he began to hint that perhaps I'd enjoy writing a mystery myself. I slaved over a story for two months and finally mailed it to him. Its inspiration was a line from one of my favorite Queen novels, *Ten Days' Wonder* (1948), and I was sure that he'd like it.

A few weeks later he invited me to Larchmont again. We had dinner at a lovely old seafood restaurant and returned to Byron Lane and sipped brandy in his living room as he ripped that story of mine apart with a surgical precision that I now realize was more than justified by the sheer unadulterated silliness of what I had written. Then we began to build the story up again. He taught me what I should have done not by telling me in so many words but indirectly, by emphasizing the wrong steps I'd taken and leaving it to me to make them right. I spent the next couple of months rethinking and rewriting that story from first word to last. Finally in fear and trembling I mailed him the revised version. And this time he sent me a contract. "Open Letter to Survivors" was published in *EQMM* for May 1972. During the month that issue was on the nation's newsstands, every time I entered a store and saw my name on that blue-and-white cover along with the names of all the other contributors it was all I could do to restrain myself from shouting "HEY!! THAT'S ME!!!" to everyone within earshot.

Over the next ten years Fred bought many more stories from me: some about law professor Loren Mensing who went on to appear in four of my novels (*Publish and Perish*, 1975, which was dedicated to Fred;

Corrupt and Ensnare, 1978; *Into the Same River Twice*, 1996, and *Beneficiaries' Requiem*, 2000); some about Milo Turner, the confidence man with an identity for every occasion, perpetually fated to solve one crime in the process of committing another, and featured after Fred's death in my novels *The 120-Hour Clock* (1986) and *The Ninety Million Dollar Mouse* (1987); some with no series character at all. Even though *EQMM* carries on today, the special thrill of working with Fred and being buoyed by his praise and instructed by his line-for-line criticism is something I shall never know again.

When Fred wanted something changed in a manuscript, the reason most of the time was that he sensed how readers would react and saw that a change was needed to forestall that reaction. I learned a vast lesson in the workings of his editorial mind from an incident in the second story I sold him and the first tale about Loren Mensing, "After the Twelfth Chapter" (*EQMM*, September 1972). In the last paragraph of the story as I wrote it, Mensing warns a black militant who has been involved in the case that the police will be keeping him under close surveillance for a while. "The black man said nothing, as though it were raining and Mensing had told him it was raining. Then he nodded, without changing expression, and walked away. Mensing felt unclean and directionless and afraid, like a man trying to fight a forest fire he knows is out of control." When the story was published I discovered that Fred had deleted the word "unclean" from the last quoted sentence. I wondered why, and after a moment's thought I saw it: the word conveyed the subtle suggestion to the reader that the black character was not on the friendliest terms with soap and water. Fred had seen this instinctively, known it wasn't what I'd intended, and cut. When I asked him later if that was indeed the reason he'd dropped the word, he replied that he'd already forgotten but it might have been something like that.

Early the following year I sent him a story in which I used the basic device of Conan Doyle's classic "The Six Napoleons" in an up-to-the-minute Loren Mensing adventure with an airplane hijacking, Arab terrorism, a conveyor belt in a dog food factory, and a band of former Green Berets turned armed robbers. My title for that story was "Six Thousand Little Corsicans." Fred thought readers wouldn't remember that the island of Corsica had been Napoleon's birthplace and so would miss the allusion to Conan Doyle — which is why the story's published title was "Six Thousand Little Bonapartes" (*EQMM*, December 1973).

I suspect that every contributor to the magazine could tell similar anecdotes about benefiting from Fred's editorial expertise. He himself told me about how Ed Hoch, the most prolific contributor in the magazine's history, had once sent him a story which was set in Victorian London and required the *fin-de-siecle* touch of a Robert Louis Stevenson but somehow failed to convey the period mood. Fred simply took down his copy of *Dr. Jekyll and Mr. Hyde* and, every time the manuscript described some action or object that was also in Stevenson's story, he replaced Ed's description with the precise words Stevenson had used, improving the tale immensely and getting the proper flavor by the most direct, economical and accurate means. For anyone wondering whether this was a violation of copyright law, it wasn't: Stevenson has long been in the public domain.

Fred did all his work at home. He never went to New York on business and never met most of the people who worked on the magazine. Every afternoon the associate editor in Manhattan would make up a package containing submissions and mail it to Byron Lane. When Fred decided a story needed changes, he would discuss them with the author over the phone or in letters, usually handwritten. I have dozens of those letters, as does everyone who ever sold a few stories to *EQMM*, but Fred's correspondence with me went way beyond the professional. Reflections about himself, remembrances of times past, health problems, gentle hints that my latest submission to him was too long, thoughts on writers and writing and editors and critics and the current scene—here are a few excerpts that I hope are representative.

October 5, 1968. "The truth is, neither Mr. Lee nor I can argue with any conviction against inconsistencies or confusions of chronology. . . . And as I read your synopses [in a preliminary draft] of early (I should have said, of the earliest) EQ novels, I felt as if I were reading about books I had never even read! (Especially *The Roman Hat*—which will be 40 years old next year . . . Good Lord!)"

October 24, 1968. "A spell of illness put me behind in work, and deadlines are made, unfortunately, of steel, not rubber.

And since it now takes me longer to do things, I continue to find myself in the mathematical predicament of always approaching being-up-to-date as a limit."

November 7, 1968. "Neither Mr. Lee nor I keeps the sort of detailed records we should have at our fingertips . . . speaking for myself, I've always been too busy, and besides, I don't have the temperament; perhaps all my senses of orderliness and logic are simply used up in EQ! (Anyway, it's a good-sounding excuse.)"

December 13, 1968. "The truth is, you know more details about the early Queen books than, after all these years, I remember. When I finish my part of Queen novels, I tend to wipe the slate of my mind clean; it's the only way I can go on to a new book. So some of the things you write about strike me—it's an odd feeling!—as unfamiliar, even at times unknown, almost from another world. . . ."

March 3, 1969. "I've been away from home (for a series of interviews relating to our 40th anniversary—the Lord knows how they'll turn out for Lee and me, if they turn out at all!) and returned to an absolutely unbelievable accumulation of proofs, correspondence, and diabolical deadlines. . . ."

March 16, 1969. "The New York Times article [by Israel Shenker, 22 February 1969] will haunt me to my grave, and beyond. Two misquotations in it have made me sound and feel foolish, and one misquotation has already re-plagued me."

August 20, 1969. "Once upon a time (so people tell me) I had a fabulous memory. It wasn't really 'fabulous,' of course, but it was good enough, so that if I had to check on something I'd read in a story, I could go to the right shelf, take down the right book, and *almost* turn to the right page. Alas, I am getting old(er), and my memory has lost the 'in' of infallible."

September 29, 1969. "We're back in Larchmont now, and I feel as if I had no rest or relaxation at all this past summer. We're talking now of going away for a month early next year—perhaps to Florida. The only problem is EQMM— but I've handled that from Texas, Europe, and Larchmont, so I should, with planning and advance work, be able to manage things from Florida—or wherever."

October 23, 1969. "I had a foot infection (as you may remember) for a whole year, with great pain. The doctors were reluctant to operate because of my diabetes, but finally they did . . . (Try typing with one foot on a pillowed chair.)

". . . If Professor [Robin] Winks is right, then EQ has been 'dead' creatively for 15 years. Speaking only for myself, I find this hard to believe—as I find it hard to believe that the Professor has read everything produced by EQ since 1954. . . . It is so-called 'serious' criticism like Professor Winks's that makes a writer cease to write.

"Further, his 'suspicions' as to working methods are, almost needless to say, all wrong. In fact, his description of the division of work is impossible—unless he has meanings for the words he uses entirely different from the accept[ed] meanings. I haven't the faintest notion how he distinguishes between 'plotting' and 'working out the formal puzzle.' No two collaborators could possibly collaborate the way Winks 'suspects.'"

October 28, 1969. "No, I didn't mean *literally* that criticism like Winks's will make me stop working. But it is a fact that this *kind* of criticism has discouraged some writers so profoundly that they stopped writing. A man like Winks doesn't realize the depth of harm he causes. Oh, yes, if you want to be a writer you must be ready, able, and willing to stand the slings and arrows etc. Easier said than done."

August 5, 1970. "I've been ill—an acute attack (the first one I've ever had) of inflammatory arthritis in the fingers and wrists of both hands and in both shoulders. I'm better now, but I was helpless for weeks, and July was a ruined month (to say nothing of the fearful weather).

"I hope to enjoy August out here [on Fire Island]. It's a good thing that I had enough work done in advance—that is, before we got here. When I'll be able to get back to work on a full schedule, I don't know."

August 18, 1970. "We're back here now—we went home, to Larchmont, for a few days—to consult my family doctor, who had me visit the hospital for a 'million' tests. . . . I've been quite ill, and while I'm better now, I've decided not to do any important work for the rest of our stay here—to try to regain my strength. Of course, I'll have to supervise EQMM, and try to keep up to date on EQMM manuscripts—but neither task should be a strain: all the important work for EQMM was done in advance of the summer, and reading manuscripts is not hard work (it can even at times be enjoyable!)."

September 1, 1970. ". . . I feel only a little better, and am still hoping, if I stay here longer than originally planned, to get a little rest and renew my strength."

September 29, 1970. "It has taken me all this time to write. I feel better, but far from my usual self. I've made up a little joke about my health: it has improved 100%—instead of being ill every day, I'm now ill only every other day.

"I'm back on insulin now—two or three injections daily—which makes traveling a difficulty. . . ."

December 6, 1971. "Hilda's mother died last month after a long and terrible illness. Bill (Hilda) is doing as well as can be expected, and we are planning to take a trip—probably a cruise to the Caribbean. We are waiting for a confirmation of a Feb 5 sailing on the Michelangelo.

"This morning I went to the eye doctor for my annual checkup, and since I'm allergic to dilation drops, I not only can barely see but have one of my usual fearful headaches. It usually wears off by late afternoon or evening. (Hope this letter is legible—my eyesight at this moment is so jumpy I have to guess at 'horizontality.')"

January 20, 1972. "I hope I sounded all right last evening. When Bill told me you were on the phone, a shudder went through me—I thought it was some sort of bad news. (Significantly I did not think it was some sort of good news.) Late-at-night phone calls, unexpected telegrams, put cold hands on me these days."

Hilda Dannay became seriously ill on the cruise and died of cancer shortly afterwards. For the next few years I watched Fred dying by inches. Photographs of him taken in 1973 show the empty, devastated face of a man waiting for the dark to claim him.

September 19, 1972. "I haven't written you sooner because things have been, and still are, very difficult for me. I'm finally getting used to being alone in this big empty house. A few weeks ago I started to drive again—after not having driven for many years—and now I feel less trapped; at least I can get around locally.

". . . And, Mike, I think you should consider cutting the story ["Leap Day," *EQMM* July l973]—judicious cutting throughout—the story would be better if it were shorter."

May 10, 1973. "I hope the rest of your visit to N.Y. was enjoyable, and again I feel I should apologize for not being able to be more hospitable while you were in Larchmont. As you know, it's a big house for one person to rattle around in, and I've been alone so much and so long that I've forgotten even the small courtesies."

June 15, 1973. "I'm afraid I won't be much help in selecting the [*Royal Bloodline*] dust—jacket design (rough sketches returned herewith). They're too small for me to get a clear enough idea (and me an old art director!). My general reaction is they're too complicated, and adding the E, even in a different color, would, I think, complicate the design more. (Complexity in plot, yes; complexity in dust-jacket design, no.)

". . . Manny and I always used a double-tail on the Q, especially in our signatures. The double-tail indicated a collaboration of two people."

July 2, 1973. "'Because the Constable Blundered' [*Alfred Hitchcock's Mystery Magazine*, July 1974] is a good strong story. But on rereading I still have serious reservations. Not about the story itself or the writing. But about 'public policy.' Is this the kind of story that should be published at this time, especially by EQMM? It 'glorifies' the end-justifies-the-means, and in these Watergate days, it propagandizes the Watergate approach. Including murder as a means to justify the end.

"As you know, EQMM does not avoid politics altogether, but we are not a forum for political controversy. Basically, primarily, we should offer entertainment, and therefore I question if we should publish this kind of story. True, I once reprinted a similar Avram Davidson story (assassination by the government); but it took place, if I recall correctly, in the early days of the republic and was published before Watergate exploded. . . . Perhaps we should discuss this on the phone."

July 23, 1973. "Mike, I'm sure you caught more typos than I did. I used to be a good proofreader, but my eyes being what they are these days, I'm not a really dependable proofreader now. But maybe I caught one or two that escaped your eagle eyes!"

August 21, 1974. "My stay here on Fire Island has been a mixed bag—pleasure and pain. But I'm glad I came: it was a hurdle I had to get over, something I had to prove; and now, at least and at last, it won't have to be proved again.

"So soon I'll be back in Larchmont, and once again I'll be picking up the pieces and putting them together and trying to make them fit. But now—and Fire Island has helped—I'm a little more optimistic, and there's a stirring inside me that I'll become lucky again."

And he was. Between this letter and the next quote, Fred met and married the former Rose Koppel, whose love and care saved his life and gave him reason at the age of 70 to love life again.

September 27, 1976. "Mike, the story ["To Catch a Con Man," *EQMM* October 1977] is too long for best effect. I really think that pruning throughout—especially deleting adjectives and verbs—would improve reading pace.

"This typing is probably terrible—so please forgive. My arthritic fingers are having one of their bad days—they rebel at almost every command. May have to give up typing one of these days—constant striking of the wrong keys can be nerve-wearing."

September 15, 1978. "I'm beginning to write with Emily Dickinson dashes—I wish I could say, with Emily Dickinson words. . . . And how do you like my arthritic handwriting—I should get a patent on it."

During the late Seventies Fred and I served together on the board of Mystery Library, a publishing project of the University of California. Each year, very late in August or early in September, we and the other board members would be flown out to San Diego for our annual meeting. Fred was diabetic, and one of my jobs after we breakfasted each morning at the University cafeteria was to take his Prohibition-style flask and go back through the serving line and fill it with the orange juice he needed to sip during the day to maintain his blood sugar level. I often wondered (and so did he) how many UCSD students and faculty saw that flask and, like Sergeant Velie in an EQ novel, drew the obvious but wrong conclusion.

In the evenings after business and dinner were over, Fred would often hold court. We would gather around him, some of us literally sitting at his feet, and he would reminisce about his near half-century in the genre. As he talked one could almost see them coming back to life: people like Conan Doyle who was still walking the earth when Ellery Queen first appeared, and Dashiell Hammett who had been one of Fred's closest friends in the time between his return from World War II and Fred's second marriage, and so many others.

We talked on the phone every few weeks and he would always invite me to spend an evening with him in Larchmont whenever I was on the east coast. Usually I would stay for three or four hours but by my subjective clock each visit lasted just a few seconds. Our conversations ranged over the length and breadth of the genre we both loved. It was in his living room that he shared with me some of the hidden history of the Forties and Fifties. He told of how he had planned a series of Hammett story collections during World War II but was stymied by the veto of Lillian Hellman, who hated those early stories and had Hammett's power of attorney while he was serving in the Aleutians. (The collections were okayed, Fred said, only after publisher Lawrence Spivak met privately with Hellman and put some pressure on her which neither of them later discussed.) He described the poisonous atmosphere of the early Fifties, the days of Joe McCarthy and HUAC and the witch hunts, when Hammett was facing a jail sentence for refusing to reveal the contributors to a left-wing bail fund, and one of the women in Hammett's life threatened to report Fred as a communist sympathizer unless he made a large contribution, supposedly to the Hammett legal defense fund. (Fred told her to go to hell and nothing happened.) He told me of John Dickson Carr's battle with cancer and asked if I had any suggestions against the day when Carr's monthly review column for *EQMM* would have to be given to someone else. (I suggested Jon Breen, who did in fact take over from Carr and remained the magazine's reviewer for decades.) Agatha Christie, Rex Stout, Anthony Boucher, the outrageous Michael Avallone, even literary giants like Hemingway and Faulkner who occasionally had dealings with Fred, they all came alive for me in his living room during those wondrous evenings. If only I were blessed with a photographic memory, what a book I could write just from our conversations! I do remember vividly the time, perhaps a year or two after I had received an Edgar award for *Royal Bloodline*, when I stepped into the Dannay living room and saw a copy of the book prominently displayed on an end table. "How thoughtful!" I said.

"Whenever you invite a writer for a visit you put out something they wrote." Fred shook his head. "No, Mike," he said. "You don't understand. That book is *always* there." There was no mirror in the room but I would bet money I blushed.

I made a special trip to New York when Fred was guest of honor at a Lotos Club banquet celebrating the fiftieth anniversary of the publication of *The Roman Hat Mystery*, and another excursion to Waukesha, Wisconsin when Carroll College awarded Fred an honorary doctorate—one of the proudest moments of his life. The last time I saw him was in New York in the spring of 1982, the night of the annual MWA Dinner. He wasn't feeling well and had arranged for a limousine to take him and Rose back to Larchmont right after the banquet. We shook hands and said goodbye on Sixth Avenue in front of the Sheraton Central, neither of us knowing how little time he had left. On the first Friday of that September he died.

For those who were privileged to know Fred on a personal basis, his death meant the end of an infinitely precious friendship. We had many divergent interests and opinions but our feeling for mystery fiction brought us together and gave birth to our feeling for each other. We shared tragedies and triumphs, happy moments and sad. But for me the best times were when we would get together and talk for hours on end about the writers who had come before Fred and those who were his contemporaries and those who were coming after him and, as I grew older, those who were coming after me. I never felt so much a part of a living tradition as I did on those occasions. Since Fred's death that vital link has snapped and the excitement of his presence lives only in memories.

He was the closest to a grandfather I've known. Without him I would never have written a word of fiction worth reading. Every writer and reader and lover of mystery fiction owes him debts none of us can pay. What he gave us—as writer, editor and friend—will live as long as any of us live who remember.

BIBLIOGRAPHY

Note: This bibliography does not aim or claim to cover every appearance of the Ellery Queen byline, a task that would require a book in itself even if it were confined to the English language or the United States. I believe my effort offers more information on its subject than any other source, but within limits, which I'll set out here.

Sections I and III, on the novels by Dannay and Lee that were published as by Ellery Queen or Barnaby Ross, list only the first U.S. and British editions and the first U.S. paperback, plus any subsequent printings with different titles.

Section II, on the Queen short story and radio play collections, lists only those books that contain at least one previously uncollected work. Therefore it does not include *More Adventures of Ellery Queen* (Bestseller pb #B3, 1940), which consists entirely of material first collected earlier, but does cover *The Case Book of Ellery Queen* (Bestseller pb #B59, 1945), which includes three radio plays never published before (or since), and *The Best of Ellery Queen* (Beaufort, 1985), which contains one previously uncollected story.

Section VII, dealing with the Queen short stories and novelettes in the order of their publication, lists the first magazine publication of each work and each of the collections in which it appears. It also lists a large number but by no means all of the anthologies in which a given work was reprinted. Anyone looking for a more comprehensive treatment of the latter subject is referred to William G. Contento's *Index to Crime and Mystery Anthologies, 1875-2010* (Locus Press, 2011), which was invaluable to me in preparing this section of the bibliography. Where a story appeared in a magazine under one title and a Queen collection under another, for obvious reasons the latter title is usually the one used when the story is reprinted in an anthology. Where that isn't the case, I've given the anthology title. However, here and throughout the bibliography I've eliminated the words "The Adventure of" where they appear in the titles of short stories, radio plays and the like. Repeating those words hundreds of times would serve no purpose, and neither would meticulously recording when they appear and when they don't when a particular work is printed or reprinted. Likewise I've ignored the presence or absence of the definite article in a title, for example in the horse-racing story which was published in a magazine as "The Long Shot" but subsequently without the first word.

I. NOVELS AS BY ELLERY QUEEN

THE ROMAN HAT MYSTERY. Stokes, 1929; Gollancz, 1929. Pocket Book pb #77, 1940.

THE FRENCH POWDER MYSTERY. Stokes, 1930; Gollancz, 1930. Pocket Books pb #71, 1940.

THE DUTCH SHOE MYSTERY. Stokes, 1931; Gollancz, 1931. Pocket Books pb #202, 1943.

THE GREEK COFFIN MYSTERY. Stokes, 1932; Gollanca, 1932. Pocket Books pb #179, 1942.

THE EGYPTIAN CROSS MYSTERY. Stokes, 1932; Gollancz, 1933. Pocket Books pb #227, 1943.

THE AMERICAN GUN MYSTERY. Stokes, 1933; Gollancz, 1933. Dell pb #4, 1940. Mercury pb #164, 1951, as DEATH AT THE RODEO.

THE SIAMESE TWIN MYSTERY. Stokes, 1933; Gollancz, 1934. Pocket Books pb #109, 1941.

THE CHINESE ORANGE MYSTERY. Stokes, 1934; Collancz, 1934. Pocket Books pb #17, 1939.

THE SPANISH CAPE MYSTERY. Stokes, 1935; Gollancz, 1935. Pocket Books pb #146, 1942.

HALFWAY HOUSE. Stokes, 1936; Gollancz, 1936. Pocket Books pb #259, 1944.

THE DOOR BETWEEN. Stokes, 1937; Gollancz, 1937. Pocket Books pb #471, 1947.

THE DEVIL TO PAY. Stokes, 1938; Gollancz, 1938. Pocket Books pb #270, 1944.

THE FOUR OF HEARTS. Stokes, 1938; Gollancz, 1939. Pocket Books pb #245, 1944.

THE DRAGON'S TEETH. Stokes, 1939; Gollancz, 1939. Pocket Books pb #459, 1947. Pocket Books pb #2459, 1954, as THE VIRGIN HEIRESSES.

CALAMITY TOWN. Little, Brown, 1942; Gollancz, 1942. Pocket Books pb #283, 1945.

THERE WAS AN OLD WOMAN. Little, Brown, 1943; Gollancz, 1944. Pocket Books pb #326, 1945. Pocket Books pb #2326, 1956, as THE QUICK AND THE DEAD.

THE MURDERER IS A FOX. Little, Brown, 1945; Gollancz, 1945. Pocket Books pb #517, 1948.

TEN DAYS' WONDER. Little, Brown, 1948; Gollancz, 1948. Pocket Books pb #740, 1950. Signet pb #Q4907, 1972 (with stills from Claude Chabrol's film version of the novel).

CAT OF MANY TAILS. Little, Brown, 1949; Gollancz, 1949. Pocket Books pb #822, 1951. Bantam pb #F3026, 1965 (with introduction by Anthony Boucher).

DOUBLE, DOUBLE. Little, Brown, 1950; Gollancz, 1950. Pocket Books pb #874, 1952. Pocket Books pb #2874, 1958, as THE CASE OF THE SEVEN MURDERS.

THE ORIGIN OF EVIL. Little, Brown, 1951; Gollancz, 1951. Pocket Books pb #926, 1953.

THE KING IS DEAD. Little, Brown, 1952; Gollancz, 1952. Pocket Books pb #1005, 1954.

THE SCARLET LETTERS. Little, Brown, 1953; Gollancz, 1953. Pocket Books pb #1049, 1955.

THE GLASS VILLAGE. Little, Brown, 1954; Gollancz, 1954. Pocket Books pb #1082, 1955.

INSPECTOR QUEEN'S OWN CASE. Simon & Schuster, 1956; Gollancz, 1956. Pocket Books pb #1167, 1957.

THE FINISHING STROKE. Simon & Schuster, 1958; Gollancz, 1958. Cardinal pb #C343, 1959.

THE PLAYER ON THE OTHER SIDE. Random House, 1963; Gollancz, 1963. Pocket Books pb #50487, 1965.

AND ON THE EIGHTH DAY. Random House, 1964; Gollancz, 1964. Pocket Books pb #50209, 1966.

THE FOURTH SIDE OF THE TRIANGLE. Random House, 1965; Gollancz, 1955. Pocket Books pb #50508, 1967.

FACE TO FACE. New American Library, 1967; Gollancz, 1967. Signet pb #P3424, 1968.

THE HOUSE OF BRASS. New American Library, 1968; Gollancz, 1968. Signet pb #T3831, 1969.

COP OUT. World, 1969; Gollancz, 1969. Signet pb #T4196, 1970.

THE LAST WOMAN IN HIS LIFE. World. 1970; Gollancz, 1970. Signet pb #T4580, 1971.

A FINE AND PRIVATE PLACE. World, 1971; Gollancz, 1971. Signet pb #Q4978, 1972.

II. SHORT STORY AND RADIO PLAY COLLECTIONS
AS BY ELLERY QUEEN

THE ADVENTURES OF ELLERY QUEEN. Stokes, 1934; Gollancz, 1935. Pocket Books pb #99, 1941. Contents: The African Traveler (no previous magazine publication); The Hanging Acrobat (*Mystery*, May 1934, as "The Girl on the Trapeze"); The One-Penny Black (*Great Detective*, April 1933, as "The One-Penny Black"); The Bearded Lady (*Mystery*, August 1934, as "The Sinister Beard"); The Three Lame Men (*Mystery*, April 1934, as "The Three Lame Men"); The Invisible Lover (*Mystery*, September 1934, as "Four Men Loved a Woman"); The Teakwood Case (*Mystery*, May 1933, as "The Affair of the Gallant Bachelor"); The Two-Headed Dog (*Mystery*, June 1934); The Glass-Domed Clock (*Mystery League*, October 1933); The Seven Black Cats (*Mystery*, October 1934, as "The Black Cats Vanished"); The Mad Tea-Party (*Redbook*, October 1934).

THE NEW ADVENTURES OF ELLERY QUEEN. Stokes, 1940; Gollancz, 1940. Pocket Books pb #134, 1941. Contents: The Lamp of God (*Street & Smith's Detective Story Magazine*, November 1935, as "House of Haunts"); The Treasure Hunt (*Street & Smith's Detective Story Magazine*, December 1935); The Hollow Dragon (*Redbook*, December 1936); The House of Darkness (*American Magazine*, February 1935); The Bleeding Portrait (*American Cavalcade*, September 1937, as "The Gramatan Mystery"); Man Bites Dog (*Blue Book*, June 1939); Long Shot (*Blue Book*, September 1939, as "The Long Shot"); Mind Over Matter (*Blue Book*, October 1939); Trojan Horse (*Blue Book*, December 1939, as "The Trojan Horse").

THE CASE BOOK OF ELLERY QUEEN. Bestseller pb #B59, 1945. Contents: The House of Darkness (from THE NEW ADVENTURES OF ELLERY QUEEN); The Teakwood Case (from THE ADVENTURES OF ELLERY QUEEN); The Hollow Dragon (from THE NEW ADVENTURES OF ELLERY QUEEN); LONG SHOT (from THE NEW ADVENTURES OF ELLERY QUEEN); Mind Over Matter (from THE NEW ADVENTURES OF ELLERY QUEEN); The Double Triangle (CBS Radio, 28 April 1940, 30 minutes); The Invisible Clock (CBS Radio, 11 August 1940, 30 minutes); Honeymoon House (CBS Radio, 19 May 1940, 30 minutes).

CALENDAR OF CRIME. Little, Brown, 1952; Gollancz, 1952. Pocket Books pb #960, 1953. Contents: The Inner Circle (*Ellery Queen's Mystery Magazine*, January 1947); The President's Half Disme (*Ellery Queen's Mystery Magazine*, February 1947); The Ides of Michael Magoon (*Ellery Queen's Mystery Magazine*, March 1947); The Emperor's Dice (*Ellery Queen's Mystery Magazine*, April 1951); The Gettysburg Bugle (*Ellery Queen's Mystery Magazine*, May 1951, as "As Simple As ABC"); The Medical Finger (*Ellery Queen's Mystery Magazine*, June 1951); The Fallen Angel (*Ellery Queen's Mystery Magazine*, July 1951); The Needle's Eye (*Ellery Queen's Mystery Magazine*, August 1951); The Three Rs (*Ellery Queen's Mystery Magazine*, September 1946); The Dead Cat (*Ellery Queen's Mystery Magazine*, October 1946); The Telltale Bottle (*Ellery Queen's Mystery Magazine*, November 1946); The Dauphin's Doll (*Ellery Queen's Mystery Magazine*, December 1948).

QBI: QUEEN'S BUREAU OF INVESTIGATION. Little, Brown, 1955; Gollancz, 1955. Pocket Books pb #1118, 1956. Contents: Money Talks (*This Week*, 2 April 1950, as "The Sound of Blackmail"); A Matter of Seconds (*This Week*, 9 August 1953); The Three Widows (*This Week*, 29 January 1950, as "Murder Without Clues"); My Queer Dean! (*This Week*, 8 March 1953); Driver's Seat (*This Week*, 25 March 1951, as "Lady, You're Dead!"); A Lump of Sugar (*This Week*, 9 July 1950, as "The Mystery of the 3 Dawn Riders"); Cold Money (*This Week*, 20 March 1952); The Myna Birds (*This Week*, 28 December 1952, as "The Myna Bird Mystery"); A Question of Honor (*This Week*, 13 September 1953); The Robber of Wrightsville (*Today's Family*, February 1953, as "The Accused"); Double Your Money (*This Week*, 30 September 1951, as "The Vanishing Wizard"); Miser's Gold (*This Week*, 18 June 1950, as "Love Hunts a Hidden Treasure"); Snowball in July (*This Week*, 31 August 1952, as "The Phantom Train"); The Witch of Times Square (*This Week*, 5 November 1950); The Gamblers' Club (*This Week*, 7 January 1951); GI Story (*Ellery Queen's Mystery Magazine*, August 1954); The Black Ledger (*This Week*, 26 January 1952, as "The Mysterious Black Ledger"); Child Missing! (*This Week*, 8 July 1951, as "Kidnaped!").

QUEENS FULL. Random House, 1965; Gollancz, 1966. Signet pb #D2894, 1966. Contents: The Death of Don Juan (*Argosy*, May 1962); E = Murder (*This Week*, 4 August 1960); The Wrightsville Heirs (*Better Living*, January-February 1956); Diamonds in Paradise (*Ellery Queen's Mystery Magazine*, September 1954); The Case Against Carroll (*Argosy*, September 1958).

QED: QUEEN'S EXPERIMENTS IN DETECTION. New American Library, 1968; Gollancz, 1969. Signet pb #T4120, 1970. Contents: Mum Is the Word (*Ellery Queen's Mystery Magazine*, April 1966); Object Lesson (*This Week*, 11 September 1955, as "The Blackboard Gangsters"); No Parking (*This Week*, 18 March 1956, as "Terror in a Penthouse"); No Place to Live (*This Week*, 10 June 1956, as "The Man They All Hated"); Miracles Do Happen (*Ellery Queen's Mystery Magazine*, July 1957); The Lonely Bride (*This Week*, 4 December 1949, as "The Lady Couldn't Explain"); Mystery at the Library of Congress (*Argosy*, June 1960, as "Enter Ellery Queen"); Dead Ringer (*Diners' Club Magazine*, March 1965); The Broken T (*This Week*, 27 July 1963, as "Mystery in Neon Red"); Half a Clue (*This Week*, 25 August 1963, as "Half a Clue to Murder"); Eve of the Wedding (*Ellery Queen's Mystery Magazine*, August 1955, as "Bride in Danger"); Last Man to Die (*This Week*, 3 November 1963); Payoff (*Cavalier*, August 1964, as "Crime Syndicate Payoff"); The Little Spy (*Cavalier*, January 1965); The President Regrets (*Diners' Club Magazine*, September 1965); Abraham Lincoln's Clue (*MD*, June 1965).

THE BEST OF ELLERY QUEEN. Beaufort, 1985. Contents: The Glass-Domed Clock (from THE ADVENTURES OF ELLERY QUEEN); The Bearded Lady (from THE ADVENTURES OF ELLERY QUEEN); The Mad Tea-Party (from THE ADVENTURES OF ELLERY QUEEN); Man Bites Dog (from THE NEW ADVENTURES OF ELLERY QUEEN); Mind Over Matter (from THE NEW ADVENTURES OF ELLERY QUEEN); The Inner Circle (from CALENDAR OF CRIME); The Dauphin's Doll (from CALENDAR OF CRIME); The Three Widows (from QBI: QUEEN'S BUREAU OF INVESTIGATION); Snowball in July (from QBI: QUEEN'S BUREAU OF INVESTIGATION); "My Queer Dean!" (from QBI: QUEEN'S BUREAU OF

INVESTIGATION); GI Story from (from QBI: QUEEN'S BUREAU OF INVESTIGATION); Miracles Do Happen (from QED: QUEEN'S EXPERIMENTS IN DETECTION); Last Man to Die (from QED: QUEEN'S EXPERIMENTS IN DETECTION); Abraham Lincoln's Clue (from QED: QUEEN'S EXPERIMENTS IN DETECTION); Wedding Anniversary (*Ellery Queen's Mystery Magazine*, September 1967).

THE TRAGEDY OF ERRORS. Crippen & Landru, 1999. Contents: The Tragedy of Errors (Fred Dannay's synopsis for the Ellery Queen novel Manny Lee didn't live to expand to book length); Terror Town (*Argosy*, August 1956); Uncle from Australia (*Diners' Club Magazine*, June 1965); The Three Students (*Playboy*, March 1971); The Odd Man (*Playboy*, June 1971); The Honest Swindler (*Saturday Evening Post*, Summer 1971); The Reindeer Clue (ghosted by Edward D. Hoch) (*National Enquirer*, 23 December 1975). NOTE: This collection also contains 22 essays and memoirs dealing with Fred Dannay or Manny Lee or both.

THE ADVENTURE OF THE MURDERED MOTHS. Crippen & Landru, 2005. Contents: The Last Man Club (CBS Radio, 25 June 1939, 60 minutes); Napoleon's Razor (CBS Radio, 9 July 1939, 60 minutes); The Bad Boy (CBS Radio, 30 July 1939, 60 minutes); The March of Death (CBS Radio, 15 October 1939, 60 minutes); The Haunted Cave (CBS Radio, 22 October 1939, 60 minutes); The Lost Child (CBS Radio, 26 November 1939, 60 minutes); The Black Secret (CBS Radio, 10 December 1939, 60 minutes); The Dying Scarecrow (CBS Radio, 7 January 1940, 60 minutes); The Woman in Black (CBS Radio, 14 January 1940, 60 minutes); The Forgotten Men (CBS Radio, 7 April 1940, 30 minutes); The Man Who Could Double the Size of Diamonds (CBS Radio, 5 May 1940, 30 minutes); The Dark Cloud (CBS Radio, 23 June 1940, 30 minutes); Mr. Short and Mr. Long (NBC Radio, 14/16 January 1943, 30 minutes); The Murdered Moths (NBC Radio, 9 May 1945, 30 minutes).

III. NOVELS AS BY BARNABY ROSS

THE TRAGEDY OF X. Viking, 1932; Cassell, 1932. Stokes, 1940, as by Ellery Queen. Pocket Books pb #125, 1941, as by Ellery Queen.

THE TRAGEDY OF Y. Viking, 1932; Cassell, 1932. Stokes, 1941, as by Ellery Queen. Pocket Books pb #313, 1945, as by Ellery Queen.

THE TRAGEDY OF Z. Stokes, 1933; Cassell, 1933. Little, Brown, 1942, as by Ellery Queen. Pocket Books pb #355, 1946, as by Ellery Queen.

DRURY LANE'S LAST CASE. Stokes, 1933; Cassell, 1933. Little, Brown, 1946, as by Ellery Queen. Pocket Books pb #669, 1950, as by Ellery Queen.

IV. OMNIBUS VOLUMES AS BY ELLERY QUEEN

THE ELLERY QUEEN OMNIBUS. Gollancz (London), 1934. Contains THE FRENCH POWDER MYSTERY (19300), THE DUTCH SHOE MYSTERY (1931), and THE GREEK COFFIN MYSTERY (1932).

THE ELLERY QUEEN OMNIBUS. Grosset & Dunlap, 1936. Contains THE ROMAN HAT MYSTERY (1929), THE FRENCH POWDER MYSTERY (1930), and THE EGYPTIAN CROSS MYSTERY (1932).

ELLERY QUEEN'S BIG BOOK. Grosset & Dunlap, 1938. Contains THE GREEK COFFIN MYSTERY (1932) and THE SIAMESE TWIN MYSTERY (1933).

ELLERY QUEEN'S ADVENTURE OMNIBUS. Grosset & Dunlap, 1941. Contains The Adventures of Ellery Queen (1934) and THE NEW ADVENTURES OF ELLERY QUEEN (1940).

ELLERY QUEEN'S MYSTERY PARADE. World, 1944. Contains THE GREEK COFFIN MYSTERY (1932) and THE SIAMESE TWIN MYSTERY (1933).

THE CASE BOOK OF ELLERY QUEEN. Gollancz (London), 1949. Contains THE ADVENTURES OF ELLERY QUEEN (1934) and THE NEW ADVENTURES OF ELLERY QUEEN (1940).

THE WRIGHTSVILLE MURDERS. Little, Brown, 1956. Contains CALAMITY TOWN (1942), THE MURDERER IS A FOX (1945), and TEN DAYS' WONDER (1948).

THE HOLLYWOOD MURDERS. Lippincott, 1957. Contains THE DEVIL TO PAY (1937), THE FOUR OF HEARTS (1938), and THE ORIGIN OF EVIL (1951).

THE NEW YORK MURDERS. Little, Brown, 1958. Contains CAT OF MANY TAILS (1949), THE SCARLET LETTERS (1953), and THE AMERICAN GUN MYSTERY (1934).

THE XYZ MURDERS. Lippincott, 1961. Contains THE TRAGEDY OF X (1932, as by Barnaby Ross), THE TRAGEDY OF Y (1932, as by Barnaby Ross), and THE TRAGEDY OF Z (1933, as by Barnaby Ross).

THE BIZARRE MURDERS. Lippincott, 1962. Contains THE SIAMESE TWIN MYSTERY (1933), THE CHINESE ORANGE MYSTERY (1934), and THE SPANISH CAPE MYSTERY (1935).

V. NOVEL BY FREDERIC DANNAY

THE GOLDEN SUMMER, as by Daniel Nathan. Little, Brown, 1953. Note: Subsequent to its book publication, three chapters of this episodic novel were published in *Ellery Queen's Mystery Magazine* as short stories: "The Boy and the Book" (June 1956, with introduction by Anthony Boucher); "The Boy and the Money Box" (August 1956, with introduction by Stanley Ellin); "The Boy and the Law" (October 1956, with introduction by James Yaffe). "The Boy and the Money Box" also appeared in DETECTIVE DIRECTORY: PART ONE (1977), a volume in the MASTERPIECES OF MYSTERY anthology series edited by Dannay.

VI. CORRESPONDENCE BETWEEN FREDERIC DANNAY
AND MANFRED B. LEE

BLOOD RELATIONS, ed. Joseph Goodrich. Perfect Crime Books, 2012.

VII. SHORT FICTION AS BY ELLERY QUEEN
IN ORDER OF PUBLICATION

1933

The One-Penny Black. *Great Detective*, April 1933. Collected in The Adventures of Ellery Queen (Stokes, 1934). Reprinted in MY BEST MYSTERY STORY, ed. anon. (Faber, 1939); MORE ADVENTURES OF ELLERY QUEEN (Bestseller pb #3, 1940); SPORTING BLOOD, ed. Ellery Queen (Little, Brown, 1942); MAIDEN MURDERS, intro. John Dickson Carr (Harper, 1952); THE BIG APPLE MYSTERIES, ed. Carol-Lynn Rossel Waugh, Isaac Asimov & Martin H. Greenberg (Avon, 1982); A TREASURY OF AMERICAN MYSTERY STORIES, ed. Frank D. McSherry Jr., Charles G. Waugh & Martin H. Greenberg (Avenel Books, 1989); MURDER MOST POSTAL, ed. Martin H. Greenberg (Cumberland House, 2001); *Ellery Queen's Mystery Magazine*, September/October 2011.

The Affair of the Gallant Bachelor. *Mystery*, May 1933. Collected in The Adventures of Ellery Queen (Stokes, 1934) and THE CASE BOOK OF ELLERY QUEEN (Bestseller pb #B59, 1945), as "The Teakwood Case."

The Glass-Domed Clock. *Mystery League*, October 1933. Collected in THE ADVENTURES OF ELLERY QUEEN (Stokes, 1934) and THE BEST OF ELLERY QUEEN (Beaufort, 1985). Reprinted in MORE ADVENTURES OF ELLERY QUEEN (Bestseller pb #B3, 1940); THE ARBOR HOUSE TREASURY OF MYSTERY AND SUSPENSE, ed. Bill Pronzini, Barry N. Malzberg & Martin H. Greenberg (Arbor House, 1981); SLEUTHS OF THE CENTURY, ed. Jon L. Breen & Ed Gorman (Carroll & Graf, 2000).

1934

The Three Lame Men. *Mystery*, April 1934. Collected in THE ADVENTURES OF ELLERY QUEEN (Stokes, 1934). Reprinted in A CENTURY OF THRILLERS, VOLUME II, ed. anon. (President Press, 1937).

The Girl on the Trapeze. *Mystery*, May 1934. Collected in THE ADVENTURES OF ELLERY QUEEN (Stokes, 1934), as "The Hanging Acrobat." Reprinted in CHALLENGE TO THE READER, ed. Ellery Queen (Stokes, 1938); SLEIGHT OF CRIME, ed. Cedric E. Clute Jr. & Nicholas Lewin (Regnery, 1977); SHOW BUSINESS IS MURDER, ed. Carol-Lynn Rossel Waugh, Isaac Asimov & Martin H. Greenberg (Avon, 1983); THE DEADLY ARTS, ed. Bill Pronzini & Marcia Muller (Arbor House, 1985).

The "Two-Headed Dog." *Mystery*, June 1934. Collected in THE ADVENTURES OF ELLERY QUEEN (Stokes, 1934).

The Sinister Beard. *Mystery*, August 1934. Collected in THE ADVENTURES OF ELLERY QUEEN (Stokes, 1934) and THE BEST OF ELLERY QUEEN (Beaufort, 1985), as "The Bearded Lady." Reprinted in THE FOURTH MYSTERY COMPANION, ed. A.L. Furman (Lantern Press, 1946); THE PENGUIN CLASSIC CRIME OMNIBUS, ed. Julian Symons (Penguin, 1984).

Four Men Loved a Woman. *Mystery*, September 1934. Collected in THE ADVENTURES OF ELLERY QUEEN (Stokes, 1934), as "The Invisible Lover." Reprinted in MORE ADVENTURES OF ELLERY QUEEN (Bestseller pb #B3, 1940); THE HILTON BEDSIDE BOOK, ed. anon. (Hilton Hotels, 1952).

The Black Cats Vanished. *Mystery*, October 1934. Collected in THE ADVENTURES OF ELLERY QUEEN (Stokes, 1934), as "The Seven Black Cats." Reprinted in MURDER BY THE DOZEN, ed. Durbin Lee Horner (Dingwall-Rock, 1935); THE SECOND CENTURY OF DETECTIVE STORIES, ed. E.C. Bentley (Hutchinson, 1938); ALFRED HITCHCOCK'S DARING DETECTIVES, ed. anon. (Random House, 1969); THE FOURTH BEDSIDE BOOK OF GREAT DETECTIVE STORIES, ed. Herbert Van Thal (Barker, 1979); PURR-FECT CRIME, ed. Carol-Lynn Rossel Waugh, Martin H. Greenberg & Isaac Asimov (Lynx Books, 1989).

The Mad Tea-Party. *Redbook*, October 1934. Collected in THE ADVENTURES OF ELLERY QUEEN (Stokes, 1934) and THE BEST OF ELLERY QUEEN (Beaufort, 1985). Reprinted in 101 YEARS' ENTERTAINMENT, ed. Ellery Queen (Little, Brown, 1941); MY BEST MURDER STORY, ed. David C. Cooke (Merlin Press, 1955); THE GREAT AMERICAN DETECTIVE, ed. William Kittredge & Steven M. Krauzer (Mentor Books, 1978); THE WORLD OF MYSTERY FICTION, ed. Elliot L. Gilbert (University of California San Diego, 1978); THE EDGAR WINNERS, ed. Bill Pronzini (Random House, 1980); *Ellery Queen's Mystery Magazine*, November 2005.

The African Traveler. No magazine publication. Collected in THE ADVENTURES OF ELLERY QUEEN (Stokes, 1934). Reprinted in MORE ADVENTURES OF ELLERY QUEEN (Bestseller pb #B3, 1940); GREAT AMERICAN DETECTIVE STORIES, ed. Anthony Boucher (World, 1945); 14 GREAT DETECTIVE STORIES, ed. Howard Haycraft (Modern Library, 1949).

1935

The House of Darkness. *American Magazine*, February 1935. Collected in THE NEW ADVENTURES OF ELLERY QUEEN (Stokes, 1940) and THE CASE BOOK OF ELLERY QUEEN (Bestseller pb #B59, 1945). Reprinted in WORLD'S GREAT DETECTIVE STORIES, ed.

Will Cuppy (World, 1943); MURDER FOR THE MILLIONS, ed. Frank Owen (Frederick Fell, 1946); THE WICKEDEST SHOW ON EARTH, ed. Marcia Muller & Bill Pronzini (Morrow, 1985).

House of Haunts. *Street & Smith's Detective Story Magazine*, November 1935. Collected in THE NEW ADVENTURES OF ELLERY QUEEN (Stokes, 1940) as "The Lamp of God." Separately published as THE LAMP OF GOD (Dell 10c pb #23, 1950). Reprinted in MORE ADVENTURES OF ELLERY QUEEN (Bestseller pb #B3, 1940); *All Fiction Detective Stories* (1942); A TREASURY OF GREAT MYSTERIES, ed. Howard Haycraft & John Beecroft (Simon & Schuster, 1957); DETECTIVES A TO Z, ed. Frank D. McSherry Jr., Martin H. Greenberg & Charles G. Waugh (Bonanza Books, 1985).

The Treasure Hunt. *Street & Smith's Detective Story Magazine*, December 1935. Collected in THE NEW ADVENTURES OF ELLERY QUEEN (Stokes, 1940). Reprinted in *Ellery Queen's Mystery Magazine*, Fall 1941; *The Saint Detective Magazine*, June-July 1953.

1936

The Hollow Dragon. *Redbook*, December 1936. Collected in THE NEW ADVENTURES OF ELLERY QUEEN (Stokes, 1940) and THE CASE BOOK OF ELLERY QUEEN (Bestseller pb #59, 1945). Reprinted in THE SECOND ARMCHAIR DETECTIVE READER, ed. Ernest Dudley (Boardman, 1950); *Ellery Queen's Mystery Magazine*, June 1959; GREAT STORIES OF DETECTION, ed. R.C. Bull (Hutchinson, 1960).

1937

The Gramatan Mystery. *American Cavalcade*, September 1937. Collected in THE NEW ADVENTURES OF ELLERY QUEEN (Stokes, 1940), as "The Bleeding Portrait."

1939

Man Bites Dog. *Blue Book*, June 1939. Collected in THE NEW ADVENTURES OF ELLERY QUEEN (Stokes, 1940) and THE BEST OF ELLERY QUEEN (Beaufort, 1985). Reprinted in THE POCKET BOOK OF GREAT DETECTIVES, ed. Lee Wright (Pocket Books pb #103, 1941); SPORTING BLOOD, ed. Ellery Queen (Little, Brown, 1942); THE KIT BOOK, ed. R.M. Barrows (Consolidated Book Publishers, 1943).

The Long Shot. *Blue Book*, September 1939. Collected in THE NEW ADVENTURES OF ELLERY QUEEN (Stokes, 1940) and THE CASE BOOK OF ELLERY QUEEN (Bestseller pb #B59, 1945). Reprinted in THE ARMCHAIR DETECTIVE READER, ed. Ernest Dudley (Boardman, 1948); *Ellery Queen's Mystery Magazine*, March 1959; DEADLY ODDS, ed. Richard Peyton (Souvenir Press, 1986).

Mind Over Matter. *Blue Book*, October 1939. Collected in THE NEW ADVENTURES OF ELLERY QUEEN (Stokes, 1940), THE CASE BOOK OF ELLERY QUEEN (Bestseller pb #B59, 1945), and THE BEST OF ELLERY QUEEN (Beaufort, 1985). Reprinted in DOLLS ARE MURDER, ed. Harold Q. Masur (Lion pb #152, 1957); *Ellery Queen's Mystery Magazine*, September 1962; BEST DETECTIVE STORIES 2, ed. Edmund Crispin (Faber, 1964); MURDER MOST FOUL, ed. Harold Q. Masur (Walker, 1971); CLASSIC STORIES OF CRIME AND DETECTION, ed. Jacques Barzun & Wendell Hertig Taylor (Garland, 1976); MASTERPIECES OF MYSTERY: THE GOLDEN AGE, PART TWO, ed. Ellery Queen (Davis, 1977).

Trojan Horse. *Blue Book*, December 1939. Collected in THE NEW ADVENTURES OF ELLERY QUEEN (Stokes, 1940). Reprinted in SPORTING BLOOD, ed. Ellery Queen (Little, Brown, 1942); MY FAVORITE MYSTERY STORIES, ed. Maureen Daly (Dodd Mead, 1966); THE SPORT OF CRIME, ed. Carol-Lynn Rossel Waugh, Isaac Asimov & Martin H. Greenberg (Lynx Books, 1989).

1946

The Three Rs. *Ellery Queen's Mystery Magazine*, September 1946. Collected in CALENDAR OF

CRIME (Little, Brown, 1952). Reprinted in BEST DETECTIVE STORIES OF THE YEAR, ed. David C. Cooke (Dutton, 1947); *Ellery Queen's Mystery Magazine*, October 1965; ELLERY QUEEN'S ANTHOLOGY #42: EYES OF MYSTERY (Fall/Winter 1981).

The Dead Cat. *Ellery Queen's Mystery Magazine*, October 1946. Collected in CALENDAR OF CRIME (Little, Brown, 1952). Reprinted in 20 GREAT TALES OF MURDER, ed. Helen McCloy & Brett Halliday (Random House, 1951); *Ellery Queen's Mystery Magazine*, November 1965, as "The Hallowe'en Mystery"; MASTERPIECES OF MYSTERY: THE FORTIES, ed. Ellery Queen (Davis, 1978); ELLERY QUEEN'S ANTHOLOGY #45: EYE-WITNESSES (Spring 1983); MURDER FOR HALLOWEEN, ed. Michele Slung & Roland Hartman (Mysterious Press, 1994).

The Telltale Bottle. *Ellery Queen's Mystery Magazine*, November 1946. Collected in CALENDAR OF CRIME (Little, Brown, 1952). Reprinted in EAT, DRINK, AND BE BURIED, ed. Rex Stout (Viking, 1956); *Ellery Queen's Mystery Magazine*, December 1965, as "The Thanksgiving Day Mystery"; MURDER BY THE GLASS, ed. Peter Haining (Souvenir Press, 1994).

1947

The Inner Circle. *Ellery Queen's Mystery Magazine*, January 1947. Collected in CALENDAR OF CRIME (Little, Brown, 1952) and THE BEST OF ELLERY QUEEN (Beaufort, 1985). Reprinted in 20th CENTURY DETECTIVE STORIES, ed. Ellery Queen (World, 1948); A CHOICE OF MURDERS, ed. Dorothy Salisbury Davis (Scribner, 1958); *Ellery Queen's Mystery Magazine*, February 1968.

The President's Half Disme. *Ellery Queen's Mystery Magazine*, February 1947. Collected in CALENDAR OF CRIME (Little, Brown, 1952). Reprinted in MURDER BY EXPERTS, ed. Ellery Queen (Ziff-Davis, 1947); BEST DETECTIVE STORIES OF THE YEAR, ed. David C. Cooke (Dutton, 1948); 10 GREAT MYSTERIES, ed. Howard Haycraft & John Beecroft (Doubleday, 1959); BEST OF THE BEST DETECTIVE STORIES, ed. Allen J. Hubin (Dutton, 1960); *Ellery Queen's Mystery Magazine*, March 1965; MERCHANTS OF MENACE, ed. Hillary Waugh (Doubleday, 1969); THE DETECTIVE STORY, ed. Saul Schwartz (National Textbook Co., 1975); ELLERY QUEEN'S ANTHOLOGY #43: MAZE OF MYSTERIES (Spring/Summer 1982); *Ellery Queen's Mystery Magazine*, December 1994; THE BEST AMERICAN MYSTERY STORIES OF THE CENTURY, ed. Tony Hillerman (Houghton Mifflin, 2000).

The Ides of Michael Magoon. *Ellery Queen's Mystery Magazine*, March 1947. Collected in CALENDAR OF CRIME (Little, Brown, 1952). Reprinted in FOUR AND TWENTY BLOODHOUNDS, ed. Anthony Boucher (Simon & Schuster, 1950); *Ellery Queen's Mystery Magazine*, April 1965.

1948

The Dauphin's Doll. *Ellery Queen's Mystery Magazine*, December 1948. Collected in CALENDAR OF CRIME (Little, Brown, 1952) and THE BEST OF ELLERY QUEEN (1985). Reprinted in BEST DETECTIVE STORIES, ed. Edmund Crispin (Faber, 1959); *Ellery Queen's Mystery Magazine*, January 1968, as "With the Compliments of Comus"; THE LOCKED ROOM READER, ed. Hans Stefan Santesson (Random House, 1968); MASTERPIECES OF MYSTERY: THE SUPERSLEUTHS REVISITED, ed. Ellery Queen (Davis, 1979); THE TWELVE CRIMES OF CHRISTMAS, ed. Carol-Lynn Rossel Waugh, Martin H. Greenberg & Isaac Asimov (Avon, 1981); MURDER FOR CHRISTMAS, ed. Thomas Godfrey (Mysterious Press, 1982); TWELVE AMERICAN DETECTIVE STORIES, ed. Edward D. Hoch (Oxford University Press, 1997); A CENTURY OF GREAT SUSPENSE STORIES, ed. Jeffery Deaver (Berkley, 2001).

1949

The Lady Couldn't Explain. *This Week*, 4 December 1949. Collected in QED: QUEEN'S EXPERIMENTS IN DETECTION (New American Library, 1968), as "The Lonely Bride."

Reprinted in *Ellery Queen's Mystery Magazine*, December 1951; ELLERY QUEEN'S 1960 ANTHOLOGY (Davis pb, 1959); ELLERY QUEEN'S LETHAL BLACK BOOK (Dell pb #2261, 1965).

1950

Murder Without Clues. *This Week*, 29 January 1950. Collected in QBI: QUEEN'S BUREAU OF INVESTIGATION (Little, Brown, 1955) and THE BEST OF ELLERY QUEEN (Beaufort, 1985), as "The Three Widows." Reprinted in BEST DETECTIVE STORIES OF THE YEAR, ed. David C. Cooke (Dutton, 1951); *Ellery Queen's Mystery Magazine*, January 1952; THIS WEEK'S SHORT-SHORT STORIES, ed. Stewart Beach (Random House, 1953); ELLERY QUEEN'S 1963 ANTHOLOGY (Davis pb, 1962); MASTERPIECES OF MYSTERY: THE GRAND MASTERS UP TO DATE, ed. Ellery Queen (Davis, 1979).

The Sound of Blackmail. *This Week*, 2 April 1950. Collected in QBI: QUEEN'S BUREAU OF INVESTIGATION (Little, Brown, 1955), as "Money Talks." Reprinted in *Ellery Queen's Mystery Magazine*, August 1952; THIS WEEK'S SHORT-SHORT STORIES, ed. Stewart Beach (Random House, 1953); ELLERY QUEEN'S ANTHOLOGY, SPRING-SUMMER 1971 EDITION (Davis pb, 1971).

Love Hunts a Hidden Treasure. *This Week*, 18 June 1950. Collected in QBI: QUEEN'S BUREAU OF INVESTIGATION (Little, Brown, 1955), as "Miser's Gold." Reprinted in *Ellery Queen's Mystery Magazine*, April 1954; ELLERY QUEEN'S 1967 ANTHOLOGY (Davis pb, 1966); ELLERY QUEEN'S MURDER—IN SPADES! (Pyramid pb #T2036, 1969); *Ellery Queen's Mystery Magazine*, November 1971, as "Death of a Pawnbroker"; TRICKS AND TREATS, ed. Joe Gores & Bill Pronzini (Doubleday, 1976); MASTERPIECES OF MYSTERY: DETECTIVE DIRECTORY, PART TWO, ed. Ellery Queen (Davis, 1978).

The Mystery of the 3 Dawn Riders. *This Week*, 9 July 1950. Collected in QBI: QUEEN'S BUREAU OF INVESTIGATION (Little, Brown, 1955), as "A Lump of Sugar." Reprinted in *Ellery Queen's Mystery Magazine*, February 1953; ELLERY QUEEN'S 1961 ANTHOLOGY (Davis pb, 1960); ELLERY QUEEN'S 12 (Dell pb #2259, 1964); *Ellery Queen's Mystery Magazine*, March 1969, as "Murder in the Park"; ELLERY QUEEN'S MINIMYSTERIES, ed. Ellery Queen (World, 1969); THE MYSTERY READER, ed. Nancy Ellen Talburt & Lyna Lee Montgomery (Scribner, 1975); *Ellery Queen's Mystery Magazine*, September/October 2001.

The Witch of Times Square. *This Week*, 5 November 1950. Collected in QBI: QUEEN'S BUREAU OF INVESTIGATION (Little, Brown, 1955). Reprinted in *Ellery Queen's Mystery Magazine*, May 1953; ELLERY QUEEN'S ANTHOLOGY, 1965 MID-YEAR EDITION (Davis pb, 1965); ELLERY QUEEN'S MYSTERY JACKPOT, ed. Ellery Queen (Pyramid pb #T2207, 1970).

1951

The Gamblers' Club. *This Week*, 7 January 1951. Collected in QBI: QUEEN'S BUREAU OF INVESTGATION (Little, Brown, 1955). Reprinted in *Ellery Queen's Mystery Magazine*, March 1955; ELLERY QUEEN'S 1962 ANTHOLOGY (Davis pb, 1961); WIN, LOSE OR DIE, ed. Cynthia Manson & Constance Scarborough (Carroll & Graf, 1996).

Lady, You're Dead! *This Week*, 25 March 1951. Collected in QBI: QUEEN'S BUREAU OF INVESTIGATION (Little, Brown, 1955), as "Driver's Seat." Reprinted in *Ellery Queen's Mystery Magazine*, November 1955; ELLERY QUEEN'S ANTHOLOGY, 1968 MID-YEAR EDITION (Davis pb, 1968); ELLERY QUEEN'S ANTHOLOGY #46: LOST LADIES, ed. Eleanor Sullivan (Summer 1983); *Ellery Queen's Mystery Magazine*, September/October 2002.

The Emperor's Dice. *Ellery Queen's Mystery Magazine*, April 1951. Collected in CALENDAR OF CRIME (Little, Brown, 1952). Reprinted in BEST DETECTIVE STORIES OF THE YEAR, ed. David C. Cooke (Dutton, 1952); *Ellery Queen's Mystery Magazine*, May 1965.

As Simple As ABC. *Ellery Queen's Mystery Magazine*, May 1951. Collected in CALENDAR OF CRIME (Little, Brown, 1952), as "The Gettysburg Bugle." Reprinted in BUTCHER, BAKER, MURDER-MAKER, ed. George Harmon Coxe (Knopf, 1954); PLANNED DEPARTURES, ed. Elizabeth Ferrars (Hodder & Stoughton, 1958); THE QUINTESSENCE OF QUEEN, ed. Anthony Boucher (Random House, 1962); THREE TIMES THREE MYSTERY OMNIBUS, ed. Howard Haycraft & John Beecroft (Doubleday, 1964); *Ellery Queen's Mystery Magazine*, June 1965; DEAR DEAD DAYS, ed. Edward D. Hoch (Walker, 1972); GREAT SHORT TALES OF MYSTERY AND TERROR, ed. anon. (Reader's Digest Books, 1982); A TREASURY OF AMERICAN MYSTERY STORIES, ed. Frank D. McSherry Jr., Charles G. Waugh & Martin H. Greenberg (Avenel Books, 1989); FIFTY YEARS OF THE BEST FROM ELLERY QUEEN'S MYSTERY MAGAZINE, ed. Eleanor Sullivan (Carroll & Graf, 1991); THE FIFTY GREATEST MYSTERIES OF ALL TIME, ed. Otto Penzler (Dove Books, 1998).

The Medical Finger. *Ellery Queen's Mystery Magazine*, June 1951. Collected in CALENDAR OF CRIME (Little, Brown, 1952). Reprinted in *Ellery Queen's Mystery Magazine*, July 1965; MANHATTAN MYSTERIES, ed. Bill Pronzini, Carol-Lynn Rossel Waugh & Martin H. Greenberg (Avenel Books, 1987).

The Fallen Angel. *Ellery Queen's Mystery Magazine*, July 1951. Collected in CALENDAR OF CRIME (Little, Brown, 1952). Reprinted in *Ellery Queen's Mystery Magazine*, August 1965.

Kidnaped! *This Week*, 8 July 1951. Collected in QBI: QUEEN'S BUREAU OF INVESTIGATION (Little, Brown, 1955), as "Child Missing!" Reprinted in *Ellery Queen's Mystery Magazine*, June 1958; ELLERY QUEEN'S ANTHOLOGY, FALL-WINTER 1971 EDITION (Davis pb, 1971).

The Needle's Eye. *Ellery Queen's Mystery Magazine*, August 1951. Collected in CALENDAR OF CRIME (Little, Brown, 1952). Reprinted in CROOKS' TOUR, ed. Bruno Fischer (Dodd Mead, 1953); ELLERY QUEEN'S ANTHOLOGY, 1963 MID-YEAR EDITION (Davis pb, 1963); *Ellery Queen's Mystery Magazine*, September 1965; ELLERY QUEEN'S SHOOT THE WORKS! (Pyramid pb #T2129, 1969); MURDER SHORT & SWEET, ed. Paul D. Staudohar (Chicago Review Press, 2008).

The Vanishing Wizard. *This Week*, 30 September 1951. Collected in QBI: QUEEN'S BUREAU OF INVESTIGATION (Little, Brown, 1955), as "Double Your Money." Reprinted in *Ellery Queen's Mystery Magazine*, September 1955; ELLERY QUEEN'S 1968 ANTHOLOGY (Davis pb, 1967).

1952

The Mysterious Black Ledger. *This Week*, 26 January 1952. Collected in QBI: QUEEN'S BUREAU OF INVESTIGATION (Little, Brown, 1955), as "The Black Ledger." Reprinted in *Ellery Queen's Mystery Magazine*, December 1955; ELLERY QUEEN'S 1962 ANTHOLOGY (Davis pb, 1961).

Cold Money. *This Week*, 20 March 1952. Collected in QBI: QUEEN'S BUREAU OF INVESTIGATION (Little, Brown, 1955). Reprinted in *Ellery Queen's Mystery Magazine*, January 1956; ELLERY QUEEN'S 1969 ANTHOLOGY (Davis pb, 1968); ELLERY QUEEN's ANTHOLOGY #56: MEMORABLE CHARACTERS, ed. Eleanor Sullivan & Karen A. Prince (Fall 1984); DETECTIVE STORIES, ed. Philip Pullman (Kingfisher, 1998).

The Phantom Train. *This Week*, 31 August 1952. Collected in QBI: QUEEN'S BUREAU OF INVESTIGATION (Little, Brown, 1955) and THE BEST OF ELLERY QUEEN (Beaufort, 1985), as "Snowball in July." Reprinted in *Ellery Queen's Mystery Magazine*, July 1956; ELLERY QUEEN'S 1969 ANTHOLOGY (Davis pb, 1968); MIDNIGHT SPECIALS, ed. Bill Pronzini (Bobbs-Merrill, 1977); ALL BUT IMPOSSIBLE!, ed. Edward D. Hoch (Ticknor & Fields, 1981); *Ellery Queen's Mystery Magazine*, January 2005.

The Myna Bird Mystery. *This Week*, 28 December 1952. Collected in QBI: QUEEN'S BUREAU OF INVESTIGATION (Little, Brown, 1955), as "The Myna Birds." Reprinted in *Ellery Queen's Mystery Magazine*, September 1956, as "Cut, Cut, Cut!"; ELLERY QUEEN'S ANTHOLOGY,

1969 MID-YEAR EDITION (Davis pb, 1969), as "Cut, Cut, Cut!"; *Ellery Queen's Mystery Magazine*, January 2004.

1953

The Accused. *Today's Family*, February 1953. Collected in QBI: QUEEN'S BUREAU OF INVESTIGATION (Little, Brown, 1955), as "The Accused." Reprinted in *Ellery Queen's Mystery Magazine*, December 1954; ELLERY QUEEN'S 1966 ANTHOLOGY (Davis pb, 1965).

"My Queer Dean!" *This Week*, 8 March 1953. Collected in QBI: QUEEN'S BUREAU OF INVESTIGATION (Little, Brown, 1955) and THE BEST OF ELLERY QUEEN (Beaufort, 1985). Reprinted in BEST DETECTIVE STORIES OF THE YEAR, ed. David C. Cooke (Dutton, 1954); *Ellery Queen's Mystery Magazine*, November 1956; THIS WEEK'S STORIES OF MYSTERY AND SUSPENSE, ed. Stewart Beach (Random House, 1957); THE COMFORTABLE COFFIN, ed. Richard S. Prather (Gold Medal pb #S1046, 1960); ELLERY QUEEN'S 1971 ANTHOLOGY (Davis pb, 1970); MASTERPIECES OF MYSTERY: DETECTIVE DIRECTORY, PART TWO, ed. Ellery Queen (Davis, 1978); THE OXFORD BOOK OF DETECTIVE STORIES, ed. Patricia Cross (Oxford University Press, 2000); THE LONGMAN ANTHOLOGY OF DETECTIVE FICTION, ed. Deane Mansfield-Kelley & Lois Marchino (Longmans, 2004).

A Matter of Seconds. *This Week*, 9 August 1953. Collected in QBI: QUEEN'S BUREAU OF INVESTIGATION (Little, Brown, 1955). Reprinted in *Ellery Queen's Mystery Magazine*, January 1957; ELLERY QUEEN'S ANTHOLOGY #23 (Spring/Summer 1972); BOXING'S BEST SHORT STORIES, ed. Paul D. Staudohar (Chicago Review Press, 1999).

A Question of Honor. *This Week*, 13 September 1953. Collected in QBI: QUEEN'S BUREAU OF INVESTIGATION (Little, Brown, 1955). Reprinted in *Ellery Queen's Mystery Magazine*, May 1958; CRIMES ACROSS THE SEA, ed. John Creasey (Harper, 1964); ELLERY QUEEN'S ANTHOLOGY #27 (Spring/Summer 1974).

1954

GI Story. *Ellery Queen's Mystery Magazine*, August 1954. Collected in QBI: QUEEN'S BUREAU OF INVESTIGATION (Little, Brown, 1955) and THE BEST OF ELLERY QUEEN (Beaufort, 1985). Reprinted in BEST DETECTIVE STORIES OF THE YEAR, ed. David C. Cooke (Dutton, 1955); ELLERY QUEEN'S ANTHOLOGY, 1967 MID-YEAR EDITION (Davis pb, 1967); *Ellery Queen's Mystery Magazine*, May 1970.

Diamonds in Paradise. *Ellery Queen's Mystery Magazine*, September 1954. Collected in QUEENS FULL (Random House, 1965). Reprinted in CRIME FOR TWO, ed. Frances & Richard Lockridge (Lippincott, 1955); ELLERY QUEEN'S 1961 ANTHOLOGY (Davis pb, 1960); CREAM OF THE CRIME, ed. Hugh Pentecost (Holt, Rinehart & Winston, 1962); ELLERY QUEEN'S 12 (Dell pb #2259, 1964); DOWNPOUR, ed. Ed McBain (New English Library, 1969); 101 MYSTERY STORIES, ed. Bill Pronzini & Martin H. Greenberg (Avenel Books, 1986).

1955

Bride in Danger. *Ellery Queen's Mystery Magazine*, August 1955. Collected in QED: QUEEN'S EXPERIMENTS IN DETECTION (New American Library, 1968), as "Eve of the Wedding." Reprinted in ELLERY QUEEN'S ANTHOLOGY, 1966 MID-YEAR EDITION (Davis pb, 1966); ROGUES' GALLERY, ed. Walter B. Gibson (Doubleday, 1969).

The Blackboard Gangsters. *This Week*, 11 September 1955. Collected in QED: QUEEN'S EXPERIMENTS IN DETECTION (New American Library, 1968), as "Object Lesson." Reprinted in FOR LOVE OR MONEY, ed. Dorothy Gardiner (Doubleday, 1957), as "Kid Stuff"; *Ellery Queen's Mystery Magazine*, April 1958; FAVORITE SLEUTHS, ed. John Ernst (Doubleday, 1965); ELLERY QUEEN'S ANTHOLOGY #24 (Fall/Winter 1972); MIRROR MIRROR FATAL

MIRROR, ed. Hans Stefan Santesson (Doubleday, 1973); MASTERPIECES OF MYSTERY: CHOICE CUTS, ed. Ellery Queen (Davis, 1979).

1956

The Wrightsville Heirs. *Better Living*, January-February 1956. Collected in QUEENS FULL (Random House, 1965). Reprinted in *Ellery Queen's Mystery Magazine*, November 1957; ELLERY QUEEN'S ANTHOLOGY #52: MORE LOST LADIES & MEN, ed. Eleanor Sullivan (Summer 1985).

Terror in a Penthouse. *This Week*, 18 March 1956. Collected in QED: QUEEN'S EXPERIMENTS IN DETECTION (New American Library, 1968), as "No Parking." Reprinted in *Ellery Queen's Mystery Magazine*, February 1958; WICKED WOMEN, ed. Lee Wright (Pocket Books pb #1263, 1960); ELLERY QUEEN'S ANTHOLOGY, 1964 MID-YEAR EDITION (Davis pb, 1964); CRIMES AND MISFORTUNES, ed. J. Francis McComas (Random House, 1970); THE MYSTERY HALL OF FAME, ed. Bill Pronzini, Martin H. Greenberg & Charles G. Waugh (Morrow, 1984).

The Man They All Hated. *This Week*, 10 June 1956. Collected in QED: QUEEN'S EXPERIMENTS IN DETECTION (New American Library, 1968), as "No Place to Live." Reprinted in *Ellery Queen's Mystery Magazine*, March 1958; ELLERY QUEEN'S 1964 ANTHOLOGY (Davis pb, 1963); ELLERY QUEEN'S ANTHOLOGY #54: BLIGHTED DWELLINGS, ed. Eleanor Sullivan (Summer 1986).

Terror Town. *Argosy*, August 1956. Collected in THE TRAGEDY OF ERRORS (Crippen & Landru, 1999). Reprinted in BEST DETECTIVE STORIES OF THE YEAR, ed. David C. Cooke (Dutton, 1957); *Ellery Queen's Mystery Magazine*, August and September 1958, as "The Motive"; ELLERY QUEEN'S 1965 ANTHOLOGY (Davis pb, 1964), as "The Motive"; MASTERPIECES OF MYSTERY: AMATEURS & PROFESSIONALS, ed. Ellery Queen (Davis, 1978), as "The Motive"; HITCHCOCK IN PRIME TIME, ed. Francis M. Nevins & Martin H. Greenberg (Avon pb #89673, 1985).

1957

Miracles Do Happen. *Ellery Queen's Mystery Magazine*, July 1957. Collected in QED: QUEEN'S EXPERIMENTS IN DETECTION (New American Library, 1968) and THE BEST OF ELLERY QUEEN (Beaufort, 1985). Reprinted in ELLERY QUEEN'S 13th ANNUAL (Random House, 1958); 20th CENTURY DETECTIVE STORIES, ed. Ellery Queen (Popular Library pb #SP333, 1964); THE CRIME-SOLVERS, ed. Stewart H. Benedict (Dell pb #3078, 1966); KILLERS OF THE MIND, ed. Lucy Freeman (Random House, 1974); MASTERPIECES OF MYSTERY: THE FIFTIES, ed. Ellery Queen, 1978.

1958

The Case Against Carroll. *Argosy*, September 1958. Collected in QUEENS FULL (Random House, 1965). Reprinted in *Ellery Queen's Mystery Magazine*, September 1960; ELLERY QUEEN's 1970 ANTHOLOGY (Davis pb, 1969); ELLERY QUEEN'S BEST BETS (Pyramid pb #N2775, 1972); MASTERPIECES OF MYSTERY: THE SUPERSLEUTHS, ed. Ellery Queen (Davis, 1976).

1960

Enter Ellery Queen. *Argosy*, June 1960. Collected in QED: QUEEN'S EXPERIMENTS IN DETECTION (New American Library, 1968), as "Mystery at the Library of Congress." Reprinted in *Ellery Queen's Mystery Magazine*, February 1963; CRIME WITHOUT MURDER, ed. Dorothy Salisbury Davis (Scribner, 1970); ELLERY QUEEN'S ANTHOLOGY #29: ACES OF MYSTERY (Spring/Summer 1975); CHAPTER AND HEARSE, ed. Marcia Muller & Bill Pronzini (Morrow, 1985).

E = Murder. *This Week*, 4 August 1960. Collected in QUEENS FULL (Random House, 1965). Reprinted in *Ellery Queen's Mystery Magazine*, May 1961; WITH MALICE TOWARD ALL, ed. Robert L. Fish (Putnam, 1968); ELLERY QUEEN'S ANTHOLOGY #28 (Fall/Winter 1974); 101 MYSTERY STORIES, ed. Bill Pronzini & Martin H. Greenberg (Avenel Books, 1986).

1962

The Death of Don Juan. *Argosy*, May 1962. Collected in QUEENS FULL (Random House, 1965). Reprinted in BEST DETECTIVE STORIES OF THE YEAR, ed. Anthony Boucher (Dutton, 1963); *Ellery Queen's Mystery Magazine*, August 1964; ELLERY QUEEN'S ANTHOLOGY, 1970 MID-YEAR EDITION (Davis pb, 1970); MASTERPIECES OF MYSTERY: THE GOLDEN AGE, PART ONE, ed. Ellery Queen (Davis, 1977); ELLERY QUEEN'S ANTHOLOGY #49: CRIMES & PUNISHMENTS, ed. Eleanor Sullivan & Karen A. Prince (Summer 1984).

1963

Mystery in Neon Red. *This Week*, 27 July 1963. Collected in QED: QUEEN'S EXPERIMENTS IN DETECTION (New American Library, 1968), as "The Broken T." Reprinted in *Ellery Queen's Mystery Magazine*, May 1966; ELLERY QUEEN'S ANTHOLOGY #31: GIANTS OF MYSTERY (Spring/ Summer 1976).

Half a Clue to Murder. *This Week*, 25 August 1963. Collected in QED: QUEEN'S EXPERIMENTS IN DETECTION (New American Library, 1968), as "Half a Clue." Reprinted in *Ellery Queen's Mystery Magazine*, August 1966; ELLERY QUEEN'S ANTHOLOGY #30: MASTERS OF MYSTERY (Fall/Winter 1975); DETECTION, ed. James Gibson & Alan Ridout (John Murray, 1978).

Last Man to Die. *This Week*, 3 November 1963. Collected in QED: QUEEN'S EXPERIMENTS IN DETECTION (New American Library, 1968) and THE BEST OF ELLERY QUEEN (Beaufort, 1985). Reprinted in BEST DETECTIVE STORIES OF THE YEAR, ed. Anthony Boucher (Dutton, 1964); *Ellery Queen's Mystery Magazine*, January 1967; ELLERY QUEEN'S ANTHOLOGY #47: LOST MEN, ed. Eleanor Sullivan (Fall 1983); *Ellery Queen's Mystery Magazine*, June 2004.

1964

Crime Syndicate Payoff. *Cavalier*, August 1964. Collected in QED: QUEEN'S EXPERIMENTS IN DETECTION (New American Library, 1968), as "Payoff." Reprinted in BEST DETECTIVE STORIES OF THE YEAR, ed. Anthony Boucher (Dutton, 1965); *Ellery Queen's Mystery Magazine*, July 1966; ELLERY QUEEN'S ANTHOLOGY #32: MAGICIANS OF MYSTERY (Fall/Winter 1976).

1965

The Little Spy. *Cavalier*, January 1965. Collected in QED: QUEEN'S EXPERIMENTS IN DETECTION (New American Library, 1968). Reprinted in *Ellery Queen's Mystery Magazine*, September 1966; MURDER IN MIND, ed. Lawrence Treat (Dutton, 1967); ELLERY QUEEN'S ANTHOLOGY #33: CHAMPIONS OF MYSTERY (Spring/Summer 1977).

Dead Ringer. *Diners' Club Magazine*, March 1965. Collected in QED: QUEEN'S EXPERIMENTS IN DETECTION (New American Library, 1968). Reprinted in *Ellery Queen's Mystery Magazine*, October 1966; ELLERY QUEEN'S ANTHOLOGY #35: MASKS OF MYSTERY (Spring/Summer 1978); ELLERY QUEEN THE BEST OF SUSPENSE, ed. anon. (Galahad Books, 1980).

Uncle from Australia. *Diners' Club Magazine*, June 1965. Collected in THE TRAGEDY OF ERRORS (Crippen & Landru, 1999). Reprinted in *Ellery Queen's Mystery Magazine*, November 1967; ELLERY QUEEN'S ANTHOLOGY #38: SECRETS OF MYSTERY (Fall/Winter 1979); ELLERY QUEEN THE BEST OF SUSPENSE, ed. anon. (Galahad Books, 1980); *Ellery Queen's Mystery Magazine*, November 2011.

Abraham Lincoln's Clue. *MD*, June 1965. Collected in QED: QUEEN'S EXPERIMENTS IN DETECTION (New American Library, 1968) and THE BEST OF ELLERY QUEEN (Beaufort, 1985). Reprinted in BEST DETECTIVE STORIES OF THE YEAR, ed. Anthony Boucher (Dutton, 1966); *Ellery Queen's Mystery Magazine*, March 1967; BOUCHER'S CHOICEST, ed. Jeanne Bernkopf (Dutton, 1969); EVERY CRIME IN THE BOOK, ed. Robert L. Fish (Putnam, 1975); MASTERPIECES OF MYSTERY: CHERISHED CLASSICS, ed. Ellery Queen (Davis, 1978);

ELLERY QUEEN'S ANTHOLOGY #37: WINGS OF MYSTERY (Spring/Summer 1979); A SPECIAL KIND OF CRIME, ed. Lawrence Treat (Doubleday, 1982); TOP CRIME, ed. Josh Pachter (St. Martin's Press, 1983); GREAT DETECTIVES, ed. David Willis McCullough (Pantheon, 1984); CRIME CLASSICS, ed. Rex Burns & Mary Rose Sullivan (Viking, 1990); THE OXFORD BOOK OF AMERICAN DETECTIVE STORIES, ed. Tony Hillerman & Rosemary Herbert (Oxford University Press, 1996); MURDEROUS SCHEMES, ed. Donald E. Westlake (Oxford University Press, 1996).

The President Regrets. *Diners' Club Magazine*, September 1965. Collected in QED: QUEEN'S EXPERIMENTS IN DETECTION (New American Library, 1968). Reprinted in *Ellery Queen's Mystery Magazine*, July 1967; ELLERY QUEEN'S ANTHOLOGY #36: NAPOLEONS OF MYSTERY (Fall/Winter 1978).

1966

Mum Is the Word. *Ellery Queen's Mystery Magazine*, April 1966. Collected in QED: QUEEN'S EXPERIMENTS IN DETECTION (New American Library, 1968). Reprinted in ELLERY QUEEN'S ANTHOLOGY #25 (Spring/Summer 1973); MASTERPIECES OF MYSTERY: THE GRAND MASTERS, ed. Ellery Queen (Davis, 1976).

1967

Wedding Anniversary. *Ellery Queen's Mystery Magazine*, September 1967. Collected in THE BEST OF ELLERY QUEEN (Beaufort, 1985). Reprinted in ELLERY QUEEN'S ANTHOLOGY #34: FACES OF MYSTERY (Fall/Winter 1977); *Ellery Queen's Mystery Magazine*, September/ October 1999.

1971

The Three Students. *Playboy*, March 1971. Collected in THE TRAGEDY OF ERRORS (Crippen & Landru, 1999). Reprinted in *Ellery Queen's Mystery Magazine*, November 1973; ELLERY QUEEN'S ANTHOLOGY #40: WINDOWS OF MYSTERY (Fall/Winter 1979).

The Odd Man. *Playboy*, June 1971. Collected in THE TRAGEDY OF ERRORS (Crippen & Landru, 1999). Reprinted in *Ellery Queen's Mystery Magazine*, October 1975; ELLERY QUEEN'S ANTHOLOGY #39: VEILS OF MYSTERY (Spring/Summer 1980); ELLERY QUEEN THE BEST OF SUSPENSE, ed. anon. (Galahad Books, 1980).

The Honest Swindler. *Saturday Evening Post*, Summer 1971. Collected in THE TRAGEDY OF ERRORS (Crippen & Landru, 1999). Reprinted in ELLERY QUEEN'S ANTHOLOGY #41: DOORS OF MYSTERY (Spring/Summer 1981); ELLERY QUEEN MASTERS OF MYSTERY, ed. anon. (Galahad Books, 1987).

VIII. MAGAZINE APPEARANCES OF NOVELS
PRIOR TO BOOK PUBLICATION

1933

DRURY LANE'S LAST CASE. *Mystery League*, October 1933. Uncut.

1934

THE CHINESE ORANGE MYSTERY. *Redbook*, June 1934. Condensed.

1935

THE SPANISH CAPE MYSTERY. *Redbook*, April 1935. Condensed.

1936

HALFWAY HOUSE. *Cosmopolitan*, June 1936. Condensed.

THE DOOR BETWEEN. *Cosmopolitan*, December 1936. Condensed.

1937

THE DEVIL TO PAY. *Cosmopolitan*, December 1937. Condensed.

1938

THE FOUR OF HEARTS. *Cosmopolitan*, October 1938. Condensed.

1968

THE HOUSE OF BRASS. *Redbook*, January 1968. Condensed.

IX. THEMED ANTHOLOGIES EDITED BY QUEEN

CHALLENGE TO THE READER. Stokes, 1938.

101 YEARS' ENTERTAINMENT: THE GREAT DETECTIVE STORIES, 1841-1941. Little, Brown, 1941. Modern Library, 1946, with the four Sherlock Holmes excerpts in the original edition replaced by a Nick Carter story.

SPORTING BLOOD: THE GREAT SPORTS DETECTIVE STORIES. Little, Brown, 1942. Faber, 1946, as SPORTING DETECTIVE STORIES.

THE FEMALE OF THE SPECIES: THE GREAT WOMEN DETECTIVES AND CRIMINALS. Little, Brown, 1943. Faber, 1947, as LADIES IN CRIME: A COLLECTION OF DETECTIVE STORIES BY ENGLISH AND AMERICAN WRITERS.

THE MISADVENTURES OF SHERLOCK HOLMES. Little, Brown, 1944.

BEST STORIES FROM ELLERY QUEEN'S MYSTERY MAGAZINE. Detective Book Club, 1944.

ROGUES' GALLERY: THE GREAT CRIMINALS OF MODERN FICTION. Little, Brown, 1945. Faber, 1947.

TO THE QUEEN'S TASTE: THE FIRST SUPPLEMENT TO 101 YEARS' ENTERTAINMENT, CONSISTING OF THE BEST STORIES PUBLISHED IN THE FIRST FIVE YEARS OF ELLERY QUEEN'S MYSTERY MAGAZINE. Little, Brown, 1946. Faber, 1949.

MURDER BY EXPERTS. Ziff-Davis, 1947. Sampson Low, 1950.

20th CENTURY DETECTIVE STORIES. World, 1948. Includes the first version of QUEEN'S QUORUM. The second edition (Popular Library pb #SP333, 1964) omits the QUORUM and substitutes newer stories for eight of the tales in the 1948 version.

THE LITERATURE OF CRIME: STORIES BY WORLD-FAMOUS AUTHORS. Little, Brown, 1950. Cassell, 1952. Pan pb #X12, 1957, as ELLERY QUEEN'S BOOK OF MYSTERY STORIES.

POETIC JUSTICE: 23 STORIES OF CRIME, MYSTERY AND DETECTION BY WORLD-FAMOUS POETS FROM GEOFFREY CHAUCER TO DYLAN THOMAS. New American Library, 1967. Signet pb #Q4269, 1970.

MINIMYSTERIES: 70 SHORT-SHORT STORIES OF CRIME, MYSTERY AND DETECTION. World, 1969.

THE JAPANESE GOLDEN DOZEN: THE DETECTIVE STORY IN JAPAN. C.E. Tuttle, 1978.

X. ANNUAL COMPILATIONS
OF BEST EQMM STORIES EDITED BY QUEEN

THE QUEEN'S AWARDS, 1946. Little, Brown, 1946. Gollancz, 1948.

THE QUEEN'S AWARDS, 1947. Little, Brown, 1947. Gollancz, 1949.

THE QUEEN'S AWARDS, 1948. Little, Brown, 1948. Gollancz, 1950.

THE QUEEN'S AWARDS, 1949. Little, Brown, 1949. Gollancz, 1951.

THE QUEEN'S AWARDS, FIFTH SERIES. Little, Brown, 1950. Gollancz, 1952. Black's Readers Series, n.d., as THE LADY KILLER AND OTHER STORIES. Ace pb #D493, 1961.

THE QUEEN'S AWARDS, SIXTH SERIES. Little, Brown, 1951. Gollancz, 1953. Black's Readers Service, n.d., as THE ENEMY AND OTHER STORIES.

THE QUEEN'S AWARDS, SEVENTH SERIES. Little, Brown, 1952. Gollancz, 1954. Black's Readers Service, n.d., as ALWAYS TRUST A COP AND OTHER STORIES.

THE QUEEN'S AWARDS, EIGHTH SERIES. Little, Brown, 1953. Gollancz, 1955. Perma pb #M3015, 1955. Black's Readers Service, n.d., as BORN KILLER AND OTHER STORIES.

ELLERY QUEEN'S AWARDS, NINTH SERIES. Little, Brown, 1954. Collins, 1956.

ELLERY QUEEN'S AWARDS, TENTH SERIES. Little, Brown, 1955. Collins, 1957. Perma pb #M3076, 1957.

ELLERY QUEEN'S AWARDS, ELEVENTH SERIES. Simon & Schuster, 1956. Collins, 1958.

ELLERY QUEEN'S AWARDS, TWELFTH SERIES. Simon & Schuster, 1957. Collins, 1959.

ELLERY QUEEN'S THIRTEENTH ANNUAL: A SELECTION OF NEW STORIES FROM ELLERY QUEEN'S MYSTERY MAGAZINE. Random House, 1958. Collins, 1960, as ELLERY QUEEN'S CHOICE: THIRTEENTH SERIES.

ELLERY QUEEN'S 14th MYSTERY ANNUAL. Random House, 1959. Collins, 1961, as ELLERY QUEEN'S CHOICE: FOURTEENTH SERIES.

ELLERY QUEEN'S 15th MYSTERY ANNUAL. Random House, 1960. Gollancz, 1961.

ELLERY QUEEN'S 16th MYSTERY ANNUAL. Random House, 1961. Gollancz, 1962. Popular Library pb #K14, 1962.

TO BE READ BEFORE MIDNIGHT. Random House, 1962. Gollancz, 1963. Popular Library pb #SP237, 1963.

ELLERY QUEEN'S MYSTERY MIX #18. Random House, 1963. Gollancz, 1964. Popular Library pb #M2065, 1964. Nine stories from this anthology were reprinted as THE MOST WANTED MAN IN THE WORLD (New English Library pb, 1968).

ELLERY QUEEN'S DOUBLE DOZEN. Random House, 1964. Gollancz, 1965, as ELLERY QUEEN'S 19th MYSTERY ANNUAL. Popular Library pb #M2082, 1965. Nine stories from this anthology were reprinted as DEATH SCENE (New English Library pb, 1968) and another ten as L AS IN LOOT (New English Library pb, 1969).

ELLERY QUEEN'S 20th ANNIVERSARY ANNUAL. Random House, 1965. Gollancz, 1966. Popular Library pb #75-1205, 1966. Eight stories from this anthology were reprinted as A CRAVING FOR VIOLENCE (New English Library pb, 1969).

ELLERY QUEEN'S CRIME CAROUSEL. New American Library, 1966. Gollancz, 1967. Signet pb #P3267, 1967.

ELLERY QUEEN'S ALL-STAR LINEUP. New American Library, 1967. Gollancz, 1968, as ELLERY QUEEN'S 22nd MYSTERY ANNUAL. Signet pb #T3698, 1968.

ELLERY QUEEN'S MYSTERY PARADE. New American Library, 1968. Gollancz, 1969. Signet pb #Q3893, 1969.

ELLERY QUEEN'S MURDER MENU. World, 1969. Gollancz, 1969.

ELLERY QUEEN'S GRAND SLAM. World, 1970. Gollancz, 1971. Popular Library pb #445-00304-095, 1971.

ELLERY QUEEN'S HEADLINERS. World, 1971. Gollancz, 1972.

ELLERY QUEEN'S MYSTERY BAG. World, 1972. Gollancz, 1973. Manor pb #12153, 1973.

ELLERY QUEEN'S CROOKBOOK. Random House, 1974.

ELLERY QUEEN'S MURDERCADE. Random House, 1975.

ELLERY QUEEN'S CRIME WAVE. Putnam, 1976.

ELLERY QUEEN'S SEARCHES AND SEIZURES. Dial Press, 1977.

ELLERY QUEEN'S A MULTITUDE OF SINS. Dial Press, 1978.

ELLERY QUEEN'S SCENES OF THE CRIME. Dial Press, 1979.

ELLERY QUEEN'S CIRCUMSTANTIAL EVIDENCE. Dial Press, 1980.

ELLERY QUEEN'S CRIME CRUISE ROUND THE WORLD. Dial Press, 1981.

XI. ANTHOLOGIES CULLED DIRECTLY FROM THE TITLES IN SECTION X

THE QUINTESSENCE OF QUEEN, ed. Anthony Boucher. Random House, 1962. Gollancz, 1963, as A MAGNUM OF MYSTERIES. Both editions subtitled BEST PRIZE STORIES FROM 12 YEARS OF ELLERY QUEEN'S MYSTERY MAGAZINE.

THE GOLDEN 13: 13 FIRST PRIZE WINNERS FROM ELLERY QUEEN'S MYSTERY MAGAZINE. World, 1971. Gollancz, 1972. Popular Library pb #445-00316-0954, 1972.

XII. UNTHEMED ANTHOLOGIES OF EQMM STORIES

ELLERY QUEEN'S 1960 ANTHOLOGY. Davis pb, 1959.

ELLERY QUEEN'S 1961 ANTHOLOGY. Davis pb, 1960.

ELLERY QUEEN'S 1962 ANTHOLOGY. Davis pb, 1961.

ELLERY QUEEN'S 1963 ANTHOLOGY. Davis pb, 1962.

ELLERY QUEEN'S ANTHOLOGY, 1963 MID-YEAR EDITION. Davis pb, 1963.

ELLERY QUEEN'S 1964 ANTHOLOGY. Davis pb, 1963.

ELLERY QUEEN'S ANTHOLOGY, 1964 MID-YEAR EDITION. Davis pb, 1964.

ELLERY QUEEN'S 1965 ANTHOLOGY. Davis pb, 1964.

ELLERY QUEEN'S ANTHOLOGY, 1965 MID-YEAR EDITION. Davis pb, 1965.

ELLERY QUEEN'S 1966 ANTHOLOGY. Davis pb, 1965.

ELLERY QUEEN'S ANTHOLOGY, 1966 MID-YEAR EDITION. Davis pb, 1966.

ELLERY QUEEN'S 1967 ANTHOLOGY. Davis pb, 1966.

ELLERY QUEEN'S ANTHOLOGY, 1967 MID-YEAR EDITION. Davis pb, 1967.

ELLERY QUEEN'S 1968 ANTHOLOGY. Davis pb, 1967.

ELLERY QUEEN'S ANTHOLOGY, 1968 MID-YEAR EDITION. Davis pb, 1968.

ELLERY QUEEN'S 1969 ANTHOLOGY. Davis pb, 1968.

ELLERY QUEEN'S ANTHOLOGY, 1969 MID-YEAR EDITION. Davis pb, 1969.

ELLERY QUEEN'S 1970 ANTHOLOGY. Davis pb, 1969.

ELLERY QUEEN'S ANTHOLOGY, 1970 MID-YEAR EDITION. Davis pb, 1970.

ELLERY QUEEN'S 1971 ANTHOLOGY. Davis pb, 1970.

ELLERY QUEEN'S ANTHOLOGY #21 (Spring/Summer 1971). Davis pb, 1971.

ELLERY QUEEN'S ANTHOLOGY #22 (Fall/Winter 1971). Davis pb, 1971.

ELLERY QUEEN'S ANTHOLOGY #23 (Spring/Summer 1972). Davis pb, 1972.

ELLERY QUEEN'S ANTHOLOGY #24 (Fall/Winter 1972). Davis pb, 1972.

ELLERY QUEEN'S ANTHOLOGY #25 (Spring/Summer 1973). Davis pb, 1973.

ELLERY QUEEN'S ANTHOLOGY #26 (Fall/Winter 1973). Davis pb, 1973.

ELLERY QUEEN'S ANTHOLOGY #27 (Spring/Summer 1974). Davis pb, 1974.

ELLERY QUEEN'S ANTHOLOGY #28 (Fall/Winter 1974). Davis pb, 1974.

ELLERY QUEEN'S ANTHOLOGY #29: ACES OF MYSTERY (Spring/Summer 1975). Davis/Dial, 1975.

ELLERY QUEEN'S ANTHOLOGY #30: MASTERS OF MYSTERY (Fall/Winter 1975). Davis/Dial, 1975.

ELLERY QUEEN'S ANTHOLOGY #31: GIANTS OF MYSTERY (Spring/Summer 1976). Davis/Dial, 1976.

ELLERY QUEEN'S ANTHOLOGY #32: MAGICIANS OF MYSTERY (Fall/Winter 1976). Davis/Dial, 1976.

ELLERY QUEEN'S ANTHOLOGY #33: CHAMPIONS OF MYSTERY (Spring/Summer 1977). Davis/Dial, 1977.

ELLERY QUEEN'S ANTHOLOGY #34: FACES OF MYSTERY (Fall/Winter 1977). Davis/Dial, 1977.

ELLERY QUEEN'S ANTHOLOGY #35: MASKS OF MYSTERY (Spring/Summer 1978). Davis/Dial, 1978.

ELLERY QUEEN'S ANTHOLOGY #36: NAPOLEONS OF MYSTERY (Fall/Winter 1978). Davis/Dial, 1978.

ELLERY QUEEN'S ANTHOLOGY #37: WINGS OF MYSTERY (Spring/Summer 1979). Davis/Dial, 1979.

ELLERY QUEEN'S ANTHOLOGY #38: SECRETS OF MYSTERY (Fall/Winter 1979). Davis/Dial, 1979.

ELLERY QUEEN'S ANTHOLOGY #39: VEILS OF MYSTERY (Spring/Summer 1980). Davis/Dial, 1980.

ELLERY QUEEN'S ANTHOLOGY #40: WINDOWS OF MYSTERY (Fall/Winter 1980). Davis/Dial, 1980.

ELLERY QUEEN'S ANTHOLOGY #41: DOORS OF MYSTERY (Spring/Summer 1981). Davis/Dial, 1981.

ELLERY QUEEN'S ANTHOLOGY #42: EYES OF MYSTERY (Fall/Winter 1981. Davis/Dial, 1981.

ELLERY QUEEN'S ANTHOLOGY #43: MAZE OF MYSTERIES (Spring/Summer 1982). Davis/Dial, 1982.

ELLERY QUEEN'S ANTHOLOGY #44: BOOK OF FIRST APPEARANCES (Fall/Winter 1982). Davis/Dial, 1982.

ELLERY QUEEN'S ANTHOLOGY #45: EYEWITNESSES (Spring 1983).

ELLERY QUEEN'S ANTHOLOGY #46: LOST LADIES, ed. Ellery Queen & Eleanor Sullivan (Summer 1983).

ELLERY QUEEN'S ANTHOLOGY #47: LOST MEN, ed. Eleanor Sullivan (Fall 1983).

ELLERY QUEEN'S ANTHOLOGY #48: PRIME CRIMES, ed. Eleanor Sullivan (Winter 1983).

ELLERY QUEEN'S ANTHOLOGY #49: CRIMES & PUNISHMENTS, ed. Eleanor Sullivan & Karen A. Prince (Summer 1984).

ELLERY QUEEN'S ANTHOLOGY #50: MEMORABLE CHARACTERS, ed. Eleanor Sullivan & Karen A. Prince (Fall 1984).

ELLERY QUEEN'S ANTHOLOGY #51: PRIME CRIMES 2, ed. Eleanor Sullivan & Karen A. Prince (Winter 1984).

ELLERY QUEEN'S ANTHOLOGY #52: MORE LOST LADIES AND MEN, ed. Eleanor Sullivan (Summer 1985).

ELLERY QUEEN'S ANTHOLOGY #53: PRIME CRIMES 3, ed. Eleanor Sullivan (Fall 1985).

ELLERY QUEEN'S ANTHOLOGY #54: BLIGHTED DWELLINGS, ed. Eleanor Sullivan (Summer 1986).

ELLERY QUEEN'S ANTHOLOGY #55: PRIME CRIMES 4, ed. Eleanor Sullivan (Fall 1986).

ELLERY QUEEN'S ANTHOLOGY #56: BAD SCENES, ed. Eleanor Sullivan (Summer 1987).

ELLERY QUEEN'S ANTHOLOGY #57: PRIME CRIMES 5, ed. Eleanor Sullivan (Fall 1987).

ELLERY QUEEN'S ANTHOLOGY #58: MEDIA FAVORITES, ed. Eleanor Sullivan (Summer 1988).

ELLERY QUEEN'S ANTHOLOGY #59: MORE MEDIA FAVORITES, ed. Eleanor Sullivan (Fall 1988).

ELLERY QUEEN'S ANTHOLOGY #60: 11 DEADLY SINS, ed. Eleanor Sullivan (Summer 1989).

XIII. ANTHOLOGIES CULLED DIRECTLY FROM THE TITLES LISTED IN XII

ELLERY QUEEN'S 12. Dell pb #2259, 1964.

ELLERY QUEEN'S LETHAL BLACK BOOK. Dell pb #2261, 1965.

ELLERY QUEEN'S MURDER — IN SPADES! Pyramid pb #T2036, 1969.

ELLERY QUEEN'S SHOOT THE WORKS. Pyramid pb #T2129, 1969.

ELLERY QUEEN'S MYSTERY JACKPOT. Pyramid pb #T2207, 1970.

ELLERY QUEEN'S BEST BETS. Pyramid pb #N2775, 1972.

ELLERY QUEEN'S COPS AND ROBBERS. Dale pb #0-89559-001-8, 1977.

ELLERY QUEEN'S CRIMES AND CONSEQUENCES. Dale pb #0-89559-002-6, 1977.

ELLERY QUEEN'S X MARKS THE PLOT. Dale pb #0-89559-004-2, 1977.

XIV. THE MASTERPIECES OF MYSTERY SERIES EDITED BY QUEEN

THE SUPERSLEUTHS. Davis, 1976.

THE PRIZEWINNERS. Davis, 1976.

DETECTIVE DIRECTORY, PART ONE. Davis, 1977.

DETECTIVE DIRECTORY, PART TWO. Davis, 1978.

THE OLD MASTERS. Davis, 1978.

THE GOLDEN AGE, PART ONE. Davis, 1978.

THE GOLDEN AGE, PART TWO. Davis, 1978.

THE FORTIES. Davis, 1978.

THE FIFTIES. Davis, 1978.

THE SIXTIES. Davis, 1978.

AMATEURS AND PROFESSIONALS. Davis, 1978.

BLUE RIBBON SPECIALS. Davis, 1978.

CHERISHED CLASSICS. Davis, 1978.

THE GRAND MASTERS. Davis, 1978.

STORIES NOT TO BE MISSED. Davis, 1978.

THE SUPERSLEUTHS REVISITED. Davis, 1979.

CHOICE CUTS. Davis, 1979.

MORE FROM THE SIXTIES. Davis, 1979.

THE GRAND MASTERS UP TO DATE. Davis, 1979.

THE SEVENTIES. Davis, 1979.

XV. COLLECTIONS OF OTHERS' SHORT FICTION EDITED BY QUEEN

A. DASHIELL HAMMETT STORIES

THE ADVENTURES OF SAM SPADE AND OTHER STORIES. Bestseller pb #B50, 1944. World, 1945. Seven stories from this collection were reprinted as A MAN CALLED SPADE AND OTHER STORIES (Dell pb #90, 1945, and #411, 1950). The complete collection was reprinted as THEY CAN ONLY HANG YOU ONCE AND OTHER STORIES (Mercury pb #131, 1949).

THE CONTINENTAL OP. Bestseller pb #B62, 1945. Dell pb #129, 1946.

THE RETURN OF THE CONTINENTAL OP. Jonathan pb #J17, 1945. Dell pb #154, 1946.

HAMMETT HOMICIDES. Bestseller pb #B81, 1946. Dell pb #226, 1947.

DEAD YELLOW WOMEN. Jonathan pb #J29, 1947. Dell pb #308, 1948.

NIGHTMARE TOWN. Mercury pb #120, 1948. Dell pb #379, 1949.

THE CREEPING SIAMESE. Jonathan pb #J48, 1950. Dell pb #538, 1951.

WOMAN IN THE DARK. Jonathan pb #J59, 1952.

A MAN NAMED THIN AND OTHER STORIES. Mercury pb #233, 1962.

B. STORIES BY OTHERS

Stuart Palmer, THE RIDDLES OF HILDEGARDE WITHERS. Jonathan pb #J26, 1947.

John Dickson Carr, DR. FELL, DETECTIVE, AND OTHER STORIES. Mercury pb #110, 1947.

Roy Vickers, THE DEPARTMENT OF DEAD ENDS. Bestseller pb #B91, 1947.

Margery Allingham, THE CASE BOOK OF MR. CAMPION. Mercury pb #112, 1947.

O. Henry, COPS AND ROBBERS. Bestseller pb #B94, 1948.

Stuart Palmer, THE MONKEY MURDER AND OTHER STORIES. Bestseller pb #B128, 1950.

C. THE "ELLERY QUEEN PRESENTS" SERIES

#1 Erle Stanley Gardner, THE CASE OF THE MURDERER'S BRIDE AND OTHER STORIES (October 1969).

#2 Lawrence Treat, P AS IN POLICE (October 1970).

#3 Edward D. Hoch, THE SPY AND THE THIEF (December 1971).

#4 Michael Gilbert, AMATEUR IN VIOLENCE (February 1973).

#5 Erle Stanley Gardner, THE CASE OF THE MURDERER'S BRIDE AND OTHER STORIES (June 1974).

#6 Stanley Ellin, KINDLY DIG YOUR GRAVE (December 1975).

#7 Julian Symons, HOW TO TRAP A CROOK (February 1977).

#8 Erle Stanley Gardner, THE CASE OF THE MURDERER'S BRIDE AND OTHER STORIES (Fall-Winter 1977).

no # Erle Stanley Gardner, THE AMAZING ADVENTURES OF LESTER LEITH (December 1980).

XVI. CRITICAL AND BIBLIOGRAPHIC WORKS BY QUEEN

THE DETECTIVE SHORT STORY: A BIBLIOGRAPHY. Little, Brown, 1942. Biblo & Tannen, 1969, with new Introduction.

QUEEN'S QUORUM: A HISTORY OF THE DETECTIVE-CRIME SHORT STORY AS REVEALED BY THE 100 MOST IMPORTANT BOOKS PUBLISHED IN THIS FIELD SINCE 1845. Little, Brown, 1951. Biblo & Tannen, 1969, with supplements through 1967.

IN THE QUEENS' PARLOR, AND OTHER LEAVES FROM THE EDITORS' NOTEBOOK. Simon & Schuster, 1957. Gollancz, 1957. Biblo & Tannen, 1969.

XVII. PROSE VERSIONS OF FILMS AND RADIO PLAYS ABOUT ELLERY

A. MOVIE NOVELIZATIONS

ELLERY QUEEN, MASTER DETECTIVE. Grosset & Dunlap, 1941. Pyramid pb #R1799, 1968, as THE VANISHING CORPSE. Based on ELLERY QUEEN, MASTER DETECTIVE (Columbia, 1940), which in turn was based on the novel THE DOOR BETWEEN (1936) Written by Laurence Dwight Smith.

THE PENTHOUSE MYSTERY. Grosset & Dunlap, 1941. Pyramid pb #R1810, 1968. Based on ELLERY QUEEN'S PENTHOUSE MYSTERY (Columbia, 1940), which in turn was based on the 60-minute radio play "The Three Scratches" (CBS, 17 December 1939). Author unknown.

THE PERFECT CRIME. Grosset & Dunlap, 1942. Pyramid pb #R1814, 1968. Based on ELLERY QUEEN AND THE PERFECT CRIME (Columbia, 1941), which in turn was based on the novel THE DEVIL TO PAY (1937).

B. NOVELETS BASED ON QUEEN RADIO PLAYS

THE LAST MAN CLUB. Whitman, 1940. Included in THE LAST MAN CLUB (Pyramid pb #R1835, 1968). Based on "The Last Man Club" (CBS, 25 June 1939, 60 minutes). Author unknown.

THE MURDERED MILLIONAIRE. Whitman, 1942. Included in THE LAST MAN CLUB (Pyramid pb #R1835, 1968). Based on "The Gum-Chewing Millionaire" (CBS, 18 June 1939, 60 minutes). Author unknown.

C. SHORT STORIES BY QUEEN BASED ON QUEEN RADIO PLAYS

"The Three Rs." *Ellery Queen's Mystery Magazine*, September 1946. Collected in CALENDAR OF CRIME (Little, Brown, 1952). Based on "The Three Rs" (CBS, 10 September 1939, 60 minutes).

"The Dead Cat." *Ellery Queen's Mystery Magazine*, October 1946. Collected in CALENDAR OF CRIME (Little, Brown, 1952). Based on "The Dead Cat" (CBS, 29 October 1939, 60 minutes).

"The Telltale Bottle." *Ellery Queen's Mystery Magazine*, November 1946. Collected in CALENDAR OF CRIME (Little, Brown, 1952). Based on "The Tell-Tale Bottle" (CBS, 19 November 1939, 60 minutes).

"The Inner Circle." *Ellery Queen's Mystery Magazine*, January 1947. Collected in CALENDAR OF CRIME (Little, Brown, 1952) and THE BEST OF ELLERY QUEEN (Beaufort, 1985). Based on "The Millionaires' Club" (NBC, 23/25 April 1942, 30 minutes).

"The President's Half Disme." *Ellery Queen's Mystery Magazine*, February 1947. Collected in CALENDAR OF CRIME (Little, Brown, 1952). Based on "George Washington's Dollar" (NBC, 19/21 February 1942, 30 minutes).

"The Ides of Michael Magoon." *Ellery Queen's Mystery Magazine*, March 1947. Collected in CALENDAR OF CRIME (Little, Brown, 1952). Based on "The Income Tax Robbery" (NBC, 12/14 March 1942, 30 minutes).

"The Dauphin's Doll." *Ellery Queen's Mystery Magazine*, December 1948. Collected in CALENDAR OF CRIME (Little, Brown, 1952) and THE BEST OF ELLERY QUEEN (Beaufort, 1985). Based on "The Dauphin's Doll" (NBC, 23/25 December 1943, 30 minutes).

"The Emperor's Dice." *Ellery Queen's Mystery Magazine*, April 1951. Collected in CALENDAR OF CRIME (Little, Brown, 1952). Based on "The Emperor's Dice" (CBS, 31 March 1940, 30 minutes).

"As Simple As ABC." *Ellery Queen's Mystery Magazine*, May 1951. Collected as "The Gettysburg

Bugle" in CALENDAR OF CRIME (Little, Brown, 1952). Based on "The Old Men" (NBC, 28/30 May 1942, 30 minutes).

"The Medical Finger." *Ellery Queen's Mystery Magazine*, June 1951. Collected in CALENDAR OF CRIME (Little, Brown, 1952). Based on "The June Bride" (NBC, 11/13 June 1942, 30 minutes).

"The Fallen Angel." *Ellery Queen's Mystery Magazine*, July 1951. Collected in CALENDAR OF CRIME (Little, Brown, 1952). Based on "The Fallen Angel" (CBS, 2 July 1939, 60 minutes).

"Kidnaped!" *This Week*, 8 July 1951. Collected as "Child Missing!" in QBI: QUEEN'S BUREAU OF INVESTIGATION (Little, Brown, 1955). Based on "The Missing Child" (NBC, 7/9 May 1943, 30 min.)

"The Needle's Eye." *Ellery Queen's Mystery Magazine*, August 1951. Collected in CALENDAR OF CRIME (Little, Brown, 1952). Based on "Captain Kidd's Bedroom" (CBS, 11 February 1940, 60 minutes).

"The Black Ledger." *This Week*, 26 January 1952. Collected in QBI: QUEEN'S BUREAU OF INVESTIGATION (Little, Brown, 1955). Based on "The Yellow Ledger" (NBC, 17/19 December 1942, 30 minutes).

"Cold Money." *This Week*, 20 March 1952. Collected in QBI: QUEEN'S BUREAU OF INVESTIGATION (Little, Brown, 1955). Based on "The Man Who Waited" (CBS, 20 March 1946, 30 minutes).

"The Phantom Train." *This Week*, 31 August 1952. Collected as "Snowball in July" in QBI: QUEEN'S BUREAU OF INVESTIGATION (Little, Brown, 1955) and THE BEST OF ELLERY QUEEN (Beaufort, 1985). Based on "The Train That Vanished" (NBC, 25/27 November 1943, 30 minutes).

"The Myna Bird Mystery." *This Week*, 28 December 1952. Collected as "The Myna Birds" in QBI: QUEEN'S BUREAU OF INVESTIGATION (Little, Brown, 1955). Loosely based on "The Fifty-Second Card" (NBC, 29/31 January 1942, 30 minutes).

"The Accused." *Today's Family*, February 1953. Collected as "The Robber of Wrightsville" in QBI: QUEEN'S BUREAU OF INVESTIGATION (Little, Brown, 1955). Based on "The Black Sheep" (CBS, 28 July 1940, 30 minutes).

"Enter Ellery Queen." *Argosy*, June 1960. Collected as "Mystery at the Library of Congress" in QED: QUEEN'S EXPERIMENTS IN DETECTION (New American Library, 1968). Loosely based on "The Booby Trap" (NBC, 9/11 November 1944, 30 minutes).

D. SHORT STORIES BY OTHERS BASED ON QUEEN RADIO PLAYS

"Here Is a Mystery." *Radio Guide*, 26 January 1940. Based on "The Cellini Cup" (CBS, 12 November 1939, 60 minutes). Author unknown.

"The Haunted Cave." *Radio & Television Mirror*, May 1940. Based on "The Haunted Cave" (CBS, 22 October 1939, 60 minutes). Author unknown.

"The Man Who Wanted To Be Murdered." *Radio & Television Mirror*, August 1940. Based on "The Man Who Wanted To Be Murdered" (CBS, 3 December 1939, 60 minutes). Author unknown.

"The Scorpion's Thumb." *Radio & Television Mirror*, December 1940. Based on "The Scorpion's Thumb" (CBS, 31 December 1939, 60 minutes). Author unknown.

XVIII. QUEEN RADIO PLAYS PUBLISHED AS SCRIPTS

"The Last Man Club." CBS, 25 June 1939, 60 minutes. THE ADVENTURE OF THE MURDERED MOTHS (Crippen & Landru, 2005).

"Napoleon's Razor." CBS, 9 July 1939, 60 minutes. THE ADVENTURE OF THE MURDERED MOTHS (Crippen & Landru, 2005).

"The Bad Boy." CBS, 30 July 1939, 60 minutes. THE ADVENTURE OF THE MURDERED MOTHS (Crippen & Landru, 2005).

"The March of Death." CBS, 15 October 1939, 60 minutes. THE ADVENTURE OF THE MURDERED MOTHS (Crippen & Landru, 2005).

"The Haunted Cave." CBS, 22 October 1939, 60 minutes. THE ADVENTURE OF THE MURDERED MOTHS (Crippen & Landru, 2005).

"The Lost Child." CBS, 26 November 1939, 60 minutes. THE ADVENTURE OF THE MURDERED MOTHS (Crippen & Landru, 2005).

"The Black Secret." CBS, 10 December 1939, 60 minutes. THE ADVENTURE OF THE MURDERED MOTHS (Crippen & Landru, 2005).

"The Dying Scarecrow." CBS, 7 January 1940, 60 minutes. THE ADVENTURE OF THE MURDERED MOTHS (Crippen & Landru, 2005).

"The Woman in Black." CBS, 14 January 1940, 60 minutes. THE ADVENTURE OF THE MURDERED MOTHS (Crippen & Landru, 2005).

"The Forgotten Men." CBS, 7 April 1940, 30 minutes. THE ADVENTURE OF THE MURDERED MOTHS (Crippen & Landru, 2005).

"The Double Triangle." CBS, 28 April 1940, 30 minutes. THE CASE BOOK OF ELLERY QUEEN (Bestseller pb #B59, 1945).

"The Man Who Could Double the Size of Diamonds." CBS, 5 May 1940, 30 minutes. *Ellery Queen's Mystery Magazine*, May 1943 and August 2005; THE ADVENTURE OF THE MURDERED MOTHS (Crippen & Landru, 2005).

"The Fire Bug." CBS, 12 May 1940, 30 minutes. *Ellery Queen's Mystery Magazine*, March 1943.

"Honeymoon House." CBS, 19 May 1940, 30 minutes. THE CASE BOOK OF ELLERY QUEEN (Bestseller pb #B59, 1945).

"The Mouse's Blood." CBS, 26 May 1940, 30 minutes. THE FIRESIDE MYSTERY BOOK, ed. Frank Owen (Lantern Press, 1947).

"The Good Samaritan." CBS, 9 June 1940, 30 minutes. *Ellery Queen's Mystery Magazine*, November 1942.

"The Dark Cloud." CBS, 23 June 1940. THE ADVENTURE OF THE MURDERED MOTHS (Crippen & Landru, 2005).

"The Blind Bullet." CBS, 30 June 1940, 30 minutes. *Ellery Queen's Mystery Magazine*, September 1943.

"The Frightened Star." CBS, 14 July 1940, 30 minutes. *Ellery Queen's Mystery Magazine*, Spring 1942.

"The Invisible Clock." CBS, 11 August 1940, 30 minutes. THE CASE BOOK OF ELLERY QUEEN (Bestseller pb #B59, 1945).

"The Meanest Man in the World." CBS, 18 August 1940, 30 minutes. *Ellery Queen's Mystery Magazine*, July 1942.

"The Mark of Cain." CBS, 22 September 1940, 30 minutes. THE POCKET MYSTERY READER, ed. Lee Wright (Pocket Books pb #172, 1942).

"The Invisible Clue." NBC, 15/17 January 1942, 30 minutes. ADVENTURES IN RADIO, ed. Margaret Cuthbert (Howell Soskin, 1945).

"Ellery Queen, Swindler." NBC, 9/11 April 1942, 30 minutes. ROGUES' GALLERY, ed. Ellery Queen (Little, Brown, 1945).

"The World Series Crime." NBC, 8/10 October 1942, 30 minutes. Published in Japan (Gogaku

Shunjusha, 1985) as a booklet, with notes in Japanese to help youths in that country who were studying English.

"Mr. Short and Mr. Long." NBC, 14/16 January 1943, 30 minutes. THE MISADVENTURES OF SHERLOCK HOLMES, ed. Ellery Queen (Little, Brown, 1944), as "The Disappearance of Mr. James Phillimore." THE ADVENTURE OF THE MURDERED MOTHS (Crippen & Landru, 2005), under original title.

"Tom, Dick and Harry." NBC, 28/30 January 1943, 30 minutes. *Ellery Queen's Mystery Magazine*, July 1943, and THE SAINT'S CHOICE OF RADIO THRILLERS, ed. Leslie Charteris (Saint Enterprises, 1946), as "The Murdered Ship."

"The One-Legged Man." NBC, 25/27 February 1943, 30 minutes. *Ellery Queen's Mystery Magazine*, November 1943.

"Crime, Inc." NBC, 10/12 June 1943, 30 minutes. *Story Digest*, November 1946, as "The Crime Corporation" (condensed).

"The Wounded Lieutenant." 15 minutes. Broadcast date unknown. *Ellery Queen's Mystery Magazine*, July 1944. This short propaganda script, written by Dannay and Lee as part of their arrangement with the Office of War Information, clearly was not aired as part of the 30-minute radio series. Individual stations may have broadcast the program on an ad hoc basis but no information as to precise air dates has been found.

"The Glass Ball." NBC, 23/25 March 1944, 30 minutes. Based on "The Man Who Wanted To Be Murdered" (CBS, 3 December 1939, 60 minutes). CHILLERS & THRILLERS (Street & Smith pb, 1945), in a simplified version designed for military recreation halls.

"The Blue Chip." NBC, 15/17 June 1944, 30 minutes. Based on "The Wandering Corpse" (CBS, 13 August 1939, 60 minutes. CHILLERS & THRILLERS (Street & Smith pb, 1945), in a simplified version designed for military recreation halls.

"The Foul Tip." NBC, 13/15 July 1944. Based on "Box 13" (CBS, 1 September 1940, 30 minutes). CHILLERS & THRILLERS (Street & Smith pb, 1945), in a simplified version designed for military recreation halls.

"The Murdered Moths." CBS, 9 May 1945, 30 minutes. THE ADVENTURE OF THE MURDERED MOTHS (Crippen & Landru, 2005).

"The Curious Thefts." CBS, 19 December 1945, 30 minutes. *Story Digest*, September 1946 (condensed).

XIX. DRAMATIZED VERSION OF A QUEEN NOVEL

ELLERY QUEEN'S THE FOUR OF HEARTS MYSTERY, by William Rand. Chicago: Dramatic Publishing Co., 1949. William Rand is a pseudonym of William Roos (1911-1987), who was half of the husband-wife mystery-writing team of Kelley Roos.

XX. JUVENILE MYSTERIES AS BY ELLERY QUEEN, JR.

THE BLACK DOG MYSTERY. Stokes, 1941. Collins, 1942. Written by Samuel Duff McCoy.

THE GOLDEN EAGLE MYSTERY. Stokes, 1942. Collins, 1943. Written by Frank Belknap Long.

THE GREEN TURTLE MYSTERY. Lippincott, 1944. Collins, 1945. Written by Frank Belknap Long.

THE RED CHIPMUNK MYSTERY. Lippincott, 1946. Collins, 1948. Written by Samuel Duff McCoy.

THE BROWN FOX MYSTERY. Little, Brown, 1948. Collins, 1951. Written by Samuel Duff McCoy.

THE WHITE ELEPHANT MYSTERY, Little, Brown, 1950. Hodder & Stoughton, 1951. Written by Samuel Duff McCoy.

THE YELLOW CAT MYSTERY. Little, Brown, 1952. Written by Samuel Duff McCoy.

THE BLUE HERRING MYSTERY. Little, Brown, 1954. Written by Samuel Duff McCoy.

THE MYSTERY OF THE MERRY MAGICIAN. Golden Press, 1961. Written by James Holding.

THE MYSTERY OF THE VANISHED VICTIM. Golden Press, 1962. Written by James Holding.

THE PURPLE BIRD MYSTERY. Putnam, 1966. Written by James Holding.

XXI. TRUE CRIME WRITING AS BY ELLERY QUEEN

NOTE: These articles were written by Manfred B. Lee based on research materials supplied by the magazines that commissioned the pieces.

A. IN MAGAZINES

THE AMERICAN WEEKLY

09/14/52 Death of a Don Juan.

10/26/52 The Taylor Case.

09/13/53 The Grammer Case.

10/11/53 The Lake Palourde Case.

11/08/53 Terror in Texas.

02/07/54 The Lethal Lady.

03/07/54 Mrs. Holmes Solves a Murder.

05/23/54 The Clue of the White Glove. (ELLERY QUEEN'S INTERNATIONAL CASE BOOK, 1964, as "Death in Manila.")

05/30/54 The Fatal Tattoo. (ELLERY QUEEN'S INTERNATIONAL CASE BOOK, 1964, as The Beautiful Lady of El Puerto.")

06/13/54 The Adamolis Swindle. (ELLERY QUEEN'S INTERNATIONAL CASE BOOK, 1964, as "The Swindler of Adamolis.")

06/20/54 The Acid Test. (ELLERY QUEEN'S INTERNATIONAL CASE BOOK, 1964, as "The Young Man Who Lost His Eyes.")

06/27/54 Mad Murderer of Tokyo. (ELLERY QUEEN'S INTERNATIONAL CASE BOOK, 1964, as "Tokyo's Greatest Bank Robbery.")

07/04/54 No Name on the Search Warrant. (ELLERY QUEEN'S INTERNATIONAL CASE BOOK, 1964, as "Crime Wave, Balkan Style.")

07/11/54 Murder Down Under. (ELLERY QUEEN'S INTERNATIONAL CASE BOOK, 1964, as "Death Among the Aborigines.")

07/18/54 The Curse of Kali. (ELLERY QUEEN'S INTERNATIONAL CASE BOOK.)

07/25/54 The Black Swan Murder Case.

08/01/54 The Girl Who Flirted with Death. (ELLERY QUEEN'S INTERNATIONAL CASE BOOK, 1964, as "The Curious Case of the Flirt.")

08/08/54 The Gravedigger's Secret. (ELLERY QUEEN'S INTERNATIONAL CASE BOOK, 1964, as "Inspector Fosse's Last Case.")

08/15/54 Death in the Garden. (ELLERY QUEEN'S INTERNATIONAL CASE BOOK, 1964, as "Passion in the Holy Land.")

09/19/54 The Love Slaves of Orissa.

09/26/54 Murder at the Wedding. (ELLERY QUEEN'S INTERNATIONAL CASE BOOK, 1964, as "African Love Story.")

10/03/54 Mystery of the Crambling Road.

10/10/54 Masquerade for Murder. (ELLERY QUEEN'S INTERNATIONAL CASE BOOK, 1964, as "The Mysterious Shooting at the Nacional.")

10/17/54 The Crime of the Croupier. (ELLERY QUEEN'S INTERNATIONAL CASE BOOK, 1964.)

10/24/54 Murder in Lovers' Lane.

10/31/54 The Two-Way Clue.

11/07/54 Murder at the Tea Party.

11/14/54 Dream Cottage Murder.

11/21/54 Death in the Harem. (ELLERY QUEEN'S INTERNATIONAL CASE BOOK, 1964, as "Secrets of the Harem.")

11/28/54 The Clue of the Missing Hands. (ELLERY QUEEN'S INTERNATIONAL CASE BOOK, 1964, as "The Butcher of Buenos Aires.")

12/05/54 The Red Maiden of Madrid. (ELLERY QUEEN'S INTERNATIONAL CASE BOOK, 1964, as "The Red Virgin.")

12/12/54 The Claws of the Hawk. (ELLERY QUEEN'S INTERNATIONAL CASE BOOK, 1964, as "The Jaws of Death.")

01/02/55 The Clue of the Passionate Poem. (ELLERY QUEEN'S INTERNATIONAL CASE BOOK, 1964, as "The Shanghai Shootings.")

11/04/56 The Taxi Dancer and the Homesick Highlander.

11/11/56 Murder After Forty.

11/18/56 The Terrible Avenger of Karos Island.

11/25/56 The Persistent Killer.

12/02/56 The Girl Who Went Too Far.

12/09/56 The Trail of Broken Hearts.

12/16/56 Murder Over Mount Torment.

01/06/57 The Wife Who Wouldn't Let Go.

01/13/57 4 Short Cuts to Love.

01/20/57 The Body in the Trunk.

01/27/57 Why These Boys Killed Their Father.

02/03/57 The Strange Case of Napoleon Caproni.

02/10/57 10 Graves for the Pretty Widow.

02/17/57 The Tennis Racket Murder.

02/24/57 The Diabolical Lover.

03/10/57 The Strange Case of the Mad Sculptor.

03/24/57 The Friendly Killers.

03/31/57 The Girl Who Had Never Been Kissed.

04/07/57 The Murder in the Underground.

04/14/57 Sense of Guilt.

04/28/57 Love at Second Sight.

05/05/57 The Girl Who Wouldn't Go Steady.

05/12/57 Till Death Did Them Part.

05/19/57 Who Blew Up Mr. Smith?

05/26/57 Death of a Playboy.

06/02/57 Love in the Death House.

11/24/57 The Clue of the Missing Hands.

02/16/58 Mrs. Patterson's Past. (THE WOMAN IN THE CASE, 1966, as "The Amazing Mrs. Patterson.")

02/23/58 The Boomerang Murder. (THE WOMAN IN THE CASE, 1966, as "The Girl in the Snowbank.")

03/02/58 Death in the Tea Leaves. (THE WOMAN IN THE CASE, 1966.)

03/09/58 Detained at Her Majesty's Pleasure. (THE WOMAN IN THE CASE 1966, as "Death Keeps a Diary.")

03/16/58 The Secret of Iron Irene. (THE WOMAN IN THE CASE, 1966, as "The Secret of Irene Schroeder.")

03/23/58 The Trail of Lonely Hearts. (THE WOMAN IN THE CASE, 1966, as "Trail of the Lonesome Hearts.")

03/30/58 Mother Against Son. (THE WOMAN IN THE CASE, 1966, as "Witness for the Prosecution.")

04/13/58 The Killer Who Wanted To Be Caught. (THE WOMAN IN THE CASE, 1966, as "The Strange Case of Elaine Soule.")

04/20/58 She Dreamt of Murder. (THE WOMAN IN THE CASE, 1966, as "The Dream Detective.")

04/27/58 Mrs. Martin's Murder Spree. (THE WOMAN IN THE CASE, 1966, as "The Mystery of Rhonda Bell Martin.")

05/04/58 Death in Silk Stockings. (THE WOMAN IN THE CASE, 1966, as "The Silk Stocking Girl.")

05/11/58 The Hanging Woman. (THE WOMAN IN THE CASE, 1966.)

05/18/58 The Forgetful Blonde. (THE WOMAN IN THE CASE, 1966, as "The Beautiful Latvian.")

05/25/58 Death in the Temple of Love. (THE WOMAN IN THE CASE, 1966, as "The Temple of Love.")

06/01/58 Death of a Part-Time Lover. (THE WOMAN IN THE CASE, 1966, as "The Beautiful Killer of Hampstead.")

10/26/58 Two Routes to Murder.

11/02/58 Murder in the Cabbage Patch.

11/09/58 The Clue of the Naughty Word.

11/16/58 The Body in the Bathtub.

11/30/58 Double Jeopardy.

12/07/58 The Clue of the Foxtail Grass.

12/14/58 The Clue of the Shattered Watch.

01/04/59 The Hunt for the Phantom Gunman.

01/11/59 The Baby-Sitter Murder.

02/08/59 Murder—With 18,000 Suspects.

02/15/59 A Tiny Bottle Full of Death. (THE WOMAN IN THE CASE, 1966, as "The Poison Whiskey Case.")

02/22/59 The Case of the Experimental Corpse. (THE WOMAN IN THE CASE, 1966, as "The Murder Without a Body.")

03/01/59 The Killer Who Was Caught by a Thread. (THE WOMAN IN THE CASE, 1966, as "The Mystery of the Yellow Thread.")

03/08/59 Murder by Proxy.

03/15/59 The Red Herring Murder.

04/12/59 The Firebug Murders.

04/26/59 The Clue in the Wallet.

05/17/59 Album of Death. (THE WOMAN IN THE CASE, 1966, as "The Man with the Jug Ears.")

ARGOSY

03/63   A Specialist in Skulls.

THE BLADE SUNDAY MAGAZINE

02/14/71 Sweet Assassins.

FAMILY WEEKLY

11/01/59 Will the Oakes Murder Ever Be Solved?

06/11/61 Who Killed the Man Everybody Hated?

MAN'S MAGAZINE

10/63   A Matter of Wife Or Death.

04/66   The Big Dame Hunters.

07/66   The Killer Who Had Body Ardor.

OFFICIAL DETECTIVE STORIES

10/60   Plunder and Death on the High Seas.

02/61   The Case of Colorado's Millionaire Brewer Coors.

B. COLLECTIONS OF TRUE CRIME ARTICLES

ELLERY QUEEN'S INTERNATIONAL CASE BOOK. Dell pb #2260, 1964. Contents: The Beautiful Lady of El Puerto (*American Weekly*, 05/30/54, as "The Fatal Tattoo"); Tokyo's Greatest Bank Robbery (*American Weekly*, 06/27/54, as "Mad Murderer of Tokyo"); Inspector Fosse's Last Case (*American Weekly*, 08/08/54, as "The Gravedigger's Secret"); The Butcher of Buenos Aires (*American Weekly*, 11/28/54, as "The Clue of the Missing Hands"); The Swindler of Adamolis (*American Weekly*, 06/13/54, as "The Adamolis Swindle"); The Strangled Bride of Oran (*American Weekly*, title not found); The Jaws of Death (*American Weekly*, 12/12/54, as "The Claws of the Hawk"); The Curse of Kali (*American Weekly*, 07/18/54); Crime Wave, Balkan Style (*American Weekly*, 07/04/54, as "No Name on the Search Warrant"); The Mysterious Shooting at the Nacional (*American Weekly*, 10/10/54, as "Masquerade for Murder"); The Young Man Who Lost His Eyes (*American Weekly*, 06/20/54, as "The Acid Test"); Death in Manila (*American Weekly*, 05/23/54, as "The Clue of the White Glove"); Death Among the Aborigines (*American Weekly*, 07/11/54, as "Murder Down Under"); The Curious Case of the Flirt (*American Weekly*, 08/01/54, as "The Girl Who Flirted with Death"); The Crime of the Croupier (*American Weekly*, 10/17/54); African Love Story (*American Weekly*, 09/26/54, as "Murder at the Wedding"); Secrets of the Harem (*American Weekly*, 11/21/54, as "Death in the Harem"); The Shanghai Shootings (*American Weekly*, 01/02/55, as "The Clue of the Passionate Poem"); The Red Virgin (*American*

Weekly, 12/05/54, as "The Red Maiden of Madrid"); Passion in the Holy Land (*American Weekly*, 08/15/54, as "Death in the Garden".

THE WOMAN IN THE CASE. Bantam pb #F3160, 1966. Corgi pb, 1967, as DEADLIER THAN THE MALE. Contents: Trail of the Lonesome Hearts (*American Weekly*, 03/23/58, as "The Trail of Lonely Hearts"; Witness for the Prosecution (*American Weekly*, 03/30/58, as "Mother Against Son"); Detained at Her Majesty's Pleasure (*American Weekly*, 03/09/58, as "Death Keeps a Diary"); The Secret of Irene Schroeder (*American Weekly*, 03/16/58, as "The Secret of Iron Irene"); The Beautiful Latvian (*American Weekly*, 05/18/58, as "The Forgetful Blonde"); The Mystery of the Yellow Thread (*American Weekly*, 03/01/59, as "The Killer Who Was Caught by a Thread"); The Strange Case of Elaine Soule (*American Weekly*, 04/13/58, as "The Killer Who Wanted To Be Caught"); The Dream Detective (*American Weekly*, 04/20/58, as "She Dreamt of Murder"); Death in the Tea Leaves (*American Weekly*, 03/02/58); The Man with the Jug Ears (*American Weekly*, 05/17/59, as "Album of Death"); The Girl in the Snowbank (*American Weekly*, 02/23/58, as "The Boomerang Murder"); The Poison Whiskey Case (*American Weekly*, 02/15/59, as "A Tiny Bottle Full of Death"); The Amazing Mrs. Patterson (*American Weekly*, 02/16/58, as "Mrs. Patterson's Past"); The Silk Stocking Girl (*American Weekly*, 05/04/58, as "Death in Silk Stockings"); The Hanging Woman (*American Weekly*, 05/11/58); The Murder Without a Body (*American Weekly*, 02/22/59, as "The Case of the Experimental Corpse"); The Beautiful Killer of Hampstead (*American Weekly*, 06/01/58, as "Death of a Part-Time Lover"); The Temple of Love (*American Weekly*, 05/25/58, as "Death in the Temple of Love"); The Mystery of Rhonda Bell Martin (*American Weekly*, 04/27/58, as "Mrs. Martin's Murder Spree").

XXII. PAPERBACK NOVELS AS BY ELLERY QUEEN

A. POCKET BOOKS TITLES

DEAD MAN'S TALE. Pocket Books pb #6117, 1961. Four Square pb, 1967. Written by Stephen Marlowe.

DEATH SPINS THE PLATTER. Pocket Books pb #6126, 1962. Written by Richard Deming.

MURDER WITH A PAST. Pocket Books pb #4703, 1963. Written by Talmage Powell.

WIFE OR DEATH. Pocket Books pb #4703, 1963. Four Square pb, 1966. Written by Richard Deming.

KILL AS DIRECTED. Pocket Books pb #4704, 1963. Written by Henry Kane.

THE GOLDEN GOOSE. Pocket Books pb #4705, 1964. Four Square pb, 1967. Written by Fletcher Flora.

THE FOUR JOHNS. Pocket Books pb #4706, 1964. Written by Jack Vance.

BLOW HOT, BLOW COLD. Pocket Books pb #45007, 1964. Written by Fletcher Flora.

THE LAST SCORE. Pocket Books pb #50486, 1964. Written by Charles Runyon.

BEWARE THE YOUNG STRANGER. Pocket Books pb #50489, 1965. Written by Talmage Powell.

THE COPPER FRAME. Pocket Books pb #50490, 1965. Four Square pb, 1968. Written by Richard Deming.

A ROOM TO DIE IN. Pocket Books pb #50492, 1965. Written by Jack Vance.

THE KILLER TOUCH. Pocket Books pb #50494, 1965. Written by Charles Runyon.

THE DEVIL'S COOK. Pocket Books pb #50495, 1965. Written by Fletcher Flora.

THE MADMAN THEORY. Pocket Books pb #50496, 1966. Written by Jack Vance.

B. TIM CORRIGAN/CHUCK BAER SERIES

WHERE IS BIANCA? Popular Library pb #50-377, 1966. Four Square pb, 1966. Written by Talmage Powell.

WHO SPIES, WHO KILLS? Popular Library pb #60-211, 1966. Four Square pb, 1967. Written by Talmage Powell.

WHY SO DEAD? Popular Library pb #60-2122, 1966. Four Square pb, 1966. Written by Richard Deming.

HOW GOES THE MURDER? Popular Library pb #60-2168, 1967. Written by Richard Deming.

WHICH WAY TO DIE? Popular Library pb #60-2235, 1967. Written by Richard Deming.

WHAT'S IN THE DARK? Popular Library pb #60-2269, 1968. Gollancz, 1970, as WHEN FELL THE NIGHT. Written by Richard Deming.

C. DELL TITLES

LOSERS, WEEPERS. Dell pb #5034, 1966. Written by Richard Deming.

SHOOT THE SCENE. Dell pb #7845, 1966. Written by Richard Deming.

KISS AND KILL. Dell pb #4567, 1969. Written by Charles Runyon.

D. LANCER NON-SERIES TITLES

A STUDY IN TERROR. Lancer pb #73-469, 1966. Gollancz, 1967, as SHERLOCK HOLMES VERSUS JACK THE RIPPER. Novelization of the movie, written by Paul W. Fairman, with a contemporary "framing story" written by Dannay and Lee and featuring Ellery.

GUESS WHO'S COMING TO KILL YOU? Lancer pb #73-808, 1968. Written by Walt Sheldon.

E. MIKE McCALL (THE TROUBLESHOOTER) SERIES

THE CAMPUS MURDERS. Lancer pb #74-527, 1969. Written by Gil Brewer.

THE BLACK HEARTS MURDERS. Lancer pb #74640-075, 1970. Written by Richard Deming.

THE BLUE MOVIE MURDERS. Lancer pb #75277-095, 1972, Gollancz, 1973. Written by Edward D. Hoch.

XXIII. PAPERBACK HISTORICAL NOVELS AS BY BARNABY ROSS

QUINTIN CHIVAS. Trident/Simon & Schuster, 1961. Pocket Books pb #6141, 1962. Written by Don Tracy.

THE SCROLLS OF LYSIS. Trident/Simon & Schuster, 1962. Perma pb #M5083, 1963. Alvin Redman, 1964. Written by Don Tracy.

THE DUKE OF CHAOS. Pocket Books pb #6232, 1964. Written by Don Tracy.

THE CREE FROM MINATAREE. Pocket Books pb #50200, 1964. Written by Don Tracy.

STRANGE KINSHIP. Pocket Books pb #50493, 1965. Written by Don Tracy.

THE PASSIONATE QUEEN. Pocket Books pb #50497, 1966. Written by Don Tracy.

XXIV. WRITINGS ABOUT QUEEN

Adey, Robert. "The Impossible Mr. Queen." THE TRAGEDY OF ERRORS (Crippen & Landru, 1999), pp. 151-158. Discussion of the Queen novels and stories revolving around locked rooms and impossible crimes.

Aird, Catherine. "Twayblade." THE TRAGEDY OF ERRORS (Crippen & Landru, 1999), pp. 169-172. Brief discussion of Queen (meaning Dannay) as an anthologist.

Amis, Kingsley. "My Favorite Sleuths." *Playboy*, December 1966. Includes a brief critique of Queen.

Andrews, Angela. "Remembering Ellery Queen." *Paperback Quarterly*, Fall 1982, pp. 3-9. Discussion of the first 20 Queen titles reprinted in paperback by Pocket Books.

Bainbridge, John. "Ellery Queen: Crime Made Him Famous And His Authors Rich." *Life*, 22 November 1943. Lengthy profile of Dannay and Lee.

Barr, Mike W. "Challenge to the Artist: The Comic Book Stories of Ellery Queen." THE TRAGEDY OF ERRORS (Crippen & Landru, 1999), pp. 194-205. Detailed account of perhaps the least often explored aspect of EQ.

Barzun, Jacques, and Wendell Hertig Taylor. A CATALOGUE OF CRIME: BEING A READER'S GUIDE TO THE LITERATURE OF MYSTERY, DETECTION AND RELATED GENRES. Harper & Row, 1971. Second edition: Harper & Row, 1989. Queen is discussed in the first edition on pp. 351-353, 370-371, 541-546, and 607-608; in the second edition, on pp. 437-438, 461-462, 613-614, 665-670, and 738-739.

Biederstadt, Lynn. "To the Very Last: The Dying Message." *The Armchair Detective*, Vol. 12 (1979), pp. 209-210. Discussion of the dying message device in Queen novels and short stories.

Boucher, Anthony. ELLERY QUEEN: A DOUBLE PROFILE. Little, Brown, 1951. A 12-page pamphlet published on the occasion of the 25th Ellery Queen novel, THE ORIGIN OF EVIL.

"There Was No Mystery in What the Crime Editor Was After." *New York Times*, 26 February 1961. An appreciation of *EQMM* and its founding editor Fred Dannay.

Breen, Jon L. "Ellery Queen." THE TRAGEDY OF ERRORS (Crippen & Landru, 1999), pp. 107-112.

"On the Centenary of Ellery Queen." *Ellery Queen's Mystery Magazine*, January 2005, pp. 3-5.

"The Queen Letters." *Ellery Queen's Mystery Magazine*, February 2005, pp. 3-9, 63. An account of Fred Dannay's correspondence with Manny Lee, archived at Columbia University.

"The Too-Short Saga of *Mystery League*." *Ellery Queen's Mystery Magazine*, March-April 2005, pp. 8-9.

"The Misadventures of Ellery Queen." *Ellery Queen's Mystery Magazine*, September-October 2005, pp. 8-9. An account of the various pastiches and pastiches of Queen.

"The Ellery Queen Mystery: Why Is the Corpus No Longer Alive?" *The Weekly Standard*, 10 October 2005, pp. 41-43. An attempt to explain why Queen has ceased to be a factor in American crime fiction.

"EQMM After Fred Dannay." *Ellery Queen's Mystery Magazine*, December 2011, pp. 79-82. A capsule history of the magazine from Fred Dannay's death to the present.

"A Century of Thrills and Chills: Ellery Queen Meets the Critics." *Wilson Library Bulletin*, April 1942. Transcript of a radio discussion with Dannay, Lee, Howard Haycraft and others, broadcast on SPEAKING OF BOOKS, 25 November 1941.

Christopher, J.R. "The Mystery of Social Reaction: Two Novels by Ellery Queen." *The Armchair Detective*, October 1972. Essay on THE GLASS VILLAGE and COP OUT.

"Ellery Queen, Sports Fan." *The Mystery Fancier*, Summer 1988, pp. 3-24. An account of the EQ sports mysteries.

"The Case of the Broken Commandments." A paper dealing with TEN DAYS' WONDER (1948), presented at the Southwestern Conference on Christianity and Literature, 1999, but never published.

Connor, Edward. "The Four Ellery Queens." *Films in Review*, June-July 1960. Revised version: "The Films of Ellery Queen." *The Queen Canon Bibliophile*, April 1971. Critical discussion of the movies based on Queen novels.

Dannay, Douglas & Richard. "Legacy." THE TRAGEDY OF ERRORS (Crippen & Landru, 1999), pp. 113-116. Brief memoir by Fred Dannay's sons.

Dannay, Douglas & Richard. "The Authorship of Three Late Ellery Queen Novels." THE TRAGEDY OF ERRORS (Crippen & Landru, 1999), pp. 128-129. Brief note on three of the Ellery Queen hardcover novels expanded from Fred Dannay's outlines by writers other than Manny Lee.

Erisman, Fred. "'Where We Plan to Go': The Southwest in Utopian Fiction." *Southwestern American Literature*, April 1971. Includes discussion of AND ON THE EIGHTH DAY.

Fistell, Ira A. "Ellery Queen: The First 50 Years." *West Coast Review of Books*, July 1979, pp. 82-86.

Gilbert, Michael. "EQMM." THE TRAGEDY OF ERRORS (Crippen & Landru, 1999), pp. 181-183. A regular *EQMM* author's brief account of Dannay as editor.

Godfrey, Thomas. "The Lamp of God." *The Armchair Detective*, Vol. 12 (1979), pp. 212-213. Discussion of the first EQ short novel.

Haycraft, Howard. MURDER FOR PLEASURE: THE LIFE AND TIMES OF THE DETECTIVE STORY. Appleton-Century, 1941. Queen is discussed on pp. 173-179.

Hertel, Ted, Jr. "Queen's Gambit: The Life and Times of Ellery Queen." THE TRAGEDY OF ERRORS (Crippen & Landru, 1999), pp. 209-218.

Hoch, Edward D. "A Tribute." THE TRAGEDY OF ERRORS (Crippen & Landru, 1999), pp. 178-180. Brief memoir of Dannay as editor by *EQMM*'s most prolific contributor.

"Ellery Queen and the Mystery Writers of America." *Ellery Queen's Mystery Magazine*, May 2005, pp. 3-4. A brief account of Fred Dannay's role in MWA.

"The Novels of Ellery Queen." *Ellery Queen's Mystery Magazine*, June 2005, pp. 2-7, 55.

"Fred Dannay and Me." *Ellery Queen's Mystery Magazine*, December 2005, pp. 110-112.

Hubin, Allen J. "Frederic Dannay: Doctor of Humane Letters." *The Armchair Detective*, Vol. 12 (1979), pp. 236-237. An account of the ceremony in which Fred was awarded an honorary Ph.D.

Hutchings, Janet. "Legacy of an Editor," THE TRAGEDY OF ERRORS (Crippen & Landru, 1999), pp. 173-177. Discussion of Dannay's role as founding editor of *EQMM*.

Karnick, S.T. "Mystery Men." *National Review*, 6 March 2000, pp. 59-61.

Keating, H.R.F. "A Letter from an Archangel." THE TRAGEDY OF ERRORS (Crippen & Landru, 1999), pp. 187-189. An English author's brief account of Dannay as editor.

Kimura, Jiro. "Ellery Queen in Japan." *Ellery Queen's Mystery Magazine*, November 2005, pp. 57, 63.

Lachman, Marvin. "Ellery Queen And His Fans." *Ellery Queen's Mystery Magazine*, December 2005, pp. 2-3.

Lee, Rand B. "Dad And Cousin Fred Entered a Writing Contest... That's When Ellery Queen Was Born." *TV Guide*, 11 October 1975, pp. 20-24.

"Girl, Breastless, Dancing." Written 2008 and accessible on the Web. A candid memoir by one of Manfred B. Lee's sons including several stories about his parents.

"The Temple of His Word: Growing Up with Ellery Queen." THE TRAGEDY OF ERRORS (Crippen & Landru, 1999), pp. 117-127. Perhaps the most vivid and detailed account of Manfred B. Lee.

Lord, Graham. *London Sunday Express*, 13 December 1970. Interview with Dannay.

Lovesey, Peter. "Avoiding Mr. Queen." THE TRAGEDY OF ERRORS (Crippen & Landru, 1999), pp. 184-186. An *EQMM* author's brief memoir of Dannay as editor.

Maslin, Janet. "Gumshoe Who Wore Pince-Nez." *New York Times*, 5 May 2005. Account of the Queen centenary conference at Columbia University.

Mazzella, Anthony J. "Whatever Happened to Ellery Queen?" *Columbia Library Columns*, February 1986, pp. 25-34.

Mooney, Joan M. THE AMERICAN DETECTIVE STORY: A STUDY IN POPULAR FICTION. Ph.D. dissertation, University of Minnesota 1968, published in five installments in *The Armchair Detective*, January 1970-January 1971, as "Best-Selling American Detective Fiction." Includes lengthy discussions of Queen.

Mori, Hidetoshi. "Ellery Queen: One of the Most Popular Mystery Writers in Japan." THE TRAGEDY OF ERRORS (Crippen & Landru, 1999), pp. 206-208.

Nevins, Francis M. "At Work and Play with Fred Dannay." THE TRAGEDY OF ERRORS (Crippen & Landru, 1999), pp. 134-139.

"The Ellerys of the Airwaves." *Ellery Queen's Mystery Magazine*, August 2005, pp. 2-13. Discussion of the long-running EQ radio series.

"The Queens of the Small Screen." *Ellery Queen's Mystery Magazine*, November 2005, pp. 58-63. An account of the various EQ television series.

"EQMM: The Dannay Years." *Ellery Queen's Mystery Magazine*, November 2011, pp. 58-63. A capsule history of the magazine's first forty years.

Parker, Dorothy. *Esquire*, January 1959. Review of the Queen threesome THE NEW YORK MURDERS.

Penzler, Otto. "The Big Little Mystery Magazine." *New York Sun*, 12 October 2005, p. 13. A capsule history of *EQMM*.

Prescott, Peter S. *Look*, 21 April 1970. Interview with Dannay and Lee, not printed in all copies of the issue.

Routley, Erik. THE PURITAN PLEASURES OF THE DETECTIVE STORY. London: Gollancz, 1972. Queen is discussed on pp. 193-195.

Ruehlmann, Bill. "We May As Well Continue Being Carrollish: A Bow Before the Queen." THE TRAGEDY OF ERRORS (Crippen & Landru, 1999), pp. 165-168. Discusses the influence of Lewis Carroll on the Queen canon.

Scott, Sutherland. BLOOD IN THEIR INK: THE MARCH OF THE MODERN MYSTERY NOVEL. London: Stanley Paul, 1953. Queen is discussed on pp. 51-55.

Siegel, David S. "A Challenge to the Listener: Ellery Queen on the Air." THE TRAGEDY OF ERRORS (Crippen & Landru, 1999), pp. 190-193. Brief account of EQ's radio career.

Shenker, Israel. *New York Times*, 22 February 1969. Interview with Dannay and Lee on the occasion of their 40th anniversary as mystery writers.

A SILVER ANNIVERSARY TRIBUTE TO ELLERY QUEEN FROM AUTHORS, CRITICS, EDITORS AND FAMOUS FANS. Little, Brown, 1954. A 31-page pamphlet published to celebrate Queen's 25th year in the mystery field.

Smith, Richard A. "Remembering My Hanai Father." THE TRAGEDY OF ERRORS (Crippen & Landru, 1999), pp. 130-133. A memoir of Manny Lee by a young black man he helped raise.

Steinbock, Steven. "Ellery Queen—Man of God." THE TRAGEDY OF ERRORS (Crippen & Landru, 1999), pp. 159-164. Discussion of religious themes in Queen novels.

"Getting to Know Manny Lee." *Ellery Queen's Mystery Magazine*, January 2005, pp. 6, 105. A brief account of Lee as a separate personality.

Sullivan, Eleanor. "Fred Dannay and *EQMM*." *The Armchair Detective*, Vol. 12 (1979), pp. 201-202. A brief description of working with Dannay by his associate editor at *EQMM* and, after his death in 1982, the magazine's editor in chief.

Symons, Julian. MORTAL CONSEQUENCES: A HISTORY FROM THE DETECTIVE STORY TO THE CRIME NOVEL. Harper& Row, 1972. Second edition: BLOODY MURDER: FROM THE DETECTIVE STORY TO THE CRIME NOVEL: A HISTORY. Viking, 1985. Queen is discussed on pp. 121-122 of the first edition and on pp. 111-112 and 139-140 of the second.

Tolnay, Tom. "The Multiple Movie Personalities of Ellery Queen." *Ellery Queen's Mystery Magazine*, July 2005, pp. 2-11. Detailed account of the Queen-based films.

Tomasson, Robert E. *New York Times*, 5 April 1971. Obituary notice on the death of Manfred B. Lee.

Unsigned. "A Case of Double Identity." *MD*, December 1967. Lengthy profile of Dannay and Lee. Dannay's choice for the best reportage on Queen.

Unsigned. "Ellery Queen." *Coronet*, February 1956. Brief profile of Dannay and Lee, with each cousin's photograph identified as the other's.

Unsigned. "Ellery Queen Builds Collection of Rare Detective Short Stories." *Publishers' Weekly*, 20 November 1943. Illustrated article on Queen as bibliophile.

Unsigned. "Mysterious Masked Author." *Publishers' Weekly*, 10 October 1936. Brief item revealing Queen's identity for the first time.

Unsigned. "Queen, Ellery." CURRENT BIOGRAPHY, 1940. Biographical profile with checklist of earlier periodical materials on Queen.

Vande Water, Bill. "Frederic Dannay, BSI." THE TRAGEDY OF ERRORS (Crippen & Landru, 1999), pp. 147-150. Brief account of Dannay's activity as a Baker Street Irregular. A shorter version appears in *Ellery Queen's Mystery Magazine*, February 2005, pp. 80, 93, 134.

Vidro, Arthur. "Literary References in Ellery Queen's *The Finishing Stroke*." CADS 53 (February 2008), pp. 19-22.

Waugh, Hillary. "Fred Dannay and Manny Lee." THE TRAGEDY OF ERRORS (Crippen & Landru, 1999), pp. 140-141. A brief memoir.

Yaffe, James. "Tribute to Fred Dannay." THE TRAGEDY OF ERRORS (Crippen & Landru, 1999), pp. 142-146. Memoir of Dannay by an author who sold his first stories to *EQMM* when he was in his teens.

Yates, Donald A. "Remembering Fred Dannay." *Ellery Queen's Mystery Magazine*, September-October 2005, pp. 4-5.

INDEX

About the Author

Francis M. Nevins has won two Edgar awards from the Mystery Writers of America for his scholarly work on Cornell Woolrich and Ellery Queen. By training a lawyer, he has written many essays on the nexus between fiction and the law. But to mystery fans, Mr. Nevins is at least equally known as the author of a number of novels and dozens of classic detective stories, many of them collected in *Night Forms* (2010).

Also from Francis M. Nevins

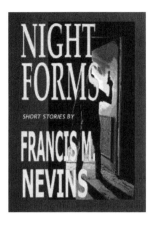

NIGHT FORMS
Francis M. Nevins
28 stories
Introduction and Afterwords
378 pages $16.95
ISBN: 978-1-935797-00-5

THE 120 HOUR CLOCK
Francis M. Nevins
A Milo Turner Scam
Afterword by the Author
134 pages $8.00
ISBN 978-1-935797-37-1

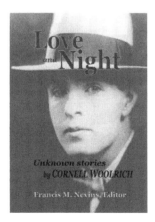

LOVE AND NIGHT
Unknown Stories
by Cornell Woolrich
Edited by Francis M. Nevins
192 pages $12.00
ISBN 978-1-935797-35-7

"A superlative book . . . jaw-dropping revelations."

WILLIAM LINK, creator of **Columbo**

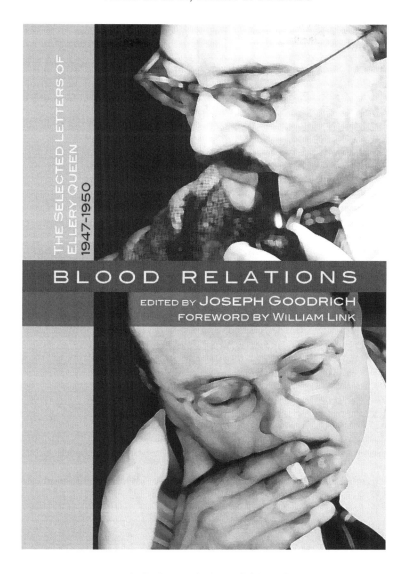

BLOOD RELATIONS
The Selected Letters of Ellery Queen 1947-1950
Edited by Joseph Goodrich
156 pages Trade Paperback $14.95
ISBN: 978-1-935797-38-8

New York author and Edgar-winning dramatist Joseph
Goodrich draws a portrait of a literary marriage made in hell.

Printed in Great Britain
by Amazon.co.uk, Ltd.,
Marston Gate.